The Arab Movements
in World War I

The Arab Movements
in World War I

Eliezer Tauber

Bar-Ilan University

FRANK CASS: LONDON

First published 1993 in Great Britain by
FRANK CASS AND CO. LTD
Gainsborough House, 11 Gainsborough Road,
London E11 1RS, England

and in the United States of America by
FRANK CASS
c/o International Specialized Book Services, Inc.,
5804 N.E. Hassalo Street,
Portland, Oregon 97213-3644

Copyright © Eliezer Tauber 1993

British Library Cataloguing in Publication Data

Tauber, Eliezer
    The Arab movements in World War 1.
    I. Title
    940.415

    ISBN 0-7146-3437-9

Library of Congress Cataloging-in-Publication Data

Tauber, Eliezer.
    The Arab movements in World War I / Eliezer Tauber.
        p.   cm.
    Includes bibliographical references and index.
    ISBN 0-7146-3437-9 (hardback)
    ISBN 0-7146-4083-2 (paperback)
    1. Arab countries—History—Arab Revolt, 1916–1918.
    2. Nationalism—Arab countries—History—20th century. 3. Middle
East—Politics and government—1914–1945. I. Title.
    DS62.9.T38   1993
    909'.0974927—dc20   91-22138
                                                             CIP

    ISBN 0 7146 3437 9
    ISBN 0 7146 4083 2 (paperback)

*All rights reserved. No part of this publication may be reproduced in any
form or by any means, electronic, mechanical, photocopying, recording
or otherwise, without the prior permission of Frank Cass and Company
Limited.*

Typeset by Regent Typesetting, London
Printed by Bookcraft (Bath) Ltd.

The Moshe Dayan Center for Middle Eastern and
African Studies
The Shiloah Institute
Tel Aviv University

The Moshe Dayan Center, through the Shiloah Research Institute and
its other constituent units, seeks to contribute by research, documen-
tation and publication to the study and understanding of the modern
history and current affairs of the Middle East and Africa. The Center,
with the Department of Middle Eastern and African History, is part of
the School of History at Tel Aviv University. This study is published in
cooperation with the Center.

Contents

Acknowledgements   ix

Abbreviations   xi

Introduction: Arab Societies before the War   1

1. Abortive Attempts   10
   The Revolt Plans of the Lebanese at the Beginning of the
   War
   The Plans of the Decentralization Party and its Emissaries
   The Revolt Plan of Amin Lutfi al-Hafiz
   The Revolt Plan of 'Abd al-Karim al-Khalil
   Rebellious Activities in the Levant during the Arab Revolt
   Subversive Activity in Iraq during the World War

2. Negligence, Treachery, and Executions   35
   Incriminating Documents
   Arrests and Executions

3. Al-Fatat, al-'Ahd, and the Origins of the Arab Revolt   57
   The Mission of Kamil al-Qassab
   Al-Fatat and al-'Ahd Combine Efforts
   Faysal in Damascus I
   The McMahon-Husayn Correspondence
   Faysal in Damascus II
   The Outbreak of the Arab Revolt

4. 'Aziz 'Ali al-Misri and the Arab Revolt   83

5. The Arab Revolt: New Features   101
   Prisoners of War, Deserters, and Others
   The Arab Legion
   The Members of the Societies and the Leadership of the
   Arab Revolt
   Iraqis, Syrians, and Others in the Arab Revolt
   Turko-Arab Peace Proposals
   The Cairo Agency

6. Syrians and Lebanese in Egypt   165
   The Syrians in Cairo
   The Declaration to the Seven and its Origins
   The Lebanese Societies in Egypt during the War

7. The Légion d'Orient and Emigré Communities in
   America   200
   The Comité Central Syrien and the Légion d'Orient
   Emigré Societies in North America

8. The Final Month of the War   231

Summary, Conclusions, and Epilogue   244

Notes   261

Bibliography   299

Index   309

Acknowledgements

I wish to express my sincere gratitude to the Dayan Center of Tel-Aviv University, which has rendered me financial help both at the research stage preceding this book and during its translation into English. Dr. Joseph A. Reif of the English Department at Bar-Ilan University translated this book from the original Hebrew, and my sincere thanks to him are hereby acknowledged. A Foreign and Commonwealth Office scholarship granted me by the British Council made it possible for me to carry out research in various archives and libraries in England in 1987.

A special note of appreciation goes to my mother, whose devotion has long been a source of strength to me.

Eliezer Tauber

Nisan 5751
Bar-Ilan, Israel

Abbreviations

AB = *Arab Bulletin*
AN = Archives Nationales
Arabie = Levant 1918-1929, Arabie-Hedjaz
Arbur = Arab Bureau
Cab = Cabinet Office
CCS = Comité Central Syrien
CIGS = Chief of the Imperial General Staff
C-in-C = Commander-in-Chief
Cmd = Command
CO = Colonial Office
CPO = Chief Political Officer
CUP = Committee of Union and Progress
CZA = Central Zionist Archives
d = despatch
DMI, Dirmilint = Director of Military Intelligence
DMO = Director of Military Operations
EEF = Egyptian Expeditionary Force
FO = Foreign Office
FRUS = *Papers Relating to the Foreign Relations of the United States*
FSI = Secretary to the Government of India in the Foreign and Political Department
GHQ = General Headquarters
GOC = General Officer Commanding
Guerre = Guerre 1914-1918
HC = High Commissioner
IJMES = *International Journal of Middle East Studies*
IO = India Office
ISA = Israel State Archives
l = letter
L/P&S = India Office, Political and Secret Departmental Records
MAE = Ministère des Affaires Etrangères
MEF = Mesopotamian Expeditionary Force
memo = memorandum
MES = *Middle Eastern Studies*
MG = Ministère de la Guerre
NA = National Archives
PA = Papiers d'Agents

Palestine = Levant 1918-1929, Palestine
PRO = Public Record Office
r = report
SSI = Secretary of State for India
Syrie-Liban = Levant 1918-1929, Syrie-Liban-Cilicie
t = telegram
USS = Under Secretary of State
WO = War Office
WP = Wingate Papers

Introduction

ARAB SOCIETIES BEFORE THE WAR

World War I was a watershed in the history of the Middle East in general and the Fertile Crescent in particular. For four centuries most of these regions were ruled by the Ottoman Empire, though several countries of the Middle East were loosened from its grip before the war. The process began with Egypt, which for all practical purposes was lost to the Empire with its conquest by Napoleon in 1798, and ended with Libya, which was occupied by Italy in 1911. Yet it was the First World War which finally brought an end to Ottoman rule over the Arab countries, and, in fact, to the Empire itself. After the war, with the capture of the Fertile Crescent by the British army, the boundaries of the modern Arab states were determined, and Syria, Lebanon, Iraq, and Transjordan were established. However, European mandates replaced Ottoman rule, and it was only in a later period that the peoples of the Fertile Crescent obtained complete independence.

The attempts of the inhabitants of the Fertile Crescent to gain some measure of independence began well before World War I. The earliest ideas for Syrian independence emerged during the 1870's. But it was in the period of 1908-1914, the years of Young Turk rule, that proto-nationalist and nationalist activity noticeably increased in the Arab provinces of the Ottoman Empire, the main cause being the deterioration of relations between Turks and Arabs. The Young Turk revolution in July 1908, which was followed by the promulgation of the constitution and the end of the era of despotism of Sultan 'Abd al-Hamid II, brought a tremendous wave of exhilaration throughout the Empire. However, the Ottoman honeymoon which followed was over soon after it began. The various nations of the Empire, including the Arabs, expected partnership and equality, but the members of the "Committee of Union and Progress" (CUP), the leaders of the Young Turks, had other plans. After suppressing an attempted counter-revolution by the

---

* The introduction is a summary of the author's *The Emergence of the Arab Movements*.

supporters of the old regime in April 1909, several of the leaders of the CUP began to put into effect the nationalist ideology that motivated them. They aspired to bring about the assimilation of all the nationalities of the Empire into the Turanian nationality. In their view the Ottoman Empire was a Turkish empire, and all its other peoples should become Turkish, willingly or not. For this purpose they began a process of Turkification of the Empire, and the Arabs saw themselves as its principal casualties. Many Arabs were removed from positions of authority, Arab officers felt discriminated against in the Ottoman army, and the Turkish language became the only language permitted in courts and government offices in the Arab provinces. These Turkish affronts against the Arabs, along with the Empire's defeats in 1911 in Libya and in the Balkan War in 1912-1913, convinced some of the Arab inhabitants that the Turks no longer had the strength to rule over the non-Turkish regions of the Empire. In order to defend the interests of the Arab provinces, Arab activists in Istanbul, in the Fertile Crescent, and outside the Empire established a series of societies, both secret and overt, during the following six years.

The first society that was founded after the Young Turk revolution was the "Arab-Ottoman Brotherhood". An open society, it was set up by former spies and functionaries of Sultan 'Abd al-Hamid, but was disbanded shortly afterwards without leaving any recognizable mark on the development of the Arab idea, which it ostensibly promoted. Its place as the representative body of the Arabs in Istanbul was taken over by the "Literary Club", which was founded in the beginning of 1910 by Arab students pursuing higher education there. The president of the club was a Shi'ite from South Lebanon, 'Abd al-Karim al-Khalil. The club functioned in the open, but as circumstances evolved it also began clandestine activities with the purpose of defending the rights of Arabs and their lands.

The first of the secret Arab societies during the Young Turk period was al-Fatat. (Its full original name was Jam'iyyat al-Umma al-'Arabiyya al-Fatat — The Society of the Young Arab Nation.) The idea for this society was conceived shortly after the revolution of 1908 by two Arab students in Istanbul, Ahmad Qadri from Damascus and 'Awni 'Abd al-Hadi from Nablus, when the two sensed the beginnings of the Turkification tendencies of the Young Turks. However, the idea of the society was not put into effect until a year later, in Paris, by 'Awni 'Abd al-Hadi and four more students, Rustum Haydar from Ba'albek, Rafiq al-Tamimi from Nablus, and Tawfiq al-Natur and

Muhammad al-Mihmisani from Beirut. The purpose of the society was to protect the "natural rights" of the Arab nation and to place it in the "ranks of living nations". The society maintained an especially high standard of secrecy; it accepted new members only after a complicated vetting procedure; it compartmentalized its activities; and it used a code for correspondence. Its most significant action in the period before the war was its organization in June 1913 of the Paris Congress in which representatives of most of the Arab societies existing at the time participated. After this Congress the centre of the society moved to Beirut.

The second secret society during this period was *al-Qahtaniyya* (named after Qahtan, a legendary ancestor of the Arabs), which was formed in late 1909 in Istanbul for reasons similar to those of *al-Fatat*. Its founders were two officers, Salim al-Jaza'iri from Damascus and 'Aziz 'Ali al-Misri from Cairo, and two civilians, Khalil Hamada, a native of Beirut, and 'Abd al-Hamid al-Zahrawi from Homs. The society sought to raise the cultural, social, and economic level of the Arabs, and to demand equal rights for Arabs and Turks in the Ottoman Empire. It had a number of branches outside the capital, and most of its members came from among Arab military officers and the ranks of the Literary Club. In 1910 Salim al-Jaza'iri and 'Aziz 'Ali al-Misri were sent to fight in Yemen, Khalil Hamada died, and 'Abd al-Hamid al-Zahrawi was forced to leave the capital because of increasing pressure from the CUP. As a result the society disbanded.

One of the foremost of the believers in a bright future for Arab-Turkish relations in the Empire, after the Young Turk revolution, was the Muslim thinker Rashid Rida. As great as his hopes were so was his disappointment when the Young Turks began to implement their Turkification policy, and this disappointment turned into blazing hatred for the men of the CUP. In 1911 he established in Cairo the "Society of the Arab Association". Its primary goals were to bring about unity among the independent Arab rulers of the Arabian Peninsula and cooperation among the various Arab societies in Syria, Iraq, and Istanbul, in the struggle against the CUP and for the future of the Arab provinces. Later he began to preach the establishment of an independent pan-Arab empire covering Syria, Iraq, and the Arabian Peninsula, whose provinces would have independent internal administration. In order to realize these ideas Rida sent emissaries to most of the rulers of the Arabian Peninsula in an attempt to unite them in the common cause, but without success.

At the time that Rida was sending his emissaries to the Arabian Peninsula there arose in Istanbul two other secret societies on the initiative of another sworn enemy of the CUP, Da'ud al-Dabbuni, a Muslim student from Mosul. The first was "The Green Flag", named after the green flag of Ibn Sa'ud, the independent ruler of Najd, who symbolized in the eyes of the founders of the society the hope of the Arab nation. It was set up in 1912 in order to strengthen the ties among the Arab students in Istanbul and to direct their attention to the rescue of the Arab nation "from the abyss into which it has fallen". Since this society was not very active, Da'ud al-Dabunni founded another one "The Black Hand", whose purpose was to assassinate Arabs who collaborated with the CUP. Nothing is known of any successful attempt by its members, and it disbanded less than a year after it was formed.

The Empire's defeats, in Libya in 1911 and in the Balkans in 1912-1913, led to a radicalization of the ideas of some of the societies, to the formation of new societies, and to a number of revolutionary ventures. The Literary Club reached the conclusion that "the Ottoman Government, whose weakness and impotence were proven in the wars in Tripoli and the Balkans, will not be able to defend the Arab countries in time of need". Therefore, it was imperative to "strengthen the Arab element in the Ottoman Empire and to turn it into one able to defend its own existence". The leaders of the Club worked to attain this purpose, mainly by propagandizing, which was done by a secret body that they set up, the "Arab Youth Society".

More revolutionary was a group of 60 officers, most of them from Baghdad, who despaired of the future of the Empire and decided to return to Iraq from Istanbul at the end of 1912 and to organize a revolt there. With the mediation of a Lebanese journalist by the name of Ibrahim Salim al-Najar they contacted diplomats from the French and British embassies in Istanbul for help in getting back to Iraq. The suggestion by a British diplomat that the officers be moved in groups of ten caused the cancellation of the plan because of the officers' fear that they would be arrested as soon as the first group of ten left.

Around the same time separatist underground activity began in Aleppo. In December 1912 a group of Muslim notables appealed to the French consul and expressed the opinion that the time had come for a revolution in all the centres of Syria, to drive out the Sultan's deputies and to deliver the country into the hands of French forces. The French lack of enthusiasm for this plan caused them to try a second approach, in April 1913, but this time to the British consul in the city. They asked him to have the British government in Egypt extend its aegis over their region, and they assured him that they could organize a popular, pro-British, movement in Aleppo, if they could get British assistance. These ideas were unrealistic, in that they were likely to complicate the diplomatic relations between Britain and the Ottoman Empire, and the British did not generate much enthusiasm for such a plan either.

Another revolutionary attempt was made in the beginning of 1913 under the leadership of Salim al-Jaza'iri. About 40 Syrian officers in Chatalja and Gallipoli arranged a secret conference under his chairmanship at which they decided, in the light of the deterioration of the Empire as evidenced in the Balkan War, to return to Syria and to start a military revolt which would bring about the expulsion of the Turks. Their ultimate goal was to gain independence for Syria and to turn it into a principality under the rule of the Egyptian Prince 'Umar Tusun. They sent a delegation of four officers to Beirut to investigate the atmosphere in that city and the readiness of its inhabitants to help in the uprising. This plan, too, was abandoned when the officers learned that they would not get the aid they were expecting from the French and that their plan was therefore unrealistic.

A plan similar to that of the Syrian officers was drawn up in March 1913 by the leaders of the Decentralization Party. This party was formed towards the end of 1912 in Cairo by a number of Syrian and Lebanese émigrés, ostensibly to work for the granting of a decentralized regime for all the vilayets of the Empire. Their real interest, however, was in improving living conditions in greater Syria and achieving for it some measure of autonomy. The party was presided over by Rafiq al-'Azm, and among its prominent figures were Rashid Rida, 'Abd al-Hamid al-Zahrawi, and Iskandar 'Ammun. However, the party soon lost all hope of bringing about any changes in the Empire by legal means. At a meeting in March 1913 the party leaders decided that the party should work towards turning Syria into an independent principality, which would include Mount Lebanon, under the rule of a Muslim prince. The party had no resources at this time for realizing such a plan, and only after the outbreak of the World War did they make any attempt to put it into effect.

While the Decentralization Party was working for a greater Syria, a number of Lebanese societies were being founded by Lebanese émigrés in Cairo, Paris, New York, and São Paulo, who focussed their efforts on Mount Lebanon alone. Though they had a common Arabic name, *al-Nahda al-Lubnaniyya* (The Lebanese Revival), these societies operated independently of each other. They all shared a common goal — maintenance of the special autonomous status of Mount Lebanon (a status granted it in 1861), extension of its privileges, and the return of various territories removed from it, of which one was the city of Beirut. The activists of the various Lebanese societies sent telegrams and petitions to the European powers calling on them to intervene on behalf of Mount Lebanon. At times they approached foreign diplomats, mainly the French, and offered to cooperate in the conquest of the region from the Ottomans. Nothing came of these offers prior to World War I, and only after the war started did the members of the Lebanese society in Cairo try to realize their aspirations for independence in cooperation with the Decentralization Party.

In 1913 a movement began spreading throughout the Arab provinces of the Empire calling for administrative reforms and the improvement of the condition of these provinces. Two open reform societies were formed in this context, one in Beirut and the other in Basra. The Beirut society not only demanded that administrative reforms be carried out in the Beirut vilayet but that advisers be brought from Europe to supervise the reforms. The society lasted only a few months. The CUP, which was in favour of a centralized government system, could not allow the existence of a reform society that demanded administrative autonomy, and in April 1913 they issued an order for its closing. In reaction the people of Beirut began a general strike and civil disobedience, and riots broke out in the streets. The governor of Beirut did not temporize, and he threw several of the society's activists into jail. The affair ended with the intervention of the British consul-general who succeeded in arranging a compromise according to which those arrested would be released and the people of Beirut would promise to maintain tranquillity. The Beirut reform society remained closed.

The Basra reform society, on the other hand, was much stronger than the one in Beirut. It was headed by Sayyid Talib al-Naqib, the "strong man" of Basra. Though this society was not a secret one, it carried out, under the inspiration of its leader, subversive activities against the authorities. In June 1913 Sayyid Talib's men assassinated Farid Bek, the military commandant of Basra, and Badi' Nuri, the mutasarrif of the Muntafik region. This was the only successful attack of this kind by any of the members of the Arab societies during this period. Sayyid Talib also had ties with another open society in Baghdad, the "National Scientific Club". There are those who claimed that this society was secretly working to drive the Turks out of Iraq.

The events of April 1913 in Beirut proved that it would not be possible to bring about change from within the Empire. Therefore, members of the secret society *al-Fatat* in Paris decided to organize a congress in that city at which representatives of the various Arab societies would put their demands to the Imperial authorities. The Paris Congress took place in June 1913 with the participation of 21 representatives from various regions of greater Syria and two from Iraq. The president of the congress was the former member of parliament 'Abd al-Hamid al-Zahrawi. Discussions dealt with administrative decentralization and its application in the Syrian provinces. The resolutions of the congress demanded administrative reforms, recognition of Arabic as an official language, broadening of the authority of the local general council in the vilayet of Beirut, financial aid to the sanjaq of Mount Lebanon, and so forth. The government in Istanbul, perplexed by the international reverberations of the congress, decided to reach an understanding with it. An emissary of the CUP arrived in Paris, accompanied by 'Abd al-Karim al-Khalil, the president of the Literary Club in Istanbul, who during this period was devising a conciliatory policy towards the CUP. These two came to an agreement with the participants of the congress concerning the reforms that the Ottoman government would have to implement in the Arab provinces. To get the application of the agreement started, 'Abd al-Hamid al-Zahrawi even went to Istanbul. But the agreed-upon reforms remained only on paper. The Ottoman government evaded implementing them, and this led to the final break between the Turks and the activists of the Arab and Syrian movements.

In mid-1913 'Aziz 'Ali al-Misri returned to Istanbul from military service in Libya, during which he led the resistance movement of the Sanusis against the Italian occupation forces. When he learned of the contacts between Arab activists and the CUP, contacts that he considered a waiver of Arab rights, he decided to form *al-'Ahd* (The Covenant — referring to "the covenant between its members and Allah in the service of the Fatherland"). The founding assembly was convened in October 1913. Among its members were many officers, such as Salim al-Jaza'iri and Amin Lutfi al-Hafiz from Damascus, Yasin al-Hashimi, Taha al-Hashimi, and Nuri al-Sa'id from Baghdad, and 'Ali Jawdat al-Ayyubi and Jamil al-Madfa'i from Mosul. The purpose of the society was to work for the establishment of a dual empire, Turko-Arab, on the model of Austria-Hungary. According to this plan the Arab provinces of this empire would be granted internal independence. But not long after the formulation of the society's platform the authorities arrested 'Aziz 'Ali al-Misri, indicted him on various charges, and intended to sentence him to death. As a result of international pressure and the intervention of the British ambassador in Istanbul, 'Aziz 'Ali was granted an amnesty and expelled to Egypt.

Branches of al-'Ahd were set up throughout Syria and Iraq, the most important ones being in Mosul and Baghdad. In 1914 the members of the Baghdad branch prepared a grandiose plan to liberate the whole region from Mosul in the north to the Persian Gulf in the south. The revolt was planned to start in Basra, where the authorities suffered from chronic weakness, and to spread from there if possible in the direction of Syria, with assistance from the al-'Ahd branch in Damascus and the tribes of central Syria. The leadership was to be offered to Ibn Sa'ud of Najd. Eventually, differences of opinion concerning the methods of implementing the plan brought about its postponement till the beginning of 1915. By then, of course, it was too late, as southern Iraq had already been occupied by the British.

There were two additional societies that were formed on the eve of the war: Al-'Alam ("The Flag", that is, the Arab flag) in Mosul, which strove for the independence of Iraq and propagandized against the Turks; and the "Arab Revolutionary Society" in Cairo, which sought to establish an Arab state on a decentralized basis and whose activity consisted of the distribution of some virulent anti-Turkish manifestos.

The political societies and revolutionary movements surveyed above were not homogeneous in character but rather were divided into a number of national currents. Some of the societies that were formed in the period from the Young Turk revolution in 1908 until the outbreak of the World War in August 1914 worked for the general Arab cause while others had local, particularistic goals. Among the former were al-Fatat, al-Qahtaniyya, and al-'Ahd as well as a pan-Arab society such as the Society of the Arab Association, which aspired to establish a pan-Arab empire covering Syria, Iraq, and the Arabian Peninsula. In contrast to these there were the particularist organizations such as the Decentralization Party, which worked on behalf of Syria, and the Society of the Lebanese Revival, which worked on behalf of Mount Lebanon. It seems also that most of the revolutionary attempts in this period were of local character, Syrian or Iraqi, rather than pan-Arab.

The activists of all the trends numbered in all only a few hundred, a drop in the ocean of five million Arab inhabitants of the Ottoman Empire. Therefore, the influence of the various societies on the Arab population of the Empire was quite limited. The societies disseminated their ideas by means of proclamations and handbills, and by such tactics as planting their people on the staffs of various Arab newspapers. It seems that the ideas of the local societies were absorbed better than those of the general Arab current. Their particularist solutions apparently seemed more realistic in the eyes of the local populations, who were seeking, at least part of them, a practical alternative to their sad state in the Ottoman Empire.

Despite the small number of members, the societies constituted a turning point in the history of the Arab Middle East: the activists and the ideologues of the various trends went from words to deeds as they attempted to realize the ideologies in which they believed. In the framework of these societies, whether of the general Arab movement or of the local ones, the national movements of the modern Arab Middle East began to take form. Besides their being the foundry of the national movements in this region these societies were also the forge that produced the Arab leadership after the First World War.

*

In August 1914 World War I broke out in Europe. The Ottoman Empire announced its armed neutrality, but on 2 August it signed a secret pact with Germany and in effect thereby joined the Central Powers. The pro-German position of the Empire found public expression later that month when it granted refuge to the German warships "Goeben" and "Breslau". These two ships led the German-Ottoman attack on the Black Sea ports of Russia at the end of October, following which Russia, France, and Britain declared war on the Empire. At the beginning of November British forces invaded southern Iraq, captured Basra, and began to move towards Baghdad. At the same time Sultan Muhammad Rashad declared a jihad against the infidels, the enemies of the Empire. World War I in the Middle East had begun, and with it began a new era in the history of the Arab countries.

Chapter 1

ABORTIVE ATTEMPTS

The Arab revolt of Sharif Husayn of Mecca in the years 1916-1918 is considered in the historical literature, both scholarly and popular, as the only revolutionary movement of the Arabs against the Ottoman Empire during World War I. Indeed, it was the only revolutionary movement that reached the stage of realization and success during this period. By no means was it the only revolt of the Arabs against the Ottomans during the World War, but its success has overshadowed the other plans and attempts at revolt and has caused them to be erased from historical memory.

In the course of this chapter the other revolt plans initiated by Arabs of the Empire will be reviewed. These were devised for the most part by Syrians and Lebanese, and their common denominator was failure. Some of them did not even reach the stage of execution and others, which did, ended within a short time with a lack of success. The main ones among them were the revolt plans devised by Lebanese activists at the beginning of the war, the plans of the Syrian Decentralization Party, the revolt plan of an *al-'Ahd* member, Amin Lutfi al-Hafiz, and the revolt plan of the former president of the Literary Club 'Abd al-Karim al-Khalil. A number of revolt attempts which were carried out in Syria and Mount Lebanon at the time of the Arab revolt will also be reviewed.

Subversive activity and attempts at revolt were not limited to the Levant. In Iraq, too, a number of revolt plans were formulated, and a number of uprisings were carried out. Most of them were directed against the Ottomans, but towards the end of the war the first buds of a resistance movement against the British began to appear. The revolutionary activities in Iraq during the war will be discussed in the final section of this chapter.

THE REVOLT PLANS OF THE LEBANESE AT THE BEGINNING OF THE WAR

When the Maronites in Mount Lebanon and Beirut learned of

the outbreak of the First World War in Europe, they openly expressed their sympathy for France. It appeared to them that France would soon occupy Mount Lebanon and would assist them in realizing their aspirations for independence. From the statements of the French consul-general in Beirut, François Georges-Picot, they understood that France was preparing to invade the region not later than three months after the Ottoman Empire entered the war. Some of them even thought that the French invasion would not be deferred for more than one month. They began collecting money for the French Red Cross, and a delegation came to Picot and informed him of the desire of Maronites to enlist in the French army.

However, not all of them were prepared to be satisfied with that. In early August 1914 a number of Maronite leaders approached the consuls-general of Britain, France, and Russia and requested the assistance of British and French soldiers and a supply of weapons and ammunition for an uprising against the Ottomans. They expressed their belief that the Muslims of Syria would join such a revolt. The British consul-general advised them not to take such an initiative because it was not in their power to challenge the Ottoman army by themselves. He cautioned them not to expect aid from Russia or France because these two countries had to worry about themselves for the time being and would not be able to open another front in Syria. A similar appeal by a group of Lebanese in Egypt to General John Maxwell, the GOC of British forces there, met with a similar response.

With Georges-Picot, on the other hand, the applicants found a sympathetic disposition to their appeal. He was unable to promise them any active assistance from France, due to its policy of trying to avoid going to war with the Ottoman Empire. Still, on his own initiative he approached the Greek consul-general with a request that the Greek government supply arms to the Lebanese. The Greek government, according to Georges-Picot, indeed expressed its readiness to transfer to the Lebanese 15,000 rifles and two million rounds of ammunition.

In the beginning of November the Allies declared war on the Ottoman Empire. The consuls-general of the Entente Powers were obliged to leave their posts, and Picot moved to Egypt where he continued his contacts with representatives of the Greek government in Alexandria. At a party held for him by members of the Lebanese community in Alexandria he promised that their country would be liberated in the near future by France and that the tricolour would fly over Syria and Mount

Lebanon. The day after he arrived in Egypt he sent a telegram to the French foreign minister, Théophile Delcassé, in which he urged France to take action in the region in order to maintain her prestige in the Levant. He pointed out that 30-35,000 Lebanese would join a landing force that came to free them from the Ottomans. There would be no need, in his opinion, for more than 1,500-2,000 French soldiers and 40 officers in order to carry out such an invasion. Additional officers would be assigned to organize the local Lebanese forces. The French foreign minister rejected Picot's invasion proposal for both military and political reasons. He was of the opinion that France should concentrate on the campaign in Europe.

A short time afterwards a delegation of Lebanese Maronites and Greek Orthodox arrived in Athens and asked the Greek government to supply them with arms to start a revolt against the Ottomans or to assist an Allied landing force on the Lebanese coast. The Greek prime minister, Venizelos, agreed to give them 3,000-4,000 rifles with ammunition and even to supply a small ship to transport the arms to the Lebanon, on condition that the operation be carried out with the agreement of the French government. Delcassé, who was not prepared to allocate French forces for an invasion of Lebanon, agreed nonetheless to the Greek aid. The British however, expressed their opposition and claimed that the amount of rifles to be sent to Lebanon would not suffice for a clash with the Ottoman army. The French responded that they were aware of the fact that the Lebanese would not be able to hold out against the Ottomans, but at the same time they could not dishearten them and certainly could not oppose the Greek government's supplying them with arms. To this the British responded sharply that it was extremely dangerous to encourage the Lebanese in such plans, even tacitly, because the Allies were in no condition to help them withstand any Ottoman reprisals which would follow a Lebanese revolt. A similar message was sent by the British to the Greek government.

In the meantime one of the Lebanese returned from Athens to the Lebanon in order to organize the landing of the weapons and ammunition. It had been prearranged that the arms would first go to Cyprus in a small ship and from there would be transferred to the Lebanese coast in small boats. Since Cyprus was under British rule it was necessary to obtain their agreement to the plan. Further discussions were held, and in the end the British consented while expressing open annoyance and sending a warning to the Lebanese to be aware of the dangerous situation in which they would find themselves should the Ottoman authorities discover the weapons and ammunition. At that point it was Delcassé who put an end to the plan when he decided that France must concentrate for the time being on the Western Front and had no interest in getting involved in an additional front in Syria.

The Lebanese plan was unrealistic and had it been put into action would have been doomed to failure. The Ottomans, who had suspicions of the Lebanese intentions and were apprehensive of French intervention in the wake of a revolt, entered Mount Lebanon on 22 November 1914 and deployed their soldiers there. They could not allow a French landing on the Lebanese coast, which would cut the supply line of the forces which were about to attack the Suez Canal.[1]

The erroneous assessment by the Lebanese that a French invasion of the Syrian coast was near at hand caused many of them in Egypt to express their desire to enlist in the anticipated invasion force. Enlistment forms were distributed and the Lebanese journalist Ibrahim Salim al-Najjar began to organize a Lebanese volunteer force. Picot encouraged this, and the British authorities were not opposed to it at first either. Within three weeks about 3,000 volunteers had been gathered, of whom 400 started military training. The Lebanese volunteer force never left Cairo. It shortly became clear that France would not take any initiative of the type suggested by Picot, and Picot himself was constrained to cool down the enthusiasm of the Lebanese. They themselves began to express their apprehensions as to the advisability of joining the recruitment initiative and thereby placing their families at home in danger of reprisals, as long as the Allies had not clarified their intentions with regard to the Lebanon. Eventually, General Maxwell ordered a halt to the mobilization activity, and with this the episode of the Lebanese volunteer force came to an end.[2]

The Lebanese in Mount Lebanon and Egypt were not the only Lebanese to make plans for a revolt against the Ottomans in this period. Shukri Ghanim, the president of the Comité Libanais de Paris, asked the French foreign minister in September 1914 to instruct Picot to remain in the Lebanon even if the Ottoman Empire should enter the war on the side of Germany. His reason for this was that Picot's "moral support" would help the Lebanese to defend themselves against an Ottoman invasion of their mountain. Ghanim expressed the opinion that it would be possible to mobilize 10-15,000 Lebanese combatants and to supply them with arms and ammunition by way of the port of

Juniyya.[3] Ghanim's suggestion was, of course, not taken seriously, and Picot left his post of assignment immediately upon France's declaration of war on the Empire.

In the beginning of November a delegation from the Lebanon League of Progress in New York came to the French ambassador in Washington and gave him a memorandum on the future of Lebanon. The French ambassador arranged a meeting of this delegation with the British ambassador and a representative of the Russian embassy so that the Lebanese could present their point of view to them. In the memorandum the members of the League expressed the aspiration of the Lebanese to be liberated from the Ottoman yoke and to gain their independence. They tried to convince the representatives of the Allies of the strategic importance of Mount Lebanon (that is, it lay across the route from Asia Minor to Egypt) and that it was an ideal site for stationing an invasion force. The Christians of the Lebanon, who made up 80 per cent of the population, were interested in helping the Allies to invade it and would be prepared to make sacrifices to achieve their freedom. Therefore, as soon as the Allied forces invaded Lebanon the local population would join them and open a revolt against the Ottomans. The authors of the memorandum purported to represent 150,000 Lebanese in North America, and claimed that they would be able to send thousands of volunteers to the Lebanon, if only they would be furnished with suitable means of transportation. They also asked the Allies to supply them with arms, ammunition, and officers.

The appeal of the Lebanese of New York did not receive a positive response, just as the other appeals of the Lebanese did not. The Allies were not ready at this stage to engage in war efforts of this type, whose chances of success were in question, and they felt that they must invest the better part of their energies in the main arenas of the war. The Lebanese did not give up. One of the authors of the memorandum, Major K. al-Aswad, appealed again in February 1915 to the British ambassador in Washington and expressed the desire of the Lebanese living in the United States to volunteer to fight the Ottomans. He suggested that a training camp be set up in Cyprus in which an organized Lebanese force would take shape and land on the Lebanese coast at the end of its training. He asked for Britain to finance the transportation of the volunteers to Cyprus and to arm them. The British foreign minister rejected the plan forthwith and instructed his ambassador in Washington not to encourage any initiatives of this sort. Other appeals during 1915 were rejected as well on the grounds that Britain could not engage in organizing an armed force on the territory of the United States, which was a neutral state.[4]

Also the Syrian community in Canada approached the Canadian government in early 1915 and informed it that a large number of Syrians in Canada, the United States, and South America wanted to volunteer in the British forces and to go to Egypt in order to fight for the liberation of Syria. They promised to enlist 30-50,000 volunteers. Nothing came of this appeal either.[5]

THE PLANS OF THE DECENTRALIZATION PARTY AND ITS EMISSARIES

After World War I broke out in Europe, and before it spread to the Middle East, the Syrian Decentralization Party and the Alliance Libanaise society of Cairo agreed to open a joint revolt against the Ottomans if and when the Empire should enter the war. The initiators of this joint activity were Iskandar 'Ammun, who was vice-president of the Decentralization Party and president of the Alliance Libanaise, and Da'ud Barakat, who was among the founders of these two bodies and a member of the executive committee of both. The planned revolt was to start in Zahla, and according to 'Abd al-Ghani al-'Uraysi, a Beiruti member of the Decentralization Party, the French minister in Cairo promised them 20,000 rifles, three warships to cover the rebels, and French officers to direct the actions.

On 20 August 1914, the Decentralization Party sent the following letter to one of its branches in the Lebanon:

The Fatherland has never needed the help of its sons as much as it does in this difficult time in which the World War is raging . . . If the Empire should enter this war, and this seems certain to many, then it will never come out of it whole. This war will most likely bring it to its end . . . In this situation the Arab countries will face the same danger that the other Ottoman countries will face and even a much greater danger . . . Inasmuch as this is the appearance of things, it is encumbent upon us, the Arab community, to contemplate the means which will keep our independence from eradication. . . . Therefore we ask you to respond as soon as possible to the following questions:
1. What forces do you have that we can depend on in the hour of need in order to carry out a general action?
2. Will it be possible for you to collect funds and send them to us, or to hold them until needed? What sums will you be able to collect?
3. Can you provide a safe refuge for one or more persons who will be called upon to lead the national movement, and to assure their

sustenance?
4. Can you send a reliable person who will represent your branch to
a place that we will designate, so that he may receive necessary
instructions?
5. If you cannot send anyone, do you see a need for a special messenger to come to you in order to deliver these instructions?
We ask that you respond immediately, for every minute that passes
will be a minute lost to Arab lives. The time has come for us to sacrifice all we have for the life of the nation.

This letter later fell into the hands of Jamal Pasha, the commander of the Fourth Ottoman Army and ruler of the Levant
(see below). The Shi'ite sheikh Kamil al-As'ad also informed
him of this plan for revolt. Jamal Pasha expressed his astonishment that the Decentralization Party, which had a pan-Syrian
tendency, should agree to cooperate with the Alliance Libanaise,
which was generally working for the Lebanon alone. Evidently
he was aware of the ideological difference between these two
bodies and of the contradiction between the Syrian idea and the
Lebanese idea. To this Kamil al-As'ad answered: "They are
working together because they believe that they must first of all
realize their primary goal, and that is to struggle against the
Ottoman Empire."[6]
The British in Cairo, who were not at all pleased by the exclusiveness of the French contacts with the Syrian and Lebanese
activists, began talks with prominent Muslim members of the
Decentralization Party. Among them were Rafiq al-'Azm, the
president of the party, and Rashid Rida, the Muslim thinker,
who was a member of its executive committee. The talks were
held without the knowledge of the Christian members of the
party (who were pro-French). They made it clear to the British
that they were interested in the liberation of the Arab countries,
even if it meant the collapse of the Empire. It was agreed that
they would put their conditions for cooperation with the British
in writing, and these would be conveyed to the British government. If the latter decided to accept the conditions, then it
should make this known officially through the Reuter News
Agency. In return for this the Arab societies would commit
themselves to incite revolts in the Arab provinces of the Empire.
It was also agreed that the party would send emissaries for this
purpose to the various Arab centres. At the behest of Rashid
Rida the British gave the party 1,000 Egyptian pounds to
finance the sending of the emissaries.
As for their political plans at this time, according to one of the
party members, they would be prepared to grant Britain priority

in the Arab countries after their liberation and to be assisted by Britain in creating a modern government. According to this person they also planned to install a new caliph in Mecca, though this caliph would focus solely on the religious sphere, while the government would be placed in the hands of an amir or governor-general.

The members of the party began sending letters to their friends in the Empire, in which they explained that no one was to enlist on the side of the Turks in the war because it was contrary to Arab interests. They reported to them that the British were prepared to supply arms and ammunition for a revolt in Syria, and they appealed to the Arab soldiers to desert from the Ottoman army. In addition to this, on 26 October 1914, two pairs of emissaries of the party left for the purpose of inciting the Muslim Arabs of the Empire to revolt. The first pair, party member Sheikh Muhammad al-Qalqili and a student of Rashid Rida by the name of 'Abd al-Rahman 'Asim, left Alexandria headed for Beirut and Syria. They arrived in Beirut on an Italian mail boat and just then they found out that the Ottoman Empire had entered the war. Muhammad al-Qalqili was terror-stricken, and they returned immediately on the same boat to Alexandria.

The second pair, deputy secretary of the Party Muhibb al-Din al-Khatib and an Iraqi by the name of 'Abd al-'Aziz al-'Atiqi, left Suez headed for the Persian Gulf, Ibn Sa'ud in Arabia, and Iraq. The British Foreign Office did inform the India Office, which was responsible for this area, about the two emissaries. But as a result of lack of coordination, when these two arrived in Bushir in the Persian Gulf, they were arrested by the British military intelligence officer there. Among their papers were found propaganda documents with a pan-Islamic and anti-Christian tone (a speech by Caliph 'Umar, in which he reassured the Arabs that even if they were few they would still be able to overcome their enemies; a speech by Caliph 'Ali on the subject of jihad; a speech by Tariq ibn Ziyad before the conquest of Andalusia; a poem by Salih ibn Sharif of Andalusia, in which he lamented the fate of his country which had been conquered by the Spaniards; and a booklet with the following instructions for incitement: 1. Denounce the government 2. Curse the Christians 3. "The giving of a helping hand to religious superstitions"). The two men did not give satisfactory answers during their investigation, and their British interrogators decided that they were propagandists working on behalf of the Ottomans. They were transferred to a jail in Basra where they spent the next seven months. The contacts between the India Office and the Foreign Office for clarification of the affair proceeded sluggishly, and Muhibb al-Din al-Khatib sent a call for help to Rashid Rida. The stunned Rida turned to the British authorities in Cairo and pressured them time and again to free the emissaries, who, after all, had been sent in coordination with them and with their financing. Finally, in June 1915 the two were released. Muhibb al-Din al-Khatib returned to Egypt, while the other emissary preferred to stay in Iraq.[7]

According to the earlier agreement between the members of the party and the British, the British chargé d'affaires in Cairo transmitted the demands of the party to his foreign minister. He pointed out that the Arabs suspected that the British intended to annex parts of the Arabian Peninsula, especially on the Red Sea coast. He therefore suggested that the British government publish a declaration that Britain had no intention to carry out any military operations in the Arabian Peninsula, unless needed for the defence of the Arabs against the Turks or in order to aid the Arabs in getting their freedom from the Turks. The next day, 14 November 1914, he received the approval of the foreign minister for the wording that he had suggested for the declaration, and immediately afterwards Reuter Agency in Cairo published the following announcement:

> Reuters learns Government no intention undertaking any military naval operations Arabia except protect Arab interests against Turkish other aggression or support attempts Arabs free themselves Turkish Rule. Reuter.

The members of the party considered this reply vague and unsatisfactory, especially in that it referred only to the Arabian Peninsula. They expressed their bitterness over the limited British commitment and claimed that in fact the British had not promised anything definite at all. The secretary of the party, Haqqi al-'Azm, even hinted that they might discontinue their cooperation with the British. As a result of this, Arthur Henry McMahon, the British high commissioner in Cairo, reported to the foreign minister in February 1915 that it appeared that the Arab leaders in Cairo would no longer be satisfied with vague promises and would insist on a definite statement concerning the future policy of Britain. In April Reginald Wingate, the Sirdar of the Egyptian army and the Governor-General of Sudan, added his voice to this opinion and said that it was necessary to inform the Arab leaders that Britain would support the independence of the Arabian Peninsula. The Foreign Office accepted this view, and in June 1915 a declaration that Britain would insist on the independence of the Arabian Peninsula in any peace treaty was distributed by means of leaflets in Egypt, Sudan, Syria, and parts of the Arabian Peninsula. The men of the Syrian Decentralization Party were disappointed with this declaration because it essentially repeated the first British declaration about the Arabian Peninsula and made no reference to the independence of the other Arab countries. As a result they ceased their contacts with the British authorities in Cairo.[8]

Following this episode the party lost its importance and many members left it during the year 1915.[9] The party was never officially disbanded; it simply crumbled as the war went on. Its leaders turned to founding new political bodies which would better suit the changing conditions of the Arab countries of the Ottoman Empire.

THE REVOLT PLAN OF AMIN LUTFI AL-HAFIZ

As early as 1907 a British army officer had written: "A strong force landed in the Bay of Ayas or at Alexandretta could break the line of communication by marching on Adana or Aleppo, and could isolate Syria from Constantinople."[10]

The idea of invading Alexandretta, or any other point in the Gulf of Iskenderun, and thus cutting the Ottoman Empire in two and severing from its centre the entire region from Syria southward (and thereby also cutting one of the main lines of communication to Iraq), kept recurring in the minds of the British during the following years. In September 1914, even before the Ottoman Empire had entered the war, Vice Admiral Mark Kerr proposed a landing at Alexandretta following which there would be an attack on the Gallipoli Peninsula. The French Admiral Dartige du Fournet supported the idea and held that a landing force of 150,000 men in the Gulf of Iskenderun could continue south in the direction of Egypt and block a Turko-German attack on the Suez Canal.

In November the British Lord of the Admiralty, Winston Churchill, proposed to the cabinet that a landing at Alexandretta would be the correct way to defend Egypt. He was joined by War Minister Lord Kitchener, who also believed that the best way to guard against an Ottoman attack on Egypt would be to land at Alexandretta, thereby blocking the transportation routes of the Ottoman army to Syria. The British authorities in Egypt concurred in this view and asserted that the Syrian population would probably provide assistance for such a landing.

In January 1915 Churchill announced that the Dardanelles campaign would include a landing at Alexandretta. The French, who considered Syria within their sphere of influence (according to an understanding reached with Britain in 1912), were disturbed by this idea, and the French government sent its Minister of the Navy to London. He succeeded in extracting from Churchill an assurance that Britain had no intention whatsoever of taking any independent initiative in Alexandretta, and any operation of this type would be with the concurrence of both governments. A short time later the British government announced that Britain had no intention of landing at Alexandretta. A message in this spirit was sent by the foreign minister to the high commissioner in Egypt, with the explanation that a British landing at Alexandretta would cause a dispute with France.[11]

In the very same period when the plan to invade Alexandretta was rejected, an Arab officer, Amin Lutfi al-Hafiz, was awaiting the invasion on the coast of Syria. He had even prepared an extensive revolt among the Arab soldiers of the Ottoman army in Syria in order to welcome the invaders. Before the war al-Hafiz was one of the important members of the clandestine Arab society *al-Qahtaniyya* and also a member of the Literary Club in Istanbul. In the beginning of 1913 he was a member of a delegation of officers headed by Salim al-Jaza'iri, who came to Beirut to investigate the readiness of its inhabitants to assist a revolt against the Ottomans. Later that same year he was one of the founders of the secret society *al-'Ahd*, and at the beginning of the war he was the head of the Aleppo branch of the society. He held the rank of major at the time and commanded the 136th Regiment which was stationed in Antioch.

Syria in February 1915 was almost clear of Turkish units, and only two Arab divisions and one regiment of Dervish volunteers were stationed there. This was after the failure of the Ottoman attack on the Suez Canal and at the beginning of attacks by the British navy on the Dardanelles. The Ottomans had begun to remove military forces from Syria to the area of the Straits and transferred there all the artillery and machine-gun units that were stationed in Syria. At that time Jamal Pasha and his deputy Fakhri Pasha assigned Amin Lutfi al-Hafiz to organize the Ottoman fortifications in the Gulf of Iskenderun. Al-Hafiz, who was expecting a British landing, set up the fortifications so that they would be of no use to anybody. Furthermore, since he was convinced that a British landing was imminent, he decided to assist it from within and organized a revolt among the Arab units from Payas in the north of the gulf down to Latakia. He also persuaded the chiefs of the Nusayri tribes to support the revolt. Joining the revolt would also be the Arab division stationed in Homs and the Arab division of Mosul stationed in Aleppo. The rebels hoped to succeed in driving out the Turks from Syria and after that perhaps to continue on to Iraq and the Hijaz. They planned to install a temporary sultan in Syria and to recognize the Sharif of Mecca as caliph.

All the necessary preparations for the revolt were carried out, and the staff of the revolt had already cut all the telegraph lines in the region of Homs. But the British landing never took place, and the Ottomans saw to it that the Arab divisions were removed from Syria (see below) and replaced by loyal Turkish units. Amin Lutfi al-Hafiz himself was sent by Jamal Pasha to Istanbul where he was later arrested, and in May 1916 he was hanged.[12]

The idea of a landing in Alexandretta was raised a second time by the British (Kitchener and others) in October-November 1915, and once again it was thwarted by the French for political reasons. In October 1917 it was the French (Foch) who raised it a third time. This time it was the British (Jellicoe) who responded coldly and claimed that it was not practical. With this the idea was finally buried for good.[13]

THE REVOLT PLAN OF 'ABD AL-KARIM AL-KHALIL

About the time that the revolt plan of Amin Lutfi al-Hafiz was aborting another revolt was beginning to take shape, one which was also supposed to cut the lines of transportation from Anatolia to Syria and to assist an Allied landing. There were those who thought that this plan was in fact connected with al-Hafiz's plan. The initiator of this revolt was the Lebanese Shi'ite 'Abd al-Karim Qasim al-Khalil. Before the war he had completed his studies at the schools of administration and law in Istanbul, was a member of al-Qahtaniyya, founded the Literary Club in Istanbul, and served as its president until the outbreak of the war. He provided assistance to the Turkish opposition party, the "Party of Liberty and Union", and opened branches of it in Damascus and Aleppo. For a while he even served as its general secretary.

He was also a member of the Decentralization Party. In 1913 he mediated between the CUP and the participants of the Arab-Syrian Congress in Paris and succeeded in attaining an agreement between them. As a result of his mediation he was accused by some of the Arab reformists of responsibility for the splits that began to occur afterwards in the reform movement. At the outbreak of the war he took the funds of the Literary Club and left Istanbul for Syria. At the time he enjoyed good relations with Jamal Pasha and even received money from him.

The centre point of the revolt planned by 'Abd al-Karim al-Khalil was to be in Sidon, and his main partner was Rida al-Sulh, who was a native of Sidon and a former representative of the vilayet of Beirut in the Ottoman parliament. Rida al-Sulh concentrated mainly on spreading propaganda that Syria was about to fall into the hands of the Allies and that a British conquest was imminent. It seems that the revolt was to have the assistance of the Mutawali Shi'ite population of the Jabal 'Amil region, who were to aid in the landing of Allied forces. Al-Khalil tried to enlist the support of the representative of Beirut in parliament, Salim 'Ali Salam. He reported to him on the revolt, its location and the resources at the disposal of the rebels, and claimed that he would be getting aid from the British. Salam refused to have anything to do with this plan and even suggested that he cancel it. Al-Khalil rejected his advice.[14]

The revolt plans became known to the Ottoman authorities relatively quickly, and from various sources. In May 1915 attacks against the Ottoman government in general and Jamal Pasha in particular increased in the Egyptian press. Leading the attacks were members of the Decentralization Party. Jamal Pasha called in 'Abd al-Karim al-Khalil, who was a member of the party, and asked him to explain what was going on. Al-Khalil pleaded that this was contrary to his way of thinking and added that if he should be permitted to go to Egypt he would be able to convince the party leaders to halt the propaganda campaign against Jamal Pasha. This answer enraged Jamal Pasha, who claimed that the real reason for his request to be allowed to go to Egypt was to reveal to the Allies the location of Ottoman forces in Syria. He refused to permit him to go to Egypt, and from then on began to suspect his intentions concerning the Empire. However, he still did not have any specific information about al-Khalil's plan for revolt.[15]

It is believed by some that the first indication of al-Khalil's plans came to Jamal Pasha from the German intelligence agency in Beirut. According to another version it was the Jewish spy

Alter Levin who divulged al-Khalil's secret. It seems, however, that he was in fact caught as a result of a series of tip-offs by local Lebanese residents. On 20 May 1915, the intelligence services of the Fourth Army received a report which described a conspiracy against the Ottoman Empire and that one of its initiators was 'Abd al-Wahhab al-Inklizi, a civil inspector in Beirut who was also a member of the Decentralization Party. A number of meetings were held in his house in which 'Abd al-Karim al-Khalil also participated. The report was signed by someone named Ahmad Sa'id al-'Amili. An investigation by the Vali of Beirut did not turn up anyone with such a name. On 29 May another report from the same Sa'id al-'Amili was received which said:

> Two days ago 'Abd al-Karim Bek al-Khalil, who enjoys the trust of Ahmad Jamal Pasha but who is actually working against him secretly, arrived in Beirut. The day before yesterday he met with the civil inspector 'Abd al-Wahhab Bek al-Inklizi, and they discussed the organization of a revolt movement. From there 'Abd al-Karim went to the village of Burj al-Barajna, in the suburbs of Beirut, where he met with several agents, and they discussed the situation and the measures they must take in order to incite the contemplated revolt. It has become known to me that 'Abd al-Karim Bek al-Khalil will be going to Sidon in order to meet there with the leaders of a group that supports him and is led by the former member of parliament from Sidon Rida Bek al-Sulh and a number of famous leaders. These men are working against the Empire and want to incite a revolt in this country for the benefit of foreign countries that are hostile to our Islamic nation and to the exalted Empire.

On 10 June the Qa'imaqam of Sidon reported that 'Abd al-Karim al-Khalil had indeed met with Rida al-Sulh in the presence of ten other men. On 18 June another report arrived from Sa'id al-'Amili in which he reported on meetings that al-Khalil had with al-Sulh and about 30 other notables of Sidon. It was pointed out that: "The purpose of these meetings is to pave the way for the outbreak of an extensive revolt, which will begin in this region. The Pasha must start an investigation of this matter before the situation in the said region becomes completely out of control." Further investigations by the Ottoman authorities concerning the source of these reports drew a blank, and the identity of Sa'id al-'Amili remained a mystery. Later it was claimed that behind the reports on 'Abd al-Karim al-Khalil stood a Lebanese by the name of Subhi Abaza.[16]

On 21 June Sheikh As'ad al-Shuqayri, the chief mufti of the

Fourth Army, also warned Jamal Pasha that 'Abd al-Karim al-Khalil and Rida al-Sulh were preparing a revolt in the region of Tyre and Sidon with Allied assistance and were exploiting the fact that only meagre Ottoman forces were stationed there at that time. He added that Kamil al-As'ad would be able to supply further details of this matter. Kamil al-As'ad was the most important Shi'ite notable in Jabal 'Amil and represented the region in parliament. Jamal Pasha immediately ordered him to report to his headquarters in Jerusalem in order to question him. When al-As'ad received the order to come to Jerusalem for an investigation, he went immediately to Salim 'Ali Salam in Beirut in order to consult with him as to how he should proceed. Salam advised him to say that he knew nothing about this matter. To this al-As'ad responded that such an answer would not be convincing because the entire population already knew about the affair. (In another context Ahmad Qadri, one of the founders of al-Fatat, said that 'Abd al-Karim al-Khalil loved publicity.)

On 23 June Kamil al-As'ad arrived in Jerusalem and was brought before Jamal Pasha. He reported to him both about the revolt plan of the Decentralization Party in cooperation with the Alliance Libanaise (see above) and about the activity of 'Abd al-Karim al-Khalil. He told him that al-Khalil had decided to exploit the fact that most of the Ottoman forces had been sent to the Straits and was organizing a revolt in the region between Sidon and Beirut, which would prepare the ground for an Allied landing on the Syrian coast. As proof for these assertions he pointed out the meetings that had been held between al-Khalil, al-Sulh, and al-Inklizi, and also what he had heard from Sheikh Muhammad Ibrahim of the village of Ansar about the planned revolt. He stressed that this sheikh told him that the revolt was supposed to break out in the immediate future. Jamal Pasha, who was aware of the weakness of his forces in the region of Sidon, issued an order that very evening to arrest all those involved in the affair and to bring them to the military court in 'Aleyh.[17]

The judicial investigation was held during the month of July, and on 9 August the intelligence department of the Fourth Army submitted the final report on the arrests. 'Abd al-Karim al-Khalil was accused of conspiring to harm the public safety during time of war, of planning a revolt against the Empire, and of membership in the Decentralization Party. He was sentenced to death and hanged on 21 August. Rida al-Sulh was accused of cooperating in the conspiracy and of spreading propaganda against the Empire. He and his son Riyad (a future prime minister of Lebanon) were sentenced to permanent exile and deported to Anatolia. (It is possible that as a result of their being in Anatolia they were not included in the second series of executions in May 1916 — see the next chapter.) 'Abd al-Wahhab al-Inklizi remained in jail and was hanged in May 1916. Salim 'Ali Salam was summoned for investigation, denied any connection with the affair, and was released for lack of evidence.[18]

Later, weird rumours spread that Jamal Pasha himself was behind the revolt plan of 'Abd al-Karim al-Khalil, and when he suspected that the plan was discovered he hastened to get rid of al-Khalil before he could reveal the secret. According to this version, when Jamal Pasha arrived in Syria, he suggested to al-Khalil that he become a partner in his plan to sever Syria from the Empire and turn it into an independent Khedivate with him at its head, while concluding a separate peace with the Allies. Al-Khalil began to gather supporters in order to carry out this idea and even tried to gain the support of the chiefs of the tribes in the Syrian desert. When Jamal Pasha found out that the Imperial authorities had knowledge of al-Khalil's activity, he himself ordered his officers to shadow al-Khalil and al-Sulh in order to remove any suspicion from himself. This strange version was based among other things on a rumour according to which al-Khalil said before he died: "I know the real reason why Jamal Pasha is hanging me, and in the future history will know it, too."[19]

The question of contacts that Jamal Pasha did or did not have with representatives of the Allies and other factors as to the possibility of arriving at a separate peace deserves extensive research in itself. Certain archival documents and memoirs of his chief of intelligence hint that there was something in this, at least to a certain degree. Nevertheless, it would be absurd to connect this unclear matter with the revolt plan of 'Abd al-Karim al-Khalil and his execution. Even if Jamal Pasha had been conducting his own independent policy with respect to the fate of Syria, he would not have turned for help to a boastful political dealer lacking means such as 'Abd al-Karim al-Khalil.

REBELLIOUS ACTIVITIES IN THE LEVANT DURING THE ARAB REVOLT

The aborted plan of 'Abd al-Karim al-Khalil was the last revolt attempt that was carried out in Syria before the outbreak of the

Arab revolt of Sharif Husayn of Mecca and that had no connection with the activities of the secret societies *al-Fatat* and
al-'Ahd. The subversive activity of *al-Fatat* and *al-'Ahd* was
being conducted throughout this whole period and was integrated in the process which finally led to the outbreak of the
Arab revolt. A separate chapter will be devoted to this activity
and to the origins of the Arab revolt.

It is generally believed that at the time that the Arab revolt
was going on in the Hijaz, and afterwards in Transjordan, no
rebellions took place in Syria and the Lebanon because of the
reign of terror pursued by Jamal Pasha. Jamal Pasha himself
tried to create this impression in his memoirs as justification for
the policy he followed. Others (Lawrence among them) claimed
that a Syrian revolt did not take place in this period because of
the indolence of the Syrian population, who were more profi-
cient in political dealings than in subversive activity. There were
those who held that the reason for the inability to start a revolt
was the many rifts and internal conflicts among the Syrians with
all their various communities and religions.[20] There is some truth
in each of these views. Yet it should be pointed out that plans
for revolt, and even actions on a small scale, did indeed take
place in Syria during the period under discussion.

In early June 1916, shortly before the Arab revolt broke out,
Nasib al-Bakri left Damascus on his way to the Hijaz together
with several of Sharif Faysal's men, who had been staying at
that time in Damascus (see below). In order to mislead the
authorities they did not head straight to the Hijaz but rather
southeast in the direction of Jawf, the stronghold of Nawaf al-
Sha'lan, the son of Nuri al-Sha'lan, the paramount chief of the
Ruwalla tribes. When the two met, al-Bakri suggested organizing
a general tribal uprising against the Ottomans in cooperation
with the Druzes. According to this plan they were to attack
Damascus, and they hoped to be aided in this action by two
sympathetic regiments stationed in 'Aleyh and Nazareth. A delegation was sent to the camp of Faysal near Medina for the purpose of requesting 20,000 rifles. Al-Bakri waited a month for the
return of the delegation, and when they did not return he
despaired, continued on to the Hijaz, and the plan for revolt did
not materialize.

A year later, in June 1917, Fawwaz al-Sha'lan, another son of
Nuri al-Sha'lan, planned a revolt against the Ottomans. This
revolt, which was aided by professional advice from the British
spy George Wyman Bury, was to break out during the visit of
Enver Pasha in Syria. The rebel forces were to be based on the

Ruwalla tribes and on the Arab officers and soldiers who had deserted the Ottoman army and had found refuge with the Ruwalla. The revolt was to include an attack on the railroads and cutting the link with Syria, and also an attempt on the life of Enver Pasha. The German intelligence in Syria reported this plan to Jamal Pasha. The latter hastened to have Fawwaz al-Sha'lan brought to Beirut and to hold him as a hostage until the publication of a declaration of loyalty by Nuri al-Sha'lan and the departure of Enver Pasha from Syria.[21]

In June 1916 Shukri al-Ayyubi of Damascus was arrested after a letter containing harsh attacks against the Ottomans was found in his possession. An investigation which followed led to the arrest of a native of Tripoli, 'Abd al-Ghani al-Rafi'i, in whose possession was found a manifesto written by him and Shukri al-Ayyubi calling for the opening of an Arab revolt. Following this many others were arrested, from Damascus, Tripoli, Zahla, Rashaya, Hasbaya, Mu'allaqa, and Ba'albek. Among them were the prominent Arab activists Shukri al-Quwwatli, Ahmad Qadri, and Faris al-Khuri. In their trial the prosecution tried to prove that they had conspired to assassinate Jamal Pasha and to remove the yoke of the Empire. The death sentence pronounced on several of those arrested was not carried out, and they spent various periods of time in jail, some until the end of the war. Some of them were freed after bribes were paid. (For this series of arrests see below in the chapter on arrests and executions.)[22]

A more successful revolt movement, if one can call it that, was that of the Haydars of Ba'albek. When those involved in the revolt plan of 'Abd al-Karim al-Khalil were arrested, the Ottoman authorities ordered the leader of the Mutawali Shi'ites in the region of Ba'albek, As'ad Haydar, and his two sons Salih and Ibrahim to present themselves in 'Aleyh for trial. All three were members of the secret society al-Fatat, and the first two were also members of the Decentralization Party. Salih was also mayor of Ba'albek. When they received the order to report, the father As'ad complied and came to 'Aleyh. Salih and Ibrahim fled to the mountains. The authorities thereupon announced that As'ad would be executed if his two sons did not turn themselves in. The threat worked, and several members of the family disclosed the hiding place of Salih who was captured. Salih Haydar was executed on 21 August 1915, together with 'Abd al-Karim al-Khalil. As'ad Haydar and his brother Husayn (also a member of the Decentralization Party) were deported to Anatolia. Following this two members of the family, Yusuf and Muhammad, joined their cousin Ibrahim in the mountains, and together they organized a band which harassed the Ottoman forces in the neighbourhood. The authorities ordered the deportation of the entire Haydar family to Anatolia. As a result, many of its sons fled to the mountains and joined the band. They then began to engage in rebellious activities against the Ottoman soldiers and to cause them losses. Military forces sent against them were unsuccessful in suppressing them. When the Turks and Germans began their great retreat towards the end of the war, the Haydars increased their activity and cut down the laggards. They even succeeded in taking prisoner an entire Turkish regiment and held it in Ba'albek until the British came.[23]

Another revolt broke out in the region of Ba'albek in late 1916 under the leadership of the Mutawali Shi'ite Milhim Qasim. He formed a band of Mutawalis around him, roamed the villages of the area, and killed isolated Turkish soldiers who crossed his path. At first he did not dare confront the army directly, but as his band grew, apparently with the help of British agents, so did his boldness, and he succeeded in preventing the Ottoman forces from moving about freely in the region. In January 1917 Jamal Pasha issued orders to destroy the Qasim's band. Large military forces from Ba'albek, Rayaq, and Zahla attacked Qasim's men and suppressed the revolt in five days, killing 125 rebels. Qasim and the remnant of his followers fled to the mountain heights. After the situation calmed down Qasim began to reorganize his band, but in the course of 1917 he was subdued by the Vali of Damascus. His wife and children were captured by the Ottomans and held as hostages in Ba'albek. In 1918 he renewed his activity and raised an armed band of 300 men. Two attacks against him by gendarmerie failed. As a result his confidence grew, and he began sending threats to the Shi'ite leaders in the region with a demand that they join his revolt. To the Qa'imaqam of Ba'albek he sent a letter demanding the release of his wife and children. This time the Vali of Damascus responded with an attack that included four infantry battalions, artillery, and aircraft. Milhim Qasim withstood the attack, and near the end of the war his band numbered 500 armed men.[24]

A somewhat smaller band operated in 1917 in the neighbourhood of Damascus. Its leaders were the brothers 'Umar and Fa'iz al-Mu'ayyad. In May 1916 one of the heads of their family, their uncle Shafiq al-Mu'ayyad, was executed, and they and other members of their family were deported to Anatolia. Several months later the two escaped from Bursa, returned to Damascus, and organized a band that harassed the Ottomans in the area of Damascus. After activity that lasted about a year, in September 1917 they went over to the camp of Sharif Faysal in Aqaba and joined the Arab revolt. Faysal sent them on missions to incite revolt in Jabal al-Duruz, Homs, and Hama; and Fa'iz also took part in operations to destroy railroads.[25]

SUBVERSIVE ACTIVITY IN IRAQ DURING THE WORLD WAR

In contrast to the many revolt attempts in the Levant during World War I, in Iraq hardly any such ideas arose. The reason for this was that most of the Iraqi officers who were members of the Arab political societies spent their military service in Syria and were partners in the revolts that arose there (as will be explained in the chapter on *al-Fatat* and *al-'Ahd*). To this must be added that the intensive battles that took place on Iraqi soil between the British and the Ottomans from the beginning of the war until its end made activity of this kind difficult. In Syria, on the other hand, no battles between military forces took place until the final month of the war. The battles there between the British and the Ottomans were restricted to the Palestine front alone, from early 1917 till September 1918, and to southern Transjordan, which the Arab revolt army reached in July 1917.

Despite all this, there did exist in Iraq some subversive activity to a small extent and a number of revolt attempts were planned.

In late March 1915, not long before the battle of Shu'ayba, a group of Iraqi officers decided to contact the British and try to reach an agreement with them. They were prepared to render the Ottoman army ineffective in exchange for a British promise to support the establishment of an Arab state in Iraq. Several of them, such as Mawlud Mukhlis, one of the veterans of *al-'Ahd*, began spreading Arab propaganda among the tribal chiefs in the region of Shu'ayba. Mukhlis even convinced one of them to join the Arab movement. The resentment of the Arab officers towards their Turkish colleagues increased as a result of the hostile attitude of the Turkish commanders towards them, and Mukhlis planned to kill his Turkish commander. However, the Ottoman defeat in the battle of Shu'ayba in April took the group of officers by surprise and disrupted their plans to contact the British. In July 1915 a group of Iraqi officers stationed in Nasiriyya (apparently at least some of them were from the earlier group of officers) decided on the following: "1. The initiation of negotiations with the British forces on the basis of granting Iraq its independence. 2. A declaration of the separation of the Nasi-riyya division, which was mainly composed of Arab troops, from the Ottoman forces, with the retention of its arms. 3. Consultation with the chiefs of local tribes, especially the Muntafik tribes, to secure their support for the move." Eventually this plan, too, was not carried out, and the officers failed to establish contact with the British. In late July Nasiriyya fell into British hands. Several of the officers, Mawlud Mukhlis among them, deserted to the British. Others either fell into or perhaps delivered themselves into British captivity.[26]

Not only in the ranks of the army was the treatment of the Arabs by the Turks harsh. Not having gained much benefit from the Sultan's call for a jihad, they began to oppress the Arab population. They confiscated funds, valuables, and food, and offended even the clergy. All men up to age 60, including Christians and Jews, were conscripted. Shortly after the Shu'ayba defeat riots broke out in Najaf. The army, which was sent to restore order, fired cannon at the crowds, hitting Shi'ite holy places there. After a struggle lasting several days the populace overcame the army, disarmed the Turkish soldiers, and burned the government buildings.

Following the uprising in Najaf came further uprisings in Karbala, Kufa, and Hilla. The Turkish garrisons and government officials were driven out. The uprising in Karbala, the most serious of them, broke out in June 1915. It began with an attack by the Bani Hasan tribe on the government house and ended with the populace controlling the city and expelling the government officials. The city turned into a place of refuge for deserters from the Ottoman army in Baghdad, and for a while it succeeded in maintaining its freedom from the Turks. However, the Arab rebels suffered from a lack of leadership and organization. They were also unable to establish contacts with the British forces in the south because there were tribes still loyal to the Ottomans separating them. At the beginning of 1916 the city was still maintaining its freedom, but several months later the Turks recaptured it, perhaps as a result of their defeat of the British at Kut al-'Amara.[27]

In October 1915, after the British occupied Kut and it seemed that they would advance to Baghdad without hindrance, a number of notables in Baghdad gathered for a secret meeting and discussed the possibility of inciting the population to revolt against the Ottomans. It has been claimed that the initiator of the meeting was an emissary of a secret society from Syria who had arrived in Baghdad. The most important of the participants at the meeting were the Naqib of Baghdad 'Abd al-Rahman al-Kaylani and Yusuf al-Suwaydi. Al-Suwaydi had good reason to hold a grudge against the Ottomans. In August 1914 his son Thabit was murdered on instructions from the CUP after he had refused to participate in actions against the Armenians in Diarbakr where he was serving as Qa'imaqam. However, when the suggestion was made to open contacts with the British and to offer them assistance, the Naqib said that all his life he had been a loyal subject of the Ottoman Sultan and he had no intention of violating this loyalty in his old age. The meeting broke up with no results, and a short time later the authorities arrested several of the participants. One of those present, who managed to escape to the British in Basra, assumed that it was the Naqib who had informed on the participants to the Turkish authorities. Yusuf al-Suwaydi and another participant were sent to the Lebanon and jailed in 'Aleyh. After serving two months in jail, al-Suwaydi was deported to Anatolia and from there was transferred to Istanbul where he remained until the end of the war.[28]

The outbreak of the Arab revolt of Sharif Husayn of Mecca in June 1916 had no significant reveberations in Iraq, not even in the British-occupied area. The officials of the Indian government who were administering this region were not interested in spreading news about the revolt, since this might awaken Arab consciousness in Iraq and thereby damage the friendly relations that they were trying to build with the local population. However, in Mosul, which remained in Ottoman hands until the end of the war, a secret society by the name of al-'Alam (The Flag) was inciting the people against the Ottomans and spreading nationalist propaganda. This society was founded a short time before the outbreak of the World War and was headed by Thabit 'Abd al-Nur, a Christian who was also a member of al-'Ahd. The society had contacts with the Hijaz, and it distributed the manifestos of the Arab revolt. It attempted to persuade the Arab soldiers stationed in the region to desert from the Ottoman army. The leader of the society himself deserted from the army, and in 1918 he enlisted in the army of the Arab revolt.[29]

However, it seems that the most effective underground society during the war sprouted in the area under British occupation and against the British, signalling the beginning of the struggle that developed between the Iraqis and the British after the war. There are those who see in the deeds of this society the first step in the path that led to the Iraqi revolt of 1920. This society arose in Najaf in early 1918 and was called the "Society of the Islamic

Revival" (*Jam'iyyat al-Nahda al-Islamiyya*). Participating in it were Najafi notables and clergy and also several tribal chiefs from the neighbourhood. It was also supported by Sheikhs Sa'ad al-Hajj Radi, Kazim al-Subbi, and 'Atiyya Abu al-Kulal, who headed three of the four quarters of the city. The society strove to turn Najaf into a centre of religious propaganda amidst the tribes of the area and to arouse the Muslims of the country to liberate Iraq from the British.

In early February 1918 a new British governor arrived in Najaf, Captain Marshall. He discontinued the financial allowances that were being paid to the sheikhs of the town and disbanded the police force, which was made up of local Najafis, replacing them with policemen brought from Kut. He also demanded that the leaders of Najaf collect the weapons that were in the town and turn them in to him. Consequently, the society decided to liquidate Captain Marshall and set the date of his assassination for the Nawruz holiday, for which many pilgrims arrived in Najaf. They hoped that the murder of Marshall would be the first step in the elimination of the rest of the British governors in the area and in the sprouting of a revolt comprising all the tribes whose leaders were members of the society, as well as other tribes.

On 19 March 1918, several members of the society led by Hajj Najm al-Baqqal, entered the government house disguised as gendarmes and shot Captain Marshall to death. The guards who were on the roof opened fire on them, and they retreated quickly. Within a short time tumult reigned in the three quarters whose heads supported the assassins. Some of the policemen from Kut were forced to vacate the city, and others found refuge in the quarter of Sayyid Mahdi al-Sayyid Salman, the only quarter head in Najaf who did not support the rebels. During the following night supporters from outside the city joined the rebels, and the next morning a real uprising broke out in the quarter of Hajj Sa'ad al-Hajj Radi, to which the other two quarters of rebels joined. The number of rebels reached 300, and in the estimate of the British there were 2,000 additional armed men in the city who were liable to join in the revolt.

A short time after Captain Marshall's assassination Captain Balfour, the governor of Shamiyya, arrived in Najaf and laid siege to the city. The British realized the delicacy of their position in that many of the tribal chiefs in the area were waiting to see how things would develop before they decided to join the rebels, should they gain the upper hand, or to maintain silence. Therefore, the British decided that the blockade should be total until the inhabitants surrendered, and they rejected the request of the 'ulama' to permit the evacuation of women and children. They informed the Najafis that the blockade would be removed only under the following conditions: "1. The unconditional surrender of the murderers and others concerned in the plot. 2. A fine of 1,000 rifles and Rs. 50,000 to be paid, as far as possible, by the rebellious quarters. 3. The delivery from those quarters of 100 men who will be deported as prisoners of war."

The harsh British measures caused most of the tribes in the area not to join the rebels. A call for help sent by the rebels to the commander of the Ottoman forces in northern Iraq went unanswered. In Najaf itself there was enough food to last six weeks, but the town suffered from a shortage of water. Thereupon the Najafis, principally the 'ulama', began contacts with the British in order to bring an end to the siege. These contacts had the support of the Shi'ite mujtahid Muhammad Kazim Yazdi, who was considered the most important Shi'ite mujtahid in Iraq.

On 7 April Sayyid Mahdi al-Sayyid Salman aided the British to take control of the hills which dominated his quarter, and to penetrate the quarter itself, in the southwest of the town. On 10 April the British captured the quarter of the rebel sheikh 'Atiyya Abu al-Kulal, in the northwest of the city. Abu al-Kulal himself fled but gave himself up to the British 18 days later. On the day that Abu al-Kulal's quarter fell three of Captain Marshall's murderers were turned over to the British, and by then it was clear that the revolt was drawing to an end. On 13 April the leader of the assassins Hajj Najm al-Baqqal and the head of the quarter in which the revolt broke out, Hajj Sa'ad al-Hajj Radi, were captured and turned over to the British. The hundreds of pilgrims who had been trapped in the town were allowed to leave, and drinking water was brought in.

During the days that followed additional rebels were turned in to the British, in fact almost all the names specified by the British in the lists given to the Najafis. The collection and turning in of rifles began in accordance with the British conditions for removing the blockade. On 4 May the blockade was lifted. Ten tons of wheat were delivered to Muhammad Kazim Yazdi for distribution to the population. In Kufa a military court was set up with Lieutenant-Colonel Leachman presiding, and 11 rebel leaders were sentenced to death. Eight others were sentenced to periods of exile ranging from six years to life. Over a hundred others who had some connection with the revolt were deported to India. On the morning of 30 May the death sentences were carried out. Among those executed were Hajj Najm al-Baqqal, Sheikh Kazim al-Subbi, and three of the sons of Hajj Sa'ad al-Hajj Radi, two of whom had taken part in the murder of Marshall. Sa'ad al-Hajj Radi himself and 'Atiyya Abu al-Kulal were sentenced to permanent exile.[30]

Chapter 2

NEGLIGENCE, TREACHERY, AND EXECUTIONS

The Ottoman Fourth Army, which was to rule the Levant during the war, was set up on 6 September 1914. Its first commander was Zaki Pasha, but on 18 November 1914 he was replaced by the Ottoman navy minister, Ahmad Jamal Pasha "The Great". The latter, who was then one of the ruling triumvirate of the Ottoman Empire (the others were Enver and Tal'at), became the omnipotent ruler of the Levant in the course of the next three years.

A short time before he arrived in Damascus documents were seized in the French consulate which gave evidence of incriminating contacts between many Syrian notables and the French (see below). When Jamal Pasha arrived in the city, the Vali presented him with the incriminating documents. However, Jamal Pasha decided to ignore them at that stage. The first assignment given to him as commander of the Fourth Army was to attack the Suez Canal and invade Egypt. For this he had to prepare a large-scale military operation in which most of the Ottoman forces stationed in Syria would participate. He decided, therefore, that it was more important to foster good relations with the local population, to obtain its sympathy, and to mobilize it for the jihad decreed by the Sultan. The incriminating documents could wait for some other time.

'Abd al-Karim al-Khalil, the president of the Literary Club, was summoned from Istanbul to Syria for the purpose of persuading the local population to support the government and to enlist in the army. Jamal Pasha befriended him, granted him large sums of money, and through him met also the Arab activists 'Abd al-Rahman al-Shahbandar, Muhammad Kurd 'Ali, and 'Abd al-Ghani al-'Uraysi. He tried to persuade them of the need to achieve unity among Arabs and Turks in order to defend the Empire against foreign conquest, and he expressed his readiness to bring about reforms in Syria. Kurd 'Ali and al-'Uraysi were journalists, and therefore he granted them, too, sums of money so they would propagandize in their newspapers on behalf of the Empire. At a party that Jamal Pasha gave for the leading Arab activists in early 1915 he expressed his esteem for the Arabic language, the language of Islam, and for the Arab race. He explained that there was no conflict between Turkish nationalism and Arab nationalism, and that if the Arabs and Turks did not learn to live together they were both doomed to extinction.[1]

The Ottoman campaign for the Suez Canal ended in complete failure. A few Ottoman forces did succeed in crossing the Canal in the beginning of February, but they immediately fell into British captivity. The beaten Ottoman army returned to Syria. For a while Jamal Pasha continued his relations with the Arab activists. But the main consideration for the gentle treatment accorded the Syrians vanished, and he was soon to decisively change his policy towards the local population.

During the month of May the first reports of the revolt plan of 'Abd al-Karim al-Khalil reached the Ottoman authorities. On 23 June Jamal Pasha ordered the arrest of al-Khalil and all those involved in his plan, and with this began the first large-scale wave of arrests among the Arab activists in Syria. (Arrests of individual Syrians had already been made before this.) From then on Jamal Pasha began to carry out a policy of terror against the populace, a policy which earned him the deep enmity of the peoples of Syria and the Lebanon for many years thereafter. On one occasion he explained to his personal secretary Falih Rifqi the logic behind this policy:

> The Syrians and the Arabs respect only the one who beats them. If we deal with them gently they will think we are weak and will beat us. Therefore we must beat them in order to be protected from their evil.[2]

Jamal's two partners in the ruling triumvirate, Enver and Tal'at, were apparently not especially pleased with this policy of his, but they did not dare interfere. The Druze Sakib Arslan relates that when he tried to appeal to Enver Pasha to intervene on behalf of the Arab activists sentenced to death by Jamal Pasha, "I saw with my own eyes, and in a way I will never forget, the powerlessness of Enver against Jamal." Jamal Pasha also surrounded himself with governors to his own liking from among the veteran Young Turks. In July 1915 the Vali of Beirut was removed from his position and replaced by 'Azmi Bek, the former chief-of-police of Istanbul. The Vali of Damascus was replaced by Hasan Tahsin Bek. In August the Muslim Turk 'Ali Munif Bek was appointed to the position of Mutasarrif of

Mount Lebanon. This constituted a clear violation of the règlement organique of 1861, according to which the mutasarrif must always be a Christian. The règlement organique itself was officially abrogated in November 1916.[3]

The situation in Syria and Mount Lebanon rapidly deteriorated. A tax of 50 per cent was levied on personal property, and one of 25 per cent on lands, sheep, cattle, camels, crops, and oil. All the trees of the country were cut down and used to fuel trains. Wagons and beasts of burden were confiscated to tow artillery. The army took over many houses and quartered soldiers in them. As the war dragged on the situation worsened and soon a famine began which became extremely serious from 1916 on and was accompanied by the outbreak of epidemics, primarily typhus. There are differences of opinion as to the number of people who died from famine and disease in Syria and Mount Lebanon during the war. The range of numbers is: 150,000-300,000 in Syria; 130,000-150,000 in the vilayet of Beirut; and 100,000-200,000 in Mount Lebanon, which was the region that suffered relatively the worst during the war. It is important to point out that the famine was not solely the fault of the Ottoman authorities. Contributing to it was the blockade of the coasts of the Empire by the Allies, which prevented the delivery of relief to the population, especially after the United States joined the enemies of the Empire. One should also point out the profiteering in food products by several of the notables in the region. Among those suspected in this was the Beiruti notable mentioned above in another connection, Salim 'Ali Salam.[4]

In early 1914 the Ottoman authorities established an intelligence bureau whose function was to keep track of the activists of the Arab societies, of subjects who had contacts with the Allies (especially France), and of other elements considered to be opponents of the CUP. According to the memoirs of the commander of the intelligence services of the Fourth Army, this bureau spent in the fiscal year 1914/15 the immense sum of 182,500 gold Turkish liras. In 1915, the second year of its existence, it received 4,131 reports and its file of suspects contained 8,938 dossiers, which were apportioned to 513 men. In the town of 'Aleyh southeast of Beirut a military court was set up in which suspects were interrogated and tried. The suspects under interrogation were chained and beaten until their clothing stuck to their bodies from the dried and clotted blood. The interrogators would pierce them with needles and cane the soles of their feet held in the falqa. Hot boiled eggs would be put in their armpits. A special instrument would press the temples of those being tortured until they felt as though their brains were bursting through their eye sockets. They would be given bread and water once every two days, and they were kept awake for three successive nights. After the interrogation stage they would be put on trial. The final section of this chapter will deal with the results of the trials.[5]

The authorities did not always take the trouble to put the suspects on trial. In many cases they deported whole families to Anatolia without trial. The number of deported families is estimated at 300, and they included several of the most eminent families in the Levant: al-Mu'ayyad, al-Jaza'iri, al-Sham'a, al-'Abid, Haydar, 'Abd al-Hadi and others. The number of deportees during the war is estimated at 50,000. Shakib Arslan claims that Jamal Pasha would go through the various towns, gather the notables, and deport ten per cent, chosen by lot. The possessions of the deportees would be confiscated and their houses put up for sale. Such was also the fate of the property of Arab activists who succeeded in escaping from the Empire, such as Ayyub Thabit, Rizq Allah Arqash, Pietro Tarrad, Khalil Zayniyya and others.[6]

Jamal Pasha left Syria for the last time on 13 December 1917. In the memory of the people of the Levant he remained "Jamal the bloodthirsty, Jamal the fiend, Jamal the tyrant, Jamal the starver of the land". The commander of the intelligence services of the Fourth Army remarks on this as follows:

> Jamal Pasha did not deserve these titles because he did not hang a single innocent person nor did he harm any but the evil. Jamal came to Syria as a Turk who was assigned to perform a mission, and he carried it out faithfully.[7]

The question as to whether Jamal Pasha was justified in taking the extremely punitive measures that he did is not the concern of the historian. Therefore, the question as to whether the Arab activists whom he sentenced to death deserved their sentence or not will not be given an answer in the following pages. On the other hand, an answer will be given to the question as to whether the accusations made against them in the trials in 'Aleyh were true or whether they were fabricated charges, as was later claimed. To this question a factual and documented answer can be given.

INCRIMINATING DOCUMENTS

In the beginning of November 1914 France, together with the other Allies, declared war on the Ottoman Empire. Immediately upon the severance of diplomatic relations the French ambassador in Istanbul instructed the French consuls throughout the Empire not leave behind any document that might have political character. He emphasized that they should burn their codes and the documents in which there was evidence of contacts between local people and the French. This instruction came just in time. On 11 November the Ottoman authorities informed the American ambassador in Istanbul that they intended to inspect the contents of all the Allied consulates, and that they would like an American representative to be present at the inspection. Since the United States had accepted the responsibility for the assets of the Allies after the declaration of war, the American ambassador protested against this, but to no avail.[8] When the Ottomans carried out their intentions, it became clear that some of the French consuls did not heed the above mentioned instruction from their ambassador.

One of the consuls who did not act according to the instructions of the French ambassador was the French consul-general in Beirut, François Georges-Picot. The American consul-general in that city also advised him to destroy his papers. Yet despite the fact that they contained many documents dealing with the contacts of locals with the French, and even with requests that France assist them in the liberation of their country from the Ottomans, Picot nevertheless preferred not to destroy the documents. He felt for some reason that within a short time he would return to his post, and therefore he preferred to hide the documents in a secret crypt behind one of the walls of the consulate. He left the secret of their location with the Maronite Philippe Zalzal, the consulate dragoman, and promised that he would return within a fortnight. As a further security measure Picot placed the American consular seals on his consular archives.

Several days after Picot left for Egypt the authorities arrested Zalzal, together with the other dragomans of the Allied consulates, and brought them to Damascus. The authorities intended to deport them to Anatolia, but Zalzal feared that they were going to be executed. He therefore asked a cousin of his who had connections with the Germans to put him in touch with the

German consul-general in Beirut. He informed this consul that he could reveal to the authorities where the papers of the French consulate were hidden, documents which dealt with the contacts of Arab activists with France. In exchange for this he asked for an assurance that he would not be executed and that he would be permitted to return home. The German consul passed on Zalzal's offer to the authorities. At first the authorities tried to find the documents on their own, but when they did not succeed, they agreed to make the deal.

On 12 November 1914 a number of security men and Ottoman soldiers arrived at the French consulate accompanied by Philippe Zalzal. He was dressed in an Ottoman uniform, had grown a beard and was wearing dark glasses in order to conceal his identity. The American consul-general, who was handling French interests in the city, protested vehemently and tried to stop them from breaking the American seals that were on the French consular archives. The Ottomans ignored his protests, entered the consulate building and broke the American seals. (Later the French lodged a complaint with the American State Department about the behaviour of the American consul. They claimed that he did not adequately oppose the actions of the Ottoman authorities and demanded that he be dismissed from his position. Their complaint was apparently unjustified. Under the circumstances at the time the American consul could do nothing more than protest and report to his ambassador in Istanbul, which he in fact did.) Then it was Zalzal's turn. He turned to one of the walls and instructed one of the soldiers to remove a secret panel behind which was revealed the depository in which the consular documents were hidden. Many Syrians and Lebanese were to pay with their lives for this treachery of Philippe Zalzal.[9]

At this stage the Ottomans were content with the incriminating documents found in the secret hiding place and preferred not to touch the regular archives of the consulate, apparently in order to create the impression that no documents of real importance had come into their hands yet. Indeed, the American consul reported on the breaking of his seals but pointed out that the authorities had not touched the archives of the French consulate. Since the Ottoman authorities had still not publicly announced the seizure of the incriminating documents, they also did not publish them at the time that they executed the first group of Arab activists in August 1915. They preferred to publish other documents, taken from the Decentralization Party, which reached their hands under circumstances which will be described later.

On 27 September 1915 representatives of the Ottoman authorities again entered the French consulate, again removed the American seals and officially confiscated the consulate archives. Thirty-two crates full of documents were brought from the consulate to the government house and inspected there. There was nothing that the American consul-general could do besides protest. In early November the American ambassador in Istanbul joined in the protest following appeals of the French government to the American government. But only in early July 1916 did the Ottoman foreign ministry bother to respond to the protest of the American ambassador. The ministry pointed out that the obligation to respect consular immunity applied only in time of peace. During time of war they had no obligation towards their enemies. The ministry added that the Allies, too, had violated the immunity of Ottoman consulates many times during the war, and therefore they had no right to speak about international law when they themselves were not abiding by it. At the end of their reply the Ottomans pointed out with a tinge of irony that the documents found in the consulates showed that "in certain regions of the Empire where certain powers had political aims, their consulates observed an attitude which cannot be reconciled with the attributions which international law accords to them."[10]

Even after the French were apprised of the confiscation of the archives of their consulate in Beirut, they were still not aware of the amount of incriminating documents that had fallen into the hands of the Ottomans. The first hint of the magnitude of the disaster came to them when they learned of the arrest in Beirut of the Maronite notable Yusuf al-Hani, and the summoning of Ayyub Thabit, Rizq Allah Arqash, Michel Tuwayni, Khalil Zayniyya, and Pietro Tarrad. All six had signed the memorandum presented to the French consul-general in Beirut in March 1913 in which they pleaded for a French conquest of Syria, or at least of Beirut and Mount Lebanon. Al-Hani was the only one of the six who did not succeed in escaping from the Empire at the outbreak of the war, and on 5 April 1916 he was hanged.

On 6 May 1916 the authorities executed the second group of Arab activists (see below), and immediately thereafter they published several of the French documents that had fallen into their hands. At this point the dimensions of the disaster became clear to the French. The French minister in Cairo identified among the documents that were published a despatch that he had sent to Paris in March 1913 concerning a subversive session of the

Decentralization Party. In a cable which he sent to the French foreign ministry following this he gloomily noted: "There is no doubt that the entire document is in the hands of the Turks."[11]

In connection with the episode of the seizure of the French documents it should be noted that the Ottomans also raided the British consulate in the city. However, in contrast to Picot, the British consul-general spent the entire final night before he left his post in burning the documents of his consulate, and the Ottomans found nothing there. When the authorities began to arrest the notables who had contacts with the French consulate, it aroused great fear among those who had contacts with the British, but none of them were arrested.[12]

As for Philippe Zalzal, the man who caused the seizure of the French documents, he was arrested by the French immediately after they took control of Beirut at the end of the war. At the beginning of 1919 he was to have been put on trial for treason, for which he could have received the death sentence or life imprisonment at hard labour. His ultimate fate remains unknown. Picot, too, did not come away clear of his negligence which brought these disastrous results. Before the war he was very popular with the inhabitants of Mount Lebanon. This popularity came to an end following this chapter, and it turned into hostility towards him, especially among the Muslim popula tion.[13]

The papers of the French consulate in Beirut were not the only ones that fell into the hands of the Ottomans. The French consul-general in Damascus, also, did not destroy secret documents before he left his post at the beginning of the war. On instructions from War Minister Enver Pasha agents of the secret service Teşkilât-i Mahsusa (Special Organization) penetrated the French consulate in Damascus in November 1914 and broke the American seals on the doors there. They brought all the docu- ments they found to the Vali of Damascus. When Jamal Pasha arrived in Damascus shortly afterwards, the Vali showed him these documents and asked him to order an investigation of the contacts between the Arab activists and the French, as evidenced by the documents. As mentioned above, Jamal Pasha refused at this stage, for reasons detailed already. However, later on use was made of these papers, and when Jamal Pasha published his book *Idahat* after the executions of May 1916, it included nine of the documents taken from the French consulate-general in Damascus.[14]

In early December 1914 representatives of the Ottoman authorities broke the American consular seal on the door of the room in which the archives of the French and British consulates in Aleppo were stored and took them away. The American consul in Aleppo protested, but the representatives of the authorities ignored his protest, stating that they were following instructions from Istanbul. The French legations in Haifa and Jidda received similar treatment.[15] Apparently the French representatives serving in these towns were careful to destroy all documents in their possession that might have an incriminating character. There is no record of any such document having fallen into the hands of the authorities in these places.

Only some of the executed Arab activists were sentenced on the basis of the French documents. The others (mainly among the first group to be sentenced) were executed on the basis of documents of the Decentralization Party, which came into the hands of the Ottomans as the result of another act of treachery, that of Muhammad al-Shanti, a party activist. Al-Shanti was a Jaffa merchant who moved to Cairo after going bankrupt. In Cairo he started working in journalism, joined the Decentralization Party, and served as its roving agent assisting in the setting up of new branches. At the beginning of the war he took the papers of the party on the pretext that he wanted to study them, then went to Athens and turned them over to the Ottoman ambassador there, hoping to receive a large reward. The ambassador immediately sent him to Istanbul, to Interior Minister Tal'at, who in turn sent him to Jamal Pasha. The latter entertained him lavishly in Damascus and gave him large sums of money. The papers that al-Shanti turned over to the Ottoman security services included, among others, lists of names of party members and supporters as well as the letter quoted above which dealt with the party's revolt plan. The handing over of these documents had catastrophic results for the Arab activists in Syria.

Muhammad al-Shanti did not get away with this act of treachery. When the Ottoman authorities no longer needed him, Jamal Pasha ordered him executed. Some say that this was on the advice of Hajj Sa'id al-Shawa of Gaza, who was a confidant of Jamal Pasha and head of counter-espionage in his home region. It is possible that Jamal decided to do this because al-Shanti himself was a partner in the activities of the Decentralization Party, and it is also possible that the Ottoman security services wanted to conceal the source from which they obtained the party documents. Whatever the reason was, on 6 May 1916 Muhammad al-Shanti was sent to the gallows.[16]

Aside from those mentioned above, there were additional

sources available to the authorities on which they could base a prosecution when they brought the Arab activists to trial. Many Lebanese and Syrian émigrés, who were in safe places in North and South America, Africa, and Australia, used to send letters to relatives in Mount Lebanon and Syria in which they expressed the opinion that the oppressive Ottoman rule was soon to end and that a French conquest of the country was imminent. The letters were opened by the Ottoman censors, and some of the addressees were arrested and sentenced to periods of imprisonment of up to 15 years. It has been claimed that some of these letters were sent with the deliberate intention of incriminating the recipients because of personal rivalries and hostilities from the pre-war period.

However, not always were such letters sent with malicious intent. Sometimes it was simply stupidity. Thus for example, the Lebanese activist Khayrallah Khayrallah sent his family photographs of himself from France in which he was shown dressed in a French army uniform. Immediately after the letter was intercepted the court in 'Aleyh announced that if he did not appear before the court within ten days he would be tried in absentia and all his property confiscated. Later Khayrallah was sentenced to death in absentia. Far more serious was the fate of the pro-French Maronite priest Yusuf al-Ha'ik. He sent a letter to his son who was serving in the French Residency in Morocco, in which he reported on the entry of Ottoman troops into Mount Lebanon and asked that France send a military force to help the Lebanese liberate their country. On the request of his father the son conveyed the message to the president of the French parliament. The latter promptly sent al-Ha'ik a letter thanking him for his loyalty to France and for the information that he transmitted about Syria. The letter fell into the hands of the Ottoman censor, and Yusuf al-Ha'ik was arrested and executed on 22 March 1915.[17]

Another important source of information was the informing by locals on the activities of the Arab activists. Already mentioned above were the informings on 'Abd al-Karim al-Khalil and his revolt plan. The commander of the intelligence services of the Fourth Army relates in his memoirs the following typical informing, which was brought against Ahmad Hasan Tabbara, who had been a leader of the Reform Society of Beirut, had participated in the Paris Congress in 1913 and was a member of the Decentralization Party as well:

My loyalty to the exalted Empire and my disgust at the treachery of the enemies of the Empire and the religion lead me to bring to His Excellency's attention the fact that the French consul in Beirut enjoyed very good relations with Sheikh Ahmad Tabbara. As a result of this Sheikh Ahmad maintains a constant contact abroad through the Dutch consulate. You can ascertain this if you place him under surveillance.

22 February 1915   Yusuf Jamal[18]

Ahmad Hasan Tabbara was hanged on 6 May 1916.

Thus, when the Ottoman authorities brought the Arab activists to trial, they had in their possession abundant and varied incriminating information: the documents from the French consulates in Beirut and Damascus, the papers of the Decentralization Party, other letters, and informings. To this must be added the vast material that the Ottoman security services (principally the General Security Service and the police) had gathered during the pre-war period through their spies and agents within the Empire, in Cairo, and in Paris.

ARRESTS AND EXECUTIONS

The first to suffer as a result of the French documents falling into the hands of the Ottomans was Nakhla Mutran, a Greek Catholic from Ba'albek. From a document seized in the French consulate in Damascus it was learned that in January 1913 he had approached the French consul-general there and expressed before him his desire that Ba'albek and the Bika' be annexed to Mount Lebanon under French aegis. On 20 November 1914 he was arrested in Damascus, put on a wagon with his hands manacled in iron chains, and led through the streets of the city with the soldiers guarding him announcing over and over: "This is Nakhla Mutran the traitor to the Fatherland!" (*hadha nakhla al-mutran kha'in al-watan!*) Afterwards he was tried and sentenced to life imprisonment. It was decided to deport him to Diarbakr, and he was put on a train going north. From here on the reports differ as to his fate. The Turks claimed that he tried to escape from the train near Jarablus and was shot to death by his guards. According to another version, as the train passed Aleppo the guards asked him for a bribe in exchange for his release. When he refused, they ordered him to get off the train and then shot him on the pretext that he was trying to escape.[19]

The arrest of Nakhla Mutran was made on the initiative of the local authorities in Damascus. When Jamal Pasha arrived in the

Levant, he decided, as mentioned above, to adopt a policy of conciliation towards the Arabs, and it was not until March 1915 that the next political trial was held. This was the trial of the Maronite priest Yusuf al-Ha'ik, who was arrested under the circumstances described above. He was hanged on 22 March and was the first of those executed for political reasons.[20]

In late June 1915 the first large wave of arrests began, following the discovery of the revolt plan of 'Abd al-Karim al-Khalil. The authorities did not keep the arrests secret. They announced publicly that they had exposed underground Arab societies that were working to establish an Arab government. Among about 60 detainees were several of the prominent Arab activists in Syria during the period under discussion: 'Abd al-Karim al-Khalil, Rida al-Sulh, the brothers Muhammad and Mahmud al-Mihmisani, 'Ali al-Armanazi and others. The first one investigated was Muhammad al-Mihmisani, a member of the Decentralization Party. He was brutally tortured and finally revealed to his interrogators much information and the names of party members. On 9 August the summary report on the investigation of the detainees was submitted to Jamal Pasha. He instructed the military court in 'Aleyh to impose the death sentence for two crimes: participation in one or more of the Arab societies or for contacts of any form whatsoever with the enemies of the Empire. Thirteen men were sentenced to death. The verdict for 11 of them was approved by Jamal Pasha, and the sentence of the other two, Hafiz al-Sa'id, the head of the Decentralization Party branch in Jaffa, and Sa'id al-Karmi, the party representative in Banu Sa'b, was mitigated to life imprisonment because of their advanced age (the former died in prison).[21]

It seems that the only one of the detainees who realized the seriousness of the situation was 'Abd al-Karim al-Khalil. While the others cheered themselves up with the hope that they would get off with prison sentences or deportation, he told them simply: "Even if all of you manage to get out of here, me they are going to hang." The night before the executions rumours spread among them that they were being sentenced to prison terms of three months to three years. Al-Khalil stubbornly insisted that his fate was sealed. And he was right. On 20 August, at midnight, the 11 were brought from 'Aleyh to al-Burj Square in Beirut where they were to be hanged. All the approaches to the square were sealed off, and it was filled with armed soldiers and police. Entry of civilians was forbidden. The condemned were brought to the Beirut police headquarters to write their wills, and from there they were taken to the square in pairs between rows of soldiers, accompanied by armed policemen. Waiting alongside the gallows were the members of the military court and the Beirut police inspector. There are various versions of the last words of the doomed men. Al-Khalil is reported to have said: "I know the real reason why Jamal Pasha is hanging me, and in the future history will know it, too." (See the previous chapter for the interpretations that were created for this sentence.) On 21 August, by 4 am the executions were over.

A few hours later the newspapers of Beirut already published Jamal Pasha's announcement of the executions of the first group of Arab activists. The group consisted of 'Abd al-Karim al-Khalil, Salim al-Ahmad 'Abd al-Hadi, Muhammad al-Mihmisani, Mahmud al-Mihmisani, Mahmud al-'Ajam, Nuri al-Qadi, 'Abd al-Qadir al-Kharsa, 'Ali al-Armanazi, Na'if Tallu, Musallam 'Abidin, and Salih Haydar.[22]

In September Jamal Pasha ordered the investigation of a large number of other Arab activists, this time concentrating on those mentioned in the documents from the French consulates. In early November ten of the prominent Arab activists in Syria were arrested, among them the former members of parliament Shafiq al-Mu'ayyad al-'Azm and Rushdi al-Sham'a. Later the senator 'Abd al-Hamid al-Zahrawi and former member of parliament Shukri al-'Asali were arrested as well. A group of four members of al-Fatat who attempted to escape to the Hijaz were identified when they reached Mada'in Salih, arrested and sent to 'Aleyh. Three other members of this society, who sought refuge with Nuri al-Sha'lan, the paramount chief of the Ruwalla tribes, were turned over by him to the authorities although he himself was a member of the society. The number of detainees in 'Aleyh kept growing, and two senior Arab officers, Amin Lutfi al-Hafiz and Salim al-Jaza'iri were added to them as well. In the months of March-April 1916, 60 more were arrested. An agent of the British, who was staying in the area at the time, managed to steal into the jail in 'Aleyh and to meet with Shukri al-'Asali. The latter asked him: "Where are the English? Where are the French? Why are we left like this?" The agent could do nothing but promise that the Allies would soon come to save them, a pledge with no warranty.[23]

Then the authorities began interrogating the detainees. Al-Fatat member Tawfiq al-Basat did not open his mouth despite the severe tortures he underwent. His fellow society member 'Arif al-Shihabi did not make any significant confessions, and apparently society member 'Umar Hamad also remained silent. In contrast to them al-Fatat member 'Abd al-Ghani al-'Uraysi

filled page after page of statements and confessions during his
interrogation, revealing names of activists and causing serious
damage. Still, he was careful not to say a word about *al-Fatat*,
and his confessions centred only on the activity of the Reform
Society of Beirut and on the Paris Congress. Likewise he made
reference to Arab activists out of reach of the Ottomans, such as
As'ad Daghir and Rashid Rida. On the other hand, society
members Rafiq Rizq Sallum and Sayf al-Din al-Khatib did not
refrain even from this, and in their detailed confessions they gave
information also about *al-Fatat*. The information given by
al-'Uraysi, Sallum, and al-Khatib was very valuable to the
authorities, no less valuable than that drawn from the French
consular documents and the papers of the Decentralization
Party. This information constituted one of the important sources
for the preparation of the indictments against the detainees and
for their death sentences.[24]

The first one to be executed in this round was the Maronite
Yusuf al-Hani, who was arrested under circumstances described
above. When he was shown the memorandum that he and his
five friends had submitted to the French consul-general in Beirut
in March 1913, he tried to justify himself by saying that when he
signed it he was not aware of its contents (occupation of Syria
or at least of Beirut and Mount Lebanon by France). His
excuses did not help him, and he was hanged in al-Burj Square
on 5 April 1916.[25]

In April 1916 the investigations and trials of the remaining
detainees were completed, and the president of the court Shukri
Bek arrived at the military headquarters in Damascus with the
list of those convicted and the various sentences decided for
them. Before he entered Jamal Pasha's room to have the sentences confirmed, 'Ali Fu'ad, the chief-of-staff of the Fourth
Army, advised him that in case Jamal Pasha decided to increase
the sentences he should say to him: "Pasha, I ask you to consider history." When Shukri Bek entered Jamal Pasha's room
and gave him the list of those convicted, 40 in all, Jamal did not
even bother to look at it, and he wrote alongside all the names
"execution". Following 'Ali Fu'ad's advice Shukri Bek said to
him: "Pasha, I ask you to consider history." At this Jamal
Pasha reacted with fury: "History? Let it be broken over your
head!" Despite this Shukri Bek persisted and succeeded in reducing the number of those sentenced to death to 27, and later on
he succeeded in having six more death sentences commuted.
Thus, after repeated changes were made in the list it was finally
drafted only on 5 May 1916, 24 hours before the scheduled

executions.

Jamal Pasha was determined to carry out the executions without waiting for approval from Istanbul, as was customary. The law was on his side because at the beginning of the war a special law had been passed permitting immediate executions when required for the security of the state, and only after carrying out the sentences to send the papers of the condemned to the capital for retroactive approval by the government and the sultan. Despite this, when Jamal Pasha made use of this law, it aroused severe criticism in Istanbul. The Grand Vizier Sa'id Halim sent him a telegram of sharp protest. Enver, too, sent him a telegram in which he emphasized the bitterness of Justice Minister Khalil Bek over the action that Jamal Pasha had taken. Jamal reacted to the criticism with contempt, and in his memoirs he claimed that not only did he have the authority to act as he did, but that it was agreed by Minister of War Enver and Minister of Interior Tal'at that he could carry out sentences without receiving approval in advance.[26]

Even before the exact identity of those sentenced to death was made known it was already clear that the number to be executed would be large. Sharif Husayn of Mecca sent a telegram to Enver with a request for clemency, but in vain. Amir Faysal, who was at the time in Damascus, pleaded time and again with Jamal Pasha to grant clemency to the condemned, also in vain. Whereupon Faysal appealed to Sheikh Badr al-Din al-Hasani, who was considered the foremost of the 'ulama' of Damascus, and asked him to plead with Jamal Pasha. But Badr al-Din refused and proved to him from the Qur'an that the condemned deserved their punishment. Badr al-Din was not content with that, but even went himself to Jamal Pasha and showed him proofs from the Hadith to justify his actions. Also the attempt by Amir Sa'id al-Jaza'iri to intervene failed. He tried to persuade Jamal Pasha to grant an amnesty, at least to his uncle 'Umar al-Jaza'iri, and at that Jamal reacted: "Who are you, that you ask me to pardon criminals and traitors?!"[27]

The day before the executions the entire al-Jaza'iri family was deported to Bursa because of the apprehensions of the authorities that the family would mobilize its Algerian supporters to free by force those condemned to death. The condemned men were divided into two groups. One, consisting of 14 men, was transferred in wagons to the police headquarters in Beirut in order to be hanged in al-Burj Square. The other, of seven men, was taken by train to Damascus to be hanged in Marja Square.

On 5 May, at 10 pm, armed soldiers were deployed in al-Burj

Square, all civilians were ordered to evacuate it, and all the approaches were sealed off. At 3 am on 6 May, they began bringing the prisoners to the square, three at a time. Several of them heaped abuse on the Turks in general and on Jamal Pasha in particular. By 5 am, 12 had been hanged and only the officers Amin Lutfi al-Hafiz and Salim al-Jaza'iri were still alive. The two prepared to go to their deaths. Al-Hafiz, with a touch of irony, advised his guards to teach their children to grow vegetables and not to send them to military service in a state which repaid its soldiers in this way. But just then Rida Pasha, commander of the division of 'Aleyh, decided to intervene on their behalf and to try to get them an amnesty. His attempts to get Jamal Pasha by telephone came to naught, and in the end he contacted his deputy, Fakhri Pasha, and they spoke at length. Fakhri told him that there was no chance that the sentence would be cancelled. When he despaired of persuading him, Rida handed the receiver to Salim al-Jaza'iri, who himself spoke with Fakhri. The answer was the same: "Impossible." Al-Jaza'iri furiously dashed the receiver to the floor, cursed the Empire, and walked together with al-Hafiz to the gallows. At 6 am the executions were over.

Hangings were being held in Marja Square in Damascus at the same time. The square was illuminated with brilliant light in order to allow good vision, and in the centre the gallows were set up. In contrast to Beirut the residents were permitted to be present in the square at the time of the executions, and they watched in silence. The seven condemned men listened to the reading of the verdicts without reacting, and then were hanged. When Senator 'Abd al-Hamid al-Zahrawi was hanged, the rope broke because of his weight. The hangman did not hesitate. He changed the rope, and al-Zahrawi was hanged again, this time properly.

Within a few hours the newspapers of Beirut published Jamal Pasha's announcement of the execution of the Arab activists. Twenty names were listed: Shafiq al-Mu'ayyad, 'Umar al-Jaza'iri, 'Umar Hamad, Rafiq Rizq Sallum, Muhammad al-Shanti, Shukri al-'Asali, 'Abd al-Ghani al-'Uraysi, 'Arif al-Shihabi, Tawfiq al-Basat, Sayf al-Din al-Khatib, Ahmad Hasan Tabbara, 'Abd al-Wahhab al-Inklizi, Sa'id 'Aql, Petro Pauli, Jurji Haddad, Salim al-Jaza'iri, 'Ali al-Nashashibi, Rushdi al-Sham'a, Amin Lutfi al-Hafiz, and Jalal al-Bukhari. The twenty-first, whose name did not appear in the announcement, was 'Abd al-Hamid al-Zahrawi. Since he was a senator it was forbidden to execute him without a writ from the sultan, and therefore his name was not mentioned in the announcement.[28]

The name of al-Burj Square was changed after the war to "The Shuhada' (Martyrs) Square", and 6 May 1916 was established in the Republic of Lebanon as "Martyrs' Day". However, the executions did not end with these. During May the Mufti of Gaza Ahmad 'Arif al-Husayni and his son Mustafa were executed. The son, who was one of the founders in 1912 of the secret society "The Green Flag", deserted from the army and tried to escape to the Hijaz with his father. Hajj Sa'id al-Shawa, who headed the counter-espionage in the Gaza region, informed on them, and they were captured by an Ottoman patrol. They were sent to Jerusalem and executed by a firing squad. The series of executions ended on 6 June 1916 with the hanging in Beirut of the brothers Philippe and Farid al-Khazin. The two, who were members of the Society of the Lebanese Revival in Beirut, also had the position of honorary dragomans at the French consulate-general there. They had wide-ranging contacts with French diplomats and statesmen, and papers documenting these contacts fell into the hands of the Ottomans when they seized the consulate papers in Beirut. Together with the brothers an ordinary robber was hanged, apparently in order to show that the authorities considered them as nothing more than common criminals.[29]

In June 1916 the third wave of arrests began as a result of the suspicion that a number of activists in Syria and Mount Lebanon were working against the Empire, and perhaps even organizing a revolt. Over 30 were arrested throughout Syria, among them Shukri al-Ayyubi, Shukri al-Quwwatli, Ahmad Qadri, Faris al-Khuri, and the senior army officer 'Abd al-Hamid al-Qaltaqji. (The circumstances which led to this series of arrests were discussed above in the section on revolt activities in the Levant during the Arab revolt.) The detainees were held in the Khan al-Basha jail in Damascus and underwent harsh torture. One of them, *al-Fatat* member Shukri al-Quwwatli, was serving at the time as secretary of the society and knew the names of its members and where its papers were hidden. After he was caned with the falqa until he bled and his fingernails were torn out, he felt that he would not be able to hold out, and decided to commit suicide. He bribed one of the guards to bring him a razor, on the pretext that he wanted to shave, and he slashed the veins in his left arm. Fortuitously, his fellow society member Ahmad Qadri, who was in the next cell, noticed the blood seeping out from under the door. Qadri, who was a doctor, called for help and he himself bandaged al-Quwwatli's arm. Afterwards al-Quwwatli was taken to a hospital and his life was saved.

The detainees were tried in a court martial and acquitted, apparently for lack of evidence. When the presiding judge came to Jamal Pasha to have him confirm the verdicts, Jamal shouted at him: "Get out of here! I want punishment, not acquittal!" There was a re-trial, and this time death sentences were meted out to Shukri al-Ayyubi and two others and prison sentences for the rest. Several of the accused were not re-tried, after bribes were paid to senior Turkish officials. Nor were those sentenced to death executed, since the government refused to approve the sentences. The Arab revolt had already broken out, and the government, which had demurred at the way the earlier death sentences were carried out, issued a new order not to execute political prisoners without approval from Istanbul. Moreover, Sharif Husayn of Mecca sent a notice to Istanbul that if the death sentences were carried out he would execute all the Turkish prisoners in his hands, including the Vali of the Hijaz. His son Faysal threatened to kill ten Turkish officers for every Arab put to death. The appeals court in Istanbul decided to acquit all the accused on the grounds that the crimes attributed to them had not actually been committed, and Jamal Pasha was sent a stern warning not to execute the accused.

However, Jamal Pasha was not ready to give in easily, and he stubbornly insisted on at least keeping them in jail. Several of the prisoners were released later on, among them Faris al-Khuri, who bought his freedom by resigning from the parliament. Others, among them Shukri al-Ayyubi who confessed to having contacts with Faysal, were released after Jamal Pasha left Syria. Three of the prisoners remained in jail until 30 September 1918, the day the Turks left Damascus.[30]

Besides the executions, imprisonments, and deportations, the military court in 'Aleyh passed many death sentences against Arab activists living outside the Empire, far out of reach of the authorities. These were tried in absentia. They included several of the most prominent Arab activists, among them: Rafiq al-'Azm, Rashid Rida, Da'ud Barakat, Faris Nimr, Ibrahim Salim al-Najjar, Shukri Ghanim, Iskandar 'Ammun, 'Abd al-Rahman al-Shahbandar, 'Aziz 'Ali al-Misri, Sayyid Talib al-Naqib, and Najib 'Azuri. Also Sharif Husayn, Amir Faysal, and the Sultan of Egypt Husayn Kamil were ordered to appear before the court within ten days; otherwise they would be declared criminals, their civil rights annulled, their property confiscated, and they would be tried in absentia.[31]

It should be noted that the Iraqi officers were unscathed by the measures taken by Jamal Pasha against the Arab activists, although they were the backbone of the secret society al-'Ahd. The explanation for this is that these officers, who were serving in Syria, were sent from there to Istanbul and Gallipoli in the beginning of Jamal Pasha's reign, when he was still treating the Arabs with gentleness. When Jamal began his hangings they were already beyond his reach. The Syrian activists, on the other hand, mostly civilians and a few officers, were arrested later on, after the various revolt plans were exposed, and they were in the palm of Jamal Pasha's hand, in Syria.

In the proclamation announcing the executions of 6 May 1916, Jamal Pasha promised to publish shortly a book in which he would reveal all the evidence that was used to convict the defendants in 'Aleyh. And indeed, at the end of 1916 his book *Idahat* (Explanations) appeared, in which he justified the sentences issued in 'Aleyh. The book was printed at the Tanin Press in Istanbul and appeared in three languages: Arabic, Turkish, and French. Tal'at tried to prevent the distribution of the book, because he did not want to re-open the debate on the executions, but Jamal Pasha came to the capital and demanded that the book be distributed. It was based on the papers of the French consulates and the Decentralization Party, and also on the confessions of 'Abd al-Ghani al-'Uraysi, Rafiq Rizq Sallum, and Sayf al-Din al-Khatib. It included a detailed examination of the Arab societies: the Arab-Ottoman Brotherhood, the Literary Club, al-Qahtaniyya, al-'Ahd, the Arab Revolutionary Society, the Lebanese Revival, the Reform Society of Beirut, and the Decentralization Party. *Al-Fatat* was briefly mentioned in the book, also,[32] contrary to the opinion of many,[33] who mistakenly believe that it was not revealed to the authorities. At the end of the book all the sentences given in 'Aleyh and their reasons were detailed. Photographs of the documents from the French consulates and of the Decentralization Party were also included in order to prove their authenticity.[34]

Contrary to the impression that various factors hostile to Jamal Pasha tried to create, the information provided in this book is reliable and very accurate. This was in fact the first serious study that was made of the activities of the Arab societies, both secret and open. Nothing written in the succeeding decades reached its level. (This was probably because Jamal had at his disposal the means for discovering the truth which were not available, and could not possibly be available, to any of the various authors who later dealt with the subject of the Arab societies.)

After the executions of May 1916 many claimed that the condemned men were hanged for crimes they had not committed.
Rashid Rida published an article in *al-Manar* entitled "Jamal
Pasha the Bloodthirsty" in which he claimed that the Decentralization Party did not aspire to sever Syria from the Ottoman
Empire, and added that only one or two of those executed were
members of the party. Later on one of the leaders of the party
published a statement in which he declared that no one among
the executed was working on behalf of a foreign state or was in
favour of secession from the Empire. In a book published in
1917 by André Mandelstam, the former dragoman at the Russian embassy in Istanbul, Jamal Pasha was vigorously attacked,
and the assertions made in his book *Idahat* were characterized as
hypocritical excuses. In 1919 the Lebanese priest Antun Yamin
branded Jamal's explanations as mendacious arguments and as
an excuse for executing innocent men.[35] Later historians and
scholars have followed these writers.[36]

The question as to whether or not the executions were justified will not be dealt with here because this is not the concern of
the historian. On the other hand, as promised at the beginning
of this chapter, a clear answer will be given as to whether or not
the accusations made against the defendants were factually true.
That is, did they or did they not take part in the various Arab
societies and engage in subversive activity? The following data
are based on diverse and abundant documentary material, and
they refer to the two principal groups of those sentenced to
death:

Those sentenced on 21 August 1915
'Abd al-Karim al-Khalil: Member of *al-Qahtaniyya*, the Literary
    Club, and Decentralization Party. In 1915 he organized a revolt in
    the region of Sidon and southern Mount Lebanon.
Salim al-Ahmad 'Abd al-Hadi: Head of Decentralization Party
    branch in Jenin and founder of the party branch in Haifa.
Muhammad al-Mihmisani: Secretary of *al-Fatat* in Beirut and mem-
    ber of Decentralization Party.
Mahmud al-Mihmisani: Head of Decentralization Party branch in
    Beirut and member of *al-Fatat*.
Mahmud al-'Ajam: Member of Decentralization Party and *al-Fatat*.
Nuri al-Qadi: Member of Decentralization Party.
'Abd al-Qadir al-Kharsa: Member of Decentralization Party.
'Ali al-Armanazi: Head of Decentralization Party branch in Hama.
Na'if Tallu: Head of Decentralization Party branch in the Biqa'.
Musallam 'Abidin: Member of Decentralization Party.
Salih Haydar: Head of Decentralization Party branch in Ba'albek

and member of the Literary Club and *al-Fatat*.

Those sentenced on 6 May 1916

Shafiq al-Mu'ayyad: Member of the Literary Club and Decentralization Party. In 1913 he tried to convince the French ambassador in Istanbul of the need to send French armed forces to Syria.

'Umar al-Jaza'iri: Member of *al-Fatat*.

'Umar Hamad: Member of *al-Fatat*, Reform Society of Beirut and Decentralization Party.

Rafiq Rizq Sallum: Vice-President of the Literary Club and member of *al-Fatat* and Decentralization Party.

Muhammad al-Shanti: Member of Decentralization Party.

Shukri al-'Asali: Member of *al-Qahtaniyya*, Literary Club, and Decentralization Party. In 1911 he worked for the annexation of Syria to Egypt.

'Abd al-Ghani al-'Uraysi: One of the first members of *al-Fatat* and member of Decentralization Party. In early 1915 he approached Sharif Husayn with a proposal to start a revolt in Syria.

'Arif al-Shihabi: Member of *al-Fatat*, *al-Qahtaniyya*, the Literary Club and Decentralization Party.

Tawfiq al-Basat: Member of *al-Fatat*, the Literary Club and Decentralization Party. In 1915 he deserted from the army.

Sayf al-Din al-Khatib: Member of *al-Fatat* and the Literary Club.

Ahmad Hasan Tabbara: One of the leaders of the Reform Society of Beirut and member of Decentralization Party.

'Abd al-Wahhab al-Inklizi: Member of the Literary Club and Decentralization Party. He was involved in the revolt plan of 'Abd al-Karim al-Khalil.

Sa'id 'Aql: Member of the Lebanese Revival.

Petro Pauli: Was not a member of any Arab society.

Jurji Haddad: Member of the Lebanese Revival, Decentralization Party and *al-'Ahd*.

Salim al-Jaza'iri: One of the leaders of *al-Qahtaniyya* and member of the Literary Club and *al-'Ahd*. In 1913 he planned to open a revolt against the Ottomans in Syria.

'Ali al-Nashashibi: Member of *al-Qahtaniyya*, Decentralization Party, and *al-'Ahd*.

Rushdi al-Sham'a: Member of the Literary Club and Decentralization Party.

Amin Lutfi al-Hafiz: Member of *al-Qahtaniyya*, the Literary Club and *al-'Ahd*. In 1915 he organized a large-scale revolt on the northern Syrian coast.

Jalal al-Bukhari: Member of *al-Fatat* and the Literary Club. In 1915 he deserted from the army.

'Abd al-Hamid al-Zahrawi: Member of *al-Qahtaniyya*, the Literary Club, and Decentralization Party.

Thus one can see that the only one of the two groups who

was not a member of the Arab societies was Petro Pauli. (He was the owner of the newspaper *al-Muraqib*, which was pro-Decentralization Party.) It is interesting to note, on the other hand, that of the 'Aleyh defendants who were acquitted there were several who were indeed members of the Arab societies. The most important of them were Ahmad Qadri, one of the founders of *al-Fatat*, 'Ali Rida al-Rikabi, one of the leaders of the society during World War I, and 'Izzat al-A'zami, a member of the Literary Club and the Green Flag society.

Chapter 3

AL-FATAT, AL-'AHD, AND THE ORIGINS OF
THE ARAB REVOLT

With the establishment of the Ottoman Fourth Army, Damascus was made its headquarters, and the city became the centre of gravity of Syria. Many of the Arab students were mobilized as reserve officers, and therefore the administrative committee of the secret Arab society *al-Fatat* decided, in late October 1914, to transfer the centre of the society from Beirut to Damascus. A branch of the society remained in Beirut. From Damascus the society attempted to re-organize its branches in the other towns of Syria and to establish contacts with other Arab countries and the outside world. The society also decided to widen its ranks in order to increase its influence. Prior to this most of its members were students and former students from the upper class. Now it was decided to bring into the society several of the important tribal chiefs in Syria such as Nuri al-Sha'lan, the paramount chief of the Ruwalla tribes, and his son Nawaf, Sheikh Fawwaz al-Fa'iz, the chief of the Banu Sakhr tribe, and several Druze leaders from the al-Atrash family. Nonetheless, these leaders remained outside the inner circle of the society, and none of them were admitted to the administrative committee. It was a different case with the retired senior officer 'Ali Rida al-Rikabi, who joined the society at this time and became one of its key figures during the war.[1]

When the World War broke out in Europe, *al-Fatat* hoped that the Empire would not enter it. When the Empire did enter the war, the administrative committee passed the following resolution:

> The goal of the Arabs is independence, and this in order to guard the existence of the Arab countries, and not out of hostility to the Turks. Therefore, if the Arab countries will stand up to the danger of European imperialism, the Society will work alongside the Turks, together with all free Arabs to protect the Arab countries.[2]

The society at this point decided to investigate if the Arab countries would indeed stand up before the danger of European conquest.

THE MISSION OF KAMIL AL-QASSAB

Already in August 1914, after the Empire announced a general mobilization, *al-Fatat* sent its secretary-general, Muhammad al-Mihmisani, to Egypt to discuss with the leaders of the Decentralization Party what line the Arabs should take with respect to the coming war. After two days of sterile discussions it was decided that it would not be possible to arrive at any operative decisions without first coordinating with the Arab amirs of the Arabian Peninsula. Al-Mihmisani returned to Beirut empty-handed, although the leaders of the party did apprise him of the contacts they had opened up with the British, and he reported this to his comrades in the society leadership.[3]

At the end of October the society decided to send another emissary to Cairo, Sheikh Kamil al-Qassab, to study the nature of the contacts with the British. He was to inform those dealing with them that the activists in Syria would be satisfied with nothing less than full independence for the Arab countries. Al-Qassab left Damascus for Beirut, and paid a large sum of money to a sailor he knew who smuggled him onto an Italian ship sailing for Alexandria. When he arrived in Alexandria he was arrested by the British, but was released following the intervention of Rafiq al-'Azm and Rashid Rida and permitted to continue on to Cairo. There he met with the leaders of the Decentralization Party, who reported to him about the emissaries sent by the party to the Arab provinces, but their talks ended without any significant results. He visited the British Residency as well, and told them that most of the Muslims of Syria were prepared to come to an understanding with the British on the basis of establishing an independent Arab state and on condition that Syria would not be occupied by France. A British assurance in this spirit would definitely bring them over to the British side. The British were not prepared to commit themselves to any limitation on the status of France in Syria, and Kamil al-Qassab left Egypt empty-handed.

After a harrowing journey on the last Italian ship to sail from Egypt to the Empire, he disembarked safely at the port of Adalia. However, when he returned to Damascus he was arrested by the authorities, who were aware of his visit to Egypt, and he was sent to the military court in 'Aleyh. He spent 27 days isolated in a cell, and then was interrogated concerning his visit to Egypt. Al-Qassab dissembled and said that the purpose of his trip was to procure books for the high school that he ran in Damascus. It is not clear if his investigators believed him or not, but he was released, perhaps so that he could be shadowed and thus reveal the secrets of the Arab societies. Al-Qassab, who was suspicious of the intentions of the authorities and felt that sooner or later he would be returned to jail, gladly accepted the decision of *al-Fatat* to send him to the Hijaz in order to strengthen the ties with Sharif Husayn. This was after the visit of Faysal in Syria and after the members of the societies handed him the "Damascus Protocol" (see below) to give to his father. Al-Qassab was asked to pressure Husayn to expedite matters, to explain to him the dire straits of the Syrians under Turkish rule, and to make it clear to him that his colleagues in the society were not prepared to settle for anything less than complete independence.

In October 1915 Kamil al-Qassab arrived in Mecca, ostensibly on hajj. He recounted to Husayn the actions of the Turks in Syria and urged him to open a revolt. Shortly thereafter Husayn showed him the letter that he had received from Arthur Henry McMahon, the British high commissioner in Egypt, dated 24 October 1915, which became a landmark in Arab-British relations in World War I. Afterwards al-Qassab settled in Medina and served as a liaison between Syria and Mecca. However, a few weeks later his friends informed him that the authorities in Damascus had issued a warrant for his arrest. He quickly returned to Mecca where he remained until the outbreak of the Arab revolt.[4]

AL-FATAT AND AL-'AHD COMBINE EFFORTS

In 1915 the number of Arab soldiers in the Ottoman army was estimated at 100,000 (and it possibly even amounted to a third of this army, which numbered about 1,000,000 men in that year). The 23rd, 25th, 26th, 27th, 42nd, 43rd, and 44th Divisions were entirely Syrian, and the 22nd, 24th, 39th, 40th, and 41st Divisions were in part Syrian. The 35th, 37th, and 38th were entirely Iraqi, and the 36th was in part Iraqi. However, not all these divisions were stationed in the Arab provinces of the Empire. The Levant was under the control of the Fourth Army, of which the two most important forces in early 1915 were the 8th Corps, consisting of the Arab 23rd, 25th, and 27th Divisions, and the 12th Corps which consisted of the Arab 35th and 37th Divisions and the partly-Arab 36th Division.

The 12th Corps was originally stationed in Mosul, and at the outbreak of World War I was transferred to Syria, its 35th Division stationed in Aleppo and the 36th in the region of Hama. The chief-of-staff of the 12th Corps was *al-'Ahd* member Yasin al-Hashimi, and a number of other members of the society served in this corps in various functions. If the Arab officers had any hopes of starting a military revolt against the Ottomans in Syria, then it was centred on the Arab forces of the 12th Corps. Therefore this corps was called by them during this period "The Army of Salvation" (*Jaysh al-Khalas*).

Al-Fatat, which was busy widening its ranks, decided to take in Yasin al-Hashimi and thereby to acquire influence among the army officers. (Before the war the number of officers who were members of the society was negligible.) The assignment was given to 'Abd al-Ghani al-'Uraysi, who contacted al-Hashimi through a staff officer who knew them both. Al-Hashimi was sworn in as a member of *al-Fatat* and became the liaison man between *al-'Ahd* and *al-Fatat*. Then a number of other *al-'Ahd* members joined *al-Fatat*, and a period of combined activity of the two societies began.[5]

The official leader of *al-'Ahd* was 'Aziz 'Ali al-Misri. However, he was in Egypt, far from the rest of the society members. Yasin al-Hashimi, who to a certain extent competed with al-Misri for leadership of the society, became its central figure in Syria. He displayed a considerable measure of presence of mind, and when on one occasion the officer members raised the idea of assassinating Jamal Pasha, al-Hashimi held them back out of apprehension that such an act would bring about the liquidation of all Arab officers. Instead, the society concentrated on disseminating propaganda among the Arab officers and inducing them to desert. The deserters would escape to the region of the Ruwalla tribes of Nuri al-Sha'lan.[6]

In early 1915, after combining the activities of the two societies, a meeting was held with the participation of Yasin al-Hashimi and several *al-Fatat* leaders, at which it was decided to prepare a general plan for a revolt against the Ottomans. The revolt was to begin in Syria under the command of al-Hashimi, who would lead the regular Arab forces, aided by tribes of the Syrian desert whose chiefs were members of the society. Their goal was to reach a state of affairs in which they would be able to set up a temporary government in Syria. At the same time, though, they wanted the revolt to spread to the Arabian Peninsula, and for this they hoped to persuade one of the Arab rulers in the Peninsula to be its supreme leader. Al-Hashimi wanted

Ibn Sa'ud of Najd to be this leader, but emissaries of *al-Fatat* who reached Ibn Sa'ud with the proposal that he lead such a revolt were politely turned down by him. He did not have confidence in their ability to stand behind their plan, and he had his own problems with Ibn Rashid. The choice then fell on Sharif Husayn of Mecca. His noble ancestry, his status as guardian of the holy places of Islam, and the distance of the Hijaz from the main Ottoman forces made him a suitable candidate to lead the planned revolt.[7]

The task of informing Husayn of the plans of the societies and to assess his readiness to lead the revolt was given to *al-Fatat* member Fawzi al-Bakri. The relations between the Hashimite and al-Bakri families were very close, going back to 1909 when 'Abdallah accompanied the hajj procession back to Damascus and was a guest in the house of the father of the family, 'Ata' al-Bakri. At Husayn's request the Ottoman war ministry agreed that all members of the al-Bakri family who were subject to conscription would fulfill their military service obligation in the bodyguard of Husayn in Mecca. With the outbreak of the war Fawzi was drafted into the army, and in accordance with the agreement he was to be sent to Mecca. His brother Nasib al-Bakri, who was a member of *al-Fatat*, exploited the opportunity and brought Fawzi into the society, and its leaders entrusted him with a message to Husayn. The message was written by 'Ali Rida al-Rikabi, 'Abd al-Ghani al-'Uraysi, and Yasin al-Hashimi, informing Husayn that the nationalists in Syria and Iraq, including the senior Arab officers in the Ottoman army, were ready to open a revolt in order to achieve Arab independence. They asked Husayn to take upon himself the leadership of this revolt and to send an emissary on his behalf to Damascus to conclude the details. Fawzi al-Bakri arrived in Mecca at the end of January 1915. Husayn listened to what he had to say, but cautiously did not react. Instead he looked out the window as though he had heard nothing. Some time after this another emissary arrived in Mecca, a Baghdadi officer who brought to Husayn the list of all the officer members of *al-'Ahd* who had sworn allegiance to him.[8]

It is important to note·from all the above that one can see that *al-Fatat* and *al-'Ahd* had begun to aspire to absolute independence, and had established their contacts with the Hashimites before Jamal Pasha began his policy of terror and the series of arrests. (Before the war these two societies did not strive to achieve complete independence and to secede from the Ottoman Empire.) One can, thus, refute the accepted opinion that Jamal

Pasha's reign of terror was what drove the nationalists to demand absolute independence. It is apparent, therefore, that it was the outbreak of the World War which was the factor that caused the change in the societies' goals and the desire to exploit the situation to achieve independence.

FAYSAL IN DAMASCUS I

In January 1915 'Ali, the eldest son of Sharif Husayn, went to Medina together with the Vali of the Hijaz Wahib Pasha in order to take part in the drive on the Suez Canal. 'Ali's assignment was to lead the Hijazi volunteers who were to participate in the campaign, while Wahib was to command the regular Ottoman soldiers that the Hijaz was to supply. During the journey a briefcase of papers belonging to Wahib Pasha fell down and was later found by one of 'Ali's men. 'Ali could not overcome his curiosity and read the documents that were in the briefcase. To his astonishment he learned that Wahib was planning to get rid of Husayn and his sons and to put an end to the quasi-autonomy that the Hijaz enjoyed. 'Ali immediately returned to Mecca and showed the documents to his father. Husayn decided to send to Istanbul his son Faysal, who enjoyed good relations with Turkish statesmen, to register a complaint with the authorities and to have Wahib Pasha removed from the Hijaz. But after Fawzi al-Bakri arrived in Mecca with the information on the planned revolt by the Arab societies in Syria, Husayn charged Faysal with an additional mission. Besides the official and overt purpose of his mission — to register a complaint against Wahib Pasha — he was to find out how serious the plans of the Arab societies were and what real forces were available to them. In case he should find that there was real substance to their plans, he was to ascertain the position of their leaders towards the contacts that Husayn had opened with the British during this period.[9]

On 26 March 1915 Faysal arrived in Damascus, ostensibly on his way to Istanbul, and was a guest of the al-Bakri family. After Nasib al-Bakri had reassured the leaders of al-Fatat concerning the disposition of Faysal, they decided to take him into the society and to reveal their plans to him. At a meeting held in the al-Bakri house with the participation of 'Ali Rida al-Rikabi, Yasin al-Hashimi, Ahmad Qadri and others, Faysal was sworn in as a member of the society, and was offered the leadership of the revolt which was to break out simultaneously in Syria and the Hijaz. Faysal responded that he had been authorized by his father only to study the situation in Syria. However, he promised at the same time to try to persuade his father to cooperate. Later Faysal was introduced to several members of *al-'Ahd* and was quite impressed by what they said about the ability of the society to stir up a mutiny in the Ottoman army in Syria. After he was sworn in also as a member of *al-'Ahd*, Faysal disclosed to the leaders of the two societies the contacts that his father had begun with the British and the encouraging message that Kitchener had sent to his father in October 1914 (see below). He stressed that without the assistance of a European power his father would not be able to take on the responsibility of starting a revolt.[10]

After a stay of two weeks in Damascus Faysal continued on to Istanbul. The leaders of the societies met for a number of secret discussions to consolidate their stand with reference to the conditions under which they would be prepared to cooperate with the British in their war against the Ottoman Empire. At the end of their discussions representatives of the two societies formulated the "Damascus Protocol", which contained the territorial and other demands that Husayn was to present to the British:

> The recognition by Great Britain of the independence of the Arab countries lying within the following frontiers:
> North: The line Mersin-Adana to parallel 37° N. and thence along the line Birejik - Urfa - Mardin - Jazirat (Ibn 'Umar) - Amadia to the Persian frontier;
> East: The Persian frontier down to the Persian Gulf;
> South: The Indian Ocean (with the exclusion of Aden, whose status was to be maintained);
> West: The Red Sea and the Mediterranean Sea back to Mersin.
> The abolition of all exceptional privileges granted to foreigners under the Capitulations.
> The conclusion of a defensive alliance between Great Britain and the future independent Arab state.
> The grant of economic preference to Great Britain.[11]

Faysal arrived in Istanbul on 23 April. He met with the Grand Vizier and showed him the documents of Wahib Pasha that had fallen into the hands of his father. Then he met with Tal'at and Enver for the same purpose. The authorities granted his request, and Wahib Pasha was recalled to Istanbul. A new Vali was appointed for the Hijaz, Ghalib Pasha. Faysal also received from the authorities a sum of 25,000 Turkish liras in order to finance the mobilization of Hijazi volunteers to take part in the second Suez Canal campaign. (When Faysal returned to Damascus he gave 1,000 liras of this money to *al-Fatat*.) While he was in Istanbul Faysal conferred with a number of senior statesmen and reached the conclusion that the Empire was on the verge of destruction. This impression strengthened his decision to accept the revolt initiative.[12]

Faysal returned to Syria, passed through Aleppo where he met some members of the societies, and arrived in Damascus on 23 May. On his arrival representatives of the societies handed him the "Damascus Protocol". Faysal then began a series of meetings with leaders of the societies and other prominent Syrians. They would slip into the al-Bakri house in the early hours of the morning in order not to arouse the suspicions of the authorities and would discuss with Faysal the need to start a revolt.

The most important of these meetings was with Yasin al-Hashimi, who told Faysal that there was no need for any assistance and that they had all that was necessary to start the revolt. All that they were asking was for Faysal to lead it. When Faysal mentioned that it would be possible to get assistance from the Hijazi tribes loyal to Husayn, al-Hashimi answered him: "We do not need them. We have everything." These words of al-Hashimi impressed Faysal very much, inasmuch as al-Hashimi was the chief-of-staff of the 12th Corps, and one could interpret what he said to mean that the revolt would be based on the 25th, 35th, and 36th Divisions. Faysal also met with 'Ali Rida al-Rikabi, who made his view clear that it was opportune to start the revolt immediately, with Sheikh Badr al-Din al-Hasani, who expressed the support of the 'ulama' of Syria for the revolt, and with Nasib al-Atrash, who promised him the support of the Druzes. Faysal expressed his wish to meet also with Nuri al-Sha'lan, the paramount chief of the Ruwalla tribes, who was considered the most powerful leader in the Syrian desert. A member of *al-Fatat*, Fa'iz al-Ghusayn, was sent to arrange a meeting, but the wily Nuri did not want to commit himself, and he merely sent his son Nawaf to meet with Faysal.

Faysal promised his collocutors to persuade his father to conclude the contacts with the British in a positive spirit, and it was agreed that he would return from the Hijaz to Syria at the head of an army of volunteers, ostensibly to take part in the second campaign for the Suez Canal. Once they arrived in Syria the revolt would be announced under his leadership, and the rebels would be joined by the 12th Corps — "The Army of Salvation".

Before he left Damascus the leaders of the societies handed him a petition in which Husayn was authorized to negotiate with Britain in the name of the Arabs and was recognized as the king of the Arab countries. The petition was signed by Yasin al-Hashimi, 'Ali Rida al-Rikabi, Shukri al-Ayyubi, Badr al-Din al-Hasani, Salim and Nasib al-Atrash, and several important tribal chiefs. Al-Rikabi and Sheikh Badr al-Din even turned over their personal seals for Faysal to deliver to his father as proof of their consent to the declaration of revolt and to all that he should do in the name of the Arabs. The "Damascus Protocol" itself was copied in tiny letters, hidden in the lining of the boots of one of his attendants, and Faysal and his party returned to the Hijaz.[13]

Faysal arrived in Mecca on 20 June. He gave his father the "Damascus Protocol" and reported to him on the readiness of the members of the societies to open a revolt in Syria and to work together with the British, if the latter should accept the conditions of the protocol. He pointed out that, according to his impressions, there were indeed in Syria Arab divisions ready to revolt, and that the number of Turkish soldiers there was not large. Public opinion, on the other hand, was not yet ready for such a step. Faysal recommended to Husayn that he take on the leadership of the revolt and at the same time renew his contacts with the British. He estimated that if the British should agree to land forces at Alexandretta this would greatly improve the chances of the revolt. Immediately afterwards Husayn and Faysal left Mecca for Ta'if, and there they were joined by 'Ali and 'Abdallah for a family discussion of the situation. The family conference produced two decisions: (a) Faysal would return to Syria, contact the leaders of the societies and organize with them the preparations for the revolt, to break out simultaneously in Syria and the Hijaz. (The suggested time for the outbreak was the following winter.) (b) Husayn would open negotiations with Britain.[14]

Soon after Faysal's departure changes occurred in Syria which were to nullify the plan to start the revolt there. The 35th Division, which was to be one of the main forces on which the revolt would be based, was the first of the Arab divisions to be removed from Syria. As a result of the intensification of battles in southern Iraq between the Ottoman and British forces, the military staff decided to return the division to Iraq. This transfer stemmed from military considerations. The removal later of the other Arab divisions from Syria, on the other hand, was the outcome of a deliberate policy of the authorities. Already from the beginning of the war agents of the Ottoman secret service, the

Teşkilât-i Mahsusa, were suspicious of the activity of the Arab officers and placed a tail on them. Their investigations revealed that the officers intended to declare independence for Syria and were preparing to assassinate their Turkish commanders. The Teşkilât-i Mahsusa recommended their arrest, but Minister of War Enver preferred to solve the problem by sending them to Gallipoli, a solution which to a certain extent was a death sentence in itself. Thus, in June 1915 on Enver's request, Jamal Pasha ordered the removal from Syria of the 23rd, 25th, and 27th Divisions of the 8th Corps and the 37th Division of the 12th Corps. Most of the Arab forces were sent to Gallipoli, while some were sent to the Caucasus, the Carpathians, and Galicia. Turkish forces brought from Anatolia replaced them and spread out over Syria. As far as the revolt plan of the societies was concerned, the withdrawal of the 25th Division was especially serious because it was to form the backbone of the revolt, once the 35th Division had been taken out. As a result of these measures the revolt plan in Syria became, in effect, inapplicable.

The planned revolt in Syria lost not only its soldiers but also its leaders. For some time the authorities had suspected that Yasin al-Hashimi was the leader of the officers, and they now decided to send him to Istanbul. Some of the more junior officers were arrested in Aleppo and interrogated, but after no evidence against them was found they were released, and they, too, were ordered to Istanbul. A group of officers left for Istanbul in mid-June, but not before they got together in Aleppo for a secret meeting in which it was decided that they should try to desert the army at the first opportunity in order to join Sharif Husayn. Among those present at the meeting was a young Iraqi officer, a member of al-'Ahd, by the name of Muhammad Sharif al-Faruqi. This junior officer was soon to become a key figure in the formation of Arab-British relations during World War I.[15]

The fact that the Arab officers who were members of the societies were sent mostly to the battlefronts outside of Syria saved their lives. Had they remained in Syria many of them probably would have been included in the series of arrests which began only a few days after they left, and which ended in executions. The fate of the civilian members was different. Some time after the Arab units began to leave Syria Muhammad al-Mihmisani and others approached the Vali of Beirut with a demand to stop sending Arab soldiers to distant battlefields. The Vali accused the soldiers of treachery and said that the government was forced to remove them from Syria out of fear that they would start a revolt. The argument became heated, and al-Mihmisani said that if the Turks did not trust the Arabs, then they should leave their country and let them defend themselves. The Arabs had no need for Turkish soldiers. The Vali immediately ordered his arrest, and al-Mihmisani, against whom much incriminating evidence had been collected from the papers of the Decentralization Party of which he was a member, was executed on 21 August 1915. His arrest was a serious blow to *al-Fatat* because he knew where the society's documents were hidden, in a grave next to his house. Thereupon the sister of Salih Haydar, also a member of *al-Fatat* (and executed together with al-Mihmisani), came to Beirut and together with al-Mihmisani's sister took out the papers from the grave and burned them. Great damage to the society was thus averted, for al-Mihmisani had broken down under interrogation and had revealed many secrets.[16]

When the authorities began to remove the Arab units from Syria, a huge wave of desertions began. An Arab officer by the name of 'Izz al-Din al-Saruji stood in the streets of Aleppo and spoke before Arab soldiers about the need to desert and to stop fighting for the Turks, the oppressors of the Arabs. According to one estimate 300 Syrian soldiers deserted as a result of this. Jamal Pasha issued an order to take the officer dead or alive, but he escaped to the Syrian desert and from there continued on to the British in southern Iraq. The main place where deserting officers found refuge was in Jabal al-Duruz. *Al-Fatat* aided dozens of officers and also the sons of notables from Damascus, Homs, and Hama to reach the mountain, where they were protected by the al-Atrash family.

In contrast to this, the success of the society in rescuing its own members was smaller. On 23 July 1915 Fa'iz al-Ghusayn was arrested by the authorities after he was informed against for having brought Nawaf al-Sha'lan to Damascus to meet with Faysal. On the same day the administrative committee of *al-Fatat* convened and decided that danger was imminent for 'Abd al-Ghani al-'Uraysi, 'Arif al-Shihabi, and Tawfiq al-Basat, and that they should immediately leave Syria and flee to the Hijaz. The three hid out for a while in Jabal al-Duruz, where they were joined by their fellow member 'Umar Hamad, who was being pursued by the authorities for the offense of membership in the Decentralization Party. The four then turned to Jawf, for refuge with society member Nawaf al-Sha'lan, but he feared the reaction of the authorities and asked them to continue on their way. They decided to continue on to the Hijaz taking the Hijazi railway, disguised as bedouins. Instead of keeping themselves inconspicuous in the interior of the train, they sat by the windows, and when they arrived at the Mada'in Salih station they attracted the attention of a doctor from Damascus who was astonished to hear bedouins speaking French to each other. When he came closer to this odd group he saw a gold tooth sparkling in the mouth of one of them and soon identified him as his schoolmate 'Arif al-Shihabi. The four were captured, sent to 'Aleyh, and hanged with the second group of those sentenced to death. Three other society members, Jalal al-Bukhari, Ahmad Muraywid, and Tahir al-Jaza'iri, wanted to follow in their path, but when they found out about the arrest of the four they decided to remain under the protection of the al-Sha'lan family. A short time after they came to him Nuri al-Sha'lan turned them over to the Ottoman authorities, and al-Bukhari was added to the list of those executed. His two companions remained in jail.[17]

It should be pointed out that despite the severe blows suffered by the society, *al-Fatat* continued to exist, and new members joined it during that very same period.

THE MCMAHON-HUSAYN CORRESPONDENCE

In 1893 Sharif Husayn was compelled to leave Mecca for Istanbul as the "guest" of Sultan 'Abd al-Hamid II. He spent 15 years with his family in the capital, and only with the Young Turk revolution did he have the opportunity to return to the Hijaz. After the dismissal of the previous Sharif of Mecca, Sharif 'Ali Haydar was the CUP's favourite for this position. Husayn, who wanted this job for himself, turned to the Grand Vizier Kamil Pasha and to the Sultan and persuaded them to give him the position. These two, who were trying their best to reduce the influence of the CUP, readily granted Husayn's appeal and appointed him to the office. From here on, and up to the outbreak of World War I, there were strained relations between Husayn and the CUP. The tension increased when Husayn proposed to the Ottoman authorities that he be appointed Vali of the Hijaz (prior to this his influence was confined to Mecca and Ta'if alone). They began to be wary of his ambitions, and instead of granting his request they sent the Vali Wahib Pasha to the Hijaz with explicit instructions to rule the region with firmness. Wahib was a tough vali, and in the past had already declared that he would suppress any Arab separatist movement.

On his arrival he demanded that Husayn return 100 Mauser rifles that were in the hands of his bodyguard. Husayn refused. After that Wahib's plan to liquidate the Sharifite family and to put the entire Hijaz under direct rule of the Empire was discovered. Husayn sent his son Faysal to Istanbul to demand the removal of Wahib Pasha (see above). Wahib was indeed brought back to Istanbul, but the new Vali, Ghalib Pasha, ordered the removal of Arab officers from the Hijaz.[18]

As a result of the deteriorated relations between Husayn and the CUP and their attempts to impair his status, or even to remove him entirely, Husayn resolved to revolt against the Empire, if he could get outside assistance to insure its success. Husayn wanted such outside assistance from Britain. Already in 1914 he had sent to Egypt his second son 'Abdallah, who intimated to Kitchener, then consul-general in Egypt, and to other British diplomats that his father was prepared to revolt against the Empire if he should receive appropriate outside help. 'Abdallah's discussions during 1914 did not bring any results because Britain was still adhering to the policy of maintaining the integrity of the Ottoman Empire. However, these conversations bore fruit with the outbreak of the World War followed by the change in Britain's policy vis-à-vis the Empire. Kitchener, now war minister, decided to further the relations with Husayn. On 31 October 1914 he sent Husayn the following letter, which, though limited and vague, was the first British promise to Husayn:

> If the Sharif and Arabs in general assist Great Britain in this conflict that has been forced upon us by Turkey . . . Great Britain will guarantee the independence, rights and privileges of the Sharifate against all external foreign aggression, in particular that of the Ottomans . . . It may be that an Arab of true race will assume the Khalifate at Mecca or Medina, and so good may come by the help of God out of all the evil which is now occurring.[19]

Encouraged by this message, Husayn continued to cultivate his relations with the British. In July 1915, after the family conference in Ta'if at which it was decided to accept the societies' proposal to start a revolt in Syria and the Hijaz, he decided to enter negotiations with the British regarding the conditions under which the two sides would cooperate in the war against the Ottoman Empire. On 14 July 1915 Husayn sent to the British high commissioner in Egypt, Arthur Henry McMahon, the first of the series of letters known as "The McMahon-Husayn Correspondence". In this letter Husayn spelt out in detail his

conditions for cooperation with the British, and on the subject
of territories he adhered word for word to the boundaries
demanded in the "Damascus Protocol":

> England to acknowledge the independence of the Arab countries,
> bounded on the north by Mersina and Adana up to the 37° of lati-
> tude, on which degree fall Birijik, Urfa, Mardin, Jezirat (ibn 'Umar),
> Amadia, up to the border of Persia; on the east by the borders of
> Persia up to the Gulf of Basra; on the south by the Indian Ocean,
> with the exception of the position of Aden to remain as it is; on the
> west by the Red Sea, the Mediterranean Sea up to Mersina.[20]

McMahon was startled by Husayn's demands, because he
considered him only a tribal chief who represented just himself
and not the Arabs in general. Therefore, in the reply he sent to
Husayn on 30 August he contented himself with a repetition of
the general promise of Kitchener of October 1914, pointing out
that it was still too soon to talk about borders. To this letter
Husayn sent on 9 September an angry response, in which he
demanded a specific reference to the question of borders. He
insisted that he was speaking in the name of the entire Arab
nation and not just in his own name. However, already before
these two letters were sent an incident occurred which was to
bring a complete turnabout in the attitude of the British towards
the demands of Sharif Husayn.

On 20 August 1915, during a series of bloody battles between
the Ottomans and the British on the Gallipoli peninsula, a
young Iraqi officer by the name of Muhammad Sharif al-Faruqi
deserted to the British lines. When the British realized that the
officer who had reached them carrying a white flag was an Arab
officer, they began to question him about what was going on the
Turkish side. After answering their questions he surprised them
with a declaration that he was a member of a secret Arab society
headed by 'Aziz 'Ali al-Misri, which was spreading propaganda
among the Arab officers in the Ottoman army and inducing
them to desert. Its purpose was to concentrate Arab officers in
Syria and to start a revolt there against the Ottomans. He
stressed that he was one of the important members of the society and added that he wished to meet with Sharif Husayn. He
also gave the British a list of officers who were members of
al-'Ahd and who were holding senior positions in the Ottoman
army. This information was sufficiently interesting for them to
send Faruqi to Egypt and to instruct the military authorities
there to check the truth of his statements with 'Aziz 'Ali al-
Misri.[21]

Faruqi arrived in Cairo on 1 September. In the first debriefing that he underwent he told his interrogators that the strength of his society was especially great among the Ottoman divisions in Mosul and Baghdad, though it also had influence in the other Arab provinces. The members of the society were ready to open a revolt as soon as the sign was given. He reported on the revolt plan of Amin Lutfi al-Hafiz, and added that Sharif Husayn was a partner in this plan and also that Ibn Sa'ud, al-Idrisi, and Imam Yahya had promised to help. This report was sufficiently impressive for the British to instruct the Lebanese-born intelligence man, Na'um Shuqayr, to interrogate him exhaustively. During the following days Faruqi was interrogated by Shuqayr, and it is important to note that during this period he met with the al-'Ahd leader 'Aziz 'Ali al-Misri. Therefore, at least some of the statements made by Faruqi in the following days were agreed to by al-Misri.[22]

On 12 September Faruqi wrote out a long statement describing the Arab movement's goals and the state of the movement on the eve of his desertion. He said that he was a member of a secret society composed of officers who were striving for the independence of the Arab countries. After his corps was transferred from Iraq to Syria he found out that there was another secret society in Syria, al-Fatat, and he personally had been concerned with uniting the two societies. When the officers learned of the contacts that had been made between Husayn and the British and that the British were prepared to assist Husayn in achieving independence, they decided that the northern border of the new independent state should be the Mersina-Diarbakr line. Since they were convinced of the amity of the British, the officers spread pro-British propaganda widely in Syria in order to convince the population that the British would help them achieve independence. However, shortly thereafter the Turks discovered the existence of the two societies and arrested a number of people, among them members of the societies. He himself was arrested and interrogated by Jamal Pasha. He was released for lack of evidence and sent to Istanbul, and from there he was transferred to the front in Gallipoli where he deserted.

Faruqi stated that the membership of his society included 90 per cent of the Arab officers in the Ottoman army, and after the union with al-Fatat they included also the civilian element in Syria, urban and nomad, from all the communities. He expressed his confidence that it would be possible to persuade many officers of the 35th Division in Iraq to join the British, of course after an understanding should be reached between the two sides. Faruqi concluded his statement by pointing out that he was not authorized officially to discuss with the British the programs of his society. Nevertheless, in order to shorten the negotiations, and because of his knowledge of the complexity of the problems of the Arabs among themselves and with France, and because of his recognition of Britain's goodwill, he was ready to answer any question put to him concerning the agreement that his society was willing to reach with the British. He was even prepared to introduce changes, including in the Mersina-Diarbakr line, and later would do his best to persuade his fellow members to accept these changes.[23]

To this statement Na'um Shuqayr appended a list of comments in which he detailed his impressions of Faruqi's personality, and also added further details about al-'Ahd and al-Fatat, given to him by Faruqi. Shuqayr characterized Faruqi as an intelligent man who knew several languages, and as a man prepared to sacrifice his life to realize his ideals. Faruqi had full confidence in himself and in his society and believed that the Arabs were capable of establishing immediately an Arab empire extending across the Arabian Peninsula, Syria and Iraq. For this, though, they would need British assistance in arms and advice, in return for which they were prepared to grant Britain concessions and privileges in the future state. However, they would accept assistance only from Britain. In case the French should land in Syria the population would fight them, and so would the society, even if this meant fighting alongside the Turks.

When Faruqi was asked about the structure on which the new Arab state would be based, he summarized his society's ideas regarding this as follows: (a) The new state would make a friendly alliance with the British. (b) The Arab countries included in it would be governed according to the principle of decentralization, that is, each country would be governed in the way most suited for it. However, all would be united under the caliph. (c) Sharif Husayn would be the caliph and sultan of the new state. (d) The basis of the state would be national and not religious. It would be an Arab empire and not a Muslim one. (e) Christians, Druzes, and Nusayris would have the same rights as Muslims. There would be a special law for Jews.

As for al-Fatat, Faruqi said that it had so far collected from the monthly dues of its members no less than 100,000 Turkish liras. Its centre was in Damascus, it had an undecipherable code, and its members had sworn on the Qur'an to offer their lives for the establishment of an Arab caliphate in the Arabian Peninsula, Syria, and Iraq.[24]

On 11 October Gilbert Clayton, the director of military and political intelligence in Cairo, wrote a memorandum on Faruqi summarizing the discussions held with him until then. Clayton emphasized Faruqi's statements that the members of al-'Ahd and al-Fatat had such great strength throughout the Arab provinces of the Ottoman Empire that neither the Turks nor the Germans would dare to suppress them. Faruqi declared that the Turks and the Germans had already approached the leaders of the officers and promised to grant all their demands. However, the officers, who trusted only the British, would prefer to get half of their demands from the British than all of them from the Turks and Germans. Nevertheless, if the British did not give a positive answer within a few weeks, the Arabs would be forced to join the Turks and Germans and to try to get the best possible conditions from them.

According to Faruqi, the officers had decided that the time had come to act. They understood that to set up a large Arab empire from Egypt to the borders of India was impossible for the time being. Therefore they were willing to be content with Britain helping them achieve a reasonable measure of independence and autonomous governments in those Arab countries in which the interests of Britain were greater than those of her allies. At the same time, Faruqi emphasized that independence for the Arabian Peninsula alone would not satisfy the Arabs. In order to satisfy them Britain would have to add autonomous governments — under British supervision and aegis — for Palestine and Iraq. Syria was also included in the program of the officers. However, because of French aspirations in this region the officers expected to be assisted by the good offices of Britain in solving the Syrian question in a satisfactory manner. In any case, they insisted that Damascus, Aleppo, Hama, and Homs be included in the Arab confederation. Any attempt by the French to occupy Syria by force would be met by the stubborn opposition of the Muslim population.

At this stage Faruqi pointed out that he was authorized by his society to receive the British answer to its proposals (in contrast to what he said to Shuqayr a month earlier). Clayton added that the proposals made by Husayn to the British in his letter of 14 July were surprisingly similar to those of Faruqi. There was therefore no doubt that Husayn's view reflected those of all the Arabs. The reports of Faruqi and the intelligence that was gathered during the preceding year on the Arab movement led to the conclusion that the situation was most serious and urgent. The Arabs had waited already an entire year in expectation of British aid in being liberated from the Ottoman yoke, and now it seemed that their patience was about to run out. The British were in need of all possible help in the Near East, especially help that would enable them to contend with Muslim public opinion and with the jihad declared by Istanbul. Therefore, if the British wanted to gain the friendship of the Arabs, they must give a positive response immediately. Clayton concluded his memorandum by stressing that the Arab leaders were ready to act rationally and to be satisfied with much less than what they had originally planned. If the British would comply with this, the Arabs would immediately begin operations against the Ottoman forces, beginning in the Hijaz and continuing in Syria and Palestine, and especially in Iraq where the strength of the society was great. Absence of a British response, on the other hand, would force the Arabs to join the Turks and Germans.[25]

Clayton sent the memorandum to McMahon, urging him to appeal to the foreign minister for instructions. A copy was sent to General John Maxwell, the GOC of British forces in Egypt. The next day, 12 October, McMahon sent the memorandum to Foreign Minister Grey. General Maxwell sent a telegram to War Minister Kitchener in which he stressed that "a powerful organization with considerable influence in the Army and among Arab Chiefs" had decided that the time had come to act. The Turks and the Germans were already in the midst of negotiations with this organization and were even giving it money. The members of the organization, however, preferred the British, as did Husayn, who was in contact with the former. However, if the British did not come forward with a sympathetic declaration of intentions, or if they delayed such a declaration, then the Arabs would be compelled to turn to the Turks, and Britain would face a jihad. On the other hand, if the British succeeded in gaining their cooperation, it would be highly valuable in the Arabian Peninsula, Iraq, Syria, and Palestine.[26]

On 13 October Kitchener cabled a reply to Maxwell empowering him in the name of the government to deal with the Arabs and to try to ensure that their traditional loyalty to Britain not be impaired. Kitchener also asked him to report to him urgently on the demands of the Arabs. Maxwell replied on 16 October emphasizing again that behind the appeal of the Arabs to Britain through Husayn there stood "a large and influential Arab party actually in the Turkish army". It was imperative to reach an agreement with them quickly so that they would act against the Turks. Otherwise, they would eventually join the Turks, and the British would then face new dangers, including another attempt of the Ottoman army to invade Egypt. Maxwell added that it was no longer possible to talk to the Arabs in general terms, rather it was necessary to be specific with them. He stressed that in his opinion the Arabs would be adamant about including Iraq (except for the vilayet of Basra, if the British opposed it), Aleppo, Homs, Hama, and Damascus in their future state. Maxwell's reply telegram ended with the warning that if the British did not reach an agreement with the Arabs without delay, they would find themselves confronting a united Islam.[27]

In the meantime further discussions were held with Faruqi, following which McMahon sent another telegram to Grey, on 18 October, in which he reported that it was absolutely clear that if the British did not give the Arabs immediate and satisfactory assurances, they would join the Germans. An Islamic union would then be formed against Britain. McMahon understood from Faruqi that the Arabs would accept the following promise from the British: Britain should agree to an independent Arab state within the borders proposed by Husayn and in those regions where Britain was free to act without detriment to the interests of her ally, France. Within these regions the Arabs would agree to British influence and would recognize British interests. Britain should commit itself to defend the Islamic holy places. As for the question of the northwestern borders of this state, according to Faruqi the Arabs would probably agree to modifications, provided that the districts of Aleppo, Damascus, Hama, and Homs remained in their hands. In contrast to this, they would oppose by force of arms any attempt by France to take over these regions. Faruqi also agreed that Britain should have a special status in the vilayet of Basra. McMahon concluded his telegram by stressing that Husayn and the Arabs would apparently not agree to less than this, and he asked for the foreign minister's instructions on the reply he had to give to Husayn and Faruqi.[28]

Feeling that time was running out, on 20 October McMahon sent two more telegrams, in which he again emphasized that the problem must be solved urgently and reported on the increasing nervousness of Husayn. On the same day a reply telegram was received from the British foreign minister, permitting McMahon to promise the Arabs specific borders for the future state, although with some limitations.[29] The path for the second letter of McMahon to Husayn was now open.

McMahon's letter to Husayn, of 24 October 1915, was the most important and most famous of the entire McMahon-Husayn correspondence. In this letter McMahon promised that

Britain would assist the Arabs to attain their independence and agreed to the borders that Husayn demanded in his letter of 14 July, subject to certain territorial limitations. The debate concerning the commitments that Britain took upon herself in the McMahon-Husayn correspondence in general, and over the territories that were or were not included in the McMahon letter of 24 October 1915, became an unremitting political nuisance for the British during the following decades, and more than once it strained Arab-British relations.[30]

A comparison of McMahon's first letter to Husayn, of 30 August, with his second, of 24 October, shows that the arrival in Cairo of the deserter Muhammad Sharif al-Faruqi brought a complete turnabout in the British attitude towards Husayn and the Arab movement. What he told the British, and to which they gave absolute credence, brought the British to accept the lion's share of Husayn's demands, and they considered him the authorized leader of a powerful Arab movement.

But how much truth was there in Faruqi's words? The activists of al-'Ahd did not comprise 90 per cent of the Arab officers in the Ottoman army, but only about one-half per cent, and this because the entire society numbered at the outbreak of the war only about 50 activists, of whom 40 were officers. Al-Fatat, too, numbered only about 40 activists at the beginning of the war. Faruqi's statement that Al-Fatat had collected 100,000 Turkish liras from its members' dues was utterly imaginary. So, too, were his statements that Ibn Sa'ud, al-Idrisi, and Imam Yahya had agreed to assist the Arab officers. Nothing is known of any broad pro-British propaganda spread by al-'Ahd officers. On the contrary, they did their best to guard the secrecy of their activity. But Faruqi's crowning touch was his statement that the Turks and Germans would not dare to suppress the officers and that they even approached their leaders and agreed to grant all their demands. The Turks had no intention whatsoever in this period to grant the Arabs any measure of autonomy. On the contrary, they began to suppress the Arab separatists as best they could, as has been extensively detailed above. Also, it is not plausible that the Germans would have turned to the Arab officers behind the backs of their allies the Turks. There is no evidence that they did such a thing, and it seems that they were unaware of the activity of the anti-Turkish societies at the time. Finally, Faruqi claimed a number of times that he held a high position in al-'Ahd. The central members of al-'Ahd were 'Aziz 'Ali al-Misri, Yasin al-Hashimi, Nuri al-Sa'id, and several others. Faruqi's function in the society was not central despite the impression he tried to make, and therefore his knowledge of it was limited, the more so concerning *al-Fatat*. He also was not the man who brought about the unification of activities of the two societies. This was done as mentioned above by Yasin al-Hashimi and 'Abd al-Ghani al-'Uraysi. Thus it is clear that Faruqi's statements to the British were permeated with inaccuracies, exaggerations, and lies.[31]

There were those who later on contended that the British officials in Cairo, and Clayton in particular, should not have relied on the testimony of one unknown deserter, which had no support from other sources. However, what happened was that the British believed that Faruqi's information confirmed information already in their possession. Thus, the men of the Arab Bureau in Cairo wrote about a year afterwards:

Information regarding the then position of the Arab party or parties was obtained from Aziz Bey Ali El Masri, then in Egypt; from Mohammed Sherif El Faroki, an Arab officer, who came over to our lines in the Dardanelles in September 1915; from Mukhtar Bey in Athens, as well as from the various intelligence sources available to the military authorities in Mudros and in Egypt.[32]

'Aziz 'Ali al-Misri, the leader of *al-'Ahd*, tried at the beginning of the war to persuade the British of his ability to organize a revolt in Iraq and Syria, that would lead to the establishment of an Arab state whose northern border would be Alexandretta-Mosul-Persian border (see below, in the chapter on al-Misri). Faruqi, as mentioned, met with al-Misri during his interrogation by the British, and it seems that at least some of Faruqi's declarations were agreed to by him. As to Mukhtar Bey, it is possible that the one meant was Mukhtar Bey al-Sulh, who during 1915 tried to convince several British diplomats of his broad knowledge of the Arab societies.

After the McMahon letter of 24 October 1915 six more letters were exchanged between him and Husayn — three from each side — during the succeeding months. However, the McMahon-Husayn correspondence was never formally resolved. A series of events occurred which forced Husayn to open the Arab revolt before the two sides had reached an official agreement.

FAYSAL IN DAMASCUS II

According to the earlier understanding with the Arab societies in Syria, and complying with the decisions of the family conference in Ta'if, Faysal returned to Damascus in January 1916 to make the final arrangements for the outbreak of the revolt in Syria. Arriving with him in Damascus were 50 men, several from the Sharifite family and others from the tribal chiefs of the Hijaz. Faysal introduced his entourage as the pioneer force of Hijazi volunteers who were to aid Jamal Pasha in the second march on the Suez Canal. Jamal greeted him warmly, because he considered them fine hostages for the loyalty of the Hijaz to the Empire, and at this stage he had no suspicions at all of their true intentions.

However, the Syria in which Faysal arrived was different from the one he had left seven months earlier. He learned that all the Arab divisions on which the revolt was to be based had been withdrawn, and with them the officer members of al-'Ahd. In their stead Syria was full of Turkish soldiers from Anatolia. Many of his civilian supporters had been arrested or were in hiding. At a clandestine meeting with members of al-Fatat in the al-Bakris' house, he gave them a detailed report on the contacts with the British. It was decided that under the prevailing circumstances it would not be feasible to open a revolt in Syria, and therefore the revolt would break out only in the Hijaz. Throughout this time Faysal reported constantly to his father on the situation. The messages were sent hidden in sword handles, within cakes, in the soles of his men's sandals, or written in invisible ink or in code. In one of these ways was sent the unambiguous message that in light of developments the entire burden of the revolt would fall on the Hijaz. Faysal also recommended that his father postpone the revolt until the contacts with the British were concluded, and preferably until a landing by the Allies at Alexandretta.[33]

In February 1916 Jamal Pasha and Enver visited Medina. Faysal accompanied them from Damascus together with al-Fatat member Nasib al-Bakri. When the retinue returned to Damascus, al-Bakri remained in Medina for a few more days during which he wrote a report to Husayn on the situation. Al-Bakri reported on the removal of Arab forces from Syria, but at the same time he stressed that al-Fatat still existed and was maintaining contacts with the leaders of the Druzes and other tribal chiefs. He urged therefore that Husayn should keep Faysal in Syria because, if he should leave, the movement there would be without a leader and would be destroyed. At the end of his report he proposed that the British should land on the Syrian coasts and cut the road to Alexandretta, simultaneously with the outbreak of the revolt.[34]

Faysal did remain in Syria, though not for very long. When the second group of Arab activists were about to be executed, he appealed to Jamal Pasha to commute their sentences but was refused. It is possible that this appeal caused Jamal to begin to be suspicious of him. In any case, Faysal heard that the authorities had tortured some of his friends to get them to confess to having contacts with him. At the same time a message arrived from his father that everything was ready for opening the revolt and that he should return to Medina immediately. Faysal decided to leave Damascus, but he had to find a good pretext for returning to the Hijaz. He told Jamal Pasha that it was desirable that he himself go to Medina to bring the army of Hijazi volunteers who were to take part in the second Suez Canal campaign. Jamal agreed and even gave Faysal 50,000 Turkish liras to finance the operation. In mid-May 1916 Faysal left for Medina, accompanied by Nasib al-Bakri. Jamal, ever suspicious, sent one of his confidants, Sheikh 'Abd al-Qadir al-Khatib, to keep an eye on them. However, as soon as they arrived in Medina the supervision by the sheikh became meaningless.

There was still one task left for Faysal to do before the outbreak of the revolt — to get out his 50 attendants who were still in Damascus, and in effect hostages in the hands of the authorities. He therefore instructed al-Bakri to return to Damascus and gave him two versions of telegrams: "Dispatch two cases of oranges", which meant that the revolt was postponed two months, and "Dispatch bay horse", which meant that the revolt would start in five days. In case he should receive the second telegram, al-Bakri was to send his entire family by train to the Hijaz and within five days to evacuate all of Faysal's attendants from Damascus. In order to elude a possible pursuit by the authorities, it was decided not to send them directly to the Hijaz but to go by way of the desert southeast, towards Jawf, the stronghold of Nawaf al-Sha'lan. Nasib al-Bakri returned to Damascus at the end of May. A day later a telegram arrived from Medina: "Dispatch bay horse."[35]

THE OUTBREAK OF THE ARAB REVOLT

On 16 March 1916 Husayn made a final attempt to reach an understanding with the Empire. He sent a telegram to Enver informing him that he was prepared to send volunteers from the Hijaz and to join the jihad of the Empire if the following conditions were met: "(a) A general amnesty shall be declared for all political defendants. (b) Syria and Iraq shall be granted a decentralized administration. (c) The rights of the Sharifate of Mecca shall be recognized, as agreed upon already during the reign of Sultan Salim, and it shall be passed on by inheritance." If the authorities did not accede to these demands, he would not take part in the war and would content himself with wishing the Empire success.

To this Enver reacted with a sharp reply by telegram: "Dealing with questions of war and the Arabs is none of your business. The political criminals in Syria will receive a just sentence. If you continue to concern yourself with this, the result will be no cause for you to rejoice. You will not see your son Faysal again unless you send the volunteers to the front, as you promised. If you do not do this, the result for you, as we have said, will not be good."

Husayn answered with a telegram in the same spirit as his preceding one. Two days later a reply came from Istanbul that if Husayn should send the volunteers the authorities would instruct Jamal Pasha to deal with Faysal in the matter of the political criminals. Husayn replied that the volunteers were willing to come to Syria only if Faysal came from Damascus to lead them. To this the authorities replied that Faysal was authorized to go to Medina to bring the volunteers from there to Syria. They also asked Husayn to instruct his son 'Ali, who was then in Medina, to leave the city, in the light of his very tense relations with the local Ottoman governor. To this Husayn replied that as soon as Faysal arrived in Medina 'Ali would leave it.[36]

Husayn's plan was to start the Arab revolt in August. However, when Faysal arrived in Medina he saw that the authorities intended to add a force of 3,000 soldiers to the mission headed by the German Von Stotzingen, which was to arrive in Yemen. His suspicions about its true purpose were aroused, and when he saw that the preparations for the departure of this force had reached an advanced stage, he advised his father to start the revolt immediately. In the beginning of June Husayn informed the British about the speeding up of preparations to open the revolt. He informed them that the revolt would in fact be opened by 'Ali and Faysal on 5 June, and it would be officially announced by him on 10 June.[37]

On 5 June 1916 'Ali and Faysal marched out of Medina and unfurled the banner of revolt. An attack made by them the next day on the suburbs of the town was repulsed, and they contented themselves with a sparse cordon around the town. They also attacked the Hijazi railway in several places, but before they were able to inflict any serious damage they were dispersed by Ottoman reinforcements armed with machine-guns. On 9 June, the day before the official declaration of revolt, the two brothers sent the following telegram to Jamal Pasha:

> The moderate demands of the Arabs have been rejected by the Ottoman Empire. The soldiers who were in readiness for the jihad do not believe that they must sacrifice themselves except for the cause of the Arabs and Islam. Therefore, should the conditions presented by the Sharif of Mecca not be met at once, it would be superfluous to point out that all relations between the Arab nation and the Turkish nation will be severed. 24 hours after the receipt of this telegram a state of war shall exist between the two nations.

On 10 June Husayn fired a shot from his palace towards the Ottoman army barracks, and with this he announced the outbreak of the Arab revolt. His forces opened with an attack on the Ottoman barracks and on the government house. In return the Ottoman garrison in the Jiyad fort in the south of the town began to shell the rebels, with no inhibitions about shelling the Great Mosque. Since this was summer, most of the Ottoman forces, including the Vali Ghalib Pasha, were in Ta'if. As a result, within three days Husayn took control of all of Mecca, except for the Jiyad fort, which held out until 4 July and surrendered only after being shelled by two British cannons brought from Jidda. The attack on Jidda had been begun on 9 June by about 4,000 tribesmen. The city surrendered on 16 June after being shelled by British warships and bombed from the air by amphibious planes. In the course of July the two coastal settlements north of Jidda, Rabigh and Yanbu', fell to the rebels. Ta'if was a harder nut to crack. 'Abdallah attacked it on 11 June, but the town, in which there were the Vali of the Hijaz and 2,000 Turkish soldiers, managed to hold out for three and a half months. 'Abdallah shelled the city constantly, but it was only after he had surrounded it with over 6,000 combatants that Ta'if surrendered on 23 September, in despair of the arrival of a relief force.[38]

A revolt by the Grand Sharif of Mecca, who was responsible for the holy places of Islam, against the sultan of the Ottoman Empire, who also served as caliph of the entire world of Islam, and this at a time when the Empire was engaged in a jihad against Christian powers defined as the enemies of Islam, was an event that required an explanation. On 26 June Husayn published a manifesto replete with verses from the Qur'an and proofs from the Hadith, in which he set out the reasons why he was forced to take such a drastic step.

He opened the manifesto with a statement that the amirs of Mecca had always been loyal to the Empire. However, the situation had changed since the CUP had seized control of the Empire and negated the powers of the Sultan. The men of the CUP were infidels who desecrated the religion of Islam and even actively harmed its commandments. Their desire was to nullify the laws of the Shari'a. This heretic society had involved the Empire in a war and had thus brought destruction upon it. But their greatest crime was the persecution of the Arab nation and their desire to exterminate its language, the language of Islam. They had put to death the foremost sons of the Arab nation (and here Husayn listed the names of several activists executed in May 1916), and had deported many families to Anatolia. They had brought the Hijaz to the brink of destruction, and had even bombarded the Ka'ba, almost hitting the black stone. Therefore, in order to defend the Hijaz, the hajj rituals, and the Arabs in general, there was no recourse but to declare full independence and to sever all connections with the men of the CUP. This independence would be absolute, with no foreign intervention or external rule. In effect it was his religious duty to take this step, being responsible for the Hijaz, for the hajj, and for the Arab nation in general. Husayn ended his manifesto with an appeal to Muslims throughout the world: "Let them [the Muslims] know that we have done what we have done out of strong conviction that it is the best service to Islam."[39]

Chapter 4

'AZIZ 'ALI AL-MISRI AND THE ARAB REVOLT

'Aziz 'Ali al-Misri, the founder and leader of *al-'Ahd*, was the first commander of the army of the Arab revolt. Al-Misri's personality was quite controversial. Besides his being the only Egyptian in *al-'Ahd* and in the Arab movement in general, before the war he had many ideological differences of opinion with his fellow society members concerning the goals to which they should strive. He dreamt of a "Mediterranean State", which would include the Arabs, Turks, Albanians, Bulgarians, Egyptians, Libyans and others, while the others were willing to settle for a change to a dual empire, Turko-Arab, on the model of Austria-Hungary. In the end al-Misri accepted their view and even strongly supported it for a long time afterwards, as will be shown below. Still, the relations between him and other members, particularly the Iraqis, continued to be erratic for personal reasons. Al-Misri was an introvert, yet at the same time very ambitious. Many of the officers in *al-'Ahd*, especially the Iraqi officers, were no less ambitious. After he was deported from Istanbul to Egypt the ties between him and most of the other society members were broken, and he lost his influence over them. The dominant personality in the society from then on (and until it disbanded in 1920) was the Iraqi officer Yasin al-Hashimi. However, al-Misri did not remain idle. From his domicile in Egypt he devised a series of plans for revolt against the Ottoman Empire, and when the Arab revolt broke out, he appeared to the British to be the ideal choice to lead it. The future proved that the choice was a mistake. This chapter will deal with al-Misri as commander of the Arab revolt and with his exploits during World War I in general.

In August 1914, at the outbreak of the war in Europe, al-Misri turned to a British official and proposed setting up an Arab empire under British tutelage. For this he asked to be given assistance to lead the Arab tribes in Iraq and Syria against the Ottomans. Britain had not yet decided to go to war with the Ottoman Empire, and therefore the Foreign Office directed Cairo to firmly instruct al-Misri to refrain from any involvement in Arab affairs. The job of restraining him was given to a Captain Russell of the British military intelligence. At a meeting between the two al-Misri told Russell that he had been empowered by a society, whose centre was in Baghdad, to investigate the disposition of the British towards the establishment of an independent Arab state under British aegis. This state would include all the Arabic-speaking regions, and its northern border would be the line of Alexandretta-Mosul-Persian border. The revolt that he was planning was to be based on the Arab military forces in Baghdad, Najd, and Syria, and in his opinion the Druzes and Christians would also join it. He asked the intelligence officer for British aid in money and arms (including artillery), and promised in exchange that Britain would be granted a preferential status in the future Arab state. The British officer replied that involvement in such a plan would cause Britain more damage than gain, and he stressed that Britain did not view the present moment as suitable for implementing such a plan. And since without the goodwill of Britain al-Misri's society could not act, it would be better if he were not to push Britain to act against its will, lest he lose its goodwill. Following this conversation al-Misri informed those members of *al-'Ahd* whom he was able to contact that they were not to start any hostile action against the Ottomans which would make it easier for foreign powers to conquer the region, before receiving assurances that there would be no such conquest.[1]

By late October 1914 the attitude of the British towards the Ottoman Empire had already changed, and as a result they also changed their attitude towards al-Misri. Gilbert Clayton, the director of military and political intelligence in Cairo, met with him for a private conversation and asked him if the Arabs would join the Turks — if and when the Empire entered the war — in spite of their enmity towards them and their desire for autonomy. Al-Misri answered that the Arabs would join the stronger side, which in their opinion was the Empire, especially after the Turks had succeeded in gaining the sympathy of some of the Arabs by dispensing offices. Then al-Misri resumed discussing his plans to start a revolt in Iraq. He told Clayton that he would sell his property in Egypt, hire a boat and sail to Basra, and within a month would be able to organize a force of 15,000 men to open a revolt against the Empire. Afterwards other Arab leaders would join the rebels. What Britain had to do was to assure a supply of money, rifles, ammunition, and artillery. However, it was not to send soldiers to aid the revolt because this would create the impression that it was interested in annexing Iraq.

Al-Misri suggested that when Britain did declare war on the Empire, she should open with military operations in the Persian Gulf. Such operations would cause the Empire to keep large military forces in Iraq, from which he planned to obtain the men for the revolt. He noted cynically that it would have been better to begin preparations for this plan several months earlier, but at the time the British were not even willing to listen. Clayton replied that under the present circumstances, before Britain had officially declared war on the Empire, it would not be possible to carry out such a plan.[2]

In mid-November 1914, after Britain had declared war on the Ottoman Empire and had invaded Iraq, the attitude of the Foreign Office to al-Misri's plan was totally different. The foreign minister informed his representatives in Cairo that they could give al-Misri 2,000 pounds Sterling in order to get organized, and also any other help that he would need. Al-Misri, who met again with British representatives, told them that at the moment he did not need any money. First of all, he had to contact his fellow society members who were then in Basra so that they could bring him up to date on the situation there. He asked the British to put him in touch with Nuri al-Sa'id, and if they could not locate him then with Muzahim al-Amin al-Pachachi or 'Abdallah al-Damluji. They should be told that "their friend in Egypt" wanted to contact them, and that they should prepare information "on all points" and to come to Muhammara with their ciphers.

However, at this point a new stumbling block arose in 'Aziz 'Ali al-Misri's path. Iraq was in the area of responsibility of the India Office, and not of the Foreign Office, and the former asked the Foreign Office to delay the departure of al-Misri to Basra until they received an opinion on this matter from the British authorities in Basra. When the plan was referred to Percy Cox, the chief political officer of the British Expeditionary Force in Iraq, he reported that Nuri al-Sa'id and Muzahim al-Amin al-Pachachi were indeed in Basra. However, he added that the views of these "young Arabs" were not suitable for the backward tribes of Iraq. Al-Misri's plan was therefore, in his opinion, impractical, and he requested that al-Misri be prevented from leaving Egypt. Cox's opinion was supported by the viceroy in India, and the British foreign minister had no option but to instruct his men in Cairo not to further 'Aziz 'Ali al-Misri's plans.[3]

In early December 1914 al-Misri made another attempt to interest the British in his plans. In a conversation with Philip

Graves, a former correspondent of the *Times* in Istanbul who was employed by British intelligence in Cairo, he expressed his opposition to the annexation of Iraq by the British. He suggested instead that they assist in establishing in Iraq a modern state that would extend from the Persian Gulf to Armenia and Anatolia. This state would of course be economically and financially dependent on British India, and there would even be a need for a British military presence for a long time, but establishing such a state would still be preferable to outright annexation. Al-Misri promised that if the British would pledge not to annex Iraq, he would go to Iraq and persuade the Arab officers in the Ottoman army to desert and the tribal chiefs not to oppose the advancing British forces. He warned that without his mediation the British forces advancing on Baghdad would meet with the stubborn resistance of the Arab and Kurdish soldiers, who would remain loyal to the Empire in its war against British invaders, in spite of the grievances they had against the Ottoman authorities.[4]

Al-Misri's program was not adopted by the British, who penetrated deeper into Iraq. The frustrated al-Misri felt that they were ignoring him and not properly appreciating the great influence that he believed he had in the Arab world. Furthermore, he was anxious to get out of the prolonged state of inactivity in which he was mired and to which he was not accustomed. He began contacts with the French, and in June 1915 he met for a conversation with the head of the French military mission in Egypt, whom he tried to convince that the Allies, especially France, had an interest in opening peace talks with the Ottoman Empire. This conversation exemplified the duality that al-Misri felt towards the Ottoman Empire, a duality that would characterize him throughout the entire war, and that would cause him to fail in his position as commander of the Arab revolt army. On the one hand he constantly generated plans to revolt against the Empire and to secede from it, and on the other hand he could not free himself from the original al-'Ahd program — to turn the Ottoman Empire into a Turko-Arab empire.

At the beginning al-Misri expressed his bitterness that the British had reneged and were ignoring all their decisions concerning his proposals to them at the beginning of the war. They even deported to India his emissary in Iraq (meaning Nuri al-Sa'id). Then al-Misri explained to his French conversation partner that if the war continued and the Allies wanted to conquer Istanbul they would suffer heavy casualties. Even if they succeeded, it would cost the lives of the Christians in the

Empire. Moreover, such an action would cause the Turks to be considered in the eyes of all Muslims as the bearers of the banner of Islam. The result would be that the Allies could face a sea of troubles in the East. Therefore, it would be advisable for France to act for the removal of the Empire from the war. He would not depend on Britain in this matter because they wanted to conquer Iraq, the Arabian Peninsula, and Palestine, and in effect to rule over the Islamic world. However, France, in cooperation with the Arabs, would be able to impose peace on the Empire. He himself could aid France to achieve this goal. If the British would allow him to leave Egypt and to go to Baghdad, Damascus, and Mecca, he would be able to be a counterweight there to the German influence, and within two months he would achieve his goal, a goal that all the sheikhs addicted to Britain could not achieve. This was because of his ability to influence the Arabs and to guide their views. He would explain to them that the war was unnecessary since their religion was not in danger, and they had nothing to gain from the war. The result would be that all the Arabs of the Empire would declare that they refused to participate in the war, and they would thereby become the party of peace. The Empire would then be forced to sue for peace, and in his opinion the Empire would indeed agree to this if its integrity would be assured. Al-Misri explained to his collocutor that this plan did not constitute treason to the Empire, but rather its rescue from the hands of the CUP.[5]

The French, too, ignored the appeals of al-Misri. But in October of that year it seemed to him that things were finally beginning to move. The British showed him the terms in McMahon's letter to Husayn of 24 October, and at least according to them he agreed in general. At this juncture he and the British began to look into how he could contribute to the struggle against the Ottomans. It was decided that the British authorities in India would seek out suitable Arab officers from among the prisoners of war in their hands, and he and Faruqi would contact them and join them to the Arab movement. One of the first officers whom al-Misri contacted was Nuri al-Sa'id, who was permitted at the end of that year to leave India for Egypt. Al-Misri and Faruqi also began to look for suitable officers among the prisoners of war in Egypt. There soon gathered around al-Misri a circle of Arab activists who would meet for discussions in his house every week.[6]

However, once again it seemed to al-Misri that matters had slowed down, and he decided to speed up the plans to bring about Arab independence by making a direct appeal to the

British war minister Kitchener. In February 1916 he wrote him a long letter in which he explained to him that in light of the stalemate on the western front the solution to the war lay in the east. If Britain would make a covenant with the Arabs, this would ensure the outcome of the war. The Arab nation would assist Britain during the war, and this would also secure a stable balance of power in the East after the war. The entry of the Arabs on the side of the Allies would have a great effect. It would erase the impression that Britain was the enemy of the Muslims, and would even create the opposite impression. Even the Muslims of India would be grateful to the British for the aid to their coreligionists, to the nation from which Islam emerged.

The Arab nation wanted Britain to help it achieve its freedom. Among the Arabs there were two trends. One wanted complete secession from the Empire and the establishment of an Arab empire, whose borders would be: In the north, the vilayets of Adana and Van; in the east, Persia, the Gulf of Basra and the Sea of 'Uman; in the west, the Mediterranean Sea, Egypt, and the Red Sea; in the south, the Indian Ocean. The second trend wanted to become a Hungary of a Turko-Arab empire. Both trends agreed that British assistance was necessary, with the second trend wanting to sever the Ottoman Empire from its alliance with Germany and to bring it into a pact with Britain. An Arab empire that would arise with the aid of Britain would always be its ally. A modern and well-equipped Arab army, stationed in the Arabian Peninsula, Iraq, and Syria, would be able to prevent an attack by hostile forces on the routes to India and to Egypt.

The Arab nation wanted its freedom as a result of the nationalist idea that had begun to pulsate within it. Arab youth was prepared to pay with their lives in order to achieve this goal. They were desirous of the friendship of the British, but not of being dominated by them or being a protectorate of theirs. The Arab nation would never consent to be under foreign rule. An invasion by a foreign conqueror would only bring a rapprochement between the Arabs and the Turks, which would serve the interests of the Germans. The current advance of the British in Iraq endangered the future of the Arab nation and was impelling it to come to terms with the Turks. These acts were sufficient to weaken the hands of those who believed that the future of the Arabs was bound up with an alliance with Britain. Therefore, his responsibility to the Arabs, his spiritual tie to Britain, which was created as a result of Kitchener's intervention on his behalf (in 1914 when he was sentenced to death in Istanbul and amnestied following British intercession), and the fact that all the proposals that he had made for the good of both nations had been rejected had brought him to write this letter. He hoped that it would receive appropriate attention, and that the matter would be brought before the British cabinet.

Al-Misri ended his letter by stating that the time to act had come. If his plan was accepted, then he would place himself at Kitchener's disposal, either in Egypt or in Britian should he be asked to come there to plan the establishment of the Arab state and to organize its army.[7]

Even in this letter al-Misri's dual attitude to the Ottoman Empire finds expression. When speaking of the two trends in the Arab movement, he was actually describing the two thought processes running through his own mind. At this stage, and for the time being, the desire to bring the Arabs to independence prevailed.

It is not known if Kitchener answered this letter. However, soon afterwards al-Misri got an opportunity to contribute to the war effort against the Ottoman Empire. In March 1916 McMahon proposed sending him and Faruqi to Iraq to use their influence and the influence of their society to mobilize the support of the Arab officers in the Ottoman army. McMahon explained his proposal in that while Faysal was concentrating on getting the support of the Arab officers in Syria, "it would now seem wise" for the British to try, through these two officers, to get the support of the Arab officers in Iraq. This was at the time of the Ottoman siege of British forces in Kut al-'Amara, and the officials in Cairo felt that such an action might perhaps relieve the siege.

In exchange for performing this mission al-Misri and Faruqi demanded that the British should give a detailed assurance as to their policy towards the future Arab state. The Foreign Office reacted to this by warning their people in Cairo not to deviate from the assurances already given to Husayn. Clayton sent the officer Wyndham Deedes to have a long talk with al-Misri and his friends in which the former made it clear that Britian would not commit itself beyond the assurances given concerning Arab independence. He added that under the present circumstances in which the Arabs were only talking and the British were the ones bleeding and paying, the Arabs had no right to negotiate the details of the independence they would receive. Following another conversation that Deedes held with al-Misri and his circle, they agreed to be content with Britain's promises till then and to be on their way.

The Foreign Office and War Office approved the plan. However, the India Office, in whose jurisdiction Iraq was, once again
was aroused and sent an urgent telegram to the viceroy in India,
in which they reported on McMahon's plan and reminded him
of Percy Cox's opposition to sending al-Misri to Iraq in December 1914. In their opinion it was too dangerous "to let loose rev-
olutionaries whose actions may extend beyond our control".
They therefore asked the Foreign Office to delay the departure
of the two until an opinion on the subject was received from the
British authorities in Iraq. This opinion indeed arrived on 30
March from General Lake, the GOC of British forces in Iraq,
and it was unambiguous. There was no possibility of deriving
any benefit from the services of the two in Iraq. The Ottomans
were carrying out thorough searches for spies, and it was therefore unreasonable that al-Misri and Faruqi could penetrate their
territories. Moreover, "their political views are much too
advanced to be safe pabula for the communities of occupied territories and their presence in any of the towns of Iraq would be
in our opinion undesirable and inconvenient." Lake thus in
effect restated Percy Cox's words of late 1914, and indeed Cox
concurred and felt that Cairo proposed such a plan simply to get
rid of some impatient Arab officers. The viceroy also stated that
he completely supported Lake's opinion.

The India Office immediately transmitted Lake's telegram to
the Foreign Office, expressing their vigorous support for it. A
copy of the telegram was sent to Cairo, and McMahon, Clayton,
and Deedes met to discuss the situation. They reached the conclusion that there was no point in protesting because it would be
assuming too great a responsibility to differ with the opinion of
people on the scene (that is, Iraq). Clayton informed the War
Office that without further instructions he would take no further
action on the matter of sending al-Misri and Faruqi to Iraq.
McMahon sent a similar telegram to the Foreign Office, while
warning that this conclusion of the affair might cause disappointment and loss of British credibility among al-Misri and his
circle, just when the Turks and Germans were doing their best
to propagandize against the British.[8]

In mid-April 1916 the attitude of the British in Iraq had
already changed. These were the final days of the siege of Kut
al-'Amara, and the British forces were in a desperate situation
there. Various plans were put forward as to how to rescue the
forces under the command of General Townshend. One idea was
to bribe the Ottoman commander Khalil Bek, or other Ottoman
generals, but for this it was necessary to have an intermediary of

high standing, and the local Iraqi notables were evading getting involved in this enterprise. At this point the British authorities in Iraq agreed that al-Misri should come to Iraq and serve as intermediary in this matter, but they still wanted from Cairo clarifications of the promises made to him in exchange for his cooperation. Cairo calmed them by saying that nothing was promised that deviated from what was promised to Husayn, that is: British rule in southern Iraq, Arab autonomy in the vilayet of Baghdad with protection of British economic and political interests there, and autonomous regimes for the Arabs in remaining Arab territories where French interests would not be impaired.[9] But it was too late. General Khalil Bek would not even hear of bribery, and a few days later General Townshend surrendered and fell into Ottoman captivity with over 10,000 of his men. 'Aziz 'Ali al-Misri remained in Cairo.

In early July 1916 Faruqi was appointed Husayn's Cairo representative. Immediately on his appointment he proposed to the British that they appoint al-Misri commander of the army of the Arab revolt. He concomitantly began contacts with al-Misri to persuade him to accept this position. Al-Misri hesitated to accept because, he said, he did not know whether Husayn's purpose was to defend the Hijaz against invasion by foreign forces or to revolt against the sultan and achieve independence. Therefore he instructed Nuri al-Sa'id, who was about to leave for the Hijaz, to investigate Husayn's goals and to report back to him. When al-Sa'id arrived in the Hijaz he implored al-Misri to come, too, and he also strove to persuade Husayn to give al-Misri command of the revolt army. At the end of August Faruqi officially requested Husayn to approve al-Misri's coming to the Hijaz. The chief qadi of Mecca joined in these entreaties, and in the end Husayn granted the request, though not without hesitation. On 6 September 1916 'Aziz 'Ali al-Misri left for the Hijaz.

When he arrived in Mecca he announced that he had come only to look over the situation and had no ambition to be appointed commander of the revolt. Following pressure by several of his fellow officers, who had arrived in the Hijaz before him, he agreed finally to accept the post and met for a talk with Husayn. At the outset of their meeting al-Misri declared that he was not in favour of absolute secession from the Empire. He made clear to Husayn that what they had to do, in his opinion, was to prevent the spread of hostile actions between the Ottomans and the British into the Hijaz and to achieve Arab autonomy within the framework of the Empire. He also recommended to Husayn not to completely give up the relations with the

Empire and Germany. These statements by al-Misri did not, of course, generate confidence in him by Husayn, and from then on the latter was suspicious of him until his last day in the Hijaz. However, the British pressed Husayn to accept al-Misri because they felt that the revolt army needed officers of his calibre. Thus, 'Aziz 'Ali al-Misri was appointed chief of the general staff of the revolt army.[10]

On 14 October al-Misri left Mecca for Rabigh, a small coastal settlement north of Jidda, to organize the forces of the sharif there and to turn them from a collection of bedouins and a few officers into a regular army. When he arrived in Rabigh he found out that several of the officers whom he knew had resigned from the army because they had not received their pay. He decided to bring together all the officers for a get-acquainted meeting at which he explained the purposes of the revolt (as he understood them), and the obligations that would be placed upon them in order to achieve these purposes:

> We are not fighting out of mere desire to fight. We are not fighting out of hatred for the Turks or love for the British. We are fighting to liberate our country and to ensure its independence. Do you believe that we can realize this ambition with the forces presently at our disposal? Do you think we can enter Syria with this army, which has neither strength nor order? How will the people there receive us, if we come to them to rob and plunder, to ruin and destroy? Therefore, before we can even think about an invasion to the north we must establish a regular army, one that can be depended upon to maintain order and security in the Arab countries that we conquer.

Rabigh was a key point in the defence of Mecca. Besides its providing access to the sea, north of Jidda, enabling the bringing of British supplies from Egypt to the revolt army, it was situated at the vertex of an equilateral triangle whose base was Mecca and Medina. For topographical reasons the road from Medina to Mecca had to pass through the coastal plain, and through Rabigh. Therefore, any attempt by Ottoman forces in Medina to counterattack and suppress the Arab revolt would have to start with the capture of Rabigh. Al-Misri and the Hashimite princes were aware of this danger and began to fortify Rabigh, especially to the northeast where the road to Medina lay. Al-Misri together with Nuri al-Sa'id also took the first steps towards setting up the regular army — they organized a brigade consisting of two infantry battalions, a machine-gun regiment, and an artillery battery.[11]

While still occupied with organizing the army, al-Misri did not keep himself out of politics. At that time the French military mission arrived in Jidda, and al-Misri, who was opposed to French influence in the Hijaz, persuaded Sharif 'Ali not to accept mountain guns from the French. He also informed the British representative in Jidda that he intended to go to Cairo to discuss French ambitions in Syria with the high commissioner. While he was busying himself in politics, cracks began to appear in his authority within the revolt army. The commander of the second battalion, Rashid al-Madfa'i, quarreled with him over personal matters and began to slander and vilify him, till eventually it was necessary to transfer him to the army of 'Abdallah. Al-Madfa'i continued to hold a grudge and later on found a way to take revenge.[12]

Al-Misri was not ready to settle for the limited-size army that he had begun to organize in Rabigh, and in late October he submitted a plan for raising a regular army of 5,000 infantrymen, which would be based in Rabigh and which could hold back the expected attacks by the Ottomans. He sent the British a list of requirements for setting up this force: 4 cannons with 1,000 shells per cannon, 60 machine guns with 50,000 rounds for each gun, 5,000 khaki sweaters, material for 7,000 pairs of trousers, 7,000 tents, etc. The British were inclined to approve the idea, but at this time al-Misri faced two obstacles: On the one hand, he did not have the necessary manpower for such a program. In Rabigh there were only about 2,000 combatants, many of them tribesmen who were not enthusiastic about joining a regular force. On the other hand, Sharif 'Ali, in whose jurisdiction Rabigh was situated, was not enthusiastic about the idea either, and in general he was not inclined to take any new initiatives.

Al-Misri was not content with just the plan to set up a large regular force. In addition he planned to set up a legion of light-armed cameleers, which would operate across the enemy lines, strike the Ottomans at key points, and damage their lines of communication. The legion was to consist of five units of 200 cameleers each, which would not be dependent on supplies from the centre and could operate independently and at great distances. Neither 'Ali nor Faysal was eager at this stage to accept this novel form of activity.

Al-Misri, who was frustrated by the tepid reception of his ideas, suggested to the British that all the regular forces, those being prepared and those in the planning stage, be transferred from Rabigh to Yanbu', a small coastal settlement north of Rabigh. This way he thought he could distance himself from the Sharifite princes and gain more independence for his operations.

He also thought that this way he would be able to maintain direct communications with the British and to receive money and supplies directly from them, and not through Husayn and his sons. However, the British were not inclined to accept the idea of moving to Yanbu' because it would expose Rabigh to Ottoman attack, with all the danger that that would bring to Mecca itself, as explained above (plus the fact that the local sheikh of Rabigh was considered disloyal to Husayn).

The successive obstacles that were placed in the way of carrying out his plans began to discourage him. He decided to focus on his second plan, to set up a mobile force of cameleers, of limited scope, which he himself would lead on attacks on the Ottoman lines of communication and the Hijazi railway. He hoped by means of this force to gain some measure of independence from the supervision of the Sharifites and that success by this force would give him enough popularity so that later on he could realize his plan to set up a large regular force. At a meeting held in mid-November 1916 with the participation of al-Misri, Nuri al-Sa'id, Faysal, and the British advisors, al-Misri again set forth his plans, and once again Faysal rejected them. In early January 1917 al-Misri was ready to settle for a force of only 500 cameleers, but despite the British recommendations to Husayn to finance this force he ran into obstacles even in purchasing the camels.

Al-Misri's plans came to naught. There were not at this stage sufficient volunteers for the force of 5,000 regulars. The idea of a mobile and independent legion seemed too revolutionary for the sharif and his sons, and it is also possible that Husayn feared that forces under the exclusive command of al-Misri might be a threat to his rule. It should be pointed out, however, that the idea of setting up mobile guerilla units was put into operation at a later stage of the revolt by Colonel Lawrence. Lawrence also claimed for himself the credit for inventing this method of warfare, although, as mentioned above, the originator of the idea was 'Aziz 'Ali al-Misri.[13]

The failure of al-Misri's plans for organizing the army is an example of the shaky relations that prevailed between him and Husayn and his sons from the day he arrived in the Hijaz until he left it. The Sharifites were suspicious of his intentions, and as was proven later, not without foundation. To this it must be added that both Husayn and al-Misri were stubborn men, and al-Misri's refusal to obey Husayn blindly, plus his obstinacy in carrying out his own plans, did not serve to lessen the tension between them. Also, al-Misri himself did not trust Husayn.

From the beginning he believed that the leader of the Arab movement should be Ibn Sa'ud of Najd, but he was compelled to compromise with reality. Also, Husayn's refusal to grant him the title of amir certainly impaired the relations between them.

Al-Misri's frustration found expression in a conversation he had with Ronald Storrs, the Oriental Secretary of the British Residency in Cairo, several days after he arrived in Rabigh. He criticized before him Husayn's methods of operation, and his own appointment as chief of the general staff he characterized as mere words (*kalam farigh*). The British liaison officers in Rabigh and Jidda reported that Sharif 'Ali was not giving al-Misri any authority. Although in principle 'Ali approved his plans, still he did nothing to have them carried out, apparently on orders from his father. The British had a feeling that the Sharifite family was wary of al-Misri becoming a second Enver (the Ottoman war minister, who was one of those who deposed Sultan 'Abd al-Hamid II). In fact, 'Abdallah even remarked to the British representative in Jidda that his father was suspicious of anyone who ever had any connection with the Young Turks (and al-Misri had been a member of the CUP at the time of the Young Turk revolution). The situation reached the point where 'Ali even thwarted an attempt by al-Misri to acquire 20 camels. Al-Misri began to threaten that unless he was given the requisite authority to do his job he would return to Egypt.

In mid-November 1916, after Faysal rejected for the second time al-Misri's military plans, al-Misri finally gave up and decided to return to Egypt. The attempts of the British to dissuade him came to naught, although he promised to return in a fortnight. In Cairo he complained bitterly to the officials of the Arab Bureau about the curbs put in his path by the Sharifite family, and he claimed that Husayn's sons were jealous of him and preoccupied with quarrels among themselves. Husayn himself would change his mind from minute to minute, and with all this it was impossible to accomplish anything. If the British wanted him to succeed in organizing the army, they would have to maintain direct contact with him and to send him the necessary equipment directly, and not through Husayn and his sons. Al-Misri was also against having the regular soldiers train in Mecca, so that they should not be bothered by the local Meccan intrigues. After completing the organization of the army it would be possible to turn it over to the control of the sharif or to whoever should be appointed for this purpose. It is noteworthy that at least on this point there was uniformity of opinion between him and the Sharifites, who were also opposed to training the soldiers in Mecca, but out of apprehension for the intrigues that al-Misri might devise.

The British did their best to persuade Husayn to give al-Misri executive authority, but they decided not to force this on him against his will lest they end up being responsible for al-Misri's behaviour. They completely rejected the possibility of direct contact between them and al-Misri. Al-Misri returned to Rabigh on 9 December, disappointed with Husayn and the British alike. He decided to remain in Rabigh and not to go to Jidda before his status was clarified, lest he be accused of intriguing. Several days later Ronald Storrs arrived in Jidda and met with Husayn for discussions in which he dealt with al-Misri's status among other matters. Storrs tried to persuade Husayn that if he were apprehensive of al-Misri becoming another Enver, or that he might betray him with the Ottomans, then he must remember that he was the supreme commander over all operations and could take away al-Misri's authority whenever he pleased. Husayn was silent for a while, and then he announced that he was willing to appoint al-Misri as minister of war, with an independent budget. Storrs immediately requested that this appointment not result in al-Misri being removed from the field of battle, which was his proper place. Husayn agreed, and on 14 December 1916 he officially appointed 'Aziz 'Ali al-Misri as minister of war of the Hijazi government.[14]

However, it seems that as far as al-Misri's attitude toward the revolt was concerned it was too late. In January 1917 he met for a conversation with the commander of the British fleet in the Red Sea region. The latter reported that al-Misri told him cynically that he was working for himself and for no one else. But what was even stranger, al-Misri tried to convince him that Medina had a sufficient quantity of supplies to last a whole year and that the Ottoman soldiers there were superbly equipped. The British commander pointed out in his report that these statements by al-Misri were in clear contradiction to all the information in his possession regarding Medina. Therefore, he did not believe him and wondered if al-Misri, for reasons of his own, was trying to deceive him.[15] In fact, this was an indication of the new plans that were going through al-Misri's mind concerning the Arab revolt in general and Sharif Husayn in particular.

As mentioned above, with his joining the Arab revolt al-Misri did not forsake the old program of al-'Ahd to establish a dual, Turko-Arab empire. While he was in the Hijaz he preached to his fellow officers that Arabs and Turks must live together on the Austro-Hungarian model. He even wanted to send the planned camelry units to Syria in order to ignite there the flames of revolt, and thereby force the Turks to make peace with the Arabs. During January 1917 an Arab attack on Medina was planned. Several officers who opposed secession from the Empire came to him and persuaded him to frustrate the attack. It was agreed that when the attack was to begin three officers would slip into the city secretly and attempt to reach an understanding with the Ottoman commander there. Then, instead of attacking Medina, they would organize a combined Arab-Turkish force under his command, which would turn to Mecca and depose Husayn. After that he would conduct negotiations with the Sublime Porte for a peace treaty on the basis of granting full autonomy to the Arabs in the framework of the Ottoman Empire. This pact would apply to all the Arab countries. (His partner in this plan was the Iraqi officer, a member of al-'Ahd, 'Ali Jawdat al-Ayyubi, who tried to work for this purpose even after al-Misri was removed from the Hijaz, and in the end he, too, was removed to Egypt for several months.)

The Arab attack began on 21 January. Several Syrian officers who were in favour of Husayn and for cooperation with the British, and who were joined by al-Misri's enemy, the Iraqi officer Rashid al-Madfa'i, went to Sharif 'Ali and told him of al-Misri's plan. 'Ali immediately ordered the cancellation of the attack and the return of the Arab soldiers. According to another version, it was al-Misri who advised 'Ali to withdraw from Medina, after the Arab forces had already reached the gates of the city. He claimed that the Ottomans were about to open a counterattack with stronger and better equipped forces. 'Ali withdrew to Rabigh, and then suspicions were aroused that behind al-Misri's advice stood evil intentions. According to a third version, it was the Ottomans who attacked Rabigh, intending to continue on to Mecca. The Arab forces were sent to stop them, under the command of al-Misri. At this stage al-Misri's plan was reported to Sharif 'Ali, and he ordered the forces to return immediately to Rabigh.[16]

Whatever the exact details of the incident were, from Husayn's point of view al-Misri was finished. At the same time al-Misri also lost the sympathy of the British. On one occasion he called for the removal of the British advisors from the revolt army. On another occasion, after the British failed to turn over to him guns that they had captured from the Ottomans, he claimed that the British did not want to supply arms to the Arab army because they wanted to eradicate in one blow both the Turks and the Arabs. These statements came to the attention of the British, and a consensus was formed between them and Husayn to remove al-Misri from the Hijaz. Al-Misri, who was ill at the time, was directed by Husayn to go to Egypt "on leave". On 21 February 1917 he boarded a British warship and left for Egypt. The very next day Husayn announced that since al-Misri had left the Hijaz without permission he considered him to have resigned from his position. Al-Misri's pleas that his leave had been approved were of no avail. A few days after he arrived in Egypt he received an order dismissing him from the Arab army and banning his return to the Hijaz. His position as war minister was taken over by the Egyptian officer Mahmud al-Qaysuni. His position as commander of the revolt army was taken over several weeks later by the Iraqi officer Ja'far al-'Askari, about whom the British said that "he would not meddle in political affairs the way 'Aziz 'Ali did".[17]

In Egypt al-Misri settled in a village in the Delta, and there, after some time passed, he resolved to move to Germany. He did not believe that Britain would win the war, and he thought that if the Germans won then it would bring about the liberation of Egypt from the British and its reunification with the Ottoman Empire. Furthermore, he believed that if he transferred his support to Germany then he could get the German government to exert pressure on the Empire to establish a decentralized regime. Such a regime would enable Egypt and the other Arab countries to remain a part of the Empire, according to the formula in the platform of al-'Ahd. He thereupon requested permission from the British authorities to move to Switzerland, intending to continue on from there to Germany. The British refused. Eventually he was permitted to travel on leave to Spain, where he remained until the end of the war.

In January 1918 'Aziz 'Ali al-Misri arrived in Madrid. He met for a talk with the British ambassador and told him that since he had been saved from the gallows in 1914 as a result of Kitchener's intervention he felt a moral obligation not to fight for the Ottoman Empire against Britain. On the other hand, he could not fight on behalf of Husayn, whom he described as lacking any military talent, distrustful, and apprehensive about revolutionary activities as was Sultan 'Abd al-Hamid II in his time. Therefore he decided to move to a neutral country such as Spain. He also told the ambassador that in the past he had hoped that the Arab provinces of the Empire would become an autonomous state bound to Istanbul as Hungary was with Austria. But these hopes were dashed by the narrow-minded pan-Turanians and anti-Arabs of the CUP. However, the truth was that al-Misri had not yet given up hope of establishing a Turko-Arab empire. An exiled Turkish prince told the ambassador a month later that al-Misri was still working to oust the CUP government in order to make it possible to bring peace between the Empire and the Allies. In al-Misri's opinion, according to the Turkish prince, if the Allies would forgo the partition of the Empire it would be possible to create a mutiny in the Ottoman army and to depose the present government. Then it would be possible to set up a new, federal empire, consisting of four autonomous states: 1) European Turkey and Anatolia, 2) Kurdistan, 3) Cilicia, Syria, the Lebanon, Palestine, and Iraq, 4) the Hijaz, 'Asir, and Yemen. (Najd and Kuwait were not included in the plan because they had already in effect broken away from the Empire.) In each of these states there would be an independent internal administration, which would enable them to develop as appropriate for them. As in the past, nothing came of 'Aziz 'Ali al-Misri's plans.[18]

In February 1918 al-Misri approached the Ottoman chargé d'affaires in Madrid and asked to be taken to Istanbul by German submarine. His request was turned down. He then proposed going to Morocco to fight the French. When this suggestion also fell by the wayside, he returned to the British embassy and told them that he would have gone to Morocco to fight the French had he not given his word of honour to the British not to impair the war effort against Germany.

In April 1918 he began contacts with the heads of the German secret service in Spain. He proposed to them that he be attached to the general staff of the German army and that he be given command of a military force of 50,000 men. The Germans asked him to wait until they received instructions from Berlin, but in fact they were not at all interested in his services and suspected that he was a British agent. Following this disappointing response, in early May al-Misri turned once again to the British embassy and suggested that he be given a post in the British army, outside the Near East. The British ambassador replied that his suggestion did not seem practicable since he did not speak any English at all. At that point, al-Misri went back to the Germans, and this time they agreed to employ him in their service for 40 Egyptian pounds a month.

Al-Misri continued his contacts with German diplomats in Madrid and in other cities in Spain until the end of the war. A few days before the signing of the armistice between Germany and the Allies it was reported to the British that the German foreign ministry was considering employing al-Misri at the future peace conference in Paris, or even as their representative in the new Arab states that would be established. The British Foreign Office immediately took the necessary steps to see that al-Misri remained in Spain. World War I ended with 'Aziz 'Ali al-Misri left in exile in Spain, frustrated by the state of inactivity in which he found himself, and depressed by the Allied victory over Germany.[19]

Chapter 5

THE ARAB REVOLT: NEW FEATURES

Many books have been written about the Arab revolt of Sharif Husayn of Mecca, some of them personal memoirs and some scholarly research. The book which paved the road was Colonel T. E. Lawrence's *Seven Pillars of Wisdom*, which is considered (not necessarily justifiably) as the classic account of the revolt. The main problem of most of the writers following him was that in one form or another they retold the same stories as their predecessors did, or at least dealt with the same subjects discussed in their predecessors' books. An example is Liddell Hart's book on Lawrence, which in effect paraphrases Lawrence's book for the most part.

The purpose of this chapter is not to retell the history of the Arab revolt in chronological order, which is well-known in any case, but to consider aspects which have not yet been explored. It will specify the identity of the participants in the revolt: volunteers, former prisoners of war, deserters, escapees, and others, placing particular emphasis on their origins: Hijazis, Iraqis, Syrians, and Egyptians. A special section will deal with the exceedingly complex array of relationships that existed among these diverse elements, among themselves, and between them and the Sharifite family. These relationships had a direct influence on the evolution of the Arab revolt and its accomplishments. British and some French officers took part in the revolt, too, and the relations between them and the Arab participants will be reviewed as well. This review will be brief, though, because many books have already been written about the function and contribution of these officers, out of all proper proportion.

This chapter will also deal with the quantitative and qualitative contribution by the members of the Arab societies to the Arab revolt, determining the number of society members who participated, and estimating the general number of participants in the armies of the revolt in its various stages. To determine the contribution of the members of the societies to the revolt, their positions in the leadership of the revolt armies and their involvement in the principal battles of these armies will be examined.

The chapter will conclude with a study of two affairs

connected to the Arab revolt, which have not yet been brought to light: the attempts of the Ottomans to achieve a Turko-Arab peace in the last year of the war, and the episode of the Arab Agency which was established in Cairo after the outbreak of the revolt. The latter has not been investigated at all until now, despite its consequences for the revolt, and for the relations between Husayn and the British in particular.

PRISONERS OF WAR, DESERTERS, AND OTHERS

The largest potential reservoir of skilled manpower for the army of the Arab revolt, that is, officers and men, was in the prisoner-of-war camps in India and Egypt. Already in late June 1916 Husayn sent a message to the British, through Faruqi, that he was interested in setting up a regular army of 30,000 men. This army would be based, according to him, on the Arabs of the Hijaz and strengthened by Arab officers and men from the prisoner-of-war camps in India, Iraq, and Egypt.[1]

However, not all the Arab officers and enlisted men who had fought on the Ottoman side and had been taken prisoner by the British were prepared to join the Arab revolt. There were those who felt a religious bond with the caliph and the Muslim empire, and they therefore refused to fight against them in cooperation with the Christian Allies. Others refused to join the revolt, not out of political-religious reasons, but out of fear of harming their families who remained within the Empire, or even of injuring themselves on the battlefield. These latter preferred the safety of the prison camps.

Even among those who agreed to volunteer for the army of the revolt there were many who showed apathy, or who spent most of their time in political intrigues. Others volunteered for the material benefits which they received. Already mentioned above were the officers who resigned from the revolt army because they did not receive their pay. On one occasion Faruqi reported to Husayn that Arab officers who were to be sent to him had informed him that their families were receiving money from the Ottoman authorities. If it should become known to the Ottomans that they had joined the Arab revolt, these payments would of course be stopped. Furthermore, they could be killed or permanently maimed as a result of their participation in the revolt. Therefore, they were demanding six months' pay in advance, to be deposited in Egyptian banks. Faruqi also appended a list of what should be the pay of each of the officers.[2]

Most of the prisoners of war who joined the revolt were Iraqis. Among them were several important members of *al-'Ahd*, such as Nuri al-Sa'id, who had joined the revolt as a lieutenant and had risen to the rank of general, 'Ali Jawdat al-Ayyubi, 'Abdallah al-Dulaymi, 'Abd al-Latif Nuri, and others.

The British supported as best they could the idea of transporting Arab prisoners of war to the Hijaz so that they could join the revolt army. A few days after the outbreak of the revolt the military authorities in Cairo appealed to the viceroy in India and asked him to send as soon as possible all the Arab officers in the prison camps there, and especially artillery officers. The authorities in India had misgivings about this, and only after they had been informed that the government had approved this did they report that they had in their control 16 officers and 125 men, though it was not clear how willing they were to join the revolt. They pointed out that sending unsuitable people could have quite an embarrassing outcome.[3]

In the meantime the British in Cairo, together with Faruqi, began to organize the first group to be sent to the Hijaz from among the prisoners of war. Faruqi promised Husayn that he could send 700 soldiers, of whom 100 were artillery men, under the command of Nuri al-Sa'id. They were to be joined by some civilians, who were to be integrated into the Hijazi administration in Mecca and Jidda. However, apparently not all the Arab officers were ready to go to the Hijaz. The task of persuading them to join the Arab revolt was given to Faruqi. His success in doing this does not seem to have been great. In a secret telegram that he sent to Husayn in late July 1916 he reported on the difficulties of persuading the officers and that he actually had "been obliged to order them to go". Faruqi therefore recommended that when they arrived in the Hijaz they should immediately upon debarkation meet with some of the more persuasive religious sheikhs.

When the first group was about to be sent to the Hijaz, some of the officers suddenly announced that the cannons placed at their disposal were old ·and of inferior quality, and therefore they would not go to the Hijaz until they received new ones. After arguments most of them agreed to board the ship that was to take them to the Hijaz, with the exception of two officers, Rashid al-Madfa'i and Rasim Sardist, who insisted on remaining in Egypt. Although these two arrived in the Hijaz later on, by special request of 'Aziz 'Ali al-Misri, the officers' behaviour left a

very bad impression on the British. At the same time updated
figures arrived from India, that there were 110 Arab officers and
2,500 soldiers there who could be sent to the Hijaz. But at this
point the British in Cairo decided to wait and see how the first
group would be absorbed in the Hijaz before sending more war
prisoners there. The Foreign Office instructed McMahon to set
up a selection process and to send only those suitable to the
Hijaz. A warning was also sent from Cairo to Sharif Husayn
concerning the caution with which he should receive the volunteers. At this stage even the British began to be apprehensive
that if a large number of war prisoners should arrive in the Hijaz
and not reveal any readiness to join Husayn's army, then it
would have embarrassing results.

On 1 August 1916 the first group of war prisoners set sail for
the Hijaz, led by *al-'Ahd* member Nuri al-Sa'id. Most of them
were prisoners of war brought from India. Accompanying them
were a Lebanese army doctor and also Fu'ad al-Khatib and
Muhibb al-Din al-Khatib who were to edit and run the rebel
newspaper *al-Qibla*. Two artillery batteries, four machine guns,
and 7,000 rifles were also sent with them.

The outcome of this expedition was later described by Reginald Wingate, the governor-general of Sudan, as a "fiasco".
When the group reached Jidda, the Arab soldiers announced
that they refused to fight against their coreligionists, the Turks.
It became clear that they had known nothing in advance about
the purpose of their trip to the Hijaz, and nobody had asked
them if they agreed to fight against the Turks. They were under
the impression that they were being transferred to the Hijaz only
to stay there until the end of the war. Another consideration that
they raised was that as former Ottoman soldiers, if they were to
fall into the hands of the Turks during the course of battle, it
would mean certain death for them. The British representative in
Jidda reported gloomily that it was not clear to him if the one
responsible for what happened was Faruqi, who was to have
prepared them for the trip, but in any case it was clear that they
did not have the slightest intention of fighting. And so, ten days
after they arrived in Jidda 102 of the soldiers were sent back to
Egypt. Only Nuri al-Sa'id and the other officers were left in
Jidda, plus a small number of soldiers who agreed to remain.[4]

Every plan to set up a regular army for the Arab revolt
involved the bringing to the Hijaz of experienced officers and
men, and the largest reservoir was, as mentioned, in the
prisoner-of-war camps. Therefore, despite the sad results of the
first group, the British decided to send more. However, this time

they were determined to apply the lessons of the first experience. At the end of August a small group was sent which consisted only of a few artillery officers and doctors. At the same time, a large group of prisoners of war, officers and men, were being organized in India, though this time the British took care to choose only suitable candidates. They asked the Iraqi officer, an *al-'Ahd* member, 'Ali Jawdat al-Ayyubi, and the Syrian officer, Tawfiq Abu Tawq al-Hamawi (both captured by the British in Iraq) to come to the prison camp and to propagandize in favour of the Arab revolt. The two told the prisoners about the revolt of Husayn and also about the atrocities committed by the Ottomans in Syria, and eventually over 300 officers and men declared their readiness to volunteer for the army of the revolt. On 16 September 25 officers and 222 enlisted men sailed from Bombay. This time, for greater safety, they were headed direct to Rabigh. When the volunteers reached Rabigh ten days later, an additional wise step was taken. Immediately on their debarkation they were met by several officers who had arrived earlier, among them Nuri al-Sa'id. The trip ended with success, and all the volunteers remained in the Hijaz and joined the revolt army.[5]

Apparently the success of this journey prompted the British to decide to transport all the Arab prisoners from India to Egypt, with a stopover in Rabigh in order to persuade them to join the revolt. This plan was encouraged by the Arab officers who had already come from India to Husayn. They claimed that 80 per cent of the Arab prisoners would agree to join up with Husayn the moment they saw that the revolt was an existing fact. In early November 1916 Wingate asked India to send all the prisoners who were fit for military duty as soon as possible.

On 20 November two ships were set to sail from Bombay with a huge shipment of 90 officers and 2,100 men. However, when the British brought the prisoners from the Sumerpur camp to the ships, it was clear that many of the officers did not want to go at all, and it became necessary to use force to take them off the train which brought them and to put them on the ships. In one case they even had to use bayonets to force obstinate officers to board the ships, and one of them was seriously wounded. The ships finally sailed on 21 November, but not before the officers were promised that they would not be forced to fight for Husayn or for anyone else against their will. The viceroy in India sent a telegram to Wingate asking him to honour this commitment in any case, and Wingate sent instructions to this effect to the British representative in Jidda.

The ships with the prisoners reached Rabigh on 1 December.

Not a single one of them would go ashore, with the exception of an Egyptian journalist who was apparently arrested by mistake in Karachi, two Christian doctors, one Syrian and one Greek, and a Kurdish police officer. Consequently Nuri al-Sa'id and several other officers of the revolt army went on board in order to persuade their fellow officers to come ashore. After an emotional meeting of al-Sa'id and his friends with the officers on the ships, which lasted until 9:30 pm and during which many cups of coffee were drunk, one officer agreed to accompany them ashore. The next day, 2 December, ten officers were persuaded to come ashore in order to hear arguments for the revolt from Husayn's men. That same evening eight of them returned to their ship. Thereupon officers and men of the revolt army were brought aboard again in order to recruit volunteers, but without success. Only one officer and one sergeant-major agreed to volunteer. On 3 December Nuri al-Sa'id and other officers of the revolt army went aboard, this time accompanied by Sharif Nasir. They decided to appeal first to the group of prisoners who had signed a petition in India to join Husayn. They hoped that if they persuaded these to disembark then others would join them. However, all of these now vehemently refused to go ashore, and they announced that they refused to fight against their government, the Ottoman government. Understandably, the other prisoners also refused to volunteer. At this point it was decided to try to persuade only the Syrian prisoners, separately from the others and in small groups. This attempt also failed. After this they tried appealing to the men individually, and this time, after great effort, several were persuaded to join the revolt army, but that was all. In a last-ditch effort seven of the leaders of the prisoners were induced to go ashore and spend the night in the Arab camp, with a promise that they would be allowed to return to their ship. The hope was that they would be persuaded more by what they saw than by speeches, which proved to be futile. The next day, 4 December, six of them returned to their ship, and only one agreed to remain and volunteer for the army of the revolt. An additional, desperate attempt by the British to persuade the prisoners ended with a few isolated volunteers, and no more.

When all was done the volunteers numbered six officers and 27 enlisted men. Lieutenant-Colonel Parker, the British liaison officer in Rabigh, announced that he had no more interest in the ships remaining in Rabigh, and they continued on their way to Egypt with the rest of the prisoners. Parker also sent an angry report to Cairo describing the chain of events and making it clear that the handling of the prisoners in India before they were sent to the Hijaz was probably one of the principal factors in their negative attitude. Parker also emphasized that the quality of most of the prisoners, from a military point of view, was low, and he expressed his bitterness that no attempt was made to winnow out the hostile officers. To this he added that the prisoners arrived in Rabigh with large sums of money, an astounding phenomenon considering that they were men about to join a combat force.

The government in India carried out an investigation to find out the reasons for the débâcle, and its conclusions were officially reported to the India Office. The investigation revealed that the previous time when the two Arab officers (al-Ayyubi and al-Hamawi) persuaded prisoners from the Sumerpur camp to enlist in the Arab revolt some of them changed their minds at the last moment and did not join the group that left India in September 1916. These prisoners divulged to the others that they were being sent to join the revolt army, and thus when the present group was about to be sent the others had already been able to stiffen their resistance. Therefore it was necessary to give them a commitment that they would not be forced to fight on behalf of Husayn against their will. As for the incident of the bayonets, the men of the Indian government claimed that it was a case of an Arab officer who had begun running wild, beating and kicking his guards, and besides it was only a matter of a 1/8-inch deep wound. As for Parker's complaints about the quality of those sent, the Indian government claimed that Egypt had requested that they send to the Hijaz all the prisoners who were fit for military duty (Wingate's telegram of early November), and that was exactly what they had done. They thought that the selection of suitable men to serve Husayn would be made when the prisoners reached their destination. And as for the amounts of money in the hands of the prisoners, the Indian government explained that this was money that was due to the prisoners for the extended period that they were held, and according to practice they had to be paid all that was coming to them before they left. Since it was hoped that they would join the Arab revolt, they did not want to anger them by not giving them the payments due to them.

The Indian government's reply was worded with more than a tinge of cynicism and derision. The reader can even get the impression of not a little hidden, malicious joy of the men in India over the failure of the plan of the British in Egypt. In any case, the fact was that the greatest attempt to enlist Arab prisoners of war in the army of the revolt failed miserably.[6]

In February 1917 Fu'ad al-Khatib and Fawzi al-Bakri arrived in Egypt from the Hijaz and began to propagandize among the prisoners of war to join the army of the Arab revolt. The experienced British informed Husayn that they had doubts about the fitness of the officers and men chosen by al-Bakri, and therefore they would not be responsible for their conduct when they reached the Hijaz. Husayn, who also had the benefit of experience, immediately instructed his representative in Cairo to inform the high commissioner that he had no interest in any officer or soldier in whom the British had no confidence. He would be interested in prisoners of war only if it was agreeable to the high commissioner. When Fu'ad al-Khatib telegraphed Husayn and informed him that he was able to recruit 200 soldiers, Husayn replied that at the moment he had no need for them, and he also ordered al-Bakri to return immediately to Mecca.[7]

However, shortly afterwards a former prisoner of war joined the revolt army, one who became its outstanding officer until the end of the war. This was Ja'far al-'Askari, the man who replaced 'Aziz 'Ali al-Misri as commander of the army of the Arab revolt. In 1915 al-'Askari was sent by Enver Pasha in a German submarine to Libya to assist in organizing the forces of Sayyid Ahmad al-Sanusi and to persuade him to attack Egypt from the west. Al-'Askari, who did not trust al-Sanusi, decided to blow up his tent, while accusing the enemies of the Sanusiyya order of carrying out this assault, and then to appoint in his place a new Sanusi leader, one more amenable to the Ottomans. Al-Sanusi discovered the plot, but in the end, under pressure from the Ottoman government and after failing to come to an agreement with the British, he agreed to launch an attack on Egypt. Al-'Askari led the Sanusi forces in two successful attacks on the western border of Egypt, in December 1915, but in the third attack, on 26 February 1916, he was defeated by the British and taken prisoner.

In March 1916 Ja'far al-'Askari was transferred to the citadel of Cairo where he was confined during the following months. One day, with another prisoner, he planned an escape. The two put together three army blankets, tied the end of one of them to the window, and let them drop down outside. The other prisoner reached the ground successfully and got away. But while al-'Askari was making his way down the last blanket tore because of his weight, and he fell from a great height into a moat that surrounded the citadel, where he was found unconscious the next morning. He was taken to a hospital with a sprained ankle. (Later he was required to pay for the three blankets on the grounds that they were no longer fit for use.) In the hospital he was visited by Nuri al-Sa'id (his brother-in-law) and the Syrian activist 'Abd al-Rahman al-Shahbandar, who showed him newspaper items with proofs of the deeds of the Ottomans in Syria. When Shahbandar showed him the newspaper *al-Sharq*, which carried a report of the executions of May 1916, including that of his friend Salim al-Jaza'iri, Ja'far al-'Askari resolved to change sides and join the Arab revolt.

In September 1916 'Aziz 'Ali al-Misri and Nuri al-Sa'id approached the British representative in Jidda and officially requested that Ja'far al-'Askari be permitted to come to the Hijaz. The British were hesitant because they harboured suspicions that al-'Askari was still loyal to the Ottomans, and in addition they wondered how two such dominant personalities as al-Misri and al-'Askari would manage to get along with each other. When he saw that his transfer to the Hijaz was stalled, al-'Askari sent a personal letter to Husayn in December 1916, in which he expressed his desire to join the revolt. He turned also to Faruqi and asked him to persuade Husayn to allow him to come to the Hijaz. Faruqi in fact wrote a warm letter to Husayn about al-'Askari (who had been his instructor at the military academy in Istanbul), and added that there were Arab officers in Egypt who had faith in al-'Askari personally, and therefore if he joined the revolt they would follow. In February 1917 Fawzi al-Bakri joined the pleaders and asked that al-'Askari be allowed to come to the Hijaz. Finally, after a lengthy correspondence and after 'Aziz 'Ali al-Misri himself was removed from the Hijaz, Husayn agreed to al-'Askari's coming there, and the latter arrived in May 1917. Amir Faysal immediately appointed him as commander of his regular forces, an appointment that was not regarded at all with pleasure by Husayn, who had learned from experience not to trust the Iraqis. Faysal had to assume personal responsibility for accepting al-'Askari.[8]

In August 1917 India reported that they had in their custody 23 Arab officers and 285 enlisted men who had all sworn to serve Husayn, and that they were expecting from Iraq an additional 72 officers and 197 enlisted men. The India Office instructed India to send to Egypt all the Arab prisoners, and on 5 September 544 volunteers sailed for Egypt, of whom 84 were officers. However, these officers and men were destined this time for an experiment of a different kind — to set up an Arab legion, not under the command of Husayn. The next section of this chapter will deal with the plan to set up the Arab Legion and its consequences. In any case, this was the last large group of prisoners of war to leave India. In April 1918 India reported that they had additional Arab prisoners of war, but they emphasized that they could not guarantee the goodwill of the prisoners nor their readiness to join Husayn. The British War Office replied that if it was not possible to assure their proper conduct then they should not be sent. If there were individuals who could be trusted, then they could be sent on a personal basis. In August 1918 the Arab Bureau in Cairo reported that it did not seem feasible to mobilize additional volunteers for the revolt army from among the Arab prisoners of war in Egypt. All the prisoners still in Egypt were characterized by the Arab Bureau as pro-Ottoman, or as finding their life in captivity more pleasant than the battlefield.[9]

The prison camps were not the only reservoir of trained manpower for the Arab revolt. There were officers and enlisted men who had deserted the Ottoman army on their own initiative and had joined the ranks of the Arab revolt. However, the number of deserters who joined the revolt was smaller even than the number of prisoners who had agreed to volunteer. Deserters like Faruqi were quite a rare phenomenon, at least in the early stages of the Arab revolt. Among the more noticeable of the officers who deserted the Ottoman army and joined the Arab revolt was al-'Ahd member Mawlud Mukhlis. He deserted in July 1915 to the British lines in Iraq, and immediately after he found out about the outbreak of the Arab revolt he went to India and joined the group of prisoners who sailed to the Hijaz in September 1916. He became one of the more important officers in the revolt army (for his exploits see below). Another important deserter was al-'Ahd member Jamil al-Madfa'i (a future prime minister of Iraq), who served in the Ottoman army in the Caucasus, was sent on leave to Syria, and from there escaped to the British lines. He joined the Sharifite army in Aqaba and was appointed its artillery commander.[10]

The deserters who joined the revolt army came from the various battle fronts, from Gallipoli, Iraq, Palestine, and even from the besieged Medina. Arab deserters from Medina slipped through to the Arab rebel lines from the beginning of the revolt until the end of the war. There were suspicions of at least one of them, Ramadan al-Shallash from Dayr al-Zur, that he was really an Ottoman secret agent. He deserted from Medina in early 1917 and joined the revolt army, and after he was suspected of being in fact an Ottoman spy he was sentenced to death. He was finally pardoned through the personal intervention of Husayn, who appointed him his adjutant, and after the war he became one of the prominent members of *al-'Ahd al-'Iraqi*. Another source of deserters was the Russian front in its various flanks. In August 1916 two Arab officers, Shukri al-Shurbaji (a member of *al-Fatat*) and Ahmad Shaykha, deserted to the Russian lines in Kermanshah. They said that they had made up their minds to desert after reading propaganda leaflets dropped by Russian planes, and in which the outbreak of the Arab revolt was reported. They took advantage of their rank to lead an attack by an Ottoman patrol, and then they went over to the Russian lines and turned themselves in. The Russians turned the two over to the British, and after an intensive investigation that they underwent in London, they were sent on their request to the Hijaz and joined the revolt army. Shukri al-Shurbaji was later appointed commandant of the officers' school in Mecca.[11]

In the final stage of the Arab revolt, and especially in the last month of the war, after the fall of Damascus and when it became clear that the fate of the Ottoman army was sealed, a large wave of deserters joined the Arab army. Among them were Tahsin and 'Ali Rida al-'Askari, the two brothers of Ja'far al-'Askari, who joined the Arab army when he arrived in Hama. Nevertheless, it is important to note that, relatively speaking, only a few deserters from the Ottoman army joined the Arab army. The overall number of deserters was immense. From about a million soldiers in 1915, about half had deserted by the end of the war. Especially serious was the situation in the Fourth Army, the ruler of the Levant, of whose 100,000 soldiers at the beginning of the war there remained only 3,500 at the end.[12] However, the overwhelming majority of the Arab deserters did not join the revolt army. They deserted the Ottoman army to save their own lives and to attend to the support of their families. Thus, after their desertion they would return to their families, or go into hiding for fear of the Ottoman pursuers of deserters.

Besides the officers and enlisted men who fell into British captivity or who deserted, joining the forces of Sharif Husayn were also civilians who had fled from the oppressive Ottoman rule in Syria. Among the first civilians who joined the revolt were members of the al-Bakri family, who fled from Damascus at the time of the outbreak of the revolt, as mentioned in a preceding chapter. They filled various administrative positions in Mecca and elsewhere, and Nasib was even sent on various missions in Syria,

as will be explained below. After the occupation of Aqaba by
the revolt army in July 1917, the flow of escapees joining the
revolt increased because of the relative ease in crossing the lines
in the region of Transjordan. In the following months young
men from the al-Mu'ayyad and al-'Asali families, which had suffered greatly at the hands of the Ottomans, joined the revolt
army. These young men were integrated into sabotage units that
operated alongside the Northern Army. In June 1918 Faysal sent
an emissary to Ahmad Qadri, one of the leaders of *al-Fatat*, and
asked him to gather as many members of his society as he could
and flee with them to Aqaba. Qadri took with him Rafiq al-
Tamimi, Rustum Haydar, Salim 'Abd al-Rahman, Sa'id al-Bani,
and several others, and they fled from Damascus to the Druze
mountain disguised as bedouins. Despite the fact that the
authorities offered a reward of 500 Turkish liras for each of
them, the group managed to slip away and reach the forces of
Faysal south of Ma'an.[13]

At this point it remains to see how many of the activists of
al-Fatat and *al-'Ahd*, that were among the initiators of the idea
of Arab revolt, participated actively in it. The examination will
be done by determining the size of the societies (before and during the war), and locating their activists who participated in the
revolt. An "activist" for this purpose will be anyone whose name
appears explicitly, at least once, in any of the documents or
books on which this research is based. (There does not seem to
be any more credible way to determine the size of the societies.)
All activists known to have participated will be taken into
account, even if their participation was very brief, a few months,
or even less. Then an estimate will be made of the total amount
of participants in the various stages of the revolt, and by referring to this estimate it will be possible to draw conclusions concerning the numerical contribution (and for the present only the
numerical one) of the activists of the societies to the Arab revolt.

Table No. 1
Society Activists and the Arab Revolt

	al-Fatat	al-'Ahd
Number of activists in pre-war period	37	54
Those joining the revolt	8	16
Per cent	21.6	29.6
Number joining the society during the war	78	3
Total activists during World War	115	57
Those joining the revolt	29	17
Per cent	25.2	29.8

From the above table it can be seen clearly that *al-Fatat* tripled its strength during the war, while *al-'Ahd* remained about the same size. On the other hand, the table shows that only about a quarter of the *al-Fatat* activists participated in the revolt, and less than a third of *al-'Ahd* activists.

At the Paris Peace Conference in 1919 Faysal claimed that the Arabs had supplied about 100,000 men to the war effort.[14] This number was completely imaginary. Determining the overall number of participants in the revolt is not at all simple. Concerning this number the following was written in a British report: "The numbers are purely conjectured, since they vary in strength from time to time, almost from day to day." To this Reginald Wingate added that the exact number in the Arab revolt army "is almost impossible to obtain".[15] The figures in the following table were gathered by cross-referencing and verification from numerous and varied sources. In order to arrive at the greatest possible accuracy the table is divided according to the various armies of the Arab revolt on the one hand, and according to the chronological development of the revolt on the other.

Table No. 2
Estimate of Participants in the Arab Revolt

	Faysal's army		'Ali's army		Abdallah's army		Zayd's army	
	Reg.	Irreg.	Reg.	Irreg.	Reg.	Irreg.	Reg.	Irreg.
Beginning of Revolt July 1916		10,000 Irregulars 30,000 Irregulars						
Sept. 1916		6,000		8,000 -9,000		6,000 -7,000		6,000
Nov. 1916		5,000		2,000 -5,000		5,000		
Dec. 1916		8,000 -9,000		8,000		4,000		
June 1917	1,673		1,375	5,000 -10,000	104	5,000	610	1,500
Aug. 1917	2,000							
Nov. 1917	3,000		2,000				1,500 Joined Faysal	
Dec. 1917	4,000							
Jan. 1918	4,500	·	3,000		400 -500			
Apr. 1918	8,000	10,000		7,000				
Sept. 1918	8,000	20,000						

It should be noted about this table that the thousands of regular soldiers recorded in it were for the most part Hijazis, though most of the officers were Iraqis and Syrians. (The numbers of prisoners of war, deserters, and escapees who joined the revolt have been discussed above.) As the revolt drew closer to its end, more and more Syrians joined it. However, even these were mostly tribesmen and villagers. In September 1918 the revolt received an enormous reinforcement of irregulars when the Druzes of Sultan al-Atrash and the Ruwalla tribesmen of Nuri al-Sha'lan joined it.

If one takes into account when studying Table No.1 that six of the activists who joined the revolt were members of both *al-Fatat* and *al-'Ahd*, then the total of all activists of the societies who joined the revolt was only 40. Of course, many Iraqis and Syrians who were not members of the societies joined, but in

any case it is clear that the society activists who joined were
from a numerical standpoint a negligible minority of the participants. Furthermore, according to Table No.1 one can see that
the activists who joined the revolt were a minority of the society
activists themselves. A question of a different sort is how much
did these activists who joined the revolt contribute to it. An
answer to this question will be of an entirely different character,
and a separate section will be devoted to it in this chapter.

After the discussion of the Iraqis and Syrians who joined the
revolt, prisoners and deserters, members of the societies and
non-members, it would be appropriate to end this section with a
discussion of several of the prominent leaders of the Arab movement during this period who did not join the revolt.

The outstanding personality in the ranks of *al-'Ahd* at the
beginning of World War I was Yasin al-Hashimi. His involvement in the development of relations with Faysal and promoting
the idea of Arab revolt has been mentioned in a preceding chapter. After he was removed from Syria to Istanbul he was
appointed chief-of-staff of the 17th Corps stationed in the region
of the capital. A year later, in 1916, he received the command of
the 20th Division which fought in Galicia. He held this position
until 1918 when he was transferred to the Palestine front and
received command of the 24th Division stationed near Tul
Karm. At this point Ahmad Qadri sent him an *al-Fatat* member, Salim 'Abd al-Rahman, to persuade him to desert the army
and join a group of escapees who were to flee to Aqaba under
Qadri's leadership (see above). There are those who say that on
this occasion al-Hashimi even received an invitation from Faysal
to come and take command of the revolt army. Al-Hashimi
rejected the appeal for two reasons: (a) The British were not
faithful to Husayn, and the proof of this was that at the same
time that they came to an agreement with him on the establishment of an Arab state they also issued the Balfour Declaration
and came to an agreement with the French to give them Syria.
They also refused to call Husayn "King of the Arabs" and
referred to him only as "King of the Hijaz". (b) He was fulfilling
a military duty and could not abandon it. Later al-Hashimi was
appointed to the very senior post of commander of the 8th
Corps stationed then in Salt in Transjordan. In September 1918
he retreated with the remnants of his corps to Damascus, was
wounded on the way in an assault by tribesmen, and with the
last of his strength reached Damascus where he went into hiding
until the arrival of the Arab army. He remained in the underground until Nuri al-Sa'id and 'Ali Jawdat al-Ayyubi succeeded

in locating him. To the surprise of many, Faysal immediately appointed him chief of the general staff of the army. His first action in this position was to completely disband the army of the revolt and set up a new Syrian army, which was manned for the most part by officers and men who also had remained in the ranks of the Ottoman army until the end of the war. This act aroused bitterness among the veterans of the revolt, and one can speculate that the fact that al-Hashimi remained in the Ottoman army until the end of the war might have had at least partial influence on this decision of his.[16]

The outstanding personality in the ranks of *al-Fatat* at the beginning of World War I was 'Ali Rida al-Rikabi. He was a senior officer who had served many years in the Ottoman army and had reached the position of corps commander, though on the eve of the war he was removed from the army and put into retirement. In 1915 he received the post of mayor of Damascus. The authorities, who were suspicious of his nationalist tendencies, obliged him to resign from this post, too, in February 1917. In May 1917 there arrived secretly in Syria a mission on behalf of the Arab revolt which included among others Lawrence and Nasib al-Bakri. On 13 June Lawrence met with al-Rikabi in a place near Damascus, reported to him on the plans to occupy Aqaba, and asked in the name of Faysal that the members of *al-Fatat* should do their best to persuade the Arab soldiers in the Ottoman army to desert and join the revolt army. Al-Rikabi replied to him that in Damascus there were indeed only 500 Turkish gendarmes and three unarmed labour battalions, but added that he could not display his true feelings towards the revolt unless he received aid. When Ahmad Qadri organized in 1918 his group of escapees, he approached al-Rikabi, too, and suggested that he join them. Al-Rikabi refused. In August 1918 al-Rikabi was to head a delegation of Syrians that was to go to Switzerland by special permission of the authorities to discuss with the Ottomans in a neutral country and a free atmosphere the possibility of reconciling Arabs and Turks, on the basis of granting autonomy to Syria under the suzerainty of the Sublime Porte. In the end the delegation was headed by Rida al-Sulh, who was brought back from exile in Anatolia. On 22 September 1918 al-Rikabi was reinstated in the army, appointed commander of the Tiberian front, and assigned to block the British advance at all costs. The rapid advance of the British brought on the collapse of this front within three days, and al-Rikabi returned to Damascus where he was assigned to defend the city after the withdrawal of the Ottomans. The day before the fall of

Damascus al-Rikabi delivered himself into the hands of the British. This episode will be discussed in detail in the final chapter of this book.[17]

In this context of the figures of the Arab movement who did not go against the Ottoman Empire during the war, it is appropriate to mention the newspaper *al-Sharq*, which appeared in Syria during 1916-18 and was the mouthpiece of Jamal Pasha. The editor-in-chief was Taj al-Din al-Hasani (a future prime minister of Syria), the son of Sheikh Badr al-Din al-Hasani. One of the senior editors of the newspaper was Muhammad Kurd 'Ali, an important journalist of the Arab movement on the eve of the war. (The correspondent of the newspaper in Tripoli was the future historian Amin Sa'id, who two decades later wrote one of the most comprehensive accounts of the history of the Arab revolt and its consequences.) When Faysal left Damascus for the last time before the outbreak of the Arab revolt, he suggested to Muhammad Kurd 'Ali that he join him. Kurd 'Ali refused. After Jamal Pasha assigned him to participate in the editing of *al-Sharq*, Kurd 'Ali began a campaign of anti-Sharifite and anti-British propaganda. He attacked Husayn in his articles and reviled him for being an ally of the British.[18]

THE ARAB LEGION

The Arab Legion was a one-off attempt by the British to set up an Arab military force, which would be made up of former prisoners of war and operate independently of the command of Sharif Husayn. The author of the idea was Mark Sykes, and the basic concept was that instead of shipping war prisoners to the Hijaz they should be assembled in one training camp in which they would become a consolidated force, trained and disciplined, from which real military benefit might be derived. This force would be employed according to military necessities and in accordance with its ability. It would be possible to use it as an auxiliary force for the Sharifite forces, and also as reinforcement for British forces on the eastern front. There were those who believed that such a force would bring "cohesion" to the Arab movement, and it was therefore decided that the commanders should be Arabs, assisted by a British and a French officer as advisors-inspectors. The high commissioner in Egypt objected to involving the French in this plan. (He felt that the Arab Legion should be the British parallel to the Légion d'Orient that the

French had set up — see below.) However, his objection was overruled, and on 26 July 1917 the British foreign minister officially informed him of the approval to establish an Arab legion under Anglo-French supervision. The Legion camp was set up near Isma'iliya, and Lieutenant-Colonel Pearson was installed as supervisor for the British.[19]

The volunteers for the Arab Legion were supposed to have come from among the Arab officers and enlisted men taken prisoner by the British in Iraq and brought to prison camps in India. In order to encourage them to enlist, the British planted the impression that they were destined, at least some of them, to join the forces of Husayn, or at least they would be able when they reached Egypt to decide if they wanted to serve in the Legion or directly under Husayn. In the Legion enlistment form it was stated inter alia: "I hereby declare that I have taken upon myself to serve in the Arab Legion for the duration of the present war, in order to fight against the Turks in the Arab countries." In the oath that the officers were required to take before they sailed to Egypt it was stated: "I swear by God and on this Holy Coran and on my military honour to serve the Government of H.M. the King of the Arabs, Hussein Ibn Ali, with fidelity and loyalty." A similar wording was used for the oath required of the enlisted men. Of course these wordings gave them the feeling that they were to be sent directly to the Arab revolt, and when the truth came out later on, problems began to arise.

In early September 1917 the volunteers sailed from India on their way to Egypt, numbering about 550 soldiers, officers and men. On 13 September they reached Aden, and there they were joined by Lieutenant-Colonel Pearson, the British supervisor of the Arab Legion. The report that Pearson submitted about the continuation of the voyage was a preview to what happened later. Concerning the participants on the voyage he stated that "many seemed more fitted for a pensionnaire hospital than anything else". Furthermore, the Arab officers had almost no authority over the enlisted men, and in fact they were not even interested in them. Between them and Pearson an argument broke out as to their destination. They claimed that they had agreed to serve only Husayn and no one else. Tension began to spread on the ship, and the volunteers began to feel that they had been deceived about their destination. In order to relieve the tension Pearson convinced them that they were indeed headed for Husayn, and only if the number of soldiers in the Legion should increase considerably would they be used outside of the

Hijaz, too. The officers were convinced; the enlisted men less so. One of the soldiers started giving a speech in which he vehemently declared that he would agree to serve only under Husayn and demanded that they be put ashore either at Jidda or Rabigh, and not in Egypt. Murmurs of agreement arose from among the other soldiers. Finally, after one of the Arab officers, 'Ali Khulqi, agreed to persuade the soldiers himself, the atmosphere calmed down a bit. This action by Khulqi resulted in his being chosen as the Arab commander of the Legion camp.[20]

When they arrived in Egypt, dozens of the volunteers refused to don uniforms, claiming that they were civilians and had volunteered to serve only as such. Added to these were the volunteers of bedouin origin, who, besides refusing to wear uniforms, also refused to participate in formations. Following in their footsteps were several dozen Christians and Jews who were among the volunteers. They announced that they also refused to bear arms. Another problem arose when many of the volunteers claimed that they were non-commissioned officers in the Ottoman army and vehemently demanded that they keep their rank. However, the Legion did not need so many NCO's. Finally, it was necessary to get rid of about 40 hostile officers and also to remove the bedouins from the Legion. The Christians and Jews, on the other hand, were induced to don uniforms and participate in formations. The problem with the NCO's was more serious. Several of them, whose ranks were not recognized, began passive resistance, which they kept up until the end of the Legion.

The British and French cadre began to train the recruits in riflemanship, machine-gunnery, throwing hand grenades, fieldcraft, physical fitness, etc., but attendance at training sessions was not always full. The theoretical lessons that were given to the officers sometimes turned into political meetings. However, despite all these problems the Legion little by little began to take shape. An order of the day was set, according to which every evening after training a short ceremony was held in which they saluted Husayn. For the Legion anthem they chose a poem composed by Rafiq Rizq Sallum, one of those hanged in Syria in May 1916.

The British asked Husayn to send a telegram of encouragement in order to convince the recruits that they had not been deceived in being brought to Egypt. Concurrently, on 4 October a delegation on behalf of the Arab revolt arrived in the Legion camp, headed by Fu'ad al-Khatib and Nuri al-Sa'id. This delegation did improve the atmosphere in the camp, although in a speech by al-Khatib he emphasized that the Legion was an inseparable part of the army of the revolt. The European supervisors began to understand more and more the pointlessness of pinning hopes on using the Legion for any other purpose than the Arab revolt. Several days later al-Khatib explicitly said this to one of the French representatives in Cairo and demanded that they send units of the Legion to Aqaba as soon as possible to join the revolt army. On 29 October, 27 Christians were sent to Aqaba including carpenters, cobblers, and other artisans, and on 31 October the artillery men of the Legion were sent there. (In any case, the Legion had no cannons with which to train them.)

The problem of discipline remained the most serious one from which the Legion suffered throughout its short existence. The soldiers would go off to Isma'iliya without official leave, and the officers maintained no control of any kind over this. In fact, the officers themselves would leave the camp without permission from time to time. Rumours spread that some of the officers and soldiers were secretly receiving pay from the Ottomans. The rumours were not proven, but in any case it was clear that at least some of the soldiers were pro-Ottoman. One of them even said outright that he preferred to return to the prison camp rather than serve in the Legion. The problems of discipline reached such a degree that it was necessary to put ten soldiers in confinement, and the European supervisors were forced to take disciplinary measures. But the most serious incident from the point of view of organizing the Legion occurred when the Arab camp commander decided that he deserved identical authority to that held by the European supervisors, and he refused to cooperate except on that basis. The supervisors were finally forced to send him to Cairo, and from there he was permitted to return only after an understanding had been reached as to his status vis-à-vis the European supervisors. However, immediately on his return to the camp he began to stir up the men against the supervisors.[21]

At that point it was clear that the plan for the Arab Legion had failed. On 19 November Pearson wrote a summary report on the Legion affair. He began it with "The experiment with the Arab Legion we have had here for the last 8 weeks, it must be confessed, has been a failure." The reasons for the failure were, in his opinion: Unsuitable selection of recruits; officers who were incompetent and unwilling and interested only in their own personal ambitions (and especially the Arab camp commander, who was the principal factor in the lack of discipline among the soldiers, and who was even ready to foment a mutiny among them in order to achieve his goals); the inappropriate explanation that the recruits received in India concerning the purpose of their mobilization; the promise given to the recruits that they would keep the ranks they held in the Ottoman army, a promise that later caused a peck of troubles. Pearson ended his report expressing doubt that there was any point in making another attempt to set up an Arab force on the pattern of the Legion. The French also reached the conclusion that the Legion was useless. In an analysis they made in summarizing the affair they emphasized the xenophobia of the soldiers of the Legion, which blocked them from cooperating with any European force, either in Syria or in Palestine. The soldiers of the Legion were prepared to fight only for the Sharif, and they dreamt of setting up a large and independent Arab empire. The French therefore reached the conclusion that there was no point in continuing to foster the Legion.

In mid-December Clayton sent a letter to Sykes in which he summarized the Legion episode in the following words: "I must honestly confess, that viewed as a symbol of Arab nationalism, the Legion has been a failure. It has not been received with any enthusiasm by local Arabs, in spite of much propaganda, and it was viewed as long as it remained here with grave suspicion by the Sherif and by Feisal, who disliked the procedure and wished to get the men direct . . . If I thought it were likely to achieve the object for which it was started, I would say go on with it, but I certainly do not think so, and I recommend closing it down."[22]

Already in early November Clayton had expressed his opinion that the Arab Legion should move to Aqaba and be joined to Amir Faysal. He claimed that the officers and soldiers were impatient and suspicious, and therefore if they continued to be kept in Egypt there would be trouble. His opinion was supported by the high commissioner and the GOC, and on 20 November the men of the Legion began to move to Aqaba. Within a week a group of 28 officers and 357 men had moved there, and this was actually most of the Legion. The Arab Legion joined Faysal's forces and merged with them, and with this the episode ended.[23] The British made no further attempt during the war to repeat the experiment of setting up an independent Arab force.

THE MEMBERS OF THE SOCIETIES AND THE LEADERSHIP OF THE ARAB REVOLT

It has been shown above that the numerical contribution of the members of the Arab societies to the Arab revolt was negligible. Another question is what was their qualitative contribution. The answer to this question is completely different. An evaluation of their qualitative contribution will be given by determining their relative part in the command of the regular revolt forces and by examining their influence on the conduct of the principal battles in which the revolt army was involved. Their share in other operations connected with the revolt, such as the propaganda missions to Syria, will also be described.

After the fall of Ta'if into the hands of 'Abdallah the first stage of the Arab revolt ended, and during the following months all the forces of the Arab revolt were concentrated in the region of Medina. They were divided at this stage into three main armies: the army of 'Ali, the army of 'Abdallah, and the army of Faysal, which were known as the Southern Army, the Eastern Army, and the Northern Army, respectively, according to their location relative to each other. As time went on and the revolt spread north in the direction of Transjordan, the importance of the Southern and Eastern Armies decreased, their having remained in the region of Medina, and the importance of the Northern Army increased, and it became the central army of the Arab revolt.

Following are diagrams of the structure of the revolt armies in the various stages, with the names of their commanders and their origins, and an indication of those commanders who were society members.

October 1916

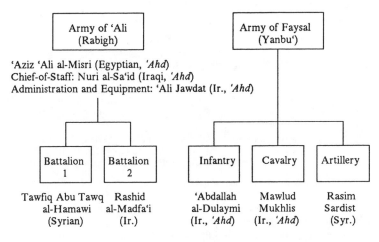

'Aziz 'Ali al-Misri (Egyptian, *'Ahd*)
Chief-of-Staff: Nuri al-Sa'id (Iraqi, *'Ahd*)
Administration and Equipment: 'Ali Jawdat (Ir., *'Ahd*)

January 1917

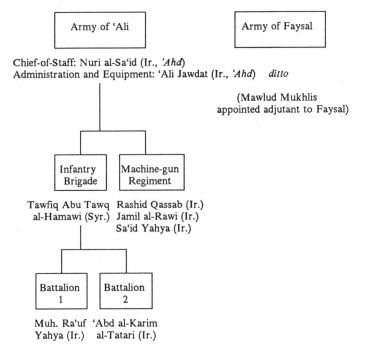

Chief-of-Staff: Nuri al-Sa'id (Ir., *'Ahd*)
Administration and Equipment: 'Ali Jawdat (Ir., *'Ahd*)   *ditto*

(Mawlud Mukhlis
appointed adjutant to Faysal)

May 1917

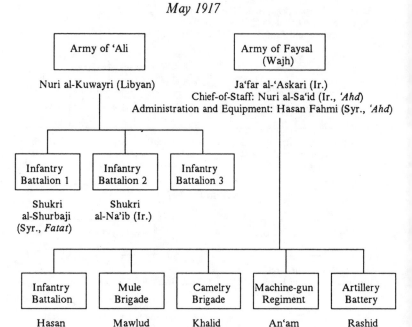

October 1917

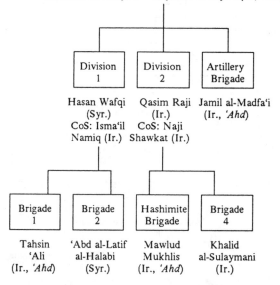

Army of Faysal
(Aqaba)

Ja'far al-'Askari (Ir.)
Chief-of-Staff: Nuri al-Sa'id (Ir., *'Ahd*)
Administration and Equipment: Shakir 'Abd al-Wahhab al-Shaykhali (Ir.)
DMO: 'Ali Jawdat al-Ayyubi (Ir., *'Ahd*)
'Abdallah al-Dulaymi — Adjutant to Faysal (Ir., *'Ahd*)

Division 1   Division 2   Artillery Brigade

Hasan Wafqi   Qasim Raji   Jamil al-Madfa'i
(Syr.)   (Ir.)   (Ir., *'Ahd*)
CoS: Isma'il   CoS: Naji
Namiq (Ir.)   Shawkat (Ir.)

Brigade 1   Brigade 2   Hashimite Brigade   Brigade 4

Tahsin   'Abd al-Latif   Mawlud   Khalid
'Ali   al-Halabi   Mukhlis   al-Sulaymani
(Ir., *'Ahd*)   (Syr.)   (Ir., *'Ahd*)   (Ir.)

The Hashimite Brigade (*al-Liwa' al-Hashimi*) was the striking force of the Northern Army. Established by Mawlud Mukhlis from former prisoners of war and bedouins, it started out as a squadron and grew to a brigade of 300 mules, 400 cameleers and a machine-gun regiment.[24]

1918

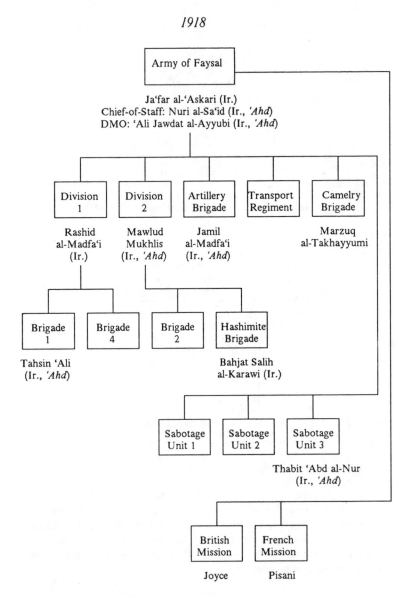

In August 1918, on the eve of the great invasion of Syria, the Northern Brigade (*al-Mafraza al-Shimaliyya*) was set up within the Northern Army as a highly mobile force to invade Syria.

The commander-in-chief of this force was Faysal, and the chief-of-staff was Nuri al-Sa'id. On the staff were also Jamil al-Madfa'i and 'Abd al-Hamid al-Shaliji (an Iraqi member of al-'Ahd). Jamil al-Madfa'i was also in command of the artillery batteries. The core of the force was 500 regular cavalrymen under the command of 'Ali Jawdat al-Ayyubi and 1,000 cameleers under the command of Tahsin 'Ali.[25]

From the above diagrams one can see clearly that almost all the commanders of the army of the revolt were Iraqis or Syrians, with the former being the majority. Furthermore, almost all the senior commanders were members of al-'Ahd. (Of those who were not members, most joined al-'Ahd al-'Iraqi after the war.) It has been pointed out above that only 17 of the al-'Ahd activists are known to have joined the revolt. It is thus clear that these few constituted the backbone of the high command of the regular forces of the Arab revolt.

At this point it would be appropriate to see how much the members of the societies influenced the course of the main battles in which the revolt army was involved. In the battles which will be reviewed here the forces involved were those of the Northern Army under the leadership of Faysal, an army which became the dominant one of the Arab revolt starting in early 1917.

On 23 January 1917 the coastal settlement of Wajh, lying about halfway to Aqaba from Rabigh and Yanbu', was captured. According to the original battle plan, the forces of Faysal were to attack Wajh from the south and east, while the British were to land 500 bedouins, under the command of Captain Bray, from the sea north of the town. However, when the time of attack arrived, Faysal's forces had not yet reached the scene. The British decided to act anyway, and under cover of shellfire from the British warships they landed the battalion of bedouins, who captured the town easily. Faysal and his men arrived only the next day, and Mawlud Mukhlis was appointed governor of the town, with the job of adapting it for use as the base of the Northern Army. According to Lawrence, neither the Arabs nor the British were aware at the time of the significance of the .capture of Wajh. This conquest was actually the first step in the great breakthrough to the north.[26]

On 1 March 1917 a mule force under command of Mawlud Mukhlis penetrated deeply northwards and attacked the railway station at Qal'at al-Mu'azzam. The Ottomans responded to the attack with heavy fire, and after the force suffered over 125 casualties, it was forced to withdraw. Mukhlis himself was wounded and broke his left hand.[27]

The occupation of Aqaba in July 1917 was the turning point in the evolution of the Arab revolt. From then on its centre of gravity shifted from the Hijaz to Transjordan. On 2 July fighters from the Huwaytat tribes under the leadership of 'Awda Abu Tayh succeeded in capturing Abu al-Lisal northeast of Aqaba, while destroying an Ottoman battalion that had arrived from Ma'an. Four days later Aqaba surrendered to the Huwaytat fighters (who were accompanied by Lawrence). After that a regular force of 500 men, under command of Rashid al-Madfa'i, entered the town. With the occupation of Aqaba the entire Hijazi coast was in the hands of the Arab rebels. Aqaba itself became the central base of the revolt army in southern Transjordan, and the operations of the Northern Army were directed from there until the final stage of the war.[28]

On 30 July 1917 forces of the Northern Army, under command of Ja'far al-'Askari, attacked the railway station at Qal'at al-Zumurrud (south of Mada'in Salih and east of Wajh) with the goal of cutting off Medina from the north. The force reached the station after midnight, and a fierce battle developed which lasted until sunset of the next day. The Arabs could not overcome the Ottoman defenders, and they suffered a serious shortage of water. They could not approach the wells which were nearby because these were within range of the Ottoman artillery. Al-'Askari ordered a retreat, but this meant that they would have to withdraw to Wajh, three days away, without water. Thereupon, Mawlud Mukhlis, who had participated in the battle as commander of the Hashimite brigade, requested al-'Askari's permission to attack the Ottoman positions that overlooked the wells. Permission was granted, and Mukhlis, at the head of his brigade, succeeded after a bitter struggle in taking the hills overlooking the wells. The Arabs were then able to supply themselves with water before the retreat.[29]

After the transfer of the Northern Army from Wajh to Aqaba was completed, Mawlud Mukhlis was sent to hold the settlement Wadi Musa (near Petra) in order to secure Aqaba against an attack from the north. On 21 October 1917 four infantry battalions and one cavalry regiment left Ma'an, under command of Jamal Pasha III (commander of Ma'an at the time), in order to attack the Arab force in Wadi Musa. The Hashimite brigade in Wadi Musa numbered about 300 regular soldiers, supplemented by 180 tribesmen. After a softening-up shelling and an aerial bombardment by a German airplane the Ottomans opened the attack. The battle lasted all day, and at first the Ottomans succeeded in pushing the Arabs from the outer fortifications of Wadi Musa. Mukhlis ordered the bedouin volunteers to retreat to the hills south of the village, while he concentrated the regulars in the hills to the north. The Ottomans, who had advanced forward from the east, found themselves under a crossfire from north and south. Towards evening the Arabs attempted to outflank them from the southeast. At that point the Ottomans were forced to retreat quickly in order to avoid being surrounded. The next day the Arabs recaptured also the positions that they had lost at the beginning of the battle. The Ottomans returned to Ma'an leaving behind 60 dead. The Arabs also suffered casualties of 40 dead and wounded, but the main significance of the successful defence of Wadi Musa was that it removed the danger of attack on Aqaba from the north. At the end of November Mukhlis even broadened the area of control of the revolt forces by capturing 'Ayn Wahida. An Ottoman attempt to recapture 'Ayn Wahida in mid-December was repulsed by Mawlud Mukhlis.[30]

On 14 January 1918 the forces of the revolt penetrated deeper to the north, and they gained an important achievement when they captured the town of Tufayla south of Karak. They took 800 prisoners, including the Qa'imaqam. Commanding the regular force which took part in the operation was the Syrian Rasim Sardist, and the bedouin volunteers were commanded by the Iraqi Isma'il Namiq. Sardist was later replaced by 'Abdallah al-Dulaymi, an Iraqi member of al-'Ahd, who had to face an Ottoman attempt to recapture Tufayla. On 25 January an Ottoman force of 800 men left Karak in the direction of Tufayla. It was attacked by the Arabs before it reached the town, and after a 24-hour battle it was completely defeated. About 500 of its soldiers were killed, about 100 were taken prisoner, and the rest made a disorderly retreat to Karak.[31]

The principal focus of the battles between the revolt army and the Ottomans during 1918 was Ma'an, the central town in southern Transjordan, with 2,000 Ottoman soldiers garrisoned in it. In early April 1918 the patience of the Arab officers ran out, and they strongly demanded a direct attack on Ma'an and the end of the tactics of attacking railway stations and tracks. Lieutenant-Colonel Joyce, head of the British mission of advisors to Faysal, and the other British advisors, opposed this. They claimed that the Arabs were not capable of attacking a fortified position in an open area, and that they suffered from artillery inferiority. At a meeting attended by the British officers, Faysal, Zayd, Ja'far al-'Askari, Nuri al-Sa'id and a number of other

Arab officers, a sharp debate broke out, with Faysal and al-'Askari supporting the British view and al-Sa'id and the other Arab officers stubbornly insisting that Ma'an should be attacked directly. Mawlud Mukhlis, who was by then a division commander, even organized a petition by the Arab officers against the British advisors, in which it was charged that the British only wanted to impede the progress of the Arab revolt. The Arab officers were fed up with serving the interests of foreigners, and from then on they would work only for the realization of their national goals. The petition ended with a threat that if their view was not accepted they would leave the army. When Mukhlis later received an order to attack the Fasu'a railway station south of Ma'an, he announced that he refused to obey it. He was immediately dismissed from command of the division and put into detention. Ja'far al-'Askari decided to take personal command of the attack on Fasu'a, but shortly after the force under his command left, a violent storm broke out, the soldiers lost their way, and they had to send for others to rescue them. Al-'Askari returned to base leaving behind many soldiers missing, and following the undermining of his authority that ensued, and pressure from the other Arab officers, Mawlud Mukhlis was released from detention and reinstated in command of his division. The path to a direct attack on Ma'an was opened.

It was decided to split the army into three columns. One would attack the Ghadir al-Hajj station south of Ma'an, a second would attack the Jardun station to the north, thus cutting off the town from both directions, and the third would attack Ma'an itself. The first two would join the third when they had completed their mission. On 11 April a column of 350 regulars and 700 bedouins under Nuri al-Sa'id's command attacked Ghadir al-Hajj. Al-Sa'id was accompanied by 'Abdallah al-Dulaymi and Jamil al-Madfa'i. Before the assault a sergeant and a private were sent out to scout the area and were discovered by the Ottomans. The private was shot and the sergeant was taken prisoner. After the attacking force captured the station they found the butchered body of the sergeant. In reprisal Jamil al-Madfa'i shot two Turkish prisoners, and 'Abdallah al-Dulaymi despatched a letter to the Ottoman commander of Ma'an warning him not to kill any more Arab prisoners. The day after the attack the Ottomans recaptured Ghadir al-Hajj. On 12 April a column of 600 regulars under the command of Ja'far al-'Askari captured Jardun and took 200 prisoners. Jardun, too, was recaptured the next day by the Ottomans. After these assaults both the southern column and the northern one continued towards Ma'an.

On 13 April the central column under Mawlud Mukhlis's command attacked the hills of Samna, about five kilometers southwest of Ma'an. Leading the assault was the 1st Brigade under Tahsin 'Ali. After a heavy battle lasting three hours the Ottoman forces began to withdraw from the hills overlooking the town. Mukhlis ordered them pursued to Ma'an, thinking that it would be possible to capture the town in the momentum of the attack. He himself led the pursuit, but as they approached the town the defenders opened fire from trenches. Mukhlis was hit by several shots and fell from his horse injured in both legs, one from a bullet and the other broken. With him in the pursuit was al-'Ahd member Thabit 'Abd al-Nur, whose horse was shot out from under him. Five other pursuers were killed, and the rest fled. Mukhlis and al-Nur were only about 100 meters from the enemy positions, and al-Nur began to drag Mukhlis until the two were out of range of fire of the Ottomans. Mukhlis was saved, but for him the Arab revolt was over. He was transferred to Egypt for medical care and was left with a crippled leg for the rest of his life.

On 13 April in the evening Nuri al-Sa'id arrived in Samna, having returned from Ghadir al-Hajj, and took over command from Mukhlis. The next day Ja'far al-'Askari, too, arrived in Samna, returning from Jardun, and took command of all three columns. On 15 April the Arabs began a general assault on Ma'an, completed its encirclement on 16 April, penetrated the town for a few hours on 17 April, and then were forced to withdraw after suffering about 250 losses. The artillery inferiority of the Arabs forced them to retreat back to Samna where al-Madfa'i began to shell the Ottoman positions. On 25 April another unsuccessful assault was made on Ma'an, and on 30 April the Arab forces withdrew to Wahida without taking the town.[32]

On 11 May regular forces commanded by Nuri al-Sa'id attacked Jardun again and occupied it. They later withdrew from it and on 17 May attacked it a second time. This time the Ottomans were waiting for them, let them enter the station, and then opened fire on them with machine-guns and hand grenades. The Arab force retreated, leaving behind seven officers and 26 soldiers killed. In early June Jardun was once more attacked and occupied, and again recaptured by the Ottomans. On 9 June Nuri al-Sa'id attacked the Jurf al-Darwish station north of Jardun, but abandoned it after the attack. On 18 June the Ottoman forces returned to it. On 21 July another, large-scale attack was staged on Jardun. The Arab forces, numbering 2,000 regulars and 600 bedouins, attacked the station in three columns, from the east, south, and west. When the first column came within about 100 meters of the station, heavy fire was opened on it, killing its commander and the commander of the Hashimite brigade which had joined it. When the second column, under command of Tahsin 'Ali, came to within 300 meters of the station, heavy fire was opened on it, too. Many of its officers and soldiers were killed, and Tahsin 'Ali himself was wounded by three bullets. The attack by the third column was also repulsed. Tahsin 'Ali ordered a retreat, but then Nuri al-Sa'id arrived on the scene and ordered a renewal of the attack. He, too, soon realized the senselessness of continuing the attack, and ordered the retreat of the Arab forces, who left behind 24 officers and about 200 soldiers killed.[33]

Ma'an held out until the end of the war, and so did Jardun. Only on 23 September, after the collapse of the Ottoman army in the face of the final offensive by General Allenby, did the Arab forces take Ma'an. (Its garrison managed to slip away, and was captured a week later near Amman.) Jardun was taken a day later, and Jurf al-Darwish was found abandoned. On 27 September 1918 Nuri al-Sa'id entered Dar'a and appointed an Arab military governor there, and with this ended the conquest of Transjordan from the Ottomans.[34]

A review of the main battles in which the Northern Army was involved in 1917-18 repeatedly brings up the names of Iraqi officers like Ja'far al-'Askari, Nuri al-Sa'id, and Mawlud Mukhlis (the latter two members of al-'Ahd). These officers, despite their small number, were the ones who led the Arab forces during the battles, and in fact they were the ones who initiated most of the battles in which the army of the revolt took part in the period under discussion.

Another important contribution of the members of the societies to the revolt, aside from their involvement in the battles, was in propaganda missions to Syria. The first mission was carried out by al-Fatat member Fa'iz al-Ghusayn in early 1917. Faysal sent him from Wajh to Nuri al-Sha'lan, the paramount chief of the Ruwalla tribes, to ask him not to assist the Ottomans and to join the Arab revolt. Al-Ghusayn was apprehensive that Nuri al-Sha'lan might turn him in to the Ottoman authorities, as he had done in the past, but this time al-Sha'lan entertained him pleasantly, although he avoided committing himself to joining the Arab revolt. (For the attitude of the Sha'lans to the revolt see the next section.)

In May 1917 a propaganda mission left Wajh for Syria

consisting of Sharif Nasir, 'Awda Abu Tayh, al-Fatat member Nasib al-Bakri, and Lawrence. 'Awda Abu Tayh went to visit Nuri al-Sha'lan with a gift of 6,000 pounds Sterling from Faysal. Nasib al-Bakri went to Jabal al-Duruz with 7,000 pounds Sterling in order to establish contacts with pro-Sharifite Druze leaders, and to discuss with them the possibility of opening a revolt on Jabal al-Duruz. Lawrence furnished al-Bakri with a list of assignments, according to which he was to do the following: To organize an intelligence service in the regions of Damascus, Dar'a, and Amman; to reconcile various Druze leaders in the cause of the common goal and to check their military needs; to establish contacts with the Druzes, the Mutawali Shi'ites, and the Maronites in Mount Lebanon; to investigate the network of roads and water supply in the region, and so forth. Al-Bakri contacted Husayn al-Atrash and later met with Sultan al-Atrash. He returned about a month later with a vague promise by the Druze leaders that they would join the revolt when the Sharifite army was near, provided that they received arms and ammunition.

In March 1918 Nasib al-Bakri was sent a second time to Jabal al-Duruz, this time accompanied by a number of young men from Damascus. He carried with him a manifesto from Faysal calling on the population to revolt, and he disseminated declarations saying that wherever the soldiers of the revolt army should reach would be recognized by the Allies as absolutely independent. He returned from his mission in early June bearing letters of allegiance from the Druze leaders, but once again the Druzes conditioned their joining on Faysal's arriving with adequate forces equipped with artillery. During this trip al-Bakri met with the Vali of Damascus, who handed him a letter from Muhammad Jamal Pasha "the Lesser" (Jamal Pasha's replacement in command of the Fourth Army), who promised him that if he should return to Damascus he would return to him all of his family's property. Al-Bakri withstood the temptation, though one of the members of his mission, from the al-'Azm family, accepted a similar offer that he received from Muhammad Jamal Pasha.

In September 1918 al-Bakri was sent a third time to Jabal al-Duruz, and he reached an agreement with Sultan al-Atrash that, in exchange for the Druzes' joining the revolt, the political independence of Jabal al-Duruz would be recognized, and it would be subject to Faysal only nominally. This time the Druzes agreed to cooperate and with large forces they joined the final attack on Damascus.[35]

IRAQIS, SYRIANS, AND OTHERS IN THE ARAB REVOLT

As explained in the preceding sections, many and varied elements participated in the Arab revolt, both from the point of view of social composition: townsmen and tribesmen, intellectuals and uneducated; and as to origin: Hijazis, Iraqis, Syrians, a few Egyptians, and also European advisors, mainly British. The purpose of this section is to examine the set of relations that existed among the various elements which took part in the revolt, and how these relations influenced its course.

The most problematic set of relations during the period under discussion was that which prevailed between the Iraqi and Syrian officers who served in the various armies of the revolt. Quarrels were constantly breaking out between them over the domination by the Iraqi officers of all the senior posts in the armies of the revolt. The Syrian officers felt discriminated against, especially since the purpose of the battles was first and foremost to liberate their own country, Syria (of which they considered Transjordan to be part and parcel). They also felt that they were not receiving positions of command commensurate with the number of Syrian soldiers serving in the revolt. To this must be added the harsh attitude of several of the Iraqi officers towards their soldiers, such as the Iraqi officer Sa'id al-Madfa'i, a difficult man who treated his soldiers so brutally that some of them went to complain about him to one of the French advisors.

The officers were actually divided into two camps: the Iraqis, headed by Ja'far al-'Askari, Nuri al-Sa'id, Mawlud Mukhlis, and others, and the Syrians headed by Hasan Fahmi, Hasan Wafqi, and others. Faysal was forced to act as mediator between the two camps, but apparently he came to prefer the Iraqis. The Syrians, of course, did not view this preference favourably, and they tried to sway Faysal towards themselves, and particularly to undermine the senior position of the commander of the Northern Army, Ja'far al-'Askari. Al-'Askari reacted by exiling several of his Syrian opponents to Mecca. The bitterness against al-'Askari increased when the Syrians claimed that he was sacrificing them on the altar of his countrymen's interests. In September 1917, following one of the quarrels among the officers, a Syrian soldier fired a pistol at al-'Askari and just missed hitting him. Faysal sentenced the soldier to flogging. In early 1918 a whisky-accompanied poker game among Iraqi and Syrian officers ended with a quarrel involving Mawlud Mukhlis and a

Syrian officer. The two drew their pistols, and Nuri al-Sa'id, who had jumped between them to defuse the situation, was slightly wounded in the hand by a bullet that was fired.

The situation reached the point that, as expressed by the Syrian activist Haqqi al-'Azm, the problem had changed from "a problem of Arabs and Turks" to "a problem of Iraqis and Syrians". The Syrians began to demand that they be formed into a single unit, which would be able to work for the outbreak of a revolt in the Hawran and thus to hasten the liberation of Syria. Syrian officers who arrived in Aqaba in late 1917 announced that they would not obey orders from Ja'far al-'Askari, and the latter was forced to send 15 of them under guard to Mecca. An attempt to improve the situation was made in early 1918 in Cairo. Arriving there were several of the prominent Iraqi officers, among them Nuri al-Sa'id and Qasim Raji. Kamil al-Qassab, who was staying at the time in Cairo, introduced them to several Syrian activists and appealed to them to end the quarrel. Nuri al-Sa'id agreed. Then al-Qassab suggested that al-Sa'id write a letter to the division commander Hasan Wafqi, who was the leader of the Syrians, and to Dr. Mahmud Hamdi Hamuda, who assisted him, in which he would propose Iraqi-Syrian cooperation in the cause of the fatherland. Al-Sa'id agreed. After that al-Qassab adjured all those present to be loyal to the Arab cause alone. Al-Qassab's attempt at mediation did not succeed, and he himself went to the camp of the Northern Army in order to reconcile the disputants. Just as he was about to succeed in this effort, an order came transferring Hasan Wafqi from command of the 1st Division to the position of inspector-general of the army. Wafqi saw this as an insult to his standing because he apparently considered his new position as inconsequential compared to the position of chief-of-staff that was held by Nuri al-Sa'id. A further dispute that broke out later between him and Ja'far al-'Askari was the last straw, and he resigned from the army and left for Cairo.

Some time later a delegation of Syrian activists arrived from Egypt, and they obtained a commitment from Faysal that officers, of whatever origin, would not be dismissed by a decision or caprice of one man alone but only after a trial. They also demanded that the command of the 2nd Division, which had been vacant since Mawlud Mukhlis had been wounded, should be given to Rasim Sardist or to Hasan Wafqi (both Syrians). The promises they received were not kept, and in May 1918 a number of Syrian officers informed a French representative in Cairo that only necessity and the high pay were still keeping them in the Arab army. Understandably, this state of affairs impaired not only the command of the Northern Army but also the ordinary soldiers, whose welfare and training were being neglected on the altar of political intrigues.[36]

The situation was no better in the armies of 'Ali and 'Abdallah, which were continuing the siege of Medina. A British officer reported on the relations between the Iraqis and Syrians as follows: "The hostility between the Syrians and the Baghdadis is very marked. The Baghdadis evidently hate everybody but themselves and are only out for making money." The Iraqis set up a sort of committee whose function was to ensure that Iraqis would get all the better-paying jobs. In this way they pushed the Syrians into an inferior condition, and most certainly they did not allow any Meccan officer to reach a senior position. In mid-1917 the members of this committee demanded that Sharif 'Ali raise their pay by one third. At this point 'Ali ordered the commander of his army, the Libyan officer Nuri al-Kuwayri, to restore order and restrain them. Al-Kuwayri's limited success in fulfilling this task will be discussed later. In any case, al-Kuwayri reported to the British that a few Iraqi officers were the real rulers in 'Ali's army and were constantly violating regulations. The Syrian officers, who constituted the majority, did not want to recognize them and were threatening to leave the army if they should be required to obey the Iraqis. In the army of 'Abdallah the tense relations between the Iraqis and the Syrians reached the point that in September 1917 a group of Syrian officers and soldiers insulted and beat Muhammad Hilmi, the Iraqi commander of 'Abdallah's regular army. 'Abdallah, of course, could not let this pass, and he sentenced the leader of the assailants to death (the sentence was later reduced to life imprisonment) and his accomplices to ten years at hard labour. In spite of all the above, the situation in mid-1918 was that most of the commanders in the armies of 'Ali and 'Abdallah and all the senior artillery commanders of the two armies were Iraqis.[37]

The situation in Mecca itself was no different. The simultaneous presence of Iraqis and Syrians in the various offices of the Hashimite administration and in the entourage of Husayn caused sharp tensions between the two elements. The Syrians found their stay in Mecca depressing and despised both the Hijazis and the Iraqis, whom they saw as lacking culture. The Meccans and the Iraqis, on the other hand, were shocked by the behaviour and European dress of the Syrians and only with difficulty considered them true believers. Husayn himself, who was aware of the lack of confidence between the Iraqis and Syrians (for his own attitude towards them see below), tried to maintain a balance. When he dismissed Faruqi (an Iraqi) as his representative in Cairo, he appointed Fu'ad al-Khatib (a Syrian) to replace him, while stating that this appointment would be only temporary, until a suitable Hijazi could be found to relieve him of this trouble.[38]

The most serious dispute between Iraqi and Syrian officers broke out in Aqaba shortly after the end of the war. Most of the Northern Army had already moved to the north, and the military governor of Aqaba was the Iraqi officer 'Abd al-Wahhab [al-Shaykhali?]. On 15 December 1918 a new governor appointed by Husayn, the qadi 'Abd al-Rahman, arrived in the town. The new governor was not satisfied with just removing 'Abd al-Wahhab from his post, but he began to check out the rumours going around concerning large financial embezzlements by 'Abd al-Wahhab. To investigate the matter 'Abd al-Rahman appointed a committee of junior Syrian officers to audit 'Abd al-Wahhab's accounts. Immediately the old feud between Iraqi and Syrian officers was renewed, with the former supporting 'Abd al-Wahhab and the latter, headed by chief army physician Dr. Mahmud Hamdi Hamuda, encouraging 'Abd al-Rahman to continue the course he had taken. 'Abd al-Wahhab immediately sent a telegram to Ja'far al-'Askari, who was in Ma'an at the time, to rescue him from his plight. The British, however, held up the telegram for fear of widening the conflict between the Iraqis and Syrians and its spreading throughout the entire army. There was also a fear that the incident would cause the beginning of a movement to remove all Iraqi office-holders from Syria. When the dispute worsened, all the Iraqi officers and soldiers in Aqaba demanded to be transferred to Amman. Then seven Iraqi officers submitted their resignations. The British believed that 'Abd al-Rahman himself did not understand the grave results caused by his decision concerning 'Abd al-Wahhab, but that he was incited by the Syrians. They therefore suggested to Zayd (Faysal was then in Europe) that he summon to Damascus both 'Abd al-Wahhab and the leader of the Syrians Mahmud Hamdi to present their cases to him, and thereby the tension in Aqaba itself would be reduced. Zayd acted accordingly, and on 23 December Mahmud Hamdi sailed for Damascus. 'Abd al-Wahhab remained in Aqaba, but on that very same day there arrived in the town a new representative of Husayn, Ibrahim Haqqi, to open an official investigation of 'Abd al-Wahhab's accounts. Ibrahim Haqqi was not identified with either side, and his investigation confirmed the suspicions that existed concerning 'Abd al-Wahhab. In any case, the incident in its wider aspect was terminated.[39]

Many of the officers mentioned in the preceding pages, Iraqis as well as Syrians, were members of *al-'Ahd*. In this state of affairs it should not be surprising that after the war the old *al-'Ahd* society split up into two separate societies: *al-'Ahd al-'Iraqi* and *al-'Ahd al-Suri*. Most of the Iraqi officers who had taken part in the Arab revolt and who were not members of *al-'Ahd* then joined the Iraqi faction, which became the dominant one.

A problem no less serious than the relations between the Iraqis and the Syrians was the problem of the relations between Iraqis and Syrians together on one side and on the other side the Hijazis in general and the Hashimite family in particular. Thus, for example, a statement made by Mark Sykes in Paris in December 1917, implying that Syria would be under the aegis of France after the war, became a pretext for the Syrian officers in Aqaba not to submit to the authority of Faysal, reasoning that they should then establish ties with France. Several of them even turned to Georges Picot, who was then in Cairo, and proposed to him that a society of officers be established which would operate in coordination with France. Apparently it was penchants of this kind that prompted Faysal to say at the time to the Syrian activist Haqqi al-'Azm that he should remember that it was the Hijazis of the Arabian Peninsula who had opened the revolt against the Ottomans. But not only the Syrians caused trouble for Faysal. In July 1918 a young bedouin killed one of Nuri al-Sa'id's soldiers. Al-Sa'id then organized a firing squad made up of friends of the slain man in order to execute the bedouin. A number of bedouin sheikhs immediately offered to substitute monetary compensation for the execution, as was customary among them. Al-Sa'id and his friends furiously rejected the offer. Faysal found himself between the frying pan and the fire — on one side the bedouin sheikhs, and on the other the Iraqi soldiers. In the end Faysal approved the execution after very heavy pressure from the soldiers.[40]

A similar situation existed in 'Ali's army. In November 1916 the Iraqi officer Hamid al-Wadi struck a Hijazi soldier who did not obey his order. In reaction 'Ali ordered al-Wadi to be put in confinement for 24 hours. The other officers, led by Sa'id al-Madfa'i and Ibrahim al-Rawi immediately announced their resignation on the grounds that 'Ali could not interfere in purely military matters and thereby cause turmoil in the army. When 'Ali heard about their decision, he became very angry, and only after Fa'iz al-Ghusayn and Lieutenant-Colonel Parker interceded was an understanding achieved between the two parties. The officers withdrew their resignation the next day. In June 1917 Major Joyce expressed himself as follows concerning the condition of 'Ali's army: "I do not consider Sherif Ali really possesses a very strong hold over these Syrian officers, and the part they take in operations is arranged more by themselves than by Sherif Ali." In 'Abdallah's army, too, there were officers, mainly Iraqis, who dictated the course of events. At first they were led by the Iraqi member of *al-'Ahd* Muhammad Hilmi, and after he was removed to Egypt (for reasons to be detailed at the end of this section), he was replaced by another member of *al-'Ahd*, 'Abd al-Latif Nuri. The latter soon quarreled with 'Abdallah and was transferred to Faysal's army. This phenomenon of officers moving from army to army, or the departure (or removal) of officers to Egypt, recurred time and again, whenever a quarrel broke out among the officers, or between them and the Hashimite princes. Apparently this was the only way to peaceably settle the internal disputes that erupted in the armies of the revolt.[41]

The relations between Husayn himself and the Syrians and Iraqis were also precarious. On one hand Husayn had to be careful not to employ too many Syrians in governmental and administrative posts in Mecca and Jidda, lest this anger the Hijazis and undermine their loyalty to him. The Hijazis saw the Syrians as invaders, who had come to the Hijaz to get all the good jobs. On the other hand, the Syrians who were employed in these towns felt isolated. They despised the Hijazi population, whom they considered retarded, and sooner or later they would leave the Hijaz and move to Egypt. Thus, for example, in October 1917 Sheikh Kamil al-Qassab and Muhibb al-Din al-Khatib left the Hijaz. Already in June 1916 al-Qassab had tangled with Husayn when he advised him to set up an organized Arab army lest he be defeated by the Ottomans. Husayn responded by asking him to confine himself to matters of education since that was his area of expertise. Al-Qassab did indeed concentrate after that on the educational affairs of the Hijaz, and even tried to reorganize it along modern lines as had been done in Syria. However, Husayn preferred that the ancient customs be retained, and eventually Kamil al-Qassab decided to retire. Muhibb al-Din al-Khatib, who was one of the editors of the rebel newspaper *al-Qibla*, later described Husayn as "a nervous, small-minded man with no capacity for objectivity and no knowledge of military matters".

The relations between Husayn and the officers were no better.

A British observer remarked about the Syrian officers that they "are not there from pure love of the Arabs, nor have they been attracted to his service from any feelings of veneration for the Grand Shereef himself . . . Their ambition is a Syria ruled by Syrians". There were officers whom Husayn simply sent away from the Hijaz. This was done with 'Aziz 'Ali al-Misri. 'Ali Jawdat al-Ayyubi was also sent away to Egypt for a while after Husayn learned of his contacts with the Ottomans in Medina. When al-Ayyubi reached Suez with several of his comrades who preferred to join him, the British authorities searched their effects, an unprecedented act, which was done according to the British by express request from Mecca. Al-Ayyubi later joined Faysal's army, following pressure on the part of the officers. Ja'far al-'Askari's joining Faysal's army, as commander-in-chief, was also much to the annoyance of Husayn, and Faysal had to accept personal responsibility for it. About Nuri al-Sa'id, Husayn said that he was busying himself in politics instead of confining himself to his duties as a soldier. Perhaps it was this state of affairs that brought the Muslim thinker Rashid Rida to suggest to Husayn that he have all the officers take an oath in writing that they would not engage in politics and would resign from all the societies in which they were members.

Husayn's aversion to the Syrians and Iraqis reached the point that when in early 1918 the idea was put forward to appoint a representative in London he announced that he refused to be represented by any Syrian or Iraqi no matter who he might be. He had confidence only in Hijazis, and he did not care even if the Hijazi chosen did not know English. In July of that year he said to the British representative in Jidda that he had no faith in any of the Iraqi or Syrian officers, and he remarked that he disliked "Syrian and Baghdadi officers on principle owing to their Turkish training".[42]

The most serious incident that occurred as a result of the soured relations that existed between Husayn and the officers happened near the end of the war, just before the army of the revolt was preparing for the great breakthrough to Syria. This incident caused the paralysis of the entire Northern Army and almost its disintegration, and also a serious rift in the relations between Husayn and Faysal.

On 18 August 1918 the British awarded a CMG decoration to Ja'far al-'Askari for his services during the war. Husayn, who already prior to this was not pleased with al-'Askari's being called commander-in-chief of the Northern Army, ordered the following announcement to be published the next day in the newspaper *al-Qibla*:

> There are those who refer to Sheikh Ja'far, one of the commanders of the Hashimite Northern Army, by the title "Commander-in-Chief", or even write this explicitly in despatches. Since this is in contradiction to the truth, inasmuch as the Hashimite Arab government has not granted such a title to anyone, nor has it at all established ranks for the commanders of its army as other governments do, and since the above-mentioned Ja'far is responsible only for administering a part of this army and no more, therefore it has been necessary to make the above announcement.

Following this official announcement from Husayn clarifications were required, and *al-Qibla* published the following complementary announcement a week later:

> Clarification from the Honourable War Ministry
> In order to avoid a lack of clarity in understanding the announcement published in *al-Qibla* No.207, that our Hashimite government has not established ranks for the commanders of the army, as other governments are accustomed to do, the intention was that our government is postponing the granting of such honours to the officers of the Arab army until after the war, since the most important mission today is the pure national mission.

Ja'far al-'Askari was in no need for clarifications. His humiliation was so great that he went into his tent and started a sit-down strike accompanied by smoking a narghileh, announcing that if his rank was not commander-in-chief, then he was not entitled to command the army. In the wake of al-'Askari's resignation the rest of the division and brigade commanders submitted their resignations, and most of the remaining officers followed them. On 29 August Faysal sent a telegram to his father in which he announced his own resignation. He pointed out that in the new situation that had been created he could no longer be responsible for the army and preferred to be considered just a simple soldier. He transferred his powers to Zayd (Husayn's youngest son, 20 years old). At this juncture chaos spread through the army. Soldiers began to refuse orders from their commanders on the ground that the latter were no longer recognized by Husayn. The rebelliousness was great particularly among the artillery men, and the Syrian officer Rasim Sardist laboured hard to prevent total anarchy among them. The frightened Zayd sent a telegram to his father informing him that all operations of the Northern Army were at a standstill, and this at a time when the enemy was only about 2,000 meters distant. He pleaded with his father to clarify the situation before there were ruinous results. To this telegram Husayn replied that his statements were already clarified in the second announcement that was published in *al-Qibla*. He again insisted that inasmuch as Ja'far al-'Askari had never been appointed by him commander-in-chief, neither officially nor semi-officially, he therefore had to deny this title to al-'Askari. Husayn added the suggestion that at the present stage al-'Askari be appointed advisor to the army, and after Ma'an was captured it would be possible to appoint him commander of the army, under the supervision of Faysal. Then it would also be possible to grant ranks to the other officers.

The British, who were seeing the Northern Army disintegrate before their very eyes, and this on the eve of General Allenby's great offensive, decided to intervene. Lawrence recommended that Husayn should apologize to Faysal and immediately appoint al-'Askari to the post of commander-in-chief. The British representative in Jidda added to this that Husayn must immediately approve the ranks of all the officers in the Northern Army, otherwise the whole Arab movement would be destroyed. On 2 September the high commissioner sent a telegram to Husayn in which he made it clear to him that he had to soon find a solution to the situation in the Northern Army. This was a crucial moment, in which the entire movement to the north stood on the border between success and failure. Therefore, in order not to endanger the Arab movement and in order to prevent the enemy from exploiting the situation, Husayn must disregard his personal reservations about al-'Askari and agree to appoint him commander of the Northern Army, under the supervision of Faysal. He also requested from him, that in order to maintain the integrity of the army, he should approve all the ranks of the officers of the Northern Army and add his good wishes for success in the missions they were about to undertake.

Apparently Husayn did not yet comprehend the seriousness of the situation. The very same day he sent a telegram to Zayd in which he characterized Faysal as a "traitor and rebel", and instructed Zayd to set up a council of three officers which would conduct the continuation of the military operations. To the British Husayn explained that the step he had taken against al-'Askari was justified since al-'Askari considered himself the supreme commander of all the armies of the revolt and not just of the Northern Army. Therefore it was necessary to clarify in *al-Qibla* that he was only one of the commanders of the Arab army. He also added that the fact that al-'Askari had pressured

for the reinstatement to the revolt army of 'Ali Jawdat al-Ayyubi
and his comrades, who were convicted of maintaining contacts
with the Ottomans, proved the justness of his attitude towards
him. And besides, "our Revolt took place before Jaafar and Nuri
and their like . . ."

Zayd, of course, was not able to cope with the task that was
assigned to him. He sent a pleading telegram to his father, in
which he defended Faysal and made it clear that Faysal was prepared to shed his blood for his country and his nation. Also, by
appointing al-'Askari commander of the Northern Army and
granting ranks to the officers, Faysal had not performed any
improper act. Zayd ended his telegram by stating that if Husayn
did not approve this, "do not hope for any further service from
your Northern Army". Immediately thereafter another telegram
arrived from the high commissioner to Husayn. He informed
him that in the light of the serious consequences that might
result from the affair, he had discussed the matter with Allenby
and their joint recommendation was that at a time of national
crisis such as this one should lay aside all personal feelings and
appoint al-'Askari commander of the Northern Army, under the
senior supervision of Faysal, of course. The high commissioner
also expressed his sorrow over the temporary lack of confidence
of Husayn in Faysal, and made it clear to him that in the
present delicate situation it would in no way be possible to forgo
Faysal. Therefore he was asking him to calm the situation by
approving all the appointments that had been decided upon by
Faysal. The telegram from the high commissioner was accompanied by a telegram from the British representative in Jidda who
asked Husayn to accede to the high commissioner's request and
to make every effort to save the situation. He also rejected
Husayn's proposal that al-'Askari be appointed commander of
the army only after the fall of Ma'an, and asked Husayn who
would lead the soldiers to take Ma'an if al-'Askari were not the
commander.

Husayn still did not understand the seriousness of the situation. In a reply telegram to the British representative in Jidda
he repeated that he was obliged to deny the title that al-'Askari
was boasting of. Husayn was astonished at the question of who
would lead the soldiers — was not Faysal the commander?! And
it was possible to appoint al-'Askari as an advisor to Faysal.
Husayn's telegram ended with the determination that as far as he
was concerned the affair was closed and there was no need to
discuss it further. The British representative gave up. He asked
Cairo to send Husayn a "very strongly worded and firm"

telegram directly from Allenby, perhaps this would break his stubbornness. On 5 September the high commissioner sent another telegram to Husayn, in which he mollified him by saying that al-'Askari had never considered himself the commander of all the Arab armies, but only as commander of the regular Northern Army. The high commissioner also stated, in his own name and in Allenby's, that if Husayn did not immediately notify Faysal of his full confidence in him and approve al-'Askari's appointment and the ranks of the other officers, then all operations of the Northern Army would be cancelled and the results with respect to the campaign for Syria would be disastrous.

This time Husayn revealed a readiness to compromise. He sent Faysal a telegram the first half of which was a sort of apology and retraction of his announcement in *al-Qibla*, but the second half repeated his old statements in new words. To Husayn's good fortune and to that of the Arab revolt in general, all the telegrams between the Northern Army and Mecca went through British channels, and in addition the British had succeeded in breaking the code used in them and read them regularly. When the character of Husayn's telegram became clear to them, Lawrence defaced the second half so that it could not be read, and the head of the British mission Joyce added a sentence to the effect that Husayn now hoped that al-'Askari would return to his post. The reworked telegram was transmitted to Faysal, who read it aloud to the officers of the Northern Army emphasizing that their honour was saved. The officers broke into shouts of joy, and the crisis was resolved.[43]

It should be pointed out that despite the positive conclusion of the crisis Ja'far al-'Askari did not participate in the great drive to Damascus, and after the war was over he was appointed to the relatively minor post of governor of Salt and remained in Transjordan. (Only in 1919 was he appointed governor of Aleppo.) One can wonder if this were not a consequence of the controversy described above, which impaired both his standing and the stability of the Arab army.

The end of the war brought a new series of problems of discipline and insubordination to the authority of the Sharifite princes. After the conquest of Damascus Sharif Zayd asked the commander of one of the forces of the Northern Army to move his men north, from Transjordan to Syria. This officer refused and even incited his soldiers to disobey the order. The result was that this force was delayed for three days, and Zayd wrote concerning this in his diary: "If everyone who violates the laws of the army is not punished, then say goodbye to this world and to independence." An even more serious situation existed in the army of 'Abdallah, which was continuing its siege of Medina (the city did not surrender until January 1919). The Iraqi and Syrian officers let it be known that they had no written contract with Husayn, and if it became clear that Iraq and Syria would not be under his sovereignty, then he had no more right to require their services. At the same time the conflict between Husayn and Ibn Sa'ud began to be reignited, and the officers found out that after Medina fell 'Abdallah would move with his army towards the Khurma oasis. Muhammad Hilmi, the Iraqi commander of 'Abdallah's army, and his senior officers, made it clear that they had volunteered for the army of the revolt in order to drive out the Ottomans. With the expulsion of the Ottomans their mission would be accomplished, and they had no intention of getting involved in the struggle of one Arab (Husayn) against another (Ibn Sa'ud). Evidently 'Abdallah understood the situation quite well, and in a conversation with a British officer he said that he intended taking only Hijazi officers with him to Khurma.[44]

Aside from Hijazis, Iraqis, and Syrians, a number of Egyptians also participated in the revolt army. Already at the beginning of the revolt the British sent two Egyptian artillery batteries to the Hijaz under the command of the Egyptian officer Sa'id 'Ali. An attempt to land the cannons at Rabigh did not go very well because of the hostile attitude of the local Arabs towards the Egyptians. The cannons were transferred to Jidda and from there Sa'id 'Ali made his way to Mecca. Soon after he arrived there Husayn complained to the British that he was "making difficulties". The British learned that Husayn had ordered Sa'id 'Ali to carry out operations that were impossible from a military point of view, and the latter refused. These incidents characterized the relations that developed from then on between the Egyptians and the other participants in the revolt. The local Arabs treated them with hostile suspicion, and the Egyptians preferred to return home at the first opportunity. Sa'id 'Ali and his men later moved to Rabigh, and Lieutenant-Colonel Parker, who visited him there in November 1916, reported that he "was sadder than usual". He told Parker that stray bullets fired by the bedouins were penetrating the tents of his men, and when the Egyptians took the trouble to prepare barriers of sandbags, the locals slipped in during the night, emptied the sacks and stole them.

One of the Egyptian officers who managed to leave the Hijaz recounted at length to the British about the hardships that his countrymen were undergoing there. He started off by saying that "Feisal himself has no notion whatever of military tactics". As a result of this lack of understanding he was giving the Egyptian artillerymen all sorts of weird orders, to move from place to place, to climb hills, to go down hills, to pack up equipment, to unpack equipment, and all for various imaginary purposes for which no benefit could be seen. The local Arabs were unwilling to extend any helping hand to the Egyptians in moving the cannons from place to place, and the Egyptians had to do all the work themselves. The Arabs even refused to supply the Egyptians with basic foodstuffs. In fact, the Arabs felt "that it would be better for Egyptian officers and soldiers to teach the Arabs to use the guns and then withdraw". The result was, of course, that the Egyptians detested their service in the Hijaz and availed themselves of any opportunity, be it of the slightest wound, to be evacuated to Egypt for medical reasons. Apparently this report by the Egyptian officer reflected reality, which was summarized by Parker simply: "The Egyptian artillery was homesick." It is interesting to note that in this harassment of the Egyptian artillerymen also a non-local participated — the Iraqi Mawlud Mukhlis, of whom Lawrence said that he "is rather a nosey sort of ass, and has upset them".[45]

'Aziz 'Ali al-Misri, the Egyptian chief of the general staff of the revolt army in its beginnings, was another who had no sympathy for the Egyptian officers, and he claimed that their camp had turned into a branch of the CUP. It is not clear on what he based his claim, but it is known that many of the Egyptian nationalists favoured the Ottoman Empire. However, al-Misri himself was eventually removed from the Hijaz, and it was the Iraqi officer Rashid al-Madf'ai and several of the Syrian officers who disclosed his plans concerning the Ottomans in Medina to Sharif 'Ali. Al-Misri's place as war minister was filled from then until the end of the war by another Egyptian officer, Mahmud al-Qaysuni. Al-Qaysuni was liked by the Syrians even less than al-Misri, and they began to demand the reinstatement of al-Misri. The situation became even more serious when al-Qaysuni issued a number of orders to the Iraqi Nuri al-Sa'id which angered him. In reaction al-Sa'id announced that he did not recognize al-Qaysuni's authority and would not obey his orders. Husayn was infuriated and ordered al-Sa'id to come immediately to Mecca where he was placed in a sort of semi-detention. At that point 'Abdallah and Faysal intervened in al-Sa'id's behalf, and Husayn agreed to transfer him to 'Abdallah's army. From there al-Sa'id moved over to Faysal's army where he served till the end of the war. Al-Qaysuni's relations with the Iraqi and Syrian officers continued to be tense, and they in fact hated him. They would submit petitions against him, and his attitude to them was reported by a British officer in 1918 as "when Northern Army Officers visit Mecca he has a habit of tearing off their badges of rank".[46]

Nuri al-Sa'id's place at the head of 'Ali's army was taken by the Libyan officer Nuri al-Kuwayri. 'Ali assigned him to restore order in his army and to restrain the Iraqi officers who were then demanding that their pay be raised by a third. Al-Kuwayri did succeed at first in removing several of the contrary officers from 'Ali's army and to install a certain measure of organization. However, after the improvement which occurred in the functioning of this army towards the end of 1917 the hatred of the Iraqi officers for al-Kuwayri increased, and they began intensive intrigues against him. In March 1918 these officers succeeded in having al-Kuwayri ousted from 'Ali's army. It became clear that 'Ali was too hesitant to impose his authority on the Iraqi officers, and his army in effect reached a state of paralysis. However, al-Kuwayri was not prepared to give in. He went to Mecca and reported to Husayn on the scandalous condition of 'Ali's army. Husayn was shocked and immediately reinstated him in his post, empowering him to take all necessary measures "without mercy" in order to improve the condition of 'Ali's army. He also asked the war minister Mahmud al-Qaysuni to accompany al-Kuwayri and to assist him in fulfilling his mission. In addition to this, five officers from the Northern Army, 12 graduates of the officers' school in Mecca, and 700 combatants were sent to 'Ali's army in order to improve its quality. In May 1918 Nuri al-Kuwayri returned to command 'Ali's army, and he removed several of the most detrimental Iraqi officers. In March 1919 al-Kuwayri left the Hijaz, despite Husayn's offer of the post of commandant of Mecca. He did not want to remain in 'Ali's army, where once again the influence of the Iraqis was increasing, and he rejected Husayn's offer also because he did not want to be under the authority of Mahmud al-Qaysuni.[47]

In connection with the attitude of the Arab rebels to the Egyptian officers who were sent to assist them, one should mention the attitude of the Egyptians in general to the Arab revolt. The outbreak of the revolt was received with surprise in Egypt, a surprise mixed with apprehensions for the beginning of foreign intervention in the holy places of Islam. The intellectuals, most of whom advocated Egyptian nationalism and were opposed to the British, reacted with hostility to the revolt. They characterized Husayn as a rebel of the realm and a tool of the British. Apparently it was people from among these circles who would follow in the streets and shout insults after the officers of the revolt army when they were on leave in Egypt. The attitude of the masses to the revolt, on the other hand, ranged from disbelief to total apathy.[48]

The last Arab element which joined the revolt were the Ruwalla tribesmen from the Syrian desert. The Ruwalla tribes numbered 5,000-6,000 tents, and their chief was Nuri al-Sha'lan, an old and cunning man, who reached his position not before liquidating two of his brothers. At the outbreak of the Arab revolt Nuri al-Sha'lan had already ruled over the Ruwalla for about 30 years, and his word had become the absolute law in the Syrian desert. Since his tribes were dependent on the markets of Damascus for supplies, and closing off these markets would have meant starving his tribes within a few months, Nuri al-Sha'lan played a double game throughout the whole war. On one hand he sent Faysal vague messages of support, and on the other he declared his allegiance to the Ottomans and even received from them considerable financial subsidies in exchange. Apparently he really hated the Ottomans, who threw him into jail in 1911 and defrauded him on a large scale in a camel-buying deal they made with him in 1914.

In early 1917 Faysal sent to him Fa'iz al-Ghusayn to persuade him to join the revolt, but Nuri al-Sha'lan evaded making any commitment. Sharif 'Ali Haydar relates that Jamal Pasha offered Nuri al-Sha'lan's son 20,000 Turkish liras for Faysal's body, and even gave him a substantial advance. Al-Sha'lan's son revealed this plan to Faysal and received from him twice as much. In June 1917 Lawrence met with Nuri al-Sha'lan and came to the conclusion that he was not prepared to take any practical step in favour of the Arab revolt. However, during this very period the authorities arrested for a while his son Fawwaz al-Sha'lan (see above, in the section on rebellious activities in the Levant during the Arab revolt), and shortly afterwards hanged in Damascus one of the tribal chiefs who supported him. Therefore, when in September 1917 Faysal sent him sharp letters demanding that he clarify his position with respect to the revolt, this time Nuri al-Sha'lan agreed to send three members of his family to Mecca carrying a message of loyalty and readiness to assist.

In March 1918 Faysal sent Nuri al-Sha'lan 25,000 pounds sterling with a concrete demand that he open a revolt against the Ottomans. He answered that he was prepared to open a revolt under three conditions: That the Druzes on Jabal al-Duruz should open a revolt simultaneously; that Faysal should sent him regular soldiers equipped with cannons; and that Husayn should not claim any sovereignty over the Ruwalla tribes. In July 1918 a quarrel broke out between the Ottoman authorities and Nawaf al-Sha'lan, and as a result he and his father informed Faysal of their readiness to cooperate immediately. A month later Nuri sent an official letter to Husayn informing him of his joining the jihad against the Turks, and in mid-September his men joined in great numbers the campaign to conquer Damascus. Concurrently all of Jabal al-Duruz under the leadership of Sultan al-Atrash revolted (the contacts which led to this rebellion were reviewed in the previous section), the Ottoman units stationed there were destroyed, and large forces of Druzes joined the drive to Damascus.[49]

The Arab revolt was assisted also by European advisors, British and French. In Jidda were the British representative Wilson (later on Bassett) and the French representative Brémond (later on Cousse). British aid was expressed in many millions of pounds Sterling and Egyptian pounds, tens of thousands of rifles, and dozens of machine-guns and cannons. French aid was more modest. The Northern Army was accompanied by a delegation of British advisors led by Major, later Lieutenant-Colonel, Joyce. (Lawrence "of Arabia" also participated in it.) Attached to it was also a French artillery battery under Captain Pisani. Many books and studies have been written about the British involvement in the Arab revolt, many of them by British officers who themselves participated in it. But there is one aspect connected to the British involvement in the revolt which has hardly been mentioned in the memoirs of these officers, but which appears at length in the documents written by these same officers while the events were occurring: the hostility of some of the Arab rebels towards the foreign officers who had come to help them.

An analysis of these documents shows that the attitude of the Arab officers to the European officers fluctuated between suspicion and hostility. It apparently arose against a religious background (Muslims versus Christians), and following the Balfour Declaration and the revelations concerning the Sykes-Picot agreement it began to have political motives, also. For the most part the hostility was pent up, but at times it burst forth in full strength. The most conspicuous example of this in Faysal's army was Mawlud Mukhlis's outburst against the British advisors during the battles for Ma'an (see the preceding section). Their military advice, which proved itself correct later on, was rejected by him on the grounds that the British had their own motives for delaying the progress of the revolt army. He organized a petition against the British and refused to obey an order given under their inspiration.

The situation in the armies of 'Ali and 'Abdallah was even worse. A British officer reported in April 1918 that all the Iraqi offidcers were exceedingly anti-British and in fact really hated them. The French representative in Jidda confirmed these tendencies. The Iraqi officer Muhammad Sa'id who was the artillery commander in 'Abdallah's army, was was considered the worst British hater. "A real bad man", who on one occasion personally insulted Lieutenant-Colonel Joyce. To balance the picture it should be mentioned that the Syrians working in the Hijaz hated the French and tried to undermine the status of the French mission in Jidda (probably against the background of their suspicions — not without foundation — concerning French ambitions in Syria).[50]

In this context of the involvement of British officers in the Arab revolt one must, of course, mention Lawrence. Instead of competing with the innumerable works written on this subject, it should suffice to quote Lawrence himself in the introductory chapter to his book *Seven Pillars of Wisdom*, an introduction which was eventually censored by Lawrence and not included in his book:

> My proper share was a minor one, but because of a fluent pen, a free speech, and a certain adroitness of brain, I took upon myself, as I describe it, a mock primacy. In reality I never had any office among the Arabs; was never in charge of the British mission with them. Wilson, Joyce, Newcombe, Dawnay, and Davenport were all over my head . . . I did my best . . . the others also did their best.[51]

The outstanding example of the negative consequences of the troubled relations among the various elements that took part in the Arab revolt was the fact that Medina managed to hold out until the end of the war. Lawrence had his own explanation for this:

> Why bother about Medina? It was no base for us, like Rabegh, no threat to the Turks like Wejh; just a blind alley for both. The Turks sat in on the defensive, immobile, eating for food the transport animals which were to have moved them to Mecca . . . They were harmless sitting there; if we took them prisoners, they would cost us food and guard in Egypt; if we drove them northward into Syria,

they would join the main Army blocking us in Sinai. On all counts they were best where they were, and they valued Medina and wanted to keep it. Let them! . . . These reasonings showed me that the idea of assaulting Medina, or even of starving it quickly into surrender was not in accord with our best strategy. We wanted the enemy to stay in Medina . . . If he showed a disposition to evacuate too soon . . . then we would have to try and restore his confidence, not harshly, but by reducing our enterprises against him.[52]

These sophisticated explanations of Lawrence, which were provided after the war (in 1920), did not reflect the complicated reality that existed during the war. The reasons for Medina's holding out till the end of the war derived not only from the remarkable tenacity of the Ottomans, but also from what was happening within the Arab army itself. Aside from the problem of the unreliability of the bedouin tribes who took part in the siege of Medina ("If a hundred of my men leave the scene of battle, all these tribes would turn their back to me", said Sharif 'Ali), the main problem was in the Arab officers who commanded the regular forces taking part in the siege. In the preceding chapter there was a detailed description of the affair of 'Aziz 'Ali al-Misri's plan to come to an understanding with the Ottoman commander of Medina and to depose Husayn with combined forces. This plan caused the failure of the Arab assault on Medina at the beginning of 1917. His partner in the contacts with the Ottomans was his fellow al-'Ahd member, the Iraqi officer 'Ali Jawdat al-Ayyubi. Al-Misri was expelled from the Hijaz after his plan was exposed, and shortly thereafter so was al-Ayyubi (though the latter was reinstated in the revolt army later on as a result of pressure by the officers).

During 1917 the siege of Medina was assigned to the armies of 'Ali and 'Abdallah. The Iraqi officers who commanded these armies demonstrated an unwillingness to engage in battle. First among them was Muhammad Hilmi, who did his best to prevent any progress and was one of the main obstacles for the plans brought by Colonel Wilson, the British representative in Jidda, for the conquest of Medina. He incited 'Abdallah not to take any initiatives, and despite the fact that 'Abdallah still continued raids on the railway, a plan for a coordinated attack by the armies of 'Ali and 'Abdallah to capture the railway north of the city was abandoned. In November 1917 Wilson left Jidda for reasons of health, and Hilmi and the other officers exploited this to increase their influence. According to a Muslim French officer attached to 'Ali's army, they not only did not want to fight, but they did not want anyone else to fight either. They even tried to incite the Muslim officers sent by the French, and asked them if they really intended to fight against their Muslim brethren the Turks. The Iraqi officer Jamil al-Rawi (chief-of-staff of 'Ali's army) went even further and would call the Ottomans killed in the battles "shuhada'" (fallen in a holy war). In one assault that was made on the railway the Iraqi officers refused to attack the Ottoman positions on the grounds that their duty was to guard Husayn and not to fight. This refusal of course caused the failure of the assault. In another assault that was made in November 1917 they stayed three to four kilometres from the centre of the battle. One Iraqi soldier even tried to desert to the Ottomans during this battle and was caught at the last moment by the bedouins. In an assault that was made in January 1918 the officers stayed 25 kilometres from the battle with the excuse that their animals were exhausted, and afterwards they were seen fleeing with their soldiers following them. The Ottomans were ready for this assault, and the British believed that they had received advance information from the Iraqi officers.

In February 1918 Muhammad Hilmi was removed from the Hijaz for several months, and this brought about an improvement in 'Abdallah's army. 'Ali's army, on the other hand, ceased all activity at Medina, both because of 'Ali's deteriorated health and because "his Syrian and Baghdadi officers are usually opposed to any proposal for action", as the British put it. In April 1918 a senior British officer attached to 'Ali's and 'Abdallah's armies reported that the Iraqi officers "will delay the fall of Medina as long as they can". Two months later he explained in another report that the Iraqi officers were acting this way because on the one hand they were pro-Ottoman, and perhaps were even being paid by the Ottoman intelligence, and on the other hand the siege of Medina was a source of income for them, a source that would be lost with the fall of the city. War Minister Mahmud al-Qaysuni confirmed this information in a report of his own and claimed that all the Iraqi officers in 'Ali's and 'Abdallah's armies were pro-Ottoman and were opposed to anything that might harm the Ottomans. Their aim was to preserve the status quo.

As for specific damage caused by the Iraqi officers, the following officers were noted: Mustafa Sa'id, (commander of the Maxim guns in 'Ali's army, "very obviously a traitor", who in an assault in May 1918 broke two Maxim guns that were in his command, and after he was ordered to shell the Ottomans with a mountain gun that he had, he broke it, too. In addition he tried to induce the British officers to come to a place which was a trap); Ibrahim [al-Rawi?], (an artillery officer who transferred from 'Ali's army to 'Abdallah's, "always intriguing", and who displayed no intention to hit the Ottomans when he was shelling them with his cannons. He, too, was accused of breaking cannons); Da'ud Sabri, (commander of artillery in 'Ali's army, who was also responsible for breaking two cannons during an assault. He and his brother Sami were suspected of selling military equipment.) In this state of affairs it was no wonder that Medina held out till the end of the war. Furthermore, even when Medina fell in January 1919, it was not because the Arab forces succeeded in taking it, but because its own officers simply decided to surrender because of the pointlessness of continuing.[53]

TURKO-ARAB PEACE PROPOSALS

A lesser-known aspect of the Arab revolt is the proposals for making a separate, Turko-Arab, peace that the Ottomans directed to the Hashimites a number of times during the last year of the war, and the varying responses of the Hashimites to them.

In November 1917 the Bolsheviks revealed in the newspaper *Izvestia* the documents of the Czarist foreign ministry, among them the exchange of letters in 1916 known as the Sykes-Picot Agreement, according to which the Arab provinces of the Ottoman Empire were divided into British and French areas of direct rule and spheres of influence. Immediately thereafter Jamal Pasha made a public speech in Beirut, in which he reported the existence of the agreement. On 26 November 1917 Jamal Pasha sent proposals for a separate Turko-Arab peace to Faysal and to Ja'far al-'Askari, and on 5 December he sent a further letter in the same spirit to 'Abdallah. He reported to the Hashimite princes on the Anglo-French agreements to divide up the Arab countries, and asked them to open peace negotiations. In addition, he reminded al-'Askari of his fighting on behalf of the Empire and against the British in Libya, and expressed his anguish that he was now fighting on behalf of the British, the occupiers of Palestine, which Saladin had defended in his time.

Faysal refused to allow Jamal Pasha's emissary to continue on to Mecca. He told him that there was no possibility of discussing a separate peace, and that the Empire should turn to the Allies in this matter. Immediately after Faysal and 'Abdallah sent on Jamal's letters to their father, Husayn ordered them to discontinue at once all contacts with Jamal Pasha and to inform him that the "sword was arbiter between them". Husayn sent on Jamal Pasha's letters to the British. A week after sending his letter to 'Abdallah Jamal Pasha left the Levant for the last time, and thus ended the first attempt to reach a Turko-Arab peace.[54]

The relative indifference of Husayn and Faysal to Jamal Pasha's statements about the Sykes-Picot agreement can be explained by these revelations not being a bolt out of the blue, despite the impression created later. Both Husayn and Faysal knew about the agreement before the Bolsheviks publicized it. In April 1917 Sykes and Picot came to Cairo, met with a group of Syrians and Lebanese, and reported to them about the principles of the agreement that concerned Syria and Lebanon. Faruqi, Husayn's representative in Cairo, immediately reported to him about the meeting and what was said in it. In May 1917 Sykes and Picot came to Jidda, and on 19 May they met with Husayn. Fu'ad al-Khatib, who was serving at the time as deputy foreign minister of the Hashimite government, was present at the meeting and gave the British a very detailed report of what was said in it. He reported that, in addition to a number of proposals made by Sykes and Picot, "no fresh information has been given the King as to the country's future except a hasty perusal and explanation (with little opportunity given him to think it over or criticise) of the Sykes-Picot agreement". According to Rashid Rida, when Sykes returned to Cairo he reported to a number of Arab activists that "Husayn agreed that the coasts of Syria should be given to France". Later Rida related that he had vehemently inveighed against Fu'ad al-Khatib for having helped Sykes persuade Husayn to accept the Sykes-Picot agreement. Al-Khatib replied that Husayn had agreed to what Sykes said and to the agreement without needing any encouragement from him. And as for Faysal, Sykes reported as follows: "On [May] the 2nd, I saw Sherif Feisul at Wejh and explained to him the principle of the Anglo-French Agreement in regard to Arab Confederation. After much argument, he accepted the principle and seemed satisfied."[55]

In February 1918 an emissary from Muhammad Jamal Pasha "the Lesser", Jamal Pahsa's replacement as commander of the Fourth Army, came to Faysal with a proposal for a Turko-Arab peace. The emissary claimed that the Ottomans were prepared to withdraw from the Arab countries. Faysal repeated the answer that was once given to Jamal Pasha that the "sword was arbiter between them", yet he pointed out that if the Ottomans would demonstrate goodwill and withdraw all their forces in the region from Medina to Amman, then he would be prepared to transmit this message to his father. Faysal reported on this to his father, and Husayn replied that the commitments of the Allies to the Arabs were the best guarantee, and that the time was not appropriate for negotiations with the Ottomans. Muhammad Jamal Pasha did not give up, and on 5 June he sent another peace proposal to Faysal. This time Faysal agreed to outline basic terms for peace negotiations, which were sent on 10 June. The terms were: All forces in Medina and in the area up to Amman shall be withdrawn to Amman; all Arab officers and enlisted men shall be transferred to Syria and joined to the Arab army; the Arab army shall be permanently under an independent command; the independence of Syria shall be comparable to that of Hungary vis-à-vis Austria; all agricultural and other products produced by Syria shall remain there and be under supervision of the Arab army; and the negotiations shall be top secret.[56]

It is not clear why Faysal consented this time to enter into negotiations. Possibly it was because of the recurrent failures of his forces to conquer Ma'an during this period. In any case, the ideas for Arab independence in the framework of the Ottoman Empire, and not outside it, did not sound so unrealistic then as it seems at first glance. It turns out that already in August 1917 the Ottoman government was looking into the possibility of giving Syria, Iraq, and the Hijaz limited autonomy. What was seen as only a passing thought in 1917 seemed more practical in 1918 when the condition of the Ottoman Empire had worsened. Even the pan-Turkish ideologue Ziya Gökalp proposed at that time that a federation of two independent states be established, a Turkish one in Anatolia and an Arab one in "Arabistan". Shakib Arslan relates that in 1918 he suggested to the German ambassador in Istanbul that after the war the Empire should be re-organized on a new basis, in which the Arab and Turkish countries would be bound to each other like Bavaria and Prussia or Hungary and Austria. The German ambassador said that he was of the same opinion and had even talked about it with Tal'at (then the Grand Vizier), who revealed a readiness to accept the idea. Several months before the end of the war Shakib Arslan, the German ambassador, and Tal'at met in Berlin, and the ambassador revealed to Arslan the contacts that had been made with Faysal. According to the ambassador, Faysal was ready to reach peace agreement on condition that the status of the Arabs in the Empire should be like that of Bavaria in Germany. The ambassador advised Tal'at to accept Faysal's terms.[57]

In early August 1918 Muhammad Jamal Pasha renewed his peace initiative. He approached Amir Sa'id al-Jaza'iri and asked him to take upon himself the task of mediating between the Empire and Faysal, in order to spare the blood of Muslims, and considering that the correspondence that had been conducted with Faysal up to then had not led to any substantive result. Al-Jaza'iri accepted the mission and informed Faysal of his desire to meet with him. Faysal replied that he had no faith in the Ottomans, but if al-Jaza'iri was interested in meeting with him then he was invited. On 11 August at night al-Jaza'iri arrived at the appointed meeting place, which was outside the headquarters of the Arab army in order to ensure the absolute secrecy of the meeting. Present at the meeting, besides Faysal and al-Jaza'iri, were Nuri al-Sa'id and Fa'iz al-Ghusayn. Al-Jaza'iri gave Faysal a letter from Muhammad Jamal Pasha, in which the latter asked him to cease his military operations and informed him of his readiness to accept the Arab demands. Faysal replied to al-Jaza'iri that the Ottomans must withdraw from the Arab countries, declare their independence, and recognize Husayn's kingship over them. The next day he gave him a letter of reply to deliver to Muhammad Jamal Pasha, in which he emphasized that he had lost all hope of reaching an agreement, and that an appeal such as this, as well as all the other appeals that he had received during the previous nine months, were a waste of time. If the Ottomans wanted to come to an understanding with the Arabs, then they had to grant the minimum that the Arabs required, and that was that their status vis-à-vis the Turks in the Empire should be like that of Bavaria vis-à-vis Germany. The Arabs wanted to be free men and would not be content with less than that. Faysal concluded his letter by saying: "I am completely prepared to enter into negotiations, if the Ottoman government accepts my proposal."

Sa'id al-Jaza'iri returned to Muhammal Jamal Pasha and gave him Faysal's letter. Muhammad Jamal Pasha immediately telegraphed to Istanbul what Faysal had said, and recommended that the Ottoman government agree to his demands. There are those who say that the Ottoman government and the sultan were inclined to agree to this. However, at this stage of the war it was too late. It is interesting to note that when Faysal reported the affair to his father, Husayn replied that there was no need at all to report to him on a matter "so unimportant".[58]

THE CAIRO AGENCY

A special chapter in the history of the Arab revolt is that of the Arab Agency in Cairo. The personality of the man who headed it in 1916-17 caused the influence of the Agency on the chain of events to exceed normal bounds and had consequences on a number of the events connected with the Arab revolt, and on the relations between Husayn and the British.

About two and a half months after he arrived in Cairo the Iraqi deserter Muhammad Sharif al-Faruqi sent a long letter to Sharif Husayn, in which he apprised him of his existence. He reported to him on his talks with the British, and at the end of his letter he asked to be allowed to come to Mecca. Husayn replied that he should stay in Cairo and continue his contacts with the British since that way he would bring the maximum benefit to the Arab cause. After a few weeks Husayn began to allocate to Faruqi 100 Egyptian pounds a month. In early June 1916, with the outbreak of the Arab revolt, Husayn agreed to Faruqi's repeated requests and allowed him to come to the Hijaz. Faruqi took part in the short siege of Jidda (his only combat participation in the Arab revolt), and then continued on to Mecca to meet with Husayn. The result of the meeting was that on 6 July 1916 he returned to Cairo bearing a letter of appointment as the official representative of Husayn in Cairo and his liaison man with the British. Thus was established the Arab agency in Cairo headed by Faruqi, who appointed as his secretary Jamil al-Rafi'i, a reckless young Syrian, who became a close partner in Faruqi's exploits during the following year. It should be noted that the British did not approve the stationing of an Arab telegraph clerk in the Cairo Agency, and Faruqi was compelled to send his telegrams to Mecca through British officials who knew Arabic. The British thus had control of the correspondence between Cairo and Mecca, and this was of consequence later on.[59]

In his new post Faruqi began a series of reports which, to put it mildly, could be called inaccurate. For example, he reported to Husayn that the Nusayris in Syria had revolted, and that "their sheikh, Sheikh Ma'ruf, I admitted to our society and swore him in when I was in Antioch". Worse yet was his report to Husayn that McMahon told him that the British government would not be sending British troops to the Hijaz because, among other reasons, it believed that the Ottoman forces there were weak and that there was nothing to fear from them. The astounded

Husayn immediately telegraphed McMahon, and the latter had to instruct his representative in Jidda to calm Husayn and smooth the difficulties.[60]

However, it seems that the worst complication in the relations between Husayn and the British was caused by Faruqi on the question of Husayn's royal title. On 10 July 1916 Faruqi sent a telegram to Husayn, in which he said that he had talked with the high commissioner on the matter of granting the title "King of the Arabs" to Husayn and found him agreeable to the idea. This telegram, like all the others that passed between Faruqi and Husayn, was intercepted by the British and deciphered before it was sent to the Hijaz. Nevertheless, they did not bother to deny it for the time being. Husayn, who already at the outbreak of the revolt had begun to debate with himself whether to take the title of "king" or "caliph", started consultations on this subject with various people who were in Mecca, among them Kamil al-Qassab, Muhibb al-Din al-Khatib, Fu'ad al-Khatib, members of the al-Bakri family, and others. Kamil al-Qassab expressed the opinion that it would not be in the interest of the Arabs if Husayn should proclaim himself caliph at that early stage of the revolt because this would incite the entire world of Islam against him. On the other hand, it would be more reasonable if Husayn were to proclaim himself king. The only one who sharply opposed these propensities of Husayn was the Muslim scholar Rashid Rida, who, during a visit to the Hijaz in October 1916 tried to dissuade Husayn from this. Obviously Rida's opinions did not make him popular with Husayn. On 29 October 1916 Husayn proclaimed himself "King of the Arab Countries" (*Malik al-Bilad al-'Arabiyya*), and 'Abdallah, in his new appointment as foreign minister, reported this to the British representative in Jidda and to the foreign ministers of France and Russia. On 4 November the coronation ceremony was held before a multitude of people, and among those pledging allegiance to him was *al-Fatat* member Sami al-Bakri as the representative of the peoples of Syria and Iraq.[61]

The announcement of Husayn's coronation was greeted coldly by the British. First of all, they were apprehensive of the reaction of the Islamic world (including the millions of Muslims in India) to this proclamation. Furthermore, they were concerned that the proclamation would impair their relations with the other Arab rulers. They also wondered if Husayn intended to include in this title also the Arabs of Egypt and Aden. The French on their part feared that Husayn would consider himself king of the Arabs of North Africa. Husayn was surprised by the chilly reaction. On 4 November he sent a telegram to Wilson, the British representative in Jidda, in which he expressed his astonishment that the British were opposed to his being called "king" when they had already addressed him by the title "caliph", which was, of course, higher than the title "king". Wilson reported this to McMahon and was asked to check with Husayn if the British had ever addressed him as "king" in any of their letters. Wilson telephoned to 'Abdallah, and the latter acknowledged that the British had indeed never sent any letter to Husayn with the title "king", nor with the title "caliph". However, in the past they had written to him: "We hope that Khalif be in your noble hold." When McMahon learned of this, he surmised that Husayn was referring to Kitchener's letter of October 1914, which included the sentence: "It may be that an Arab of true race will assume the Khalifate at Mecca or Medina." But there still remained the question why Husayn was so convinced that his title as king would be recognized by the British immediately and without problems. The answer was finally found by Wilson, who located the above-mentioned telegram from Faruqi, on 10 July, in which the latter reported that McMahon had approved of the title "King of the Arabs" for Husayn. The truth then became clear that Faruqi had reported to Husayn in this telegram on a conversation with McMahon that had never taken place. McMahon's explanations of this affair to Foreign Minister Grey are deserving of quotation in full:

[Faruqi] was in a habit — with the view doubtless of enhancing his importance — of occasionally reporting to the Sherif the purport of imaginary interviews with me and others that never took place. These came to our notice through the interception in transmission of cipher telegrams between him and the Sherif. Thus we found that on July 10th Faroki in a telegram to the Sherif said inter alia 'I have discussed with the High Commissioner regarding the title of King of the Arabs and I saw him willing to admit this idea with the greatest facility'. No such discussion ever took place. Incidentally Faroki was in Cairo and I in Alexandria . . .[62]

In Mecca, too, the matter aroused not a little confusion. On 21 November Deputy Foreign Minister Fu'ad al-Khatib sent Faruqi a telegram demanding of him to refrain from discussing with the British officials the question of Husayn's royal title until he received further instructions. He also informed him that Husayn wanted him to locate the copy of the telegram in which he reported that the British has expressed their willingness that he be called "Sultan of the Arabs". He pointed out that Husayn had expressed his astonishment at the British demurral at his coronation as king, when they had already agreed that he should receive the titles "Caliph of the Arabs" and "Sultan of the Arabs", titles that had much wider authority than the title "king". Faruqi replied in a telegram four days later in which he again quoted his telegram of 10 July about the imaginary conversation he had with McMahon, in which the latter apparently agreed that Husayn should be called "King of the Arabs".[63]

The British, in any case, had to decide how to refer to their ally who had decided to call himself "King of the Arab Countries", and in this effort they brought in the French. Wilson suggested that they call him "His Majesty the Sherif". McMahon suggested that they call him "King of the Hijaz" (and in Arabic *Malik al-Hijaz*). Wingate suggested that they call him "King of the Arabs in Hijaz". The government in India suggested that they call him "King of the Arabs in Hijaz and its dependencies". Percy Cox suggested that they call him "Sultan al-Hijaz Hamil al-Haramayn". The French government suggested calling him "Malik al-Haramayn". Finally the British government decided to accept McMahon's suggestion and to recognize Husayn only as "King of Hijaz", and on 26 December 1916 Reuter's Agency in Cairo published the following telegram: "His Britannic Majesty's Government and that of the French Republic have formally recognized His Highness the Grand Sherif of Mecca as King of the Hedjaz."[64]

Husayn was thus not recognized as "King of the Arab Countries", and this conclusion to the affair left a heavy deposit of bitterness in his heart. In addition, he began to lose confidence in his representative in Cairo. Already in September Husayn had suggested to McMahon that "in order to avoid misunderstanding", perhaps it would be better that the communication between them go through Wilson alone. Then, after the revelation of Faruqi's untruthful report about their imaginary conversation, McMahon decided to act on this suggestion, because of — as McMahon phrased it — "the undesirability and danger of some further flight of imagination of this kind". Husayn himself was angry with Faruqi not only because of his reports. He also gained the impression that Faruqi was wasting the funds being given to him. Therefore Husayn asked the British not to allow Faruqi to use his funds to buy necessities, and that anything he acquired on account of his subsidies should first receive the approval of Wilson. Moreover, when Ronald Storrs was sent to Jidda in mid-December in order to "remove any misunderstandings that exist in Sherif's mind owing to irresponsible statements by Faroki", Husayn explicitly informed him that he was "far from satisfied with the person of Faroki as his Cairo representative and wishes to appoint another, whom we [the British] are at liberty to choose, in his place".[65] In other words, at this stage Husayn had more confidence in the British than in his personal representative in Cairo. Nevertheless, in spite of it all, Faruqi remained another nine months in his position before Husayn finally decided to get rid of him.

One of Faruqi's main duties as Husayn's representative in Cairo was to recruit Arab officers and enlisted men, most of them prisoners of war, and to send them to the Hijaz to join the Arab revolt. He had to explain to these volunteers the reasons for Husayn's uprising and to persuade them to be loyal to him. Faruqi encountered difficulties in fulfilling this mission, and in a telegram sent to Husayn in late July 1916 he reported that he was left with no choice but to order the officers to sail for the Hijaz. He suggested therefore that when these officers arrived in the Hijaz they should immediately be met by persuasive religious sheikhs. As mentioned above, when this group of former prisoners of war arrived in the Hijaz in early August, most of the soldiers refused to fight against the Turks. They claimed that they were under the impression that they were being sent to the Hijaz only to stay there until the end of the war and that no one ever asked them if they were willing to fight against the Turks. There was no alternative but to send most of this group back to Suez, and Wilson, who reported on this to McMahon, wondered if this "misunderstanding" was not another one of Faruqi's deeds. In September Faruqi succeeded in persuading four Egyptian officers to serve with Husayn. However, an investigation by the British authorities revealed that two of these officers were retired, the third had resigned from the Egyptian army, and the fourth was dismissed from it. At this point Husayn had apparently despaired of Faruqi's recruits, and he informed him that he refused to accept the Egyptian officers that he had chosen. When asked by Wilson what he had against Egyptian officers, Husayn answered that what he was opposed to "are officers or anyone else selected by Faroki, but he would warmly welcome any Egyptian recommended by the Sirdar". Concurrently, Fu'ad al-Khatib sent a letter of reprimand to Faruqi for having given money to the Egyptian officers, and he asked him not to spend any more money without getting prior approval.[66]

On 8 June 1917 Faruqi again sent one of his reality-distorting reports, this time concerning the attitude of the United States towards the Arabs. He told Husayn that he had found out from a reliable source that the United States had officially expressed its opposition to the occupation of Syria by France. The reply telegram from Mecca was pathetic. Husayn wanted to inform the American representative in Cairo that he "thanks the noble American people, and that he has now learned that humanity is more perfect than he has ever imagined. His realization of the existence of such a high feeling in the world doubles his thanks to the Creator. He therefore thanks the American people for these sacred qualities . . ." Faruqi, who apparently realized that he had exaggerated a bit in his report, sent a telegram the next day in which he included several clarifications: The "reliable source" for this information was Dr. Ya'qub Sarruf, one of the owners of the newspaper al-Muqattam; the opposition of the United States was not specifically to the occupation of Syria by the French, rather it was opposed in principle to the annexation of other countries; there was a rumour here that the United States had advised all its allies of this decision; he could not ver-ify this information from an official source. The perplexed for-eign ministry in Mecca asked him that if he should somehow obtain any official information concerning American opposition, then he should inform them.[67] Faruqi, of course, could not act on this request of his foreign ministry because the United States had other worries in June 1917 than to make declarations of opposition to the occupation of Syria by France.

In the last two months of Faruqi's service as Husayn's repre-sentative in Cairo the foreign ministry in Mecca ignored him more and more, and it seems that they considered him a nui-sance. Thus, for example, Mecca did not bother to update him about the capture of Aqaba by Faysal's army in July 1917, an event that was a turning point in the Arab revolt, and Faruqi had to read about it in a newspaper. He immediately sent a pleading telegram to Mecca that they should keep him informed on what was happening. On another occasion Faruqi tried to persuade his foreign ministry to officially order all the Arab acti-vists in Cairo to refrain from discussing the policy of the Arab government in coffee houses and other public places. The answer from the foreign ministry was: "What do we have to do with Egyptian cafes and clubs? . . . It is of no importance." Faruqi insisted and sent another telegram, in which he claimed that public debates on these matters were damaging and were causing the Arab government to be looked on with contempt by the Egyptians. The response of the foreign ministry was: "We have nothing to add."[68]

Apparently, the last straw, which made Husayn decide to fire

Faruqi, was in context of Husayn's relations with the Muslim scholar Rashid Rida. Already before the war Rida had tried to persuade Husayn to accept his plan to forge an alliance among the rulers of the Arabian Peninsula. Husayn refused. In October 1916 Rida went on a pilgrimage to Mecca and offered his services to Husayn. Husayn again refused, apparently because he had reservations about Rida's anti-European tendencies. Rida returned to Egypt empty-handed, and within a short time he became hostile to Husayn (and pro-Ibn Sa'ud). As a result of a caustic article about the members of the Arab government in the Hijaz, which Rida published in his periodical *al-Manar* in early 1917, the breach between the two men became total. (A ban was even put on bringing *al-Manar* into the Hijaz.) Faruqi, together with the Syrian activist Rafiq al-'Azm, attempted to conciliate between Husayn and Rida. Husayn did not take to this very well, and in a telegram dated 24 August he informed Faruqi that he was forbidden to meet any more with Rida and that it was forbidden even to allow Rida to enter the Agency building. Faruqi replied that he accepted the prohibitions, but it seems that he continued his contacts with Rida, and Husayn therefore decided to put an end to the whole affair. In early September 1917 Faruqi was summoned to Mecca, and when he arrived there Husayn informed him of his dismissal.[69]

Fu'ad al-Khatib replaced Faruqi as Husayn's representative in Cairo. However, in the light of his past experience with both Syrians and Iraqis, and the need to maintain a balance between them in order to prevent mutual suspicion, he announced that al-Khatib's appointment was only temporary, until a suitable Hijazi could be found for this position. When such a Hijazi would be found, then al-Khatib's duty would be terminated. With the entry of al-Khatib to his new post a new secretary was also appointed — the Syrian activist (and member of both *al-'Ahd* and *al-Fatat*) Khalid al-Hakim. A year later, in September 1918, Faysal informed his father that he had learned that al-Khatib was engaging in intrigues against him. It is not clear what brought Faysal to think so, but Husayn in any case decided to summon al-Khatib to Mecca and to relieve him of his post. The British, who were very satisfied with al-Khatib's functioning as Husayn's representative in Cairo (he had also been employed in their service in Khartoum and in Cairo over a long period), tried to convince Husayn of his loyalty to him and to Faysal, but in vain. Husayn insisted that, in accordance with Faysal's request, al-Khatib's period of service be terminated. His place as Husayn's representative in Cairo was taken this time by

a Hijazi, Sharif Sharaf 'Abd al-Muhsin al-Barakati, who held
this office until June 1920.[70]

Chapter 6

SYRIANS AND LEBANESE IN EGYPT

The Syrian-Lebanese community in Egypt constituted a separate group with no connection from a political point of view with the local population, and in general was also unpopular in their eyes. The number of Syrian and Lebanese émigrés in Egypt during World War I has been estimated at 100,000, of whom 35,000 were in Cairo, and the rest in Alexandria, Tanta, Mansura, and other cities in Lower Egypt. These émigrés were educated and ambitious, and they became dominant in their new country in commerce, in the British administration, and even in the cultural life. They were generally richer than the local Egyptians. (Their total wealth has been estimated at 27 million Egyptian pounds.) They competed with local Egyptians for jobs. (For example, out of only 3,000-4,000 Syrians who lived in Sudan about 500 served in the British administration there.) They owned six of the 11 daily newspapers in Egypt in that period. They were also naturally more pro-British than the local people, and in their newspapers, (especially *al-Muqattam*) they described the British occupation as beneficial to Egypt. All this made them, as said, unpopular with the local Egyptian population in general, and with the anti-British and pro-Ottoman Egyptian nationalists in particular. The Egyptian nationalist Mustafa Kamil once called them "*dukhala*'" (foreigners), and this could characterize the feeling of the local population towards them. All this caused the many Syrians and Lebanese living in Egypt to be interested from a political point of view more in the fate of Syria and Mount Lebanon than in the fate of Egypt, the country which in certain cases they had been living in for many years. For this purpose they established various parties and societies, such as the Alliance Libanaise of Cairo and the Decentralization Party.

THE SYRIANS IN CAIRO

After the demise of the contacts between the Decentralization Party and the British in mid-1915, which resulted from the avoidance by the latter in giving concrete commitments concerning the fate of Syria, the leaders of the party and other Syrian notables met for a series of discussions about the future of Syria. The participants reached the conclusion that the Ottoman Empire would lose the war and that Syria would be occupied by the Allies. As for the desirable future for Syria after the war the discussions produced three principal possibilities: (a) Syria would be annexed by one of the European powers and would become part of it. This possibility was rejected by the conferees on the ground that annexation of the small Syrian nation to a larger one would bring about its assimilation and disappearance. (b) Syria would have administrative autonomy under the aegis of one of the powers. This power would appoint a governor-general, advisors and inspectors, but the rest of the office holders would be local people. The defence of Syria would be placed in the hands of this power, but a local gendarmerie and police force would be set up. (c) Syria would receive absolute independence within its historic borders and guaranteed by the powers. It would be headed by a prince. It would have a government half of whose ministers would be Muslim and half Christian, who would be elected from among its own parliament members. The prince and the government would appoint European advisors and inspectors to assist in the administration of the country. The seat of government would be either in Damascus or in Beirut. A parliament would be established, whose term of office would be nine years, and every three years one third of its members would stand for re-election. A third of the members of parliament would be chosen in general elections, a third would be appointed by the government, and a third by the administrative councils of the vilayets of Syria. Syria would be divided into four vilayets: the vilayet of Lebanon, the vilayet of Damascus, the vilayet of Aleppo, and the vilayet of Palestine. The governor of each vilayet would be appointed from the majority community in it, and his deputy from one of the other communities. If the governor be Muslim, his deputy would be Christian, and vice versa. Each vilayet would have an administrative council whose members would be chosen proportionally to its religious communities, preserving the rights of the minorities. This council would deal with the internal affairs of the vilayet.

It is noteworthy that from among the Muslims who participated in these discussions there was a minority who would not be satified even with the third possibility (and certainly sharply rejected the first two possibilities.) At their head stood the Muslim scholar Rashid Rida. He succeeded, though, in persuading the participants to add an amendment to their program concerning independent Syria, and that was that the prince of Syria must be a Muslim from one of the eminent families in Islam. However, he was not able to persuade those present to adopt his greater plan, to unite Syria with the Hijaz and Yemen, and thus to establish a new Arab empire, whose ruler would also be the caliph of the world of Islam.[1]

Staying in Cairo during this period was Mark Sykes, who interviewed several of the more prominent Syrian and Lebanese personages who were living in Egypt. Sa'id Shuqayr expressed his opposition to the annexation of Syria by France, an act that was liable to cause a confrontation between the Muslim and Christian Syrians (he himself was a Christian). Faris Nimr, one of the owners of the newspaper *al-Muqattam*, also expressed his opposition to annexation of Syria by France or to separation of Palestine from it. However, he added that in his opinion an independent Syria did not have a chance to maintain itself for even one day. A different opinion was of course given by Rashid Rida, who tried to convince Sykes of the need to establish an independent Arab state that would include the Arabian peninsula, Syria, and Iraq. Rida even threatened that if Britain should act against the will of the Muslims it would face the constant danger of a pact between them and Germany. These opinions earned for him the characterization by Sykes as "a hard, uncompromising, fanatical Moslem", the likes of which "it is impossible to come to understanding", and therefore "force is the only argument that they can understand". The British officer Wyndham Deedes, who was in Cairo at that time, reached the same conclusions from his conversations with Syrian activists, most of whom first and foremost were opposed to France having any foothold at all in Syria. The Syrian Muslims were prepared to prefer even the Turks over France, and the reason for this attitude was the behaviour of France in countries where it was the ruler, such as Tunisia. Even the Syrian Christians, except for the Maronites, were not interested in being ruled by France.[2]

In this context of the opinions of the Syrians regarding the future of the Arab countries after the war it is worth mentioning briefly the opinions of Habib Lutf Allah, a bizarre personality from the wealthy Lutf Allah family, which had been living in Egypt for a long time and several of whose members were later on among the founders of the "Syrian Union Party". Just before the war he was permitted to move to Syria from Egypt, but about a year later, after the Ottomans issued a death sentence in absentia against his brother Michel, he fled to Switzerland. In

Switzerland he met with the former Khedive of Egypt, 'Abbas Hilmi, and proposed to him "in the name of the Arab Congress of the Syrian Countries" to be president of Syria. After that he went to London, where he suggested to Kitchener to open an Egyptian-Arab revolt against the Ottomans, under the leadership of 'Abbas Hilmi and Husayn. The British in Egypt responded to this that Lutf Allah "is a weak vain type of Syrian with no bottom full of schemes". However, he did not give up and suggested to Foreign Minister Grey to establish a British protectorate in Syria, Cilicia, and Palestine, with a Christian prince, and an Arab monarchy in Baghdad headed by 'Abbas Hilmi, under British aegis. At the end of 1915 he returned to Egypt where he told everybody who was interested that the British foreign minister had approved his programs. He also asked to meet with the sultan of Egypt as the representative of 'Abbas Hilmi, but the sultan rejected him angrily and even worked to expel him from Egypt. In late January 1916 McMahon ordered him to leave Egypt within 48 hours, with a warning that his personal future and that of his property in Egypt were dependent on his behaving properly in the future. Habib Lutf Allah deposited with him a letter in which he committed himself to abstain from political activity. However, a month after his expulsion from Egypt he was already in Madrid and proposing to the British ambassador there as follows: (a) 'Abbas Hilmi will officially recognize the sultan of Egypt. (b) 'Abbas Hilmi's son shall be recognized as the crown prince of the son of the sultan of Egypt. (c) The vilayets of Aleppo, Beirut, Damascus, Mosul, Baghdad, and Basra, and the sanjaqs of Mount Lebanon and Jerusalem shall become a confederation under the presidency of 'Abbas Hilmi. (d) Husayn, the ruler of the Hijaz, shall be recognized as caliph. (e) In Yemen a separate state shall be set up under the rule of al-Idrisi and Imam Yahya. (f) An Anglo-Egyptian force under the command of 'Abbas Hilmi shall attack Baghdad, concurrently with an additional force that shall attack Syria from the direction of Egypt. The Foreign Office in London instructed its ambassador in Madrid to completely ignore this "quite irresponsible" man. Habib Lutf Allah remained in Spain until the end of the war and continued to send letters in this spirit to the British Foreign Office. His letters were filed in the archives as soon as they were received.[3]

If in 1915 and the first half of 1916 the idea for establishing one large Arab state, in which Syria would be included, was confined to a the Muslim ideologues of the type of Rashid Rida, the outbreak of the Arab revolt changed the picture among the

Syrians and Lebanese in Cairo, and the idea began to amass supporters. Contributing to the spread of this idea were Syrians who held various posts in the Arab administration in the Hijaz, and who from time to time came to Cairo on leave. In early January 1917 several of them organized a conference in Cairo, in which the heads of the Alliance Libanaise society participated as well as Faruqi and Ja'far al-'Askari. The conclusions of the conference were that Syria must be under the sovereignty of Husayn, though it would have autonomy and could administer its internal affairs separately from the Hijaz. Iskandar 'Ammun, the president of the Alliance Libanaise who was present at the meeting, joined in this decision in the name of the Lebanese, on the assumption that Mount Lebanon would gain in the framework of this state the privileges that it had before the war, and that its boundaries would be expanded, as the Lebanese had been demanding for a long time.[4]

In February 1917 Rafiq al-'Azm, the past president of the Decentralization Party, wrote a long letter to Sharif Husayn. He explained in his letter that in order to unite the scattered people of the Arab nation one must establish unity among the Arab amirs. This could be done only by assuring the amirs that their rights and authority in the countries they rule would be maintained even in the framework of the new Arab empire that would arise. If Husayn would agree to make a guarantee in this spirit to the rulers of the Arabian Peninsula, they would agree to unite with him, and it would then be possible to establish an Arab union on the pattern of the German states or the United States of America. The status of Husayn would then be majestic like that of the German Kaiser (and as in Germany, the fact that the king of Bavaria ruled in his own country did not impair the authority of the Kaiser, so also the internal rule of the Arab amirs would not impair the status of Husayn). On the other hand, if Husayn did not succeed in achieving unity with the other rulers of the Arabian Peninsula, then the Ottomans would engage in intrigues as was their wont, and eventually they would persuade these rulers to declare war on Husayn. A situation such as this could be exploited in the future by a foreign power, a colonialist one, which would dominate the country. This outcome could be prevented only by Arab unity, under a supreme central government. Only thus would it be possible to establish an Arab empire on solid foundations.

Three weeks later Husayn sent his answer to Rafiq al-'Azm's proposal. He congratulated him on the high intelligence which he demonstrated in his letter and on his loyalty to the Arab movement. But as for his concrete proposal, Husayn replied by listing a long series of historical events that occurred between him and his neighbours, the various amirs of the Arabian Peninsula, and during which his conduct testified to his good intentions towards them. Their behavious towards him, on the other hand, was "what they call nowadays 'diplomacy'". He recalled to al-'Azm that when he was crowned king Syrian representatives were also present, and recognized him as king in the name of their countrymen from Syria and Iraq (he was referring to Sami al-Bakri's speech at the coronation ceremony), and pointed out that he had started the revolt in full knowledge that he had no supporters except Allah "and those who promised to remain faithful to us". Husayn ended his letter with an expression of hope that Rafiq al-'Azm would continue to provide him with his valuable advice. In mid-April 1917 he invited al-'Azm to come to Mecca for consultations "on important matters". Al-'Azm replied that he could not go for reasons of health, and it is not clear if it was his poor health that caused him to send this answer or perhaps his disappointment at Husayn's earlier lack of cooperation.[5]

In mid-1917 voices began to be heard again with misgivings about the wisdom of including Syria in a greater Arab state in which the Hijaz would be dominant. These voices were heard mainly among Christians such as Faris Nimr and Sa'id Shuqayr, or George Lutf Allah who explicitly told Faruqi that he had no faith in the Arab revolt. At the same time also Rafiq al-'Azm sent a telegram to the French parliament, which he signed with the title President of the Decentralization Party. The foreign ministry in Mecca understood correctly that the purport of this title was that Rafiq al-'Azm still adhered to the idea of decentralization, namely "local independence without Syria being conjoined to the Arab government, and we are sorry [about this]". Faruqi hastened to calm his foreign ministry that the idea of the Decentralization Party was not relevant to the current time, and that al-'Azm remained "the most loyal to the movement and to Arab unity". Faruqi also promised to work for a change in the platform of the party (which in fact no longer existed) and to accommodate it to the idea of Arab unity.

In late June Faruqi met with a group of Syrian activists which included the former leaders of the Decentralization Party, the leaders of the Alliance Libanaise, and other activists, and he explained to them Husayn's policy regarding Syria. He told them that Husayn was striving for Arab unity, though he is cognizant of the fact that Mount Lebanon had a special status and therefore it would remain completely independent in the future Arab state, and only in the political, security, and economic spheres would it be connected to the Arab government. According to Faruqi, the Lebanese who were present at the meeting expressed their satisfaction with this arrangement. Faruqi then appealed to those present with a request that they abandon the names of their old parties and unite in the establishment of a new society which would work to free their country. A debate then began among those present as to the ways in which they could act on behalf of Syria. Apparently Faruqi was not allowed to enter the discussion on the future of Syria, and certainly not to speak in Husayn's name. Nor did the views heard during the above debate please the ears of the foreign ministry in Mecca, and Faruqi received strict instructions to leave the issues of Syria alone.[6]

The Syrians in Cairo, Decentralization Party members and others, were involved during the war in propaganda activities on behalf of the British. Already mentioned in a preceding chapter were two pairs of propagandists who were sent by the Decentralization Party to Syria and Iraq at the beginning of the war. These missions ended in failure, but Sheikh Muhammad al-Qalqili, one of the propagandists sent to Syria, continued his contacts with the British for a long time and assisted them in the propaganda effort against the Ottomans. In July 1915 he wrote a propaganda pamphlet in which he called for the establishment of an independent Arab state in Syria under British aegis. The pamphlet was dropped through Syria by plane. In the pamphlet he compared the poor condition of the Syrians with the improved condition, according to him, of the Egyptians under British rule. He attacked the Ottoman Empire and claimed that it was not defending the religion of Islam but was pursuing Muslims and giving in to Germany, which wanted to dominate the world of Islam. The pamphlet included a sort of dialogue between a Syrian sheikh and a pro-Ottoman Egyptian youth. The sheikh demonstrated to the young Egyptian the crimes of the Ottoman authorities in Syria, and at the conclusion of the dialogue the young Egyptian "was convinced" that he must abandon his support of the Empire, admitting that the current regime in Egypt was better than what any man could wish for himself. Muhammad al-Qalqili thus worked into this pamphlet, doubtlessly under British influence, both anti-Ottoman propaganda and propaganda against the pro-Ottoman Egyptian nationalists.

In August 1916 al-Qalqili began to publish a propaganda

newspaper by the name of *al-Kawkab*, of which he was the director but his instructions were received from Gerald Brackenbury of the Office of Public Instruction, and the newspaper's policy was coordinated with the Arab Bureau through Philip Graves. The editor-in-chief was the Syrian activist 'Abd al-Rahman al-Shahbandar, who was also a former member of the Decentralzation Party. At first the origin of the newspaper was to be kept secret and it was to be distributed clandestinely in Syria, but the great demand that it won among the Syrians in Egypt itself brought about its unrestricted distribution in about 1,000 copies from Algeria to the Persian Gulf. The newspaper would appear every Tuesday, and among its writers were prominent personalities such as Rafiq al-'Azm. It supported the Arab revolt, worked for strengthening the ties between the Arabs and Britain, and propagandized against the misdeeds of the Ottoman authorities in Syria and Iraq.

Besides *al-Kawkab*, there would arrive from London a propaganda newspaper in Arabic called *Haqiqat*, and in addition Faris Nimr would accept willingly any propaganda suggestion by the British and publish it in his newpaper *al-Muqattam*. In late 1916 the Syrian activists got together, with British assistance, for an exceptional propaganda effort. They published in the printing house of *al-Muqattam*, in 500 copies, a 250-page book on "The Arab Revolt: Its Origins, Reasons, and Results" (*Thawrat al-'Arab: Muqaddimatuha, Asbabuha, Nata'ijuha*). The book was written anonymously by As'ad Daghir, who was also a former member of the Decentralization Party, and who was employed at the time as an assistant editor of *al-Muqattam*. The book covered the history of the overt Arab societies that operated in the Ottoman Empire before the war, and detailed the wrongs done to the Arabs by the Turks before and during the war. It included as well the manifesto that Husayn disseminated at the outbreak of the revolt. The book was distributed in the Hijaz, Iraq, Sudan, and Tangier, and, at least according to the British, it had quite an effective influence.[7]

During 1917 the Syrians and Lebanese in Cairo were constrained to begin to relate to the agreements and declarations that were signed or made by the British concerning the division of the Arab provinces of the Ottoman Empire, and at least in Arab eyes they were perceived as either partially or completely contradicting the commitments given by the British to Husayn about the independence of the Arab countries. In April 1917 Sykes and Picot arrived in Cairo on their way to the Hijaz for the purpose of explaining to Husayn the Sykes-Picot agreement.

Before they left for Jidda the two met together with Syrian representatives, and at least according to Sykes they reached an understanding with the Syrians on the establishment of a state or autonomous Arab confederation in the area parallel to areas A and B of the Sykes-Picot agreement, and which would be assisted by Britain and France in defence matters and would grant these two powers a monopoly in its territory in economic and financial matters. It was made clear to them that it was decided to give the entire Syrian coast ("the blue area") to France, and, according to Sykes, agreement was reached that Palestine would not be included in the new state. After this meeting Sykes by himself met privately with the Syrian representatives and discussed the future of Baghdad with them. In contrast to the optimistic reports by Sykes on these meetings, 'Abd al-Rahman al-Shahbandar claimed that he and Rafiq al-'Azm were among those who met with Sykes and that there conversation with him was difficult.

Picot, too, arranged a separate meeting with the Syrian and Lebanese activists in the Shepheard's Hotel, and reported to them that the Allies had already made a decision concerning Syria and Lebanon. These regions would be under French aegis, with Lebanon under direct French rule, and the regime in internal Syria would be "consultative". He noted that his title was already High Commissioner of Syria. Faruqi reported to Husayn about this meeting and noted that some of those present at it were pleased with Picot's statements while others criticized him severely. One of the results of Picot's meeting with the Syrians and Lebanese was the boost in morale among the supporters of France among them, who since the outbreak of the Arab revolt under British sponsorship had been keeping a low profile. In June 1917 they set up with the encouragement of the French representation in Cairo the "Society for the Defence of the Rights of Syria and Lebanon". Heading the society was the Lebanese Christian 'Abdallah Sufayr Pasha, and most of its other members were also Christian, though not all of them. The society strove to put Syria, including Palestine and Lebanon, under French aegis or mandate. The new state would have an independent internal administration, while Lebanon, in its expanded borders including Tripoli, Tyre, Sidon, and the Biqa', would obtain its own independent administration.[8]

The second event that required a Syrian response during 1917 was the Balfour Declaration concerning the establishment of a Jewish national home in Palestine. As soon as the declaration became known in Cairo Fawzi al-Bakri and Sulayman Nasif (a

Lebanese Christian lawyer) went to the Arab Bureau bearing a telegram signed by them and by Rafiq al-'Azm and Faris Nimr in which they declared to Balfour that Palestine was an inseparable part of Syria. The two representatives also demanded from the British that the Syrians should have the same rights in Palestine as the Jews, in all fields. The British promised first to send on their telegram to London, but after they kept it for almost a month they informed the Syrians that their telegram could not be sent at that time, and they also recommended to them to desist from that path of protest. In mid-December a delegation of Syrian Muslims left Cairo for Aqaba, headed by Haqqi al-'Azm, to persuade Faysal to protest against the policy of Britain on the Zionist question. (Haqqi al-'Azm had additional reasons for his trip to Aqaba, which will be explained below.) Faysal indeed expressed his misgivings about the Balfour Declaration, but he refused to protest against it to the British. Haqqi al-'Azm tried to convince him that in his position as one of the Arab leaders he was obligated to protest, and certainly was his father the "King of the Arab Nation" obligated to protest against it. Faysal stood by his refusal. An attempt by the Syrians to appeal to Husayn himself, through his representative in Cairo, had the same result, with Husayn stressing that he was well aware of the British plans for the Jews in Palestine. The attitude of Faysal and Husayn on the subject of the Balfour Declaration caused a feeling among the Syrians in Cairo that Husayn was totally under British control and that he had even committed himself to them not to interfere in their policy in Palestine.[9]

In the meantime Mark Sykes was in London trying to begin steps to reach an Arab-Armenian-Jewish understanding. Beginning to profess the realization of the aspirations of these three peoples for freedom, he set up a combined committee which included Syrian representatives (among them al-Fatat member 'Abidin al-Hushaymi), Armenians, and Zionists (Weizmann). In mid-November 1917 he sent to several of the Syrian leaders in Cairo, who had gotten together at that time in the "Syria Welfare Committee", a letter in which he proposed to them that in the interests of liberating their country they must cooperate with the Armenians and the Jews. He stressed in his letter that all that the Zionists wanted was to be given the right to settle in Palestine and to conduct their national life there. On his request Clayton also joined in the attempts to convince the Syrians in Cairo of the benefit that would accrue from their joining the Arab-Armenian-Zionist triumvirate that Sykes was planning. The men of the above-mentioned Syrian society, led by

Sulayman Nasif, discussed the matter and reached the conclusion "that their best and only policy was to co-operate with the Jews on the lines suggested". They informed Clayton that out of their awareness of the strength and status of the Jews they were then interested in disseminating propaganda in Palestine on behalf of Syrian-Jewish brotherhood. This could be accomplished by sending a delegation of members of the society to Palestine. Along with this they began contacts with representatives of the Zionist movement in Cairo. In January 1918 members of the society, among them Sulayman Nasif, Rafiq and Haqqi al-'Azm, Fawzi al-Bakri, and Faris Nimr, sent a letter of reply to Mark Sykes in which they informed him that from his letter to them they understood that all that the Zionists wanted was to settle in the country and to benefit from the same rights and the same obligations as the local inhabitants. Therefore they accepted with sympathy his proposals for Arab-Armenian-Zionist cooperation, and were ready on their part to send a delegation to Palestine to preach in this spirit. Sykes answered their letter in mid-February, informing them in the name of the London Syrian-Armenian-Zionist committee of the impending arrival in Egypt of a Zionist delegation headed by Weizmann.[10]

Nothing came of Sykes' Syrian-Armenian-Zionist committee plan. Contributing to its demise was also Husayn's refusal to send a representative to this committee on the grounds that he was the sole spokesman for the Arab nation. Nevertheless the contacts between the Zionists and Syrians in Cairo continued. In March 1918 the Zionist delegation headed by Weizmann arrived in Egypt, and on the 27th of the month it met with the representatives of the Syrian society, Sulayman Nasif, Faris Nimr, and Sa'id Shuqayr. Prior to the meeting Nasif had compiled a list of demands, the principal ones of which were: (a) The Arabs should have equal rights in the government of Palestine. (b) Arabic should be the official language. (c) Until the end of the war no sale of lands should be permitted. When these points were raised at the meeting, Weizmann agreed to them, and even added that he had personally requested of Balfour that until the end of the war purchase and sale of lands in Palestine should not be permitted. Weizmann emphasized that the Zionists had no intention of setting up a Jewish government in Palestine, and that they regarded the place as a refuge that would be a national and intellectual home for them. Weizmann also spoke of the economic welfare and development that the Zionists movement would bring to Palestine, from which the Muslim and Christian inhabitants would also benefit. The Syrian representatives who participated in the meeting were quite satisfied with Weizmann's clarifications and even promised to send a calming letter to the Arabs of Palestine.

In early April the Zionist delegation continued on to Palestine. There it was received with hostility by the local Arabs, whose suspicions concerning the intentions of the Zionists with regard to Palestine were only strengthened by its visit. In early May the British permitted the Syrian society to carry out its plan to send a delegation to Palestine in order to calm the fears of the population about the Zionist plans. The delegation included Rafiq al-'Azm, Sulayman Nasif, and Mukhtar al-Sulh, and it was decided to define it as private visit and not as an official delegation under British sponsorship or on behalf of the Syrian society. The delegation spent about two weeks in Palestine, during which it visited Jerusalem and Jaffa. In these two cities the delegation encountered very hostile feelings towards the Zionists, and its explanations that there was nothing to fear from the Zionists since they did not intend to set up a Jewish government in Palestine and since steps had been taken to prevent Jews from buying land in Palestine did not help. The local Arabs saw the delegation as an official mission that had come to deal with their problems, and they began to pour out their troubles. Rafiq al-'Azm promised that the delegation would assist them as best as it could, and indeed when the delegation returned to Cairo it suggested a number of measures to reduce the feelings of distress of the Arabs of Palestine, also on the economic plane. In any case, in its principal objective of calming the Arabs of Palestine with regard to the Zionist plans it failed, and with this ended the episode of the attempt to bring the Syrian society and the Zionists closer.[11]

In the first half of 1918 the particularistic tendencies among the Syrian activists in Cairo began to increase, tendencies which later resulted in the establishment of Syrian parties such as the "Syrian Unity Party", and contributed at least indirectly to the issuance of the "Declaration to the Seven". Already in late 1917 it began to become clear that it was precisely the "team-work"of the Syrians and Hijazis following the establishment of the Hashimite government in the Hijaz which had caused constantly growing qualms on the part of the Syrians about the idea that after the war they would be ruled by Husayn. Clayton expressed himself on this phenomenon as follows: "There is no doubt a very real fear amongst Syrians of finding themselves under a Government in which patriarchalism of Mecca is predominant. They realize that reactionary principles from which Sherif of

Mecca cannot break loose are incompatible with progress on modern lines. Increased touch between Syrian intellectuals both Christians and Moslems and Mecca accentuates rather than diminishes this feeling."

In other words, the enthusiasm of the Syrians for Husayn began to fade, and there began to be heard among them voices against their being ruled by a "religious fanatic" such as he. Those who felt this way shuddered at the very thought that "the undisciplined riffraff of the king's army would enter Damascus". Some of these people were prepared to recognize Faysal as the ruler of Syria, but only if he would recognize on his part the unity of the Syrians and the need to develop Syria according to modern methods and under European patronage. Syria, according to their conception, had to be independent, without being united with any other Arab country, or at least autonomous. The autonomists among them emphasized more than the others the need for protection by the powers, and individuals among them — Christians — even wanted Syria to be annexed to France. In April 1918 the American representative in Cairo divided the Syrian Muslims there into three trends: The Syrians who were loyal to Husayn, and who wanted him to rule over Syria as the sultan of a new Arab empire which would include besides Syria the Arabian Peninsula and Iraq as well; the Syrians who were interested in having Faysal ruling over an independent Syrian principality, or at least over a Syrian autonomy within an Arab confederation; and the Syrians who wanted Syria to be semi-independent under the guidance and assistance of a European power, though with Faysal as its constitutional prince, but without any connection to the Hijaz.[12]

The Syrian society which was active in Cairo in late 1917 and early 1918 then broke up, after its members could not reach agreement as to the desirable future government for Syria after the war, and this because of the opposition of Rafiq al-'Azm and Fawzi al-Bakri to the pro-European supervision leanings of the other members. Faris Nimr, one of the other members, then began to develop pro-American leanings, after he came to the conclusion that Britain would not take upon itself the control of Syria. He rejected outright the possibility of a French protectorate over Syria, and he claimed that even the Maronites were no longer interested in French protection. This idea of an American aegis over Syria formed one of the basic lines of the "Moderate Syrian Party", which was established after the war, and it gained many supporters during the visit to Syria of the King-Crane commission. Faris Nimr was also opposed to the possibility of

Husayn being king of Syria, and in a conversation with the British he told them of the apprehensions of the Syrians that British aid to Husayn and his declaring himself king meant that the British would help him to become king of all the Arab countries including Syria. He explained to the British that the Syrians were indeed prepared for Faysal to be the consitutional ruler of Syria, but under no circumstances as the representative of his father. Nimr also rejected an appeal of pro-Hashimite Syrian Muslims that he join the supporters of the idea of establishing a new Arab empire which would include the Arabian Peninsula, Syria, and Iraq. He told them that the idea was unrealistic and that it would be better for them to concentrate on obtaining independence for Syria. They offered him financial support for his newspaper *al-Muqattam* if he would propagandize in the spirit of their views, and Nimr answered that he was prepared to spend 5,000 Egyptian pounds from his own pocket for propaganda in favour of the independence of Syria under American protection.[13]

Haqqi al-'Azm, another member of the above-mentioned Syrian society, became at this time one of the enthusiastic supporters of France among the Muslim Syrians. Already noted above was his participation in the delegation of Syrian Muslims that went to Aqaba in mid-December 1917 to persuade Faysal to protest against the Balfour Declaration. Haqqi al-'Azm had additional reasons for going to Aqaba. He tried to convince Faysal that the Syrians would never agree to accept as their ruler the king of the Hijaz because it was unacceptable that a rich and cultured country such as Syria should be ruled by the Hijaz. The Syrians would indeed be prepared to accept Faysal as the governor of Syria, but only on condition that he realized that Syria needed the patronage of a foreign nation, and that this nation could only be France. To this Faysal replied: "And as for me, I would go to war against France, for the sake of Syria." In this state of affairs it is quite clear why Faysal rejected Haqqi al-'Azm's offer to serve as his private secretary, and al-'Azm returned to Cairo empty-handed.

Haqqi al-'Azm then began to attack sharply the idea of establishing the great Arab state. He explained the lack of reality in achieving this idea: Iraq had already been occupied by the British after suffering heavy casualties, and they would not relinquish it in favour of the Arab state; the independent rulers of the Arabian Peninsula, such as Ibn Sa'ud and Ibn Rashid, would not agree to be included in this state; it had already been decided by the Allies that Palestine would be an international area and that a Jewish national home would be set up in it; and above all, the fanatical and backward Hijaz, "which is only a little bit different from the condition it was in during the time of Adam and Eve", was not capable of ruling the more progressive Syria. And as for the future Syria, al-'Azm outlined the following program: (1) A Greater Syria should be established (whose northern border would be southern Anatolia, the eastern border - Iraq, the southern border - northern Hijaz to Aqaba, the western border - Palestine, if indeed it should be under international administration). (2) Syria should be divided into five cantons (or six if it included also Palestine): Lebanon in its expanded borders (including Beirut, Tripoli, Sidon, and the Biqa'), Damascus (including the Syrian desert, Hama, Homs, Jabal al-Duruz, Transjordan, Nablus, Acre, and Haifa), Aleppo (including Latakia, Antioch, and Alexandretta), Dayr al-Zur, and Mardin. (3) The cantons would be united on the Swiss pattern or that of the United States. (4) The chief-of-state would be an amir who was not a Syrian, and who would be chosen the first time by the Allies, after which his eldest son would inherit his place. The amir would be subject to the constitution. (5) The government of Syria would be democratic and secular. It would be assisted by authoritative foreign advisors with for a period of at least 15 years, until the state became accustomed to a democratic regime. (6) Each canton would have an elected council with the right to make laws. The council would choose the governor of the canton from among its residents. (7) Syria would have a general council, in which representatives of all the cantons would participate, and which would deal with the general affairs of the country. (8) The union of the cantons would be expressed in four areas only: foreign affairs, defence, customs duties, and finances. Each canton would pay an annual sum to the capital for defence expenses. (9) Office holders in the cantons would be appointed by the local governors. (10) The official language of Syria would be Arabic.

This program of Haqqi al-'Azm, which was published in various Arab newspapers, evoked criticism in Meccan circles. He responded to this criticism with a strong press campaign against Husayn and his ambitions concerning Syria. He published an article with the headline "The Lebanese and almost all Christian Syrians are afraid of a king whose authority is based on religion and who will establish a theocratic government; many Muslims concur". In the body of the article he wrote: "The King of the Hijaz, who owes his authority to the religion . . . cannot be but a religious sovereign, and adopt a policy that is perhaps beneficial in the Hijaz, but would harm Syria and sooner or later bring about a civil war . . . And besides, there is no political, economic, or cultural connection between the Hijaz and Syria."[14]

THE DECLARATION TO THE SEVEN AND ITS ORIGINS

After the dissolution of the above-mentioned Syrian society a new group of activists began to form in Cairo, which included Kamil al-Qassab, 'Abd al-Rahman al-Shahbandar, Rafiq al-'Azm, Rashid Rida, Khalid al-Hakim, and others, and which formed the basis for establishing later on the "Syrian Union Party". The basis for their cooperative activity was the constantly increasing dissatisfaction with Husayn who was, in their opinion, a stubborn man inconsiderate of the opinion of others. They also feared that Husayn would agree to the partition of Iraq and Syria between Britain and France in order to assure his personal position in the Hijaz. They decided therefore that they had to act on behalf of Syria independently and without relying on Husayn.

A short time after the new party was organized, Kamil al-Qassab was summoned to the Arab Bureau where he went together with 'Abd al-Rahman al-Shahbandar and Khalid al-Hakim. When they arrived there, they were received by Clayton and Osmond Warlond, an official of the Bureau who was considered an expert on the Arab societies. Clayton spoke to them sternly and warned them not to do anything which would harm British interests of those of their allies, and Warlond added a personal warning to al-Qassab that if it should become necessary the British would not hesitate to exile him to some distant island. Al-Qassab replied that the Arabs wanted only to protect their rights and he protested the tone in which he was being addressed, which was unbecoming for a conversation between allies. Clayton answered that he had had no intention at all of threatening him, and in fact he wanted to reach an understanding with them and explain to them the importance of working together for the common goal. With this the conversation ended, but two days later Warlond appeared at al-Qassab's house and informed him as follows: "We consider the Arab societies and parties our allies and friends, as we consider Husayn and his sons, and we give them full honour and esteem. We are prepared to discuss with you the Arab problem." He requested from him that the Arab parties should choose two representatives to open discussions, maintaining strict secrecy. He also made clear to him that the results of these discussions would be brought to Husayn for his knowledge and approval. In this context it should be noted that Warlond himself believed in the need to establish a number of states or a confederation of states in the Arab provinces of the Ottoman Empire. He also supplied to Syrian activists with documents such as the constitutions of the United States and Switzerland, translated into Arabic. Following this the Syrian activists chose 'Abd al-Rahman al-Shahbandar and Rafiq al-'Azm as their representatives in their contacts with the British.[15]

On 26 April 1918 seven of the Syrian activists prepared a memorandum which they gave to Warlond for him to pass on to the high commissioner Reginald Wingate. In the preamble of the memorandum, which was addressed to the British government, they presented themselves as the representatives of the various Arab societies who "have been given full power to voice the expression of their tongues". They explained that among the Arabs doubts had begun to arise concerning the intentions of Britain and apprehensions that with the end of the war the British would abandon the Arabs. These doubts and apprehensions increased with the appearance of the pro-French societies (referring mainly to the Comité Central Syrien in Paris, see the following chapter), which did not actually represent the will of the Syrians. Therefore they saw it as their duty to their compatriots across the enemy lines to express the true views of the Syrians. Their right to express these views derived from their representing four fifths of the population of Syria. The societies in whose name they spoke represented all layers of the nation, and especially the intellectuals, the religious leaders, and the aristocracy. They also had ties with the chiefs of the bedouin tribes. Therefore, the British government would, in their opinion, be making a most serious mistake to ignore this appeal.

In order to remove the misunderstandings and to achieve full cooperation with the British, they decided to present before the British government the following questions and clarifications: (1) Could they assure their compatriots that it was the intention of the British government to grant full independence to the Arab countries? If the answer to this question should be positive, then the Arab societies would commit themselves to give all assistance to the Allies. (2) When the people of the Arab movement referred to the Arab countries, they meant the Arabian Peninsula, Syria, Iraq, the vilayet of Mosul, and a large part of the vilayet of Diarbakr. (3) Did the British government intend to aid

the inhabitants of these countries to establish a decentralist government, such as that of the United States, for example, which
would suit the local conditions, or perhaps it was relating to all
the Arab countries as one piece? (4) The Syrians would indeed
be happy to join a federal Arab government, but it should be
kept in mind that already long before the war they were striving
to achieve a decentralist regime in Syria, according to which it
would be divided into provinces which would administer their
internal affairs by themselves. This principle could be applied to
all the Arab countries which would gain their independence. (5)
The Arabs had always relied on the friendship of Britain, and
they were asking it to be the protector of the Arab race, which
would demonstrate its loyal friendship to it. (6) The declarations
of Britain that it would not harm the Turkish vilayets, while not
making any such declarations concerning the Arab vilayets, were
causing despair among the Arabs because they believed that
they, the allies of the British, were more deserving of independence for their country than the Turks, the allies of Germany.
(6b) Although there were well-known differences of opinion
among the amirs of the Arabian Peninsula, they could all be
conjoined in the federal Arab government if Britain would aid it.
(7) Despite the fact that the Arab revolt broke out in the Hijaz,
its cornerstone had been laid in Syria, which had the greatest
share in the intellectual movement. The Hijaz had an enduring
tie with Syria, and Husayn and his sons had worked in full coordination with the Arab societies there and in Egypt. If the Syrians had not had full confidence in the faithfulness of Britain to
the Arabs in general and to Syria in particular, they would not
have sacrificed from the beginning of the war the best of their
sons for the independence of the Arab countries. They had no
doubt that the men of justice of Britain would not allow their
blood to have been shed in vain, whatever might be the political
situation in Europe.[16]

The authors of the memorandum asked that it be kept secret
in light of the fact that Syria was still under Ottoman rule and
tens of thousands of its sons were serving on distant battlefields
for the Ottomans. A public disclosure of the memorandum
could cause Ottoman revenge on Syria and the Syrians. Also the
names of the seven authors remained confidential. According to
the common version that appears in historical literature on the
Arab movement, the seven Syrians were: Rafiq al-'Azm (the former president of the Decentralization Party), 'Abd al-Rahman
al-Shahbandar (a former member of this party), Kamil al-Qassab
(a member of al-Fatat), Fawzi al-Bakri (a member of al-Fatat),

SYRIANS AND LEBANESE IN EGYPT

Khalid al-Hakim (a member of *al-Fatat* and *al-'Ahd*), Mukhtar al-Sulh, and Hasan Hamada (a past member of *al-Qahtaniyya*). However, Warlond himself listed their names in a letter he sent afterwards to Clayton, and his list included the name of Muhibb al-Din al-Khatib (a member of *al-Fatat*, and also a former member of the Decentralization Party) instead of Fawzi al-Bakri. A third version of the seven also includes Muhibb al-Din al-Khatib, but in place of Khalid al-Hakim.[17]

In order to strengthen their appeal the seven authors added to it a synopsis of the history of the Arab societies in the years 1908-1915 — "the true story", as they put it. In this synopsis there was but a small grain of truth and a very large collection of imaginary items. According to it there had existed a central Arab society, which already in 1908 had planted one of its members in the leadership of the CUP in order to learn all the secrets of the Young Turks. In 1909 this society instructed its members in Istanbul, who included also members of parliament, officers and soldiers, to set up the "Liberal Moderate Party". (The truth was that this was a Turkish party in opposition to the CUP.) In the same year the society also opened branches throughout Syria and Palestine and began to foster brotherhood among the Muslim and Christian Arabs. It also sent delegations which propagandized in favour of the Arab idea to Iraq, Anatolia, Rumelia, and Libya. It began to consolidate cooperative activity of the Iraqi and Syrian officers stationed in Istanbul, aided Arab students in the city to complete their higher studies, and brought about the election of anti-government members of parliament such as Shukri al-'Asali. In 1910 the society instructed its members who were serving as Ottoman army officers in Yemen to induce the Imam Yahya to sign an armistice with the Ottomans in order to prevent the needless shedding of Arab blood. In 1911 the society arrived at a coordination with the Armenians. It also warned the Imperial government against the impending invasion of Libya by Italy, but the government ignored its warning. When Italy invaded Libya, the society instructed its officer members to volunteer for service there. 911 officers volunteered, and the Ottoman authorities which was overwhelmed by this large number of Arab officers, eventually accepted only 72 of them. In 1913 the society began widespread Arab propaganda in the light of the failures of the Empire in the Balkans. In 1914 the society propagandized against the involvement of the Empire in the World War, which would only have caused agony to the Arab people. Jamal Pasha began to remove the Arab officers from the Arab countries and to replace them with Turks. In 1915 the

CUP began to work towards the realization of their final goal — "extermination" of the Arabs.[18]

A series of events then began, which testified to the British being carried along by the statements of the Arab activists concerning the strength and influence of the Arab societies, in a way very similar to what happened before the despatch of the McMahon letter of 24 October 1915. After the presentation of the memorandum of the seven and the synopsis attached to it, Warlond conducted his own research on the Arab societies, and the results of this research were summarized in a report that he wrote and which was published in slightly condensed form in the *Arab Bulletin*, an internal intelligence bulletin issued by the officials of the Arab Bureau in Cairo. This report did contain a number of inaccuracies, but in general it showed that the British had much information on the Arab societies. However, what the British lacked was a reliable assessment of the true strength and influence of these societies. At the end of his report Warlond wrote that the strength of *al-Fatat* was very great (he did not refer to its name explicitly because it was "still held in secrecy" by its members, but it was clear that he was referring to *al-Fatat*), and it had representatives in all the important Arab families, in all branches of the Ottoman administration, and in all units of the Ottoman army. In a later letter Warlond adopted the words of the Syrian activists, that *al-Fatat* numbered on the eve of the World War 150,000 members. (The number of society activists on the eve of the war was 37, and the number of activists during the war was 115. See the preceding chapter.)

These data gave the British in Cairo the feeling that there was a need to respond positively to the appeal of the seven Syrians. To this were added a number of other elements, which in the opinion of the British increased the importance of strengthening their ties with the Arabs. The signing of the peace treaty between Bolshevik Russia and Germany in March 1918 raised the fear that additional German forces could then stream into the Ottoman Empire by way of the Black Sea and would perhaps be steered to a new attack on Iraq. There was also a new political consideration: For the first time a number of Syrian activists declared openly (apparently Faris Nimr and his circle) that they preferred an American aegis over Syria to a British or French one. In a conversation with Warlond these Syrians explained that since the United States had no interests in the region, while Britain and France did, therefore they preferred that this power should be the one to assist the Syrians in establishing their new state. They had confidence only in the United

States that it would depart once Syria was capable of managing its affairs by itself.[19]

At the end of his report Warlond stressed that *al-Fatat* was prepared to activate its members only for full Arab independence, and as long as the policy of the Allies remained unclear they would refrain from acting. On 7 May 1918 High Commissioner Wingate received the memorandum of the seven, including Warlond's recommendations, and on the same day he sent it to London. In the despatch accompanying the memorandum Wingate stressed that the seven "were well qualified to represent Syrian Moslem opinion in Egypt". As for the societies to which they belonged, several of them died out as a result of the actions of the Ottoman authorities against them, but the others "are said to have a large membership and ramifications throughout the Arab-speaking countries". Therefore he was of the opinion that the British should not ignore them, considering that the CUP had already proved how great the influence of a secret society could be in this part of the world. These men promised to cooperate vigorously with the Allies against the Ottomans, provided that their demands were accepted. And since at that time the military situation of the Allies was not exciting, and the enemy was disseminating intensive propaganda in the Arab regions, there was a danger that if a reply were not forthcoming from the British, or that the reply were unsatisfactory, then these men "will feel themselves free to modify their pro-Ally inclinations and ultimately, if necessity in their eyes demanded it, to enter into communications with the enemy". Wingate stressed that he was indeed aware of the fact that the British government could not give the far-reaching promises that the authors of the memorandum were demanding, but on the other hand it would not be wise to ignore their aspirations, which in his opinion expressed the desires of the majority of Muslim Syrians and a considerable part of the Christian Syrians. Therefore he felt "that a sympathetic reference to our desire to see local self-government combined with progress towards political union of the (Asiatic) Arabic-speaking peoples would be opportune and well received".[20]

The memorandum of the seven received the "earnest attention" of the British government, and on 11 June 1918 Mark Sykes drafted the government's answer, which became known later on as "The Declaration to the Seven". (Some months later it turned out that one of the main interested parties, General Allenby, the commander-in-chief of British forces in the region, had not been brought into the secret of the consultations that preceded the declaration.) In this declaration the British in fact agreed with the central idea embodied in the memorandum — they did not relate to the Arab countries as a single bloc:

> The areas mentioned in the memorandum fall into four categories:
> 1. Areas in Arabia which were free and independent before the outbreak of war;
> 2. Areas emancipated from Turkish control by the action of the Arabs themselves during the present war;
> 3. Areas formerly under Ottoman dominion, occupied by the Allied forces during the present war;
> 4. Areas still under Turkish control.

The British government would recognize the absolute independence of the Arabs who were inhabitants of the first two categories and would assist them. (This paragraph had great significance, since it implied that the British would recognize the independence of any territory that would be conquered by the Arabs themselves by the end of the war.) In the regions that would be occupied by the Allies a government would be set up based on the consent of the local population. As for the territories of the fourth category, the British would do their best to see that their inhabitants would also achieve their freedom and independence.

The declaration was sent to Cairo, and on 22 June Hogarth and Warlond gave it to the two representatives of the seven, 'Abd al-Rahman al-Shahbandar and Rafiq al-'Azm. Al-Shahbandar asked for clarifications, and Hogarth replied that he could not depart from the text of the declaration. Nonetheless he told him that the British would recognize Arab governments that would be established according to the declaration. Al-'Azm expressed his general satisfaction with the declaration, but he took advantage of the occasion to make a long speech about the disappointment that the Arabs felt because of the British refusal to accept all the borders proposed by Husayn (in the McMahon-Husayn correspondence), and about the personal discomfort caused him by the existence of a secret agreement between the British and the French (referring to the Sykes-Picot agreement). In accordance with what was agreed in advance between the British and the Syrians in Cairo, the British sent a copy of the declaration to Husayn. Kamil al-Qassab on his part sent a copy to Faysal so that he would persuade his father to agree to it, but Husayn did not respond. He apparently understood very well the discrepancy between the declaration and his plans to establish one large Arab state under his direct rule.[21]

At the same time that discussions began between the British and the group of Syrians Hogarth held a conversation also with Faris Nimr about his views on the future of Syria. Nimr completely rejected the suggestion that he participate in a delegation of Syrians to Husayn, and this because of his opposition in principle to any possibility that Syria should be ruled by the Hijaz or that it should be included with it in the framework of a single state. As for the future Syria, Nimr said that he yearned for an integral and independent Syria, which would indeed be a member of an Arab federation but would have its own prince or king. This ruler could not under any circumstances be the King of the Hijaz because then the regime in Syria would be theocratic, the status of the Christians in it would be inferior, and it would not be truly autonomous. Nimr stressed that he preferred that the ruler of Syria be a native Syrian; however, since he was not able to indicate a suitable Syrian, he was prepared to agree on one of Husayn's sons. He said that he recognized the fact that the Syrians were not yet capable of running an independent state, and therefore he was interested in having Syria under foreign patronage, but only temporarily and without impairing the sovereignty of the Arabs. As for the identity of this foreign patron, Nimr then suggested Britain, and if it could not be arranged, then the United States, but under no circumstances France. Nimr suggested to the British that they should regard Syria as a unit by itself and not as one bound to Iraq or the Hijaz. "Let the Federal Unity come later, and be formed piece by piece."[22]

Nimr was not the only one opposed to Husayn, yet prepared to accept one of his sons. Haqqi al-'Azm, one of the strongest opponents of Hijazi influence in Syria, proposed to Faysal in August 1918 that he become king of Syria under French aegis. He advised him to begin immediate negotiations with the French government and also offered himself as mediator between Faysal and the French. Faysal, of course, did not even bother to respond to this proposal, which was totally unacceptable to him. However, what activists such as al-'Azm feared came to pass with the ending of the war when the Hijazi "tribes" entered Damascus and began to interfere in Syrian politics. Al-'Azm and 200 other shocked Syrians and Lebanese sent a sharp protest in late October 1918 to the representatives of the Allies in Cairo (Britain, the United States, France, and Italy), in which they angrily rejected the possibility of the primitive Hijazis ruling the progressive Syrians, which would be a humiliation and an insult to the Syrians. They demanded therefore that the Syrian question be completely separated from the Arab question and that a regime based on its political unity and integrity should be set up in Syria, a Syria totally separated and independent of the other Arabic-speaking countries.[23]

During these final months of the war an incident occurred which was to remove from Husayn the last of his supporters among the Syrians in Cairo. This incident, indeed, had no political character, but its influence caused the loss of the last bit of credit that any of the Syrian activists still gave to Husayn. In June 1918 three ordinary criminals escaped from jail in Mecca. One managed to get away, but the other two were caught. They were sentenced to amputation of their right hands and feet, according to Islamic law. The sentence was approved by Husayn and carried out immediately on one of them. The Allied representatives in Jidda immediately appealed to Husayn, who insisted that the sentence was properly executed and according to Islamic law, though at the same time he granted an amnesty to the second. Also amnestied was another convict whose tongue was to be cut out.

The Syrian activists in Cairo were occupied at that time with sending a memorandum to President Wilson in which they requested him to assist the Arabs in achieving full independence, which would include the Arabian Peninsula, Iraq, Syria, and Palestine. Concurrently Kamil al-Qassab initiated a meeting in the Arab Agency in Cairo in which it was decided to sent a delegation of Muslims and Christians to Jidda in order to press Husayn to establish an Arab confederation with him as its head, with Damascus as its capital and including Syria, Palestine, Iraq, and the entire Arabian Peninsula. Husayn himself announced his consent to receive the delegation and also instructed his representative in Cairo to assist them. But in that very period an issue of the newspaper *al-Qibla* arrived in Cairo carrying a detailed report of the amputation of the hand and foot of the recaptured criminal in a public ceremony to the delight of the crowd of spectators. The newspaper reported the incident in glowing terms, with expression of open satisfaction with the upholding of the laws of Islam in letter and spirit. The Syrian activists were shocked. It was enough to confirm the worst of their fears about being ruled by the "primitive and backward" government of Husayn. This time the fears and sharp expressions enveloped even the most enthusiastic supporters of Husayn among the Syrians, and the same activists who were to participate in the delegation to Jidda came to the Arab Agency in Cairo and gave notice that they would not be able to go.[24]

At the same time the quarrel between the Syrian and Iraqi

officers in the army of the Arab revolt worsened, and attempts at mediation by Kamil al-Qassab and others were not crowned with success. All this, along with the effect of the "Declaration to the Seven", brought the Syrian activists in Cairo to the conclusion that they should work for the severance of the Syrian problem from the general Arab problem and strive for the establishment of an independent Syrian entity which would suit the degree of Syria's development and the will of its inhabitants. In November 1918 Britain and France issued a joint declaration concerning the necessity of establishing local governments according to the will of the inhabitants in the regions liberated from the Ottomans. It seems that this declaration was the final incentive for the formation of the "Syrian Union Party" (*Hizb al-Ittihad al-Suri*) in the following month. This party, under the leadership of Michel Lutf Allah, Rafiq al-'Azm, Kamil al-Qassab, 'Abd al-Rahman al-Shahbandar, and even the pan-Arabist Rashid Rida, strove for the creation of an independent and united Greater Syria on the basis of a decentralized regime.[25]

THE LEBANESE SOCIETIES IN EGYPT DURING THE WAR

With the outbreak of World War I the Alliance Libanaise society of Cairo decided not to content itself any more with its traditional demands to preserve the autonomous rights of Mount Lebanon and to expand its borders, and it began to strive for the achievement of independence for the mountain. At the beginning of the war it began combined activity with the Decentralization Party (through the mediation of its president Iskandar 'Ammun, who was also vice-president of the party), and the two organizations planned an armed revolt against the Ottomans with French assistance. The plan was never carried out, as explained at the beginning of this book. The demise of this plan also symbolized the end of the strong pro-French tendency that characterized the society before the war. In the years prior to the war this society adopted a distinctly pro-French policy, and so did the other branches of the network of Lebanese societies, "The Lebanese Revival", which were dispersed in Mount Lebanon itself and throughout the Lebanese émigré communities in Europe and America. Several of the Lebanese activists even appealed then to French diplomats with an explicit request that France occupy the region or at least for a French protectorate. This orientation was to change completely during the course of the war.

Before the war the society in Cairo benefited from influence both in Mount Lebanon and among the Lebanese émigré communities abroad. The very fact that it was physically close to Mount Lebanon enabled it to be informed on its problems and needs, and on the other hand the fact that it was abroad enabled it to stay out of the local political disputes strewn in it, and thus to be cloaked in the mantle of a society which was working on behalf of the interests of all the populations of the mountain. This status of the society was lost with the outbreak of the war and the severance of the tie between it and the inhabitants of the mountain.

The leaders of the society in the period prior to and in the early years of the World War were three: Iskandar 'Ammun - the president of the society, a Maronite lawyer who had been serving a long time in the legal system of the Egyptian government; Antun al-Jumayyil - the founder of the society, a Maronite who was editor of the newspaper *al-Ahram* and later employed in the Egyptian finance ministry; Da'ud Barakat - a Maronite who was editor-in-chief of *al-Ahram*. This triumvirate directed the activities of the society unchallenged until the crisis which befell it in mid-1917, as will be explained further on.[26]

After the death of the revolt plan in which it was involved, the society kept a low profile for quite a long time in order, as it claimed, not to give the Ottoman authorities a pretext for starting reprisals against the inhabitants of Mount Lebanon. Concurrently in this period there began to be heard the first protests — though still faint — against the possibility that France would take over Mount Lebanon and perhaps even turn it into a part of greater Syria. In February 1917 it became known to the society members that the imperial authorities had abrogated the règlement organique of Mount Lebanon, and this time they decided to break their silence and to start a campaign of protests against the authorities of the Empire. Iskandar 'Ammun, the president of the society, and Yusuf Darian, the Maronite archbishop in Cairo, presented a combined protest to the Allied representatives in Cairo in which they detailed all the special rights that the mountain had acquired according to the règlement organique, and they protested against the incessant attempts by the Empire to impair the special autonomous status of the mountain, attempts that had culminated in the total nullification of the règlement organique, which was guaranteed by the European powers. It is needless to point out that the protest was useless because it was directed to the wrong address. In a reply to Archbishop Darian the French foreign ministry conveyed the sympathies of France, which would not forget the Lebanese in their difficult hour.[27]

From then on the members of the society began intensive activity on behalf of the Lebanon, and the Lebanon alone, until Faruqi, Husayn's representative in Cairo, remarked about them: "They speak only about the Lebanon . . . because they are first of all Lebanese and only afterwards Arabs." They then formed an ideology that strove for "absolute independence of the Lebanon, within its natural borders, under the guarantee of the great powers". They thus expressed their desire not only for the formation of Greater Lebanon, but also for the end of the exclusiveness of French aegis over Lebanon and its replacement by a guarantee of all the powers. It is noteworthy that this view of theirs was not necessarily acceptable to all the Lebanese in Egypt. Many of these Lebanese had reservations about the chilly policy that the society had begun to form towards France.[28]

The most important branch of the Alliance Libanaise outside of Cairo was in Alexandria. The society there was established in 1910 by the lawyer Yusuf al-Sawda, who headed it during the following years until 1921. He was anti-French, and the society's policy was framed according to his views in this spirit. With the outbreak of the war al-Sawda decided that the society should work from then on to achieve absolute independence for Mount Lebanon in its expanded borders. In late 1917 at a general conference of the society he informed them about the desire of the Allies to grant Lebanon absolute independence. This declaration, which of course was not consonant with reality, aroused the anger of the French diplomats in Egypt, who had not displayed excessive sympathy towards him even before this.[29]

In April 1917 Sykes and Picot arrived in Cairo and clarified to the Syrian and Lebanese activists there the principles of the Sykes-Picot agreement (an event which was examined in detail at the beginning of this chapter). The statements of the two on the subject of placing Lebanon under direct French rule were received with severe criticism by some of the Lebanese activists (although not by all of them). From then on the Alliance Libanaise of Cairo went over to open anti-French activity, and it began a series of protests against the intentions of France concerning Lebanon. There were Lebanese who wanted to present to the United States representative in Cairo a protest against any foreign domination of Lebanon whatsoever, and Faruqi, Husayn's representative there, exploited this situation and suggested to his foreign ministry to organize a delegation of Lebanese to go to the United States and propagandize there on behalf

of the Arab question. He explained to his superiors that the success of such a mission was assured considering the Syrian and
Lebanese émigré communities that existed there. The positive
response of Mecca to this idea was not long in coming. The
deputy foreign minister Fu'ad al-Khatib asked him to meet with
Iskandar 'Ammun on the matter of the mission and to transmit
to him the following word for word: "The object of our aspirations is to see the children of our race and nation in Lebanon
benefiting from full independence, without any restriction, not
on our part nor on the part of others."

Faruqi transmitted the message to Iskandar 'Ammun, who
received it with overt joy. At this stage 'Ammun in effect went
over to the camp of the staunch supporters of Husayn. This
ideological reversal was to inflict terminal damage to his standing
in the Alliance Libanaise. In late June Faruqi tried to convince
the other leaders of the society of Husayn's good intentions. He
told them at a well-attended meeting that Husayn recognized
that Lebanon had a special status, and therefore it would remain
independent in the framework of the future state, and only in the
political, defence, and economic areas would it be bound to its
government. Faruqi reported to Mecca that his listeners
expressed their satisfaction with this arrangement. However,
Yusuf al-Sawda (who did not attend the meeting), relates in his
memoirs that the reply of the members of the society was that
they were not prepared to agree to anything except that Lebanon should have complete independence.[30]

During this period there began to circulate in Mecca the idea
of sending ambassadors to London, Paris, Rome, and Petrograd.
Faruqi recommended that one of the ambassadors should be a
Christian and suggested Iskandar 'Ammun as a candidate. The
whole idea of the ambassadors was unrealistic, considering the
unwillingness of the British to approve it, but Iskandar 'Ammun
— and also his fellow society members — received the impression
that his appointment as ambassador would go through soon.
This fact, together with the fact that 'Ammun had begun to
advocate at this time the idea of establishing the greater Arab
state, of which Lebanon would be an autonomous province,
brought the members of the Alliance Libanaise to the conclusion that 'Ammun "had sold his fatherland to the Arabs" in
exchange for the ambassadorship. The matter aroused deep
anger among the members of the society, and his two partners in
the leadership, Antun al-Jumayyil and Da'ud Barakat, demanded
unequivocally that he resign from the presidency of the society.
'Ammun assented immediately, and on 30 June 1917 he

submitted his resignation as president of the society. In his letter of resignation he claimed that since he had accepted a senior post from Husayn, which would give him a wider field of operation for the Lebanese cause, he could not fulfill both posts simultaneously, and therefore he had decided to resign from the presidency of the society. His place as president was taken by Auguste Adib Pasha, a respected personality, who was a former senior official in the Egyptian finance ministry. However, from then on the office of president of the society became more an honorary one than one with practical influence. 'Ammun's place in the leading triumvirate of the society was taken by Jubra'il Taqla, the owner of the newspaper al-Ahram, who became the motivating force of the activity of the society until the end of the war and who contributed not a little to the exacerbation of its anti-French orientation. (According to the French, it was because of his disappointed hopes of receiving funds from them to subsidize al-Ahram).[31]

Iskandar 'Ammun was not the only Lebanese who became pro-Hashimite in this period. He was followed by Lebanese activists such as Emile Yazbak, Emile al-Khuri, Farid al-Khazin (not the Farid al-Khazin who was executed in Beirut in 1916) and others. Several of them even joined Faysal's army in Aqaba. It is noteworthy that the Alliance Libanaise itself began towards the end of the war to receive 30 Egyptian pounds a month from the government of the Hijaz, and one of its leaders, Da'ud Barakat, received ten Egyptian pounds a month personally. Members of the society began a propaganda campaign among the wealthy Syrians in Egypt to get them not to contribute funds for the benefit of the families of Syrians who had volunteered for the French Légion d'Orient (on this see the following chapter). Also Iskandar 'Ammun, who at first had seen positively the recruiting for the Légion d'Orient, and had even sent his son Sa'id to volunteer for it, changed his attitude towards this army after he came to the conclusion that the Lebanese recruits who had volunteered for it would not be used for the liberation of their fatherland but for imposing French sovereignty on their mountain. In fact, already at the beginning of his contacts with Husayn he instructed his son (at the last moment) not to carry out his volunteering for the Légion d'Orient, and instead he sent him to Faysal's army. Sa'id 'Ammun participated in raids by the army of the revolt on the railways and in early 1918 he was commissioned an officer. Iskandar 'Ammun himself was recommended in 1918 by Kamil al-Qassab as information emissary to Europe on behalf of the Arab revolt. Husayn accepted this recommendation and also instructed the Arab Agency in Cairo to grant 'Ammun 1,000 Egyptian pounds to finance his trip to Europe. However, while 'Ammun was preparing for the trip to Europe the story of the amputation of the hand and foot of the criminal who tried to escape from the jail in Mecca was published (an affair described in detail in the preceding section), and among the damages caused by this affair was also the non-departure of 'Ammun for Europe.[32]

In December 1917, shortly after the public disclosure of the Sykes-Picot agreement by the Bolsheviks, the Alliance Libanaise held a general meeting in which it was decided to publicly demand that Mount Lebanon be granted absolute independence, guaranteed by all the powers, and not just France. In accordance with the spirit of the meeting, on 8 January 1918 the society issued a *Mémorandum sur les aspirations des Libanais* which dealt with the condition and goals of the Lebanese. The memorandum was delivered to the British high commissioner in Egypt and to the representatives of France, the United States, Italy, and the Vatican in Cairo. The memorandum opened with a statement that the Lebanon had always had full administrative autonomy and with a description of the special status which the mountain had enjoyed since 1861. After this came a description of the anguish of Mount Lebanon during the war, which had caused the loss of more than a third of its population. The demand was then made that the mountain should gain its independence, but not in its present borders, which were suffocating the population and had caused the emigration of 300,000 Lebanese to foreign countries. The borders demanded were the "natural" borders of the mountain, which would include all the districts belonging to it geographically, economically, and historically. These included, in the opinion of the authors of the memorandum, the Biqa' and Ba'albek, Beirut, Tripoli, Sidon, Tyre, Marj 'Ayun, Hasbaya, and Rashaya. And this independence should be guaranteed by all the powers.[33]

The American representative in Cairo in this period explained that the motivation for these actions of the Lebanese was that they saw themselves not as Arabs but as descendants of the Phoenicians, a people completely separate from the Arabs or Syrians. They did not want to exchange the yoke of Ottoman occupation for rule by Muslim Syria. On the other hand they did not want to become a French protectorate, in which they would be governed by French officials who considered them an inferior race. Therefore their desire was that Mount Lebanon become an independent state, with no political tie to Syria, a country whose fate did not interest them at all. Auguste Adib, the president of the society, put forward his views to the American representative concerning the future government that would have to prevail in the future independent Lebanon. The regime in the new state should be a democratic, constitutional princedom or a republic. A founding assembly of 200 to 300 members would decide which of the two options to choose. In the event that it should choose a princedom, it would also decide if the prince would be a local person or a foreigner, and it would also choose the prince or the first president. The chief of state who would be chosen would form a government whose ministers would appoint the other functionaries of the government. Every four years a parliament would be chosen in general and proportional elections, with each member representing 20,000 inhabitants. In the new state there would be absolute equality for all citizens before the law, and the rights of minorities would be preserved.[34]

The anti-French positions of the society aroused the anger of several Syrian-Lebanese societies in various places. The Comité Central Syrien of Paris protested the memorandum of the society and claimed that the society's demand to exchange the aegis of France for that of all the powers would return Lebanon to the communal strife of times past, with every Lebanese appealing to a differenc consul with a request for aid. At a meeting that the society of Paris held in March 1918 it decided to protest vigorously against the attempt by the Alliance Libanaise to designate itself as the representative of the Lebanese and as empowered to speak in their name, when the truth was that the Lebanese were loyal to France with all their might. In April the Syria-Mount Lebanon League of Liberation in New York joined the protests, and in a letter that it sent to the Comité Central Syrien it condemned the lack of patriotism and loyalty of the Alliance Libanaise of Cairo. It expressed the loyalty of the Syrians and Lebanese in America to France, their traditional friend. The Alliance Libanaise did not remain in debt to its castigators, and in an open letter to the president of the society of Paris the names of several of the members of the society were listed in order to show that they indeed were respected figures entitled to speak in the name of the Lebanese. Also listed were names of the Comité Central Syrien in order to prove that they were the ones not entitled to speak in the name of the Lebanese and Syrians, since some of them had held French citizenship for many years and the others were unimportant people. In another article that the society of Cairo published it characterized its opponents

as representing the opinion of a marginal and insignificant
minority within the Syrian and Lebanese émigré communities.[35]

Towards the end of the war the society radicalized its anti-
French positions. In early June 1918 it held a conference in
Alexandria at which it protested against the inclusion of the
Lebanon in a French protectorate. In July it held another, well-
attended, conference in Cairo. It was represented as a literary
meeting, but actually it served as a platform for raising the
demands of the society for granting absolute independence to
Mount Lebanon, in its expanded borders, under the guarantee of
all the powers, and totally rejecting any possibility of a French
protectorate. The president of the society Auguste Adib suggested the idea at the meeting that similar societies be set up
throughout the Lebanese émigré communities with their centre
being the society in Cairo. Yusuf al-Sawda, the president of the
society of Alexandria, was also among the speakers at the meeting, and he presented a series of historical and geographical arguments to explain the need to expand the borders of Mount
Lebanon. He, too, emphasized that all the powers must be guarantors for the mountain's independence. The French in Egypt
seethed with anger and turned to the British high commissioner
with a demand that further meetings of this kind be banned.
This request perplexed the British, who were afraid that if they
forbade the society to hold meetings it would cause bitterness
and hostility against them among the Syrian and Lebanese
émigrés in Egypt (who in general were pro-British) and would
only increase the prestige of the society. Therefore they decided
not to forbid the society to hold meetings as long as they did not
disturb the public order, and to pressure the society's leaders not
to express views that would affront the French. On the other
hand, when the society requested British approval to publish a
new newspaper that would express their views, that is, independence for Lebanon under international aegis and with no preference for a specific power, the French had no difficulty
persuading the British not to grant the desired licence.[36]

However, the French did not content themselves with appeals
to the British authorities to curb the activity of the Alliance
Libanaise. As noted in the preceding section, already in June
1917 they encouraged the establishment in Egypt of the pro-
French "Society for the Defence of the Rights of Syria and
Lebanon", headed by 'Abdallah Sufayr Pasha. Regarding Lebanon the society strove for the establishment of an independent
state under French aegis, in expanded borders which would
include Tripoli, Sidon, Tyre, and the Biqa'. The members of the

society sent a telegram to the French premier, in which they expressed the loyalty to France of the Lebanese and Syrians living in Egypt and their desire to bind their destiny with that of France. The telegram ended with "Vive La France". Apparently this society did not carry out any further significant actions because in March 1918 the French foreign ministry turned to its representative in Cairo and requested him to encourage the establishment of a new society which would be connected with the Comité Central Syrien in Paris. It recommended that he make efforts to include also Muslim Syrians in the society, persuading them to accept the French plan for Syrian autonomy. The contacts to set up this new society went along lazily, with those involved being mainly the activists of the "Society for the Defence of the Rights of Syria and Lebanon". They were indeed ready to work along the lines of action suggested by the French, but they insisted that the new society be independent of the one in Paris. The society was eventually established officially only after the Anglo-French declaration of November 1918 regarding the establishment of local governments according to the will of the inhabitants in the regions liberated from the Ottomans. It included mainly Christians, Maronites and Greek Orthodox, and a small number of Muslims (led by Haqqi al-'Azm). The society, which was called "The Lebanese-Syrian Society of Egypt", grew quickly, and in January 1919 it already had branches in Alexandria, Tanta, and Mansura, with its central committee located in Cairo. The society strove for the establishment of a Syrian federation, which would be composed of autonomous provinces, in whose framework would be preserved the special autonomous status of Mount Lebanon. The relations of Mount Lebanon with the other parts of Syria would be conducted as circumstances developed. The territorial integrity of Syria and its political unity would be guarded under the responsibility, guidance, and protection of France. The Syrian question would be completely separated from the Arab question, in the light of the substantive differences existing between the Syrians and the Arabs.[37]

In addition to the pro-French societies the French employed a number of Lebanese activists for the purpose of disseminating pro-French propaganda among the Lebanese and Syrian circles. The most prominent of these were the journalists Khalil Zayniyya and Rizq Allah Arqash. Both of them were members of the "Lebanese Revival" society in Beirut before the war, and they fled to Egypt when it began. Khalil Zayniyya was described by the French minister in Egypt as "responsible for securing the propaganda service among the Syrian element". He received generous monetary support from the French foreign ministry to finance his newspaper *al-Mir'a* (at a certain stage the French minister in Cairo wondered if the French were not wasting too much money on it, more than its true importance justified), and he also sent articles to the United States by means of the diplomatic pouch of the French legation. Rizq Allah Arqash also sent articles to the Arabic press in the United States by means of the French legation in Cairo. Most of his articles dealt with the connection between Syria and France, and on one occasion he wrote a satire on the personality of Iskandar 'Ammun and the fickleness of his political views on the future of Syria.[38]

The anti-French views of the Alliance Libanaise were not the sole reason for the discord which broke out between it and other Syrian and Lebanese activists. In early 1918 Haqqi al-'Azm stirred up another question, which until then had been kept in low profile by both Syrian and Lebanese activists. The demand for granting complete independence for the Lebanon meant not only its non-inclusion in the future Arab empire, but its severance from the rest of Syria, also. Therefore he attacked the Alliance Libanaise for its desire to sever the Lebanon from the rest of Syria and to grant it complete independence. He claimed that cutting off the Lebanon from Syria would cause damage to both countries because Mount Lebanon could not maintain itself alone, just as Syria could not live without it. Therefore the two regions had to be in permanent contact from the commercial, agricultural, economic, and political point of view. Al-'Azm did indeed express his understanding of the apprehension of the Lebanese about the entry of the Hijazi army into Syria and of their fear of being ruled by a king who based his authority on religion, but that was no reason to sever Lebanon from Syria. These fears of the Lebanese were common also to the other Christians of Syria and even to many of its Muslims. (A similar view, against severance of Lebanon from Syria, was expressed in May 1918 by Georges Samné of the Comité Central Syrien of Paris.)

In late June 1918 Antun al-Jumayyil responded to the arguments of Haqqi al-'Azm in a letter that he sent to *al-Qibla*. Al-Jumayyil claimed that Mount Lebanon had always been independent, even before the règlement organique of 1861, whose innovation was only the provision of guarantees by the powers for its independence. Therefore, when his society demanded the "independence of the Lebanon, within its natural borders, under the guarantee of the powers", it was not asking anything exceptional. All that the Lebanon wanted was to be liberated from the yoke of the Ottoman Empire, which had violated its commitments to it according to the treaty of 1861. Al-Jumayyil spoke about the existence of a Lebanese nationalism (*jinsiyya*), to which the Lebanese were attached, and wished the Syrians that they, too, would wake up to demand their Syrian nationalism. What the Lebanese were opposed to was the desire of some Syrians "that there should be no trace of the Lebanese question".[39]

Chapter 7

THE LEGION D'ORIENT AND EMIGRE
COMMUNITIES IN AMERICA

With the outbreak of World War I in Europe a number of
Maronites came to the French consulate-general in Beirut
requesting to be recruited into the French army. Their request
was rejected since they were Ottoman subjects. Later, after the
Empire entered the war, the French agreed to accept Syrian and
Lebanese volunteers for the Foreign Legion. However, from the
beginning of the war various Syrian groups turned to the French
government with a request that it be made possible for Syrians
in France, Egypt, and America to fight against the Ottomans in
an organized form under French command. Appeals of this kind
gained the support of the French foreign ministry and of statesmen from the French colonialist circles. Both of these felt that
the setting up of a Syrian volunteer force by France would give
proof of the traditional amity of France towards the Syrians and
of its readiness to help them realize their ambition to fight the
Ottomans.

Consequently the French war ministry decided on 15 December 1916 to form the Légion d'Orient to be composed of Syrians, Arabs, and Armenians, and to work for the liberation of
their countries under French command. It was decided that the
base of the Légion would be in Cyprus. Volunteers from the two
Americas, recruited by emissaries of the Syrian societies, would
be sent to the French ports of Le Havre, Bordeaux, and Marseille, in possession of a certificate from the French consul in the
country of departure or from the president of one of the Syrian
or Armenian societies recognized by France. Syrian volunteers
resident in France would be able to volunteer in Paris or in
Marseille. Afterwards all the volunteers would be sent to Port
Said where they would be joined by Syrians volunteering in
Egypt, and from there the recruits would be transferred to
Cyprus. Advance contacts were arranged with the British authorities in Egypt to assure their cooperation in this matter.

The first recruits for the Légion d'Orient were from the Armenians evacuated from Musa Dagh. Also joining it were soldiers
from the Ottoman army who had been taken prisoner by the

Allies, and Syrian exiles and émigrés from Europe and South America. In mid-1917 the Syrian volunteers mobilized in Egypt and also volunteers from the island of Irwad (a French-occupied island near the Syrian coast to which Syrian and Lebanese refugees were fleeing) were transferred to the base in Cyprus. Later that same year the United States government announced that it would permit the recruitment of Lebanese and Syrians residents for the Légion d'Orient. It would also permit those who were in the American army to transfer to the Légion.

Despite all this, the number of Syrian recruits in France, the Americas and the Levant together amounted in early August 1917 to only 208. There were also serious discipline problems among the Syrian volunteers, who revealed very little willingness to go into battle. The commander of the Légion, Lieutenant-Colonel Romieu wondered what their true value would be when they had to actually fight. In November 1917 the number of Syrian volunteers came to 300. The number of Armenian recruits at the same time was eight times as large. Discipline problems and the lack of readiness to make sacrifices among the Syrians continued. In addition tense relations began to develop between the Syrian and Armenian soldiers in the Légion (and in fact mutual loathing prevailed also between the Christian Syrian soldiers, who were the majority, and the Muslim Syrians). The Armenians, in contrast to the Syrians, displayed a readiness to fight, were disciplined, and apparently also better educated. However, with the Armenians a different problem arose. They were prepared to sacrifice themselves for the liberation of their regions of origin. They revealed, on the other hand, a complete lack of interest in the Syrian territories, to the point that the French command wondered whether from a military point of view there would be any sense in employing the Légion outside of the Armenian regions. Still, after considering everything, the French then reached the conclusion that recruitment of additional volunteers for the Légion d'Orient should be done only among the Armenians and not to recruit any more Syrian volunteers. A trickle of Syrian volunteers nevertheless continued to arrive, and in mid-1918, on the eve of its being sent to the front the Légion numbered over 5,600 men, of whom about 550 were Syrians. At this stage it was already clearly divided into two parts — Armenian and Syrian.

The first combat unit of the Légion d'Orient was already set to go in February 1917. Despite this, it began to operate on the Palestine front only in July 1918, among other reasons because of the fear of reprisals that the Ottomans might take in reaction to its operation. The Légion comprised an important component of the French expeditionary force which accompanied the forces of Allenby in Palestine, and it then included three Armenian battalions and one Syrian company. The single important battle in which it participated was on 19 September 1918, at Nablus, as part of the great autumn offensive of General Allenby to demolish the Ottoman front. The French expeditionary force was responsible for a sector in the western part of the front, and to the right of the French force stood the Légion d'Orient. According to the French, the Armenian and Syrian Legionnaires distinguished themselves in battle. After that the Légion continued on with the French to Beirut, and its Armenian contingent continued further north with them till Cilicia.[1]

THE COMITE CENTRAL SYRIEN AND THE LEGION D'ORIENT

In Paris at the outbreak of World War I a number of Syrian and Lebanese organizations were active, all of them with a small number of participants. "Count" Cressaty, an eccentric Christian banker from Damascus who had already spent more than half his life in France, formed the "Comité Franco-Syrien" and devoted his efforts to total annexation of Syria to France. In early 1915 the society was joined by Nadra Mutran, a Greek Catholic from Ba'albek who was deeply involved in Syrian political activity before the war and also participated in the Arab-Syrian Congress held in Paris in 1913. Mutran, however, was working towards a different goal, the granting of autonomy to Syria, and the dispute between the two men brought about the withdrawal of Cressaty from the society. Mutran, apparently with the support of French colonialist circles, then began to plan an invasion of Syria by a French military force led by Algerian officers. The idea was that such a force could be assisted by the many Algerians living in Syria in order to take over the country from the Ottomans. The French foreign ministry totally rejected the plan for a number of reasons, among them the fear of damage to French prestige in the east and reprisals by the Ottomans against the Syrian population should such an expedition fail. Thereupon the foreign ministry decided that it should exercise strict supervision of Mutran and remove him from Paris with the first intrigue he should try to carry out. Mutran indeed desisted from plans of this kind, and in February 1915 he established a new society called "Comité Littéraire Arabe", which was

supposed to work through political means for the liberation of
the Syrians from the Ottomans and the assurance of autonomy
for Syria. Two young Muslim activists also took part in this new
society, Jamil Mardam and 'Awni 'Abd al-Hadi. The society
professed to be a liaison between the Syrians and the governments of France and Britain, but apparently it came to an end
soon after it was set up.[2]

After his retirement from the above-mentioned society,
"Count" Cressaty began to give lectures on the merits of
France's ties to Syria. In his lectures he was supported by various French colonialist organizations. In 1915 he published a
tract with the title *La Syrie française*, in which he tried to demonstrate the important interests that France had in Syria from an
economic, industrial, strategic, and political point of view, and
the overt love that the Syrians felt for France "like a son for his
mother". In this tract he also defined the borders of Syria
according to him: The Taurus mountains in the north, Iraq and
the Syrian desert in the east, the Arabian Peninsula in the south,
and Egypt and the Mediterranean Sea in the west. A year later
(the year of his death) Nadra Mutran, too, published a book,
entitled *La Syrie de demain*, in which he gave in detail his out-
look on the fate of Syria. He expressed in it his opinion that the
annexation of Syria to France was not a good solution because
of the current lack of accord of the Syrians with French ways.
His solution therefore was that the French should send to Syria
a resident or high commissioner who would administer it on
behalf of France. Under the resident there would be local ministers, who would be assisted in the first stage by French advisors.
All the different parts of Syria would be united and under one
authority and uniform laws. Still, its provinces would enjoy a
certain measure of administrative decentralization in local affairs.
Although Mutran included in his vision a general assembly,
which would mainly comprise the members of the administrative
councils of the provinces, he was against there being an elected
parliament and senate in the future Syria. According to him,
post-war Syria would have to work very hard to rebuild itself,
and it would not have the leisure nor the capability to waste on
election campaigns and political quarrels, not to mention that
members of parliament would anyway serve only themselves and
not their fatherland. Motivated by his pan-Syrian views, Mutran
also set out against the Lebanese separatists who aspired to
obtain independence for their country, and he claimed that the
educated Lebanese would only gain from the union of Lebanon
with Syria. Justice and equality, which would reign in the future

Syria, would prevent any possibility of harm to the Christians by the Muslim majority.[3]

A bit larger than the societies mentioned above was the "Comité Libanais de Paris", which was founded in 1912. Its president was Shukri Ghanim, a Maronite born in Beirut who had already spent about 25 years in France and had connections with various French political and colonialist circles. The secretary of the society was Khayrallah Khayrallah, a Maronite who served as an editor at the highly influential Paris newspaper *Le Temps*. (Both Ghanim and Khayrallah participated in the Arab-Syrian Congress held in Paris in 1913.) With the outbreak of the war Khayrallah enlisted in the French army and served in it for a period of time. When he left his military service and returned to the society, a serious dispute broke out between him and Ghanim, a dispute which caused the break-up of the society. It seems that beyond the exacerbation of the personal relations between them (Ghanim apparently felt that Khayrallah was impinging on his authority as president of the society), there was also an ideological basis for the quarrel between them. While Khayrallah still clung to the goal of the society from before the war, that is, to achieve full autonomy for Mount Lebanon and to be content with only French protection, Ghanim was active during this period on behalf of uncompromising loyalty to France. Khayrallah published in *Le Temps* various documents of the society, without Ghanim's permission, in order to support his claims. In late May 1915 he gave a public lecture in which he emphasized that the Lebanese desired the return of their national sovereignty and were opposed to colonialism. Their hope was that France would assist them in achieving their autonomy and freedom.

At that point Ghanim decided to expel Khayrallah from the society, but all its members were opposed to it. On 25 June Ghanim convened the members and delivered a long and tiring speech to justify his position. He detailed all his actions on behalf of Mount Lebanon in order to prove his faithfulness both to the Lebanon and to his duty as president of the society. He pointed out that he had no personal interest in this activity of his, and emphasized that, as before the war, he was still in favour of the Lebanon attaining its rights. Moreover, the opinions that Khayrallah was then bringing up were in fact Ghanim's. What Khayrallah did not understand was that times had changed, and in accordance with this it was necessary to change both goals and means of expression. Demonstrative actions of the kind that Khayrallah was performing would only keep away from the society French statesmen who were sympathetic to it. Everyone desired that the Lebanon should have autonomy, but one must find the proper time to say this, and the proper time was not then. Khayrallah's public statements were liable to start a debate on the subject of the Lebanon, which the Lebanon had no interest in starting then. It was also not the time to enter into a confrontation with France, their host, but to tighten the bond between the Lebanon and Syria to France. Ghanim also attacked Khayrallah for having published documents of the society without its approval, and he concluded his speech with the hope that the members of the society would express their confidence in him as they had done until then.

The members of the society refused to grant his appeal, and the result was that Ghanim took advantage of his position as president of the society to prevent its having further meetings. Attempts by the society members to convene it in order to elect a new administrative committee were thwarted by him a number of times, and the society in fact ceased to exist. In the following months Ghanim concentrated on an extensive correspondence with the French foreign ministry in the course of which he gave it the addresses of Lebanese activists in Paris (among whom were former members of his society), who, in his opinion, were working against French interests. He had especially harsh things to say against Bishop Faris, the representative of the Maronite patriarch in Paris, whom he characterized as an anti-French intrigant. He claimed that this bishop was using the Maronite Church in Paris for his personal interests and to conduct an anti-French policy.[4]

In May 1916 Ghanim, together with Georges Samné, a Greek Melchite writer born in Damascus who had spent many years in France and who maintained connections with the colonialist circles, started publishing again his periodical from before the war *Correspondance d'Orient*. The aim of the periodical was to prove the desire of the Syrians for French protection. In July, a month after the outbreak of the Arab revolt, it was stated in the periodical: "There is no Arab race, no Arab nation . . . There is no Arab question, but Arab questions." From then on the periodical began to work for the Syrian idea, which was perceived by its editors as not identical to the revolt which broke out in the Hijaz. In a conversation that Ghanim held around the same time with one of Mark Sykes' agents he attacked those Arabs who were demanding full independence as having an unrealistic view of the situation or personal interests. According to him, the Arabs were not yet ripe for independence and for taking the government into their own hands. If such a thing should happen, the result would be total anarchy. The Arabs needed at the present time the protection and guidance of France and Britain, who must divide the Arab provinces among themselves into spheres of influence, and set up high commissioners to direct their development, while giving a certain autonomy to the local inhabitants.[5]

The controversy between the uncompromising supporters of France among the Syrians and Lebanese and those who were in favour of obtaining independence for Syria and Mount Lebanon, together or separately, or even sympathized with the Arab revolt, found expression also in the Arabic press which appeared in Paris. Starting in March 1916, Ghanim and Samné published the newspaper *al-Mustaqbal*. It appeared once a week and was intended for dissemination of propaganda in the Muslim world, in the Middle East, and in Africa. At first *al-Mustaqbal* expressed pro-Arab views and sometimes even pan-Arab ones, and proclaimed that it would be the clarion of the awakening Arab nation. However, this tendency, which was explicitly contrary to the views of Ghanim and Samné, resulted from the leanings of its two editors, 'Awni 'Abd al-Hadi and Ibrahim Salim al-Najjar, who were both prominent members in a number of Arab societies, secret and overt, in the pre-war period. And indeed, within a short time a split occurred between the owners of the newspaper and the editors. Ghanim asked 'Abd al-Hadi to publish on the front page of the newspaper an article in which Ghanim praised the policy of France. 'Abd al-Hadi refused, and then Ghanim informed him that the newspaper was supported by the French foreign ministry, and it was they who wanted the article published. 'Abd al-Hadi resigned from his job. Al-Najjar also resigned soon after, for similar reasons, although with him an additional consideration played a part — besides being an advocate of the Arab movement he was also in favour of independence for the Lebanon, an idea that was contrary to the views of Ghanim and Samné. From then on the newspaper became the organ for French sympathizers among the Syrians and Lebanese, and it was supported intensively, as mentioned, by the French foreign ministry, to the point that there were those who considered it an official propaganda instrument of the ministry, which it was not. In addition to its pro-French proclivities, the newspaper began, inspired by Ghanim and Samné, to spread propaganda in favour of the Syrian idea (in contrast to the Arab idea, or the particularist Lebanese one).

Ibrahim Salim al-Najjar did not sit idle after his departure from *al-Mustaqbal*. In late 1916 he began to publish *L'Orient Arabe*. In this newspaper, which appeared every two weeks, he worked not just for his fatherland Lebanon but for the general Arab cause, which he professed to guard against those who wished to harm it. The newspaper was considered by the French to be hostile to them and acting against their policy concerning Syria, and apparently in these tendencies al-Najjar was being assisted by Khayrallah. Therefore, when in August 1917 al-Najjar sent an erroneous report to *al-Muqattam* about a declaration made by the French premier, in which he supposedly said that France had no plans or intentions to occupy Syria, the French did not content themselves with a denial. They took advantage of the opportunity to send al-Najjar to a detention camp for Ottoman subjects. When shortly afterwards *L'Orient Arabe* demanded the release of its editor, the authorities responded by suspending the newspaper for three months. In August 1918 the newspaper was suspended for good. Al-Najjar remained in the detention camp until the end of the war.[6]

In April 1917 Shukri Ghanim came up with a new idea. In a letter to the French premier he proposed using the French-occupied island of Irwad facing the Syrian coast for setting up a refugee centre for Lebanese refugees and as a supply base for arms and food. The island could receive supplies from Port Said, which was not too far away, and it would be possible to communicate from the island with the inhabitants of Tripoli, who according to him were faithful to France, and with the Mutawali Shi'ites and the Nusayris in the region. Ghanim proposed that he himself be sent to Irwad by France, with arms, ammunition, and a number of artillerymen and machine-gunners. He then would be able to turn the island into a "resistance" centre, which, when the day should arrive, would serve France as a springboard for intervention in Syria. He made clear that all his proposals were for the sake of France's prestige, for which he was prepared to sacrifice his life. He would do his utmost for the common interests of his "fatherland by choice" (France) and his "motherland" (Lebanon, or perhaps he in fact meant all of Syria).

The French were in no need of his advice concerning the island of Irwad, which without it had become a centre for refugees fleeing from the continent and a French intelligence base. Still, because the French foreign ministry considered Ghanim a man who was known "for his loyalty to French interests in Syria" and in whom they had confidence, it was decided to allow him to go to Irwad whenever he thought that the time had

arrived to carry out his plans, and also to give him aid in realizing these plans.[7] However, for Ghanim, the whole affair of Irwad
was a passing idea, and a few days later he had already taken a
new initiative — the establishment of the Comité Central Syrien.

On 25 April 1917 most of the Syrian émigrés in Paris held a
meeting on the initiative of Shukri Ghanim and in the presence
of a senior official of the French foreign ministry. It was decided
to form the "Comité Central Syrien" (CCS), which would unite
the Syrians in the city and work first of all to collect funds to
finance sending a recruiting mission to America and to aid the
families of the recruits to the Légion d'Orient. On 2 May the
founding convention was held, again with the participation of
senior French statesmen. The platform of the society was
approved without opposition, and a unanimous message was
sent to the French premier, expressing the unswerving loyalty of
the society's members to France and their confidence that it
would assist the Syrian people to be liberated from the Ottomans and to achieve autonomy under French aegis.

However, the society came up against serious problems at the
next meeting, on 19 May, when Ghanim proposed that the temporary administrative council of the society be elected as its permanent council. His argument was that there was insufficient
time to elect new people since the French foreign ministry was
waiting for him to present the members of the society's recruiting mission to America. He hastily announced that the temporary council had been elected as the permanent council and left
the meeting. This irregular election procedure angered those
present. They grumbled about this dictate of Ghanim's, which,
they said, reminded them of the election procedures in the Ottoman Empire. Even if they were willing to accept his electing
himself president of the society, many of them were opposed to
his choosing in this way Georges Samné as its secretary-general.
They claimed that Samné was not an authentic Syrian at all, but
an Egyptian who had received Spanish citizenship and later on
French citizenship. (Samné indeed had French citizenship, but it
is not clear why they thought he was not of Syrian origin, he
was a native of Damascus.) Ghanim in any case was not prepared to yield on the appointment of his faithful partner, and
perhaps this was the reason why he proceeded as described
above.

On 29 May the society convened for another meeting, and
several members made a motion to cancel the illegal elections
held at the previous meeting and to hold new, secret elections.
Ghanim protested vigorously and claimed with passion that it

was his right to choose who would work together with him in the organization that he had founded. His words aroused strong opposition, and eventually a compromise was reached that the council would remain as it was but as a temporary one until new elections could be held. New elections were never held, and this state of affairs caused many of the members of the Syrian community in Paris to announce that they did not recognize the right of the society to speak in their name.

Despite all this, the French foreign ministry announced its official recognition of the society. It consented to Ghanim's proposal to attach a senior official of the ministry to the society's emissary who was sent to Marseille to apprise the large Syrian community there of the founding of the society and its goals. The society's emissary to Marseille and one other who was sent to Bordeaux succeeded in collecting 100,000 francs to finance the recruiting activities of the society. The society received also generous financial aid from the French foreign ministry itself, and it was supported in addition by the Comité de l'Orient, a French colonialist society of which Georges Samné was also the secretary-general. Money was contributed to the society also by French firms and financiers who had economic and other interests in Syria. Within a short time it was perceived by the official authorities in France and its statesmen as the representative body of Syrian émigré communities, a status that, as will be shown further on, it far from enjoyed.[8]

Soon after its founding the society published a manifesto in which it explained its goals, which were summed up as "liberation of Syria under French aegis". The four principal lines of action that the society would take to realize this goal would be: "(1) To continue and even increase the recruitment for the Syrian Legion. No task is more urgent than this. (2) To set up an aid fund, which would be able to be used to finance the primary needs of the country on the morrow of its liberation. (3) To concentrate all activities for the liberation of Syria. (4) To discuss the form of the future regime of Syria, in coordination with the French government." The society made clear that it would act in cooperation with the French political and military authorities, and it would in effect serve as a mediator between them and the Syrian émigré communities in Allied and neutral states. It would endeavour to unify the efforts made by the Syrians to realize their aspirations because unity was the essential condition for their success. For this purpose it would send representatives to all the various Syrian societies in order to ensure that their activities would be coordinated. (For this reason the society was called the Comité Central.)

An examination of the society's goals, as expressed in this manifesto, in its platform, and on other occasions, shows that the society was in effect working towards the pan-Syrian idea, that is, the establishment of an integral and federal Syria. Mount Lebanon was to be included in this Syria, though with an autonomous status, and the members of the society repeatedly emphasized the many bonds that existed between it and the rest of Syria. However, the supreme goal of the society was the tightening of the bonds between Syria and France and emphasizing the absolute loyalty of the Syrians to France. Not without cause did the French foreign ministry inform its representative in Cairo, about a month and a half after the founding of the society, that "its platform accords with our views", and added, "We have the ability to supervise and direct its activity."[9]

The first article of the CCS's platform stated, among other things: "The goal of this society is to unite all the Syrians scattered throughout the Allied and neutral countries and all the local groups . . . The ultimate goal of the society is the liberation of Syria and the achievement of its independence, under the aegis of France, with its help and guarantee, by way of a federal regime of provincial autonomies, in whose framework the various regions (the Lebanon — which already enjoys an autonomous regime — Palestine, etc.) will maintain their unique character and the unhampered development of their legitimate aspirations."[10]

The *Correspondance d'Orient*, which became the official organ of the society, began a propaganda campaign for the unity of Syria. It explained to its readers that in spite of the differences in beliefs among the Syrians in the various regions they actually constituted a single nation and their country was a single geographical unit. Their entire future depended on their ability to implement this unity and to establish a strong national and liberal government in Syria. This government would require the assistance of technical advisors sent by a friendly power, and this of course could be only France. The future Syria would extend from the Taurus mountains to the Suez Canal, it would be secular, and all religious communities would be represented in its government. A free Syria could arise only if its inhabitants allowed love of the fatherland to cover all the religious differences that existed among them. The periodical also sharply attacked the desire heard from the Hijaz to annex Syria. In an article entitled "The Dangers of Pan-Arabism", Samné denounced the ambition of the Hijazi government to occupy

Syria, when in fact there was no connection between the Hijaz and Syria. Samné's words implied that he actually did not consider the Syrians Arabs. The French censored the more caustic sections of the article (and its title), but somebody took the trouble to send a large number of the original version to Egypt and the Hijaz in sealed envelopes. Mecca reacted with anger, and so did Faysal, whom a copy of the article reached in Aqaba. The British, too, complained to the French about the damage to the relations of the Allies with the Hijaz that Samné's foolish behaviour was causing.[11]

The views of the CCS angered not only the adherents of the Arab movement but also those who supported the Lebanese idea. Heading the latter in Paris was Bishop Faris of the Maronite Church, who stubbornly continued to oppose Ghanim's political line and organized an opposition to the CCS. The idea of establishing a greater Syria, even if it should be federal, was unacceptable to the Lebanese activists, who would not be satisfied with less than total and separate independence for Mount Lebanon. Also among the Syrian émigrés living in Paris there were many who opposed the CCS, for various reasons, and even circulated a protest petition against it which received many signatures. At a certain point the CCS addressed a call to the Syrian and Lebanese émigrés in Egypt to form local societies which would be affiliated with it. A number of them met in the editorial office of the Cairo newspaper *al-Muqattam*, and after a long discussion they decided to reject completely the proposal of the CCS. The Lebanese especially were against this idea, which they saw as part of the French plot to occupy their mountain.

The charge that the CCS was serving French colonialism was the dominant accusation that its opponents made against it. They emphasized time and again the fact that the leaders of the society, Ghanim and Samné, held French citizenship, and they claimed that their whole aim was to bring about the occupation of the Levant by France. They also held against them that having been residents of France for so many years they had in effect lost the right to speak in the name of Syria and the Syrians. The opposition that the society aroused in many circles caused the French general security service at one point to wonder if the society indeed represented the Syrians. The foreign ministry hastened to reassure it that the society was a liaison between the French government and the Syrian communities in France and abroad, and that from the day of its founding it had not failed to follow "our official instructions". The opponents of the society, according to it, were no more than a few anti-French individuals or those motivated by personal ambitions.[12]

The first assignment that the CCS took upon itself when it was founded was to send a recruiting mission to South America to propagandize for the volunteering by Syrian and Lebanese émigrés for the Légion d'Orient. The mission was originally supposed to number three emissaries: Dr. César Lakah, a Greek Catholic Syrian with French citizenship, Jamil Mardam, a Muslim native of Damascus (member of *al-Fatat*) who was in Paris when the war broke out and decided to remain there, and Sheikh Yusuf al-Khazin, a Lebanese Maronite journalist who had lived for many years in Egypt. The latter was urgently summoned to Paris at the expense of the French government (after being chosen for this by French sympathizers among the Lebanese in Cairo) in order to represent the Lebanese element in the recruiting mission. However, when he arrived in Paris, he was apprised, as he put it, of Ghanim's ambitions to assist in the occupation of the Levant by France; and he announced his refusal to participate in the mission. Attempts by Ghanim to persuade him to retract his refusal came to naught, and on 20 May 1917, after they were officially presented to the secretary-general of the French foreign ministry, Lakah and Mardam set out on their journey. Yusuf al-Khazin returned to Egypt. This composition of the mission did not bode well. It included only two Syrians, one a French citizen and the other a Muslim with Arab tendencies. There was no Lebanese in it despite its being directed also to the Lebanese communities in South America. This caught the eye of the Lebanese, and even the French sympathizers among them grumbled that no other Lebanese was chosen instead of al-Khazin.[13]

On 8 June 1917 the recruiting mission arrived in Brazil. The two important émigré societies in Brazil at the time were the "Renaissance Libanaise" of São Paulo under the presidency of Faris Najm, and the "Syrian-Lebanese Patriotic Society" of Rio de Janeiro under the presidency of Ni'ma Jafet. The Renaissance Libanaise, which was founded back in 1912, set as its goal during the war to work for the independence of Mount Lebanon in its original boundaries under French aegis. This ideology of the society was in contradiction to the pan-Syrian views of Shukri Ghanim. Despite this, during the war a correspondence was carried on between them in matters concerning Lebanon, principally in connection with the society's appeals to President Wilson, the King of Spain, the French foreign ministry, and the Pope, to exert their influence to aid the starving Lebanese population. (The King of Spain responded positively to this appeal.)

In August 1916 the society also informed Ghanim that it was opening an initiative to recruit Syrian and Lebanese volunteers with the intention of forming an expeditionary force of émigrés, which would work for the liberation of Syria under Allied command. Towards the end of 1916 12,000 men had already advised of their readiness to enlist, though only a few of them began active military training. The relations of the society with the French consul in São Paulo were good, especially because the latter would give the Lebanese and Syrian émigrés travel certificates when needed without their having to come in contact with the local authorities. On the other hand, around May 1917 a congress of representatives of the Lebanese societies in South America was held in São Paulo, and the demand for full independence was raised in it, along with expressions of opposition to any foreign influence, occupation, or mandate.[14]

When the mission arrived in Brazil it began to tour the country, arranging meetings and assemblies in the various cities and exhorting the Syrian and Lebanese émigrés to enlist in the Légion d'Orient in order to liberate their country. During its stay in Brazil the mission was supported by the French minister in Rio de Janeiro, who was also present at many of the conferences that it arranged. The largest and most important of the sessions were held in Rio de Janeiro and São Paulo with the participation of the senior members of the Renaissance Libanaise and the Syrian-Lebanese Patriotic Society. The deputy foreign minister of Brazil honoured one of the conferences with his presence, and the meeting was concluded with the Brazilian national anthem and the Marseillaise.

Several of the speeches given at these meetings are worth mentioning. Ni'ma Jafet, president of the Syrian-Lebanese Patriotic Society, called upon his listeners to exchange the religious bond with the national bond and extolled the mobilization for the Légion d'Orient in the cause of liberating Syria and Lebanon. Jamil Mardam said: "Brothers! The Muslims already know that they and their Christian brothers have one fatherland and a common interest . . . This is the new spirit which rules the heart of every Syrian Muslim . . . Yes, it is so! The Muslims erred in the past by thinking that the religious bond was stronger than the national one, but they soon realized their error and have begun to atone for their past misdeeds." Lakah emphasized in his speeches the love of the Syrians for France "because of the principles of freedom which bind us to her, and for her noble feelings and freely given services to the weak and oppressed". At a certain point the emissaries were asked by the local people what was in store for the future Syria. When this question was sent to Shukri Ghanim he telegraphed them immediately: "The liberation of Syria and achieving a regime of freedom under the aegis of France". The French foreign ministry approved this wording, ex post facto.

However, the emissaries were not received everywhere with cordiality. It seems that they were more sympathetically received in Rio de Janeiro than in São Paulo. Several contradictory statements that the two had made concerning Syria and Lebanon caused the members of the Harmoun Club in São Paulo (émigrés from Hasbaya, Rashaya, and Marj 'Ayun) to dissociate themselves from the mission and to notify in the press that they would not cooperate with it until they had consulted with their countrymen in Egypt. (Immediately thereafter they sent a letter in this spirit to Faris Nimr, who was one of the prominent opponents of the CCS.) In several places the emissaries encountered an even more biting attitude, when they were met with insulting and mocking posters in which they were called traitors and sell-outs to France. When several newspapers published the names and pictures of émigrés who had agreed to volunteer for the Légion (against the advice of the two not to publish it), the opponents of the mission hastened to the volunteers to persuade them with threats and other means to withdraw.[15]

Despite all their difficulties the emissaries collected over 100,000 francs to finance the recruitment activities, and they sent to France the first detachment of volunteers. They also succeeded in setting up a super-committee to coordinate the activities of the societies in Rio de Janeiro and São Paulo. The French foreign ministry, which was not well aware of the difficulties that the mission had encountered, was quite excited about its accomplishments till then and decided to allocate 10,000 additonal francs to finance the travels of the emissaries. The ministry also budgeted 40,000 francs from its "Fonds Spéciaux" for support of pro-French Syrian newspapers in Brazil which supported the policy of France towards Syria. The payments were to be transferred to these newspapers as if in the name of the CCS. After the mission returned to Paris Lakah recommended giving additional financial subsidies to a list of Syrian newspapers in Brazil. However, this time the French minister in Rio de Janeiro expressed determined opposition to doing so. In his opinion the general picture of the recruiting mission episode showed that the Syrian communities in Brazil were indifferent towards the Allies in general and towards France in particular and even towards their own people in Syria. The recruiting attempt for the Légion d'Orient was, in his words, a "fiasco", both as to the number of recruits and their quality.[16]

On 26 September 1917 the mission arrived in Montevideo, the capital of Uruguay. It was received by the local Syrian and Lebanese with sympathy, garlands of flowers, and tricolor flags. On his arrival Lakah organized a "Lebanese-Syrian Patriotic Society" with the French minister in Montevideo elected as its honorary president. The goals of the society were: "(1) To serve the interests of Mount Lebanon and Syria . . . (2) To declare the independence of Mount Lebanon in its ancient borders, under a French protectorate. (3) To support the expeditionary force that the glorious French nation was preparing . . . (4) To encourage the recruitment of volunteers for this expeditionary force. (5) To collect funds for the above-mentioned objectives." And indeed, the mission succeeded in recruiting 20 volunteers, whose physical fitness was checked personally by Lakah, a physician by profession. The 20 were sent later on to France, and it was characterized as a success by the French consul, who prior to the arrival of the mission was not able to recruit even a single volunteer. After several meetings with the participation of notables from the Syrian-Lebanese community in Montevideo, the mission continued on its way to Argentina.[17]

On 12 October 1917 the mission arrived in Buenos Aires. The very large Lebanese community of Argentina was composed mainly of Maronites. The dominant society among these was the "Union Libanaise" of Buenos Aires, which was founded close to the outbreak of the World War. It strove during the war for the complete independence of Mount Lebanon in its ancient borders under French aegis. This ideology was destined to bring it into a confrontation with the mission from Paris. The relations of the society with the French minister in Buenos Aires were good. The latter thought he could use it as a tool to recruit volunteers for the Légion d'Orient, and therefore he worked to persuade Syrians in northern Argentina to join it. His efforts did not go well, mainly because of the hostility that existed between the various Syrian and Lebanese communities. The Maronites objected to any idea of cooperation with the Greek Orthodox, the Melchites, or the Armenians, and most certainly they were opposed to cooperation with the Druzes or Muslims. Still he succeeded in bringing the society close to France. On the 14 Juillet of 1916 the society sent a telegram of congratulations to the newspaper *al-Mustaqbal* and the large newspapers of Paris. On the 14 Juillet of 1917 it held a large party in honour of this day with the participation of the French minister and other

French diplomats and notables. On the eve of the arrival of the Parisian mission to South America the society was still able to ensure the patronage of the French legation in Buenos Aires for all the Lebanese in Argentina. The Argentine government announced consequently that in case of a declaration of war between Argentina and the Empire the Lebanese émigrés would not be considered Ottoman subjects. However, the good relations between the society and the French were about to change.[18]

The leaders of the Union Libanaise received the recruiting mission coldly and expressed their chagrin at the non-inclusion of even one Maronite in it. They refused to cooperate either in disseminating propaganda or in recruiting volunteers despite the efforts of the French minister to bring the two sides together. The leaders of the society especially refused to establish any contact with the CCS. The minister asked the members of the society to work on their own then to carry out the recruitment programs. However, following the controversy that arose between the society leaders and the emissaries from Paris the former informed the French minister that they would do so only if he would make an official commitment that after the liberation of Syria by the Allies, the Lebanese — and especially the Maronites — would attain a special autonomous regime.

The society also opened a vigorous propaganda campaign in its newspaper *al-Ittihad al-Lubnani* against the mission. It announced that it was loyal only to the Lebanon and its independence and that it had full confidence that France would help realize this aspiration. Pursuant to this ideology it would refuse to maintain any connection with a non-Lebanese society (meaning the CCS), or one that was not striving for the independence of the Lebanon. "The Syrian question is one question and the Lebanese question is another, and we are unable not to separate the one from the other." Furthermore, the society not only sharpened the contrast between the Lebanese idea and the Syrian idea and expressed unequivocal opposition to any possibility of annexing Lebanon to Syria, but it also explicitly accused the mission and the CCS of not working for the independence of the Levant, but rather for its occupation. The society's newspaper accused the mission from Paris that in its desire to connect the recruiting activities and even the Union Libanaise itself with the CCS it would only cause the recruitment effort to fail. The newspaper informed the French that it would respond to their appeal concerning the recruitment if the French government would recognize the independence of the society's activities in this area from those of the CCS and its mission.

The mission encountered opposition not only from the Union Libanaise and the Maronites. It met opposition of a different type from pro-German newspapers, who greeted it with open hostility because of the very fact that it was working on behalf of the Allies. They attacked the idea of recruiting for the Légion d'Orient and accused the CCS of aspiring to bring about the annexation of Syria to France. After the mission returned to Paris it suggested to the French foreign ministry to set up "black lists" of Syrians disloyal to France in Buenos Aires, who were apparently under German influence. On the other hand, Lakah suggested granting financial subsidies to a series of pro-French Syrian newspapers in Buenos Aires so that they would struggle against the German influence.[19]

The mission spent almost four months in Argentina, but aside from a number of meetings it held in Buenos Aires and several other cities it did not record any noticeable achievement. The number of volunteers who agreed to join the Légion d'Orient came to 14 (according to another version 17), all of them Syrians. The French minister in Buenos Aires judged its activity as "almost a total failure". On the other hand it managed to cause a break in the good relations that had existed prior to its arrival between the French legation and the Union Libanaise. The members of this society stubbornly held to the idea of Lebanese independence and to separation from the activity on behalf of all Syria. At a certain point they even sent a letter to the French minister threatening to sever all ties with the legation if it continued to support the tendencies which found expression in the views of the mission from Paris. Apparently the leaders of the society themselves then felt that they had gone too far, and later they began an information campaign in their newspaper, in which they emphasized that they wanted an independent Lebanon under French aegis and had never accused France of wanting to turn Lebanon into a colony. The CCS was the one who was interested in that, and the dispute was therefore between the society and the CCS and not between it and France. They described the statements of the CCS against them as outright lies and stressed that the Lebanese had nothing against the Syrians. Their acting separately was due only to the special status of their mountain. The society also made known its readiness to work with all its strength on behalf of the recruitment. It thought that with this it had succeeded in restoring its good relations with the French legation to what they had been. However, from a report by the French minister in late 1919, it seems that the legation

did not forgive the society for its conduct at the time the recruitment mission came, and considered it a disloyal element. It
therefore recommended not to give its members certificates for
passports to Syria because their presence there might be detrimental to French interests. As for the recruitment mission itself,
it continued on for a short visit to Chile, and according to its
own account was well received by the local émigrés, who disso-
ciated themselves from the conduct of the Lebanese of Buenos
Aires. According to the French minister, on the other hand, its
success in Chile was not much greater than in Argentina. In
February 1918 the mission returned to Paris.[20]

In July 1917, while the mission was making its first steps in
South America, Shukri Ghanim came up with a new idea. He
suggested to the French war minister that instead of the attempts
that were being made since the beginning of the war to drag
France into military involvement in the Levant, a real Syrian
army should be formed which would be assigned the task of liberating Syria. Ghanim estimated that it would be possible to
recruit for this army in the two Americas, in Egypt, and in the
French possessions in Africa 12,000 to 15,000 men. With the
landing of this army in Syria it would be joined by another
15,000 to 20,000 locals from Mount Lebanon, Tripoli, Beirut,
and other places, and a general revolt would break out against
the Ottomans in the entire region. Ghanim stressed that if
France should adopt this plan, it would enhance its prestige
among the Syrians and among Muslims in general.

The French war ministry weighed Ghanim's proposal and
came to the conclusion that it was without any serious foundation. The attempt to recruit volunteers for the Légion d'Orient
had already proved that even if the Syrian émigré communities
showed sympathy for France, they still did not show any extra
enthusiasm to be actually mobilized. Moreover, even the few
volunteers had turned out to be of poor quality. The sad experience of recruiting Syrians for the Légion d'Orient brought the
war ministry to the conclusion that at most it would be possible
to recruit 1,000 to 2,000 men for the army that Ghanim proposed. In addition, it considered Ghanim's proposal an unnecessary duplication of the Légion d'Orient, which already existed,
and to which it would be possible to add the new recruits that
Ghanim professed to bring. It therefore decided that it would be
a waste to allocate French officers and military equipment for
this force. In September 1917 a polite letter of reply was sent to
Ghanim thanking him for his proposal and bringing to his attention that the Légion d'Orient was designed to be able to absorb

many additional volunteers, many more than it had at the time. Under these conditions it seemed unnecessary to set up an additional military force, and any Syrian who wanted to volunteer for the liberation of his fatherland could join the Légion d'Orient.[21]

In December Ghanim made a new proposal. The background to this proposal was the rapid advance of the British on the Palestine front, which led Ghanim to fear that they would soon penetrate into Syria and become the dominant force there. In order to preserve the influence of France in the Levant, and being aware that France could not send substantial forces to the region at that time, Ghanim proposed that the moment the first square kilometre of Syrian soil would be liberated, a local Syrian government on behalf of France should be set up there. This government would call for help from the French forces accompanying Allenby on the Palestine front, headed by the French high commissioner of Syria (a function then being fulfilled by Georges-Picot), who would be given the task of organizing a local regular army. This action would not require large forces nor opening a new front, nor would it encounter opposition from the allies of France, who had already recognized its rights over Syria. On the other hand, this would be the last chance for France to maintain its status and influence in Syria.[22] Nothing is known of any serious consideration of this plan by the French, other than its being filed away in their foreign ministry files.

The danger of an increase in British influence in Syria worried Ghanim throughout the entire period and especially after Allenby succeeded in breaking through the Ottoman front in the third battle of Gaza. He warned the French foreign minister that the Syrians would consider the British their sole liberators and complained that the impression was being created that France was neglecting Syria. He urged him therefore not to lose time and to take immediate action to prevent British hegemony in the east. Ghanim did not have to be concerned for long about the status of France in Syria. In November 1917 the Bolsheviks exposed the Sykes-Picot agreement. On 23 December 1917 the CCS held a conference with the participation of French statesmen, among them Jean Gout, a senior official in the foreign ministry. The guest of honour at the conference was Mark Sykes. After a short opening address by Ghanim about the devotion of the Syrians to France, Sykes made a long speech in which he made it clear that Britain and France were completely united in their policy towards the non-Turkish regions of the Ottoman Empire. He suggested to the Syrians that they achieve internal unity among themselves in order to be able to set up in Syria a regime of development, culture, and freedom. He added that they should aspire to receive the vital assistance of France, which they would need until they were able to administer their affairs by themselves. Gout spoke after Sykes and confirmed in the name of the French foreign ministry what Sykes had said about the full agreement that existed between France and Britain concerning the future of the non-Turkish population in Asia Minor. Gout also pointed out that the two powers had no colonialist intention. They had decided — each one in its sphere of influence — to guide to autonomy, development, and a better future the Arabic-speaking people living between the heights of Anatolia and the Indian Ocean. "Friendly advisor of civilization, this was the duty that France and Great Britain were prepared to take upon themselves, the one in the north and the other in the south." His words were greeted with thunderous applause. Several days later the French foreign minister gave a speech in the Chamber of Deputies, in which he asserted the traditional rights of France in Syria and its natural duty as its liberator. The CCS considered the speech a confirmation of the statements by Sykes and Gout. It hastened to express to the foreign minister the gratitude of the Syrians and the Lebanese for the interest which France had shown in them and their hope that its friendship and support for them would last forever.[23]

On 7 March 1918 the administrative council of the CCS held a conference on the occasion of the return of the recruitment mission from South America. The main speech at this conference was given by Shukri Ghanim, who pointed out that the results of the mission could have been better had they not encountered counter-propaganda on the part of some individuals with personal interests, who did not hesitate to cause substantive damage to Syria. Moreover, in the war of the columns that they carried on in the press they attacked not only the CCS but France itself. On 16 March the CCS held a party in honour of the members of the mission with the participation of prominent French statesmen. The first of the speakers was Ghanim, who emphasized that the liberation of Syria would be achieved with the aid of "our mother France", to which the Syrians were faithful "to death". Then Samné gave a detailed report of the trip of the mission, almost skipping over the sad chapter of the mission's visit to Argentina. In contrast to this, Dr. Lakah, who spoke after him, dwelt on the difficulties encountered by the mission. Concluding the array of speeches was Jamil Mardam, who called on the Syrians to unite for the liberation of their common fatherland.[24]

With the end of the war and the liberation of Syria from the Ottomans the CCS flooded the French foreign ministry with congratulatory telegrams for the French government. These had reached the society from various Syrian and Lebanese organizations with whom it had been in contact in North and South America and West Africa. The society of course sent its own warm telegram for the part played by France in the liberation of Syria and on the occasion of the entry of the French to Beirut. However, on 10 October 1918 the society decided to register also a protest with the French foreign minister, in its name and in "the name of all the societies affiliated with it throughout the world", against the Sykes-Picot agreement. What disturbed the CCS about this agreement was not the turning of the region into a protectorate or sphere of influence of a foreign power — the cause of disturbance for the other Arab elements — but the very fact that Syria was divided according to this agreement between two powers, and not placed in its entirety under the sole aegis of France. The society was therefore protesting against the partition of Syria and the severance of Damascus from its main ports, from the fertile fields of the Hawran, and from the important cities such as Aleppo and Homs. They strongly demanded the establishment of a democratic and federal Syria, maintaining the national unity of the Syrians, and with the vital assistance of France.

The ideology that was then guiding the society found expression in a pamphlet published by its secretary-general Georges Samné entitled *La Question Syrienne*: "There exists a Syrian question . . . Syria demands to be established as a free nation. It demands along with this freedom the integrity of the country and its unity within its natural borders from the Taurus to Sinai and from the Mediterranean Sea to the desert. . . . In order for Syria to be a strong state, united and prosperous, it needs a constitutional regime . . . it needs a federal constitution . . . and it needs finally the support of a friendly great power. France alone fulfills these conditions. . . . Therefore, European interest, Allied interest, Syrian interest, and French interest, all these lead to the establishment of a federative Syria under French aegis." The future Syrian state was perceived by Samné as a democratic, secular state, and he rejected entirely the possibility of a Hijazi sovereignty over Syria. And until the new Syria was properly organized Samné recommended the stationing of a French high commissioner in Damascus.[25]

Following the new circumstances in Syria Shukri Ghanim

suggested to the French foreign ministry to take a series of measures to enhance French prestige in the Levant and to neutralize
the influence of the liberating British forces. He proposed opening an intensive propaganda campaign, not only among the Syrian communities abroad, but also in Syria itself. This
propaganda would be spread by means of the press, leaflets,
meetings, and especially by verbal propaganda, the most effective
of all. In order to prevent tension between the Allies, the
employment of these means of propaganda should be entrusted
to the CCS. Ghanim therefore requested an initial sum of
500,000 francs to finance this activity, and recommended close
cooperation between the society and the French authorities in
the administrative organization of Syria and in the selection of
suitable people to carry out this assignment.

The French foreign ministry examined Ghanim's proposal and
then came to the inescapable conclusion that Ghanim and his
society were not the suitable factors to carry out an operation of
this type. A summation of the CCS's activity brought out that it
was not successful in becoming a unifying factor among the Syrian communities and societies in America and in Europe. Moreover, even in France it had not succeeded in achieving an
authoritative status among the Syrian and Lebanese émigrés,
many of whom (and not only its outstanding opponents such as
Bishop Faris and Khayrallah) disagreed with it. Ghanim himself
was indeed considered a respected personality, but he had been
absent from Syria for many years and had no supporters there.
Therefore it would be unwise to send him to Syria or to use his
society as a propaganda instrument of the French government
among the population of Syria. The foreign ministry decided to
inform him therefore that since the military operations in Syria
were not yet concluded it would not be possible for any civilian
to enter it. On the other hand, it was decided to grant the society
50,000 francs to distribute among needy Syrians and for sending
packages to the soldiers and the wounded of the Légion d'Orient
in Palestine. It was also recommended to tell Ghanim that his
remaining in Paris would be of greater benefit to Syria because
the foreign ministry could then avail itself of his precious
advice.[26]

EMIGRE SOCIETIES IN NORTH AMERICA

The Syrian and Lebanese communities in the United States at the time of World War I numbered about 300,000 people, about two thirds of whom were Christians and the rest Muslims and Druzes. This was apparently the country with the largest community of emigrants from the Levant. The pan-Arab idea was not widespread among these émigrés, and those among them who were interested in what was happening in the Ottoman Empire focused on Syria and Lebanon alone. The largest émigré communities were in New York, where the two more active societies during the early part of the war functioned, the "Syrian Union Society" and the "Lebanon League of Progress".

The Syrian Union Society (two of whose members participated in the Arab-Syrian Congress in Paris in 1913) worked, as its name attested, for all of Syria. According to pronouncements of the editor of the veteran newspaper *Mir'at al-Gharb*, which was under the influence of the society, it seems that its leaders did not believe in the ability of the Syrians to rule themselves alone after the war, and were in favour of a British protectorate. The last known activity of this society was the sending of a petition to the American Secretary of State in May 1916 in which they requested the intervention of the United States to rescue the Christians of Syria from the sad fate of the Armenians.[27]

More important than this society was the Lebanon League of Progress (*al-Nahda al-Lubnaniyya* in Arabic), which tried in the beginning of the war to persuade the representatives of the Allies in Washington to invade Mount Lebanon with the assistance of thousands of potential Lebanese volunteers from North America. This initiative of the society was rejected by the Allies. The Lebanon League of Progress strove for the establishment of an independent constitutional principality in Mount Lebanon in its original boundaries. This principality would be ruled by an elected foreign prince, who would bequeath the post to his descendants, and it would be under the aegis of France. The attitude of the society to France was very warm, as was also the attitude of its president, the Maronite Na'um Mukarzal (also a participant in the Arab-Syrian Congress in Paris in 1913), who was the owner of the veteran pro-French newspaper *al-Huda*.

In late May 1915 the society sent a letter to the French ambassador in Washington in which they informed him once more of their loyalty to France and added that the inhabitants of

Mount Lebanon were anxiously awaiting the moment when France would decide to use their services (that is, would invade Mount Lebanon). The Lebanese were ready to bear French rifle and bayonet in order to realize their national aspirations under the wings of their protector these many generations, France. Several days later the ambassador received a further memorandum, in which the sad situation of Mount Lebanon was described and the oppressions of its inhabitants by the Ottoman authorities were detailed. The society stated that it indeed understood that in the current situation the Allies could not allocate soldiers for a landing on the coasts of the Lebanon. Still it was asking the Allies to enable the Lebanese to defend themselves by aiding the transportation to Lebanon of volunteers from among the Lebanese émigrés, and the shipment of arms and ammunition. The society suggested that the problem of American neutrality be solved by way of Canada.[28]

The proposals of the society did not earn the serious attention of the French. In mid-1915 it decided to arrange a general Lebanese congress in which representatives of all the Lebanese communities and societies in the two Americas would participate. The congress was to have opened in early September and to last a week. In the announcement the society disseminated it pointed out that considering the disregard by the Ottomans of the international agreements concerning Mount Lebanon, and since on account of the war the powers guaranteeing its status could not intervene on its behalf, therefore the society had decided to convene a congress to discuss ways to restore to Mount Lebanon its independence and even to broaden it. The society made clear in its announcement that it was striving to obtain complete independence for Mount Lebanon with a foreign prince as constitutional ruler. It also noted that in addition to this subject the congress would discuss the means to unite the various Lebanese émigré communities and their societies. Apparently the society could not carry out its plans. No congress was held in September. At first the organizers announced that it was only postponed. But in early October the society announced that it considered it unnecessary to hold the congress because the Allied governments had decided by themselves to be responsible for "the defence and freedom of the small nations".[29]

During the course of 1916 the society continued to bring the French ambassador's attention to the systematic violations of the special status of Mount Lebanon being committed by the Ottomans. The society especially protested the replacement of the Christian governor of the mountain by a Muslim governor, which was contrary to the règlement organique of the mountain to which the European powers were guarantors. It claimed that in effect the Ottomans had terminated the autonomy of the mountain and had annexed it to the vilayet of Damascus. And indeed in November 1916 the Empire officially announced the abrogation of the règlement organique. When this became known to the society, it hastened to send a sharp protest to the French ambassador, in which it explained that the Lebanon had always enjoyed autonomy, its regime was different from that of the rest of Syria, and it was not in fact considered a regular province of the Empire. By abrogating its special status the Empire had violated its treaties with the powers that were guarantors for the autonomy of the mountain. At present the Lebanese were of course unable to oppose it, but they were raising their voice in vehement protest and hoping that when the day arrived in which international disputes would be settled, this injustice would also be redressed.[30]

Another subject which occupied the society during the war was the question of the connection or lack of connection that there would be between Lebanon and Syria after the war. Already in January 1916 Na'um Mukarzal had made a special trip to Washington to find out if France had changed its intentions concerning his country. He explained to the French ambassador that rumours were spreading that France intended to establish a greater Syria in which there would be a Muslim majority, and made it clear to him that the Lebanon was interested in becoming a principality or republic that would be run by itself. In July 1917 Mukarzal sent a telegram to the French premier in which he demanded complete independence for Mount Lebanon under French aegis, and he did not forget to stress at the end of the telegram: "We refuse to be included in Syria, in which most of the population are Arabs or Muslims. We are not Arabs, and the calamities that we have suffered were caused only by religious laws that do not accord with our civilization." In October of that year Mukarzal visited the French consul-general in New York and forcefully informed him that "in the light of history, tradition, and differences of race and religion, there should be set up in Lebanon and Syria two totally separate states. The Maronite Christians do not want to be included in a greater Syria, in which the Arabs and Muslims of all races would be the majority. . . . Each one, Lebanon and Syria, should have its independence and its own autonomous administration." Mukarzal emphasized that the Maronites desired a French protectorate and would regret to see the establishment of a combined protectorate of the Allies over a Greater Syria which would include Lebanon. These views of Mukarzal and the Lebanon League of Progress were about to bring them into conflict with a new society that was formed in New York a short time earlier.[31]

On 7 May 1917 the "Syria-Mount Lebanon League of Liberation" was founded in New York. Its president was Ayyub Thabit (a future president of Lebanon), who was one of the prominent activists of the Reform Society of Beirut before the war, and had participated in the Arab-Syrian Congress in Paris in 1913. Thabit, who was vehemently anti-Turkish, did not return to Beirut after the Congress, but moved to the United States and acquired great influence in the Syrian community in New York. A death sentence in absentia was issued against him in the Empire. At first Thabit was in favour of granting autonomy to Syria under the supervision of the powers, and he hoped for an Allied landing on the Syrian coast. However, since he was staunchly pro-French he very soon began a newspaper propaganda campaign in favour of a French protectorate over Syria. This was the political line that he advocated until the end of the war. His colleagues in the leadership of the society were in effect the intellectual elite of the Syrian and Lebanese émigrés in the United States. The vice-president was the author and historian Amin al-Rihani. The two secretaries of the society were the authors and poets Jubran Khalil Jubran and Mikha'il Nu'ayma. Under the influence of the society were the émigré newspapers *al-Sha'b*, *al-Fatat*, *al-Sa'ih*, and *al-Funun*.

The society was striving for the liberation of Syria and Lebanon with the help of France and its allies, but it preferred not to enter into the question of the relationship that would exist between the liberated Syria and Lebanon. It hoped that all the regions of Syria would have after the war administrative autonomy in the running of their internal affairs. The platform of the society laid down the following: "(1) The liberation from Turkish rule and Turkish sovereignty, whether it be actual or nominal. (2) Extending the aegis of France over Syria. (3) Postponement of the discussion of the form of internal government in Syria and of the relationship of Lebanon to the other parts of Syria until after the above two articles are implemented. (4) Total separation of the Arab question from the Syrian question." In addition to the above the society was active in trying to persuade Syrians and Lebanese to volunteer for the Légion d'Orient. These tendencies of the society brought it very close to the CCS. On the other hand, its human composition and goals brought it into confrontation with Mukarzal's Lebanon League of Progress. While Thabit's society was working on behalf of all of Syria and was made up of people from all its communities, Mukarzal's society was working on behalf of Mount Lebanon alone and was made up solely of Maronites. This ideological confrontation brought about a split in the ranks of the Syrian and Lebanese activists in New York which lasted until the end of the war.[32]

On 18 June 1917 the Syria-Mount Lebanon League of Liberation held a meeting in Brooklyn, and its resolutions were sent to the President of the United States and to the ambassadors of France, Britain, Italy, and Russia in Washington. The conferees called upon the Allies to act in the cause of liberating the oppressed peoples of Syria and Lebanon from the yoke of Ottoman oppression. They also decided to start a propaganda campaign to persuade the Syrians and Lebanese in the countries where they had emigrated to volunteer for the Allied armies and thus to contribute their share in halting the German attempt to dominate the world. Afterwards the society decided to arrange a general meeting of representatives of all the Syrian émigré communities. In a public statement it promised to assist with all means at its disposal in the founding of leagues among the émigrés who supported its ideas and who were interested in spreading its views. It would be the central league for them. The society invited the representatives of these leagues to the general meeting in order to coordinate the lines of action in the various Syrian issues and to awaken in the Syrians the idea of personal and national independence. The conference was held in August, attended by over 600 people, among them the consul-general of France in New York, and during its course Thabit read out the society's platform.[33]

The declarations of Sykes and Gout concerning the future status of France in Syria, made before the CCS in December 1917 (see above), were welcomed by the Syria-Mount Lebanon League of Liberation, as was the speech of the French foreign minister on the rights of France in Syria, which had been given several days later in the French Chamber of Deputies. Another opportunity to demonstrate the loyalty of the society to France was afforded it after the publication of President Wilson's Fourteen Points. (The twelfth point spoke about assuring the autonomous development of the non-Turkish peoples of the Ottoman Empire.) In May 1918 the society sent a memorandum to President Wilson thanking him for his statements concerning the Ottoman Empire, which applied also to Syria. At the same time it made clear that in order for Syria to be able to develop autonomously it needed the guidance, assistance, and protection of France. The society explained that international guarantees for Syria would perhaps protect its Christian minority against the return of the Ottoman tyranny, but it would not be able to prevent Turkish intrigues which would arouse the fanatical elements among the illiterate masses, who were the majority. The progress of Syria towards national unity and autonomous development would then be prevented. Therefore, Syria needed the direct guidance and protection of a democratic Christian power, and this had to be France, its traditional protector. In an accompanying letter sent to the American Secretary of State the society pointed out that by these statements it was expressing the will of all Syrians, except for a few "fanatical Muslims", who were incorrigibly "pro-Turko-German".[34]

During 1918 the society worked for the recruitment of volunteers for the Légion d'Orient, and it retained a physician to examine the recruits. Those found suitable were sent to Bordeaux and from there to the Légion d'Orient. Several of them participated in battles in Palestine. However, the society dedicated its main efforts during this period to a comprehensive propaganda campaign to strengthen the relations between Syria and France, availing itself of the four émigré newspapers which were under its influence. (The editors-in-chief of these newspapers were members of the executive committee of the society.) Ayyub Thabit himself wrote 30 pro-French articles in the name of the society, many of which were reprinted in the Syrian press in South America. Thabit, who reported on all this to the French consul-general in New York, pointed out that "Our viewpoint of the Syrian question, in its relation to France, is exactly the same as the 'official' view" (of the French), that is, the liberation of Syria and the demand for a French protectorate. On this occasion Thabit emphasized that the dissemination of these ideas would be more successful if "certain organizations" in the two Americas were forbidden to use the name of France in their separatist activity on behalf of Lebanese "independence". Thabit made clear that this separatist activity was not only irrational but was also causing rifts among the Lebanese themselves. (Many of the members of the Syria-Mount Lebanon League of Liberation were Lebanese.) By these statements Thabit of course meant first of all Mukarzal's society. The French consul-general on his part did his best to reconcile the two societies and to bring about unity among the Syrian and Lebanese activists in New York. He explained to them the importance of presenting a

unified viewpoint to the American authorities and public opinion in the United States, but his efforts were in vain.[35]

The rift between the two societies and their supporters found
expression in October 1918 when they held two separate parties
to celebrate the victories of the Allies in Palestine and Syria. The
Lebanon League of Progress held a party to which only Maronites were invited. In contrast to this, Syrians and Lebanese of
all communities and religions were invited to the party held by
the Syria-Mount Lebanon League of Liberation. The French
consul-general in New York was invited to both parties. To the
second were invited also Colonel House and Professor Shotwell
of Columbia University, who afterwards participated in the
American delegation to the Paris peace conference. The main
speech at the party of the Syria-Mount Lebanon League of Liberation was given by its president Ayyub Thabit. He emphasized
in it the desire of the Syrians to be completely freed of the Ottoman yoke, in any form whatsoever, and their yearning for all of
Syria (including the Lebanon) to be placed under the protectorate of a single power. This power could only be France, which
was bound to Syria since the time of the Crusades. With the
help of France Syria would be able to achieve a liberal regime
and national development. He pointed out that these statements
of his were acceptable not only to the Christians but also to the
Muslims of Syria. Several of the Syrians who participated in this
meeting expressed to the French consul-general their fears of the
expansion of the Arab kingdom of the Hijaz into Syria with the
support of Britain. The consul-general calmed them by saying
that the question of the northern borders of the Arab kingdom
had not yet been settled, but he was convinced that it would not
include the coastal region of Syria and the Lebanon.[36]

In addition to the above-mentioned societies there were many
other societies of Syrian and Lebanese émigrés in the United
States. In New York itself there were the "Lebanese Cedar"
society, which demanded absolute independence for Mount
Lebanon, and the "American Lebanese Union", which
demanded independence for the Lebanon under French control.
In Cleveland "The New Spirit Society" was founded, which
strove for the attainment of the independence of the Syrian
nation (which, according to it, included the inhabitants of Lebanon and Palestine) and the establishment of a democratic, constitutional, and decentralized government in Syria within its
natural borders. Lebanon was to keep its special autonomous
status in the framework of this Syria. In early 1918 this society
convened a congress in Cleveland, to which were invited Syrians,

Lebanese, and Palestinians from the neighbouring communities to discuss the Syrian question. There also existed émigré societies in Mexico, of which the "Syrian-Lebanese Society" of Merida in Yucatan should be mentioned. This society was distinctly pro-French, and in March 1918 it sent a telegram of thanks to the French premier for the encouraging declarations made by Sykes and Gout before the CCS in December 1917 (see above), and for the speech made by the French foreign minister afterwards on the same subject. In Havana, Cuba, there was the "Lebanese-Syrian Liberation Society", which from time to time sent modest sums of money to the CCS in Paris.[37]

Chapter 8

THE FINAL MONTH OF THE WAR

Major-General Barrow was busy with his breakfast in the early hours of 30 September 1918 when General 'Ali Rida al-Rikabi was brought before him. Major-General Barrow was the commander of the 4th Cavalry Division, which was the main force of the eastern column of the British forces preparing for the final assault on Damascus. 'Ali Rida al-Rikabi was one of the prominent members of *al-Fatat* during World War I. On 22 September he was returned to the Ottoman army after several years in forced retirement, appointed commander of the Tiberias front, and assigned to halt the British advance at all costs. The rapid British advance caused this front to crumble in three days. Al-Rikabi returned to Damascus and was then assigned to defend the city after the departure of the Ottomans. On 30 September al-Rikabi surrendered himself to the British, seven miles south of Damascus, and was brought before Major-General Barrow. Al-Rikabi did not content himself with turning over all the information that he had on the plans for the defence of Damascus and on the general condition of the Ottomans in the city. He cheerfully told the British general that before his desertion he had stationed the Ottoman soldiers in the south of the city in positions that could not be defended and had organized the heavy artillery positions around Damascus such that they could not hold out because of lack of water.[1]

While al-Rikabi was bringing Barrow up to date on what was happening in Damascus, the situation in the city itself was quickly changing. The Ottomans, who had decided to leave the city, appointed Shukri al-Ayyubi its governor in order to ensure the neutrality of the inhabitants during their retreat. Al-Ayyubi immediately went to the prison of the citadel and released the 4,000 prisoners who were in it, among them murderers, thieves, and drug addicts. At the same time a number of Syrian leaders gathered in Damascus for a secret meeting to organize the takeover of the government after the Ottomans withdrew. In the middle of the meeting the brothers Muhammad Sa'id and 'Abd al-Qadir al-Jaza'iri burst in and announced that they were taking the reins of the government into their own hands.

The brothers al-Jaza'iri were the grandsons of Amir 'Abd al-Qadir al-Jaza'iri (their father, 'Ali al-Jaza'iri, was vice-president of the Ottoman parliament during a certain period). Before the war Sa'id had relations both with the French and with the Germans and had also maintained good relations with the Ottoman authorities as well. He became famous for killing three men in pistol incidents and breaking the head of a fourth. His younger brother 'Abd al-Qadir had studied before the war at the school for administration in Istanbul and was on the administrative committee of the "Literary Club". In 1916 their uncle 'Umar was hanged by the authorities for his contacts with the French, and at the same time the entire al-Jaza'iri family was deported to Anatolia. 'Abd al-Qadir escaped from his place of exile, and after a trek of hardships covering thousands of kilometres he managed to reach Mecca in September 1917. Husayn gave him a flag for him to wave in Damascus on the day of its liberation, and 'Abd al-Qadir went on to Faysal's camp in Aqaba. His relations with Faysal were apparently less good. There are those who believe that the tensions that built up between them derived from their being both men of dominant and ambitious personalities. Others believe that 'Abd al-Qadir did not think well of the influence the Iraqi officers had over Faysal.

In October 1917 Faysal asked him to assist Lawrence in blowing up the bridge in Wadi Khalid near Tall al-Shihab. The blowing up of this bridge was intended to cut the Ottoman lines of transportation in the Yarmuk valley, as part of the preparations for General Allenby's great offensive. Because in the region of the bridge there were villages in which there lived Algerians who supported the al-Jaza'iri family, Faysal thought that 'Abd al-Qadir could be of use in carrying out the mission successfully. From the outset 'Abd al-Qadir demonstrated an unwillingness to take part in the plan on various grounds, but Faysal pressured him to join Lawrence. The sabotage team left on its way, but two days before the planned attack, and at a distance of 50 miles from the bridge, 'Abd al-Qadir disappeared. He reappeared in Damascus and reported the plan to the authorities. The Ottomans did not believe him and arrested him. In the meantime the sabotage team reached the bridge, but when they approached its foundations in order to plant the sacks of explosives there, the rifle of one of them dropped. One of the bridge guards noticed them and opened fire. The men began a hasty escape for fear that the bullets would hit the sacks of explosives and blow them up. The operation failed and the force withdrew, leaving behind a number of dead. At this point the Ottomans were convinced

of the correctness of 'Abd al-Qadir's statements, and a reconcili-
ation was achieved between them, which included the return of
the al-Jaza'iri family from exile. 'Abd al-Qadir then began to
acquire great influence in Damascus, but between him and Lawrence an account was opened, which was to bring about his
doom.[2]

In early September 1918 Jamal Pasha "the Lesser" charged
Sa'id al-Jaza'iri with gathering together the Algerians in Syria
and forming a local force which would assist in maintaining
order and also help the Ottoman army. 'Abd al-Qadir was
placed at the head of the force, and he received from Jamal
Pasha 1,000 rifles and 70 crates of ammunition. The German
commander Liman von Sanders also gave Sa'id a substantial
sum of money for the defence of the Rayaq railway junction. At
first 'Abd al-Qadir did turn south with his army of volunteers in
order to come between the Arab army and Jabal al-Duruz, but
with the collapse of the Ottoman army in the face of General
Allenby's offensive and its retreat towards Damascus, 'Abd al-
Qadir returned there, too. At this juncture it was clear to the al-
Jaza'iri brothers that the Ottomans could no longer hold out. At
noon on 30 September 1918 'Abd al-Qadir al-Jaza'iri appeared
at the headquarters of Jamal Pasha "the Lesser" fully armed and
with his supporters waiting for him outside. He informed Jamal
Pasha that among the inhabitants there was a fear that the Germans wanted to burn down Damascus before its evacuation.
Therefore the Turks and the Germans had to leave the city
immediately, and he and his men would take upon themselves
the job of maintaining order during the withdrawal of the Ottoman forces. Jamal Pasha "the Lesser" was left with no option
but to accept the dictate of 'Abd al-Qadir, and at 14:00 he left
the city. At 14:30 the al-Jaza'iri brothers declared the independence of Syria under the temporary rule of Sa'id and in the
name of Husayn. (As a matter of fact, four days earlier Faysal
had sent a letter to Sa'id al-Jaza'iri, in which he enjoined him to
declare the establishment of a temporary Arab government in
Syria immediately on the withdrawal of the Ottomans. However,
because of the confusion that reigned around Damascus at that
time, the bearer of the letter, Fa'iz al-Ghusayn, could not deliver
the message to Sa'id.)

The flag which Husayn had handed to 'Abd al-Qadir was
hoisted by Sa'id from above the government house in the presence of the notables of the city, among them Shukri al-Ayyubi
and Faris al-Khuri. The Turkish and German soldiers who were
withdrawing from the city at the time passed by the waving flag

in total apathy. 'Abd al-Qadir on his part concentrated a force of about 1,500 Algerians and began to patrol the streets of the city and instill order. A proclamation signed by the two brothers was disseminated in the city and it called upon the inhabitants to maintain the peace. Severe punishments were assured for those who violated it. A guard was also stationed at the banks, over the foreign residents and over the Christian and Jewish minorities. Two young Syrians, supporters of Sa'id al-Jaza'iri, took over the Damascus telegraph office, and the news about the establishment of the Arab government was broadcast in all the cities of Syria.

With the fall of darkness a number of Ruwalla horsemen arrived in the city, sent by Sharif Nasir, the commander of the Arab force which was to have entered the city the next day. Their function was to locate 'Ali Rida al-Rikabi and to inform him that he was to head the new government and to await the entry of the Arab army the next day. But al-Rikabi was, as mentioned, with Barrow, and thus, at the end of the day, 30 September 1918, Sa'id al-Jaza'iri was left as the sole ruler of the city. Sa'id remained in the government house all night, issuing orders and trying to establish an orderly Arab government. He appointed a gendarmerie commandant, a general security service commander, and even a state council. But the entire government that he set up was to come to an end within a few hours.[3]

One of the most controversial questions in the history of the First World War in the Middle East is the question of who conquered, or to be more exact, who reached Damascus first. The controversy over this question resulted not only from considerations of national and political prestige, but also because in the Declaration to the Seven the recognition by the British of the independence of the areas liberated by the Arabs themselves was promised. This question can be resolved only by studying the reports of the British and other army officers who were in the city on the day it was conquered, on the one hand, or the reports of the local residents who were witnesses to this event, on the other. For this reason those who base themselves, for example, on Allenby's reports reach incorrect conclusions,[4] because Allenby arrived in the city only on 5 October, and his knowledge of what happened in Damascus on 1 October was not first-hand. In fact, on 1 October the Desert Mounted Corps (the force responsible for the occupation of Damascus) reported to British headquarters as follows:

Outskirts of Damascus were entered from the North West by Aus.

Div. last night. Col. Lawrence and Arabs entered this morning. Our troops keeping clear of Town . . .

This report was quite accurate. In the diary of the headquarters this was recorded at 13:40:

At 06:00 Damascus was taken. Understand Lawrence's Arabs have entered.

And at 14:00 a telegram was sent from Allenby to the War Office:

We took Damascus at 06:00 today. Details follow.

However, in the promised telegram, which was sent on the same day, the facts were already put together in the following form:

Last night the Australian Mounted Division entered the outskirts of Damascus from the north-west. The town was occupied by the Desert Mounted Corps and the Arab Army at 6 am to-day.

And in the final report that Allenby wrote on 31 October the following picture emerged:

Shortly after midday on Sept. 30 the Australian Mounted Division overcame the enemy resistance at Katana. By the evening it had closed the exits from Damascus to the north and the north-west, while the 5th Cavalry Division had reached the southern outskirts of the town. At 06:00 on Oct. 1, the Desert Mounted Corps and Arab Army entered Damascus . . .[5]

The exact facts were a bit different, as will be shown here, relying on British, French, Australian, and Arab sources. Lieutenant-General Chauvel, commander of the Desert Mounted Corps, wrote on 2 October a report on the taking of Damascus, in which the following was said, inter alia:

Late in the evening of the 30th, however, the Australian Mounted Division . . . had penetrated into the north-western outskirts of the city.

The British officer Willson, who was among those who entered Damascus, adds the following:

As a matter of fact, the Arabs were second-best in that race: on the evening of September 30th the Australian Mounted Division, with a brigade of which the Chasseurs d'Afrique were co-operating, and the British 5th Cavalry Division gained the suburbs of Damascus.

But then they received an order not to enter the city and to wait until the Arab army arrived. It turns out that not all the forces acted in accordance with this order. The French officer Pichon relates:

> The forces of General Allenby marched in two columns: the eastern column was composed of the British-French-Arab detachment of Lawrence and Faysal (with the French artillery battery of Pisani) and of the Indian 4th Cavalry Division (under Major-General Barrow); the western column was composed of the Australian Mounted Division of Major-General Hodgson (which included the three French squadrons of spahis and chasseurs d'Afrique under Commandant Lebon), and the Indian 5th Cavalry Division (under Major-General MacAndrew). The eastern column was delayed, and therefore the attack was led by the western column. The Australian division outflanked Damascus from the north, with the French regiment leading. At the moment when he was about to penetrate the city Commandant Lebon suddenly received an order to halt. It was the 3rd Australian Brigade which despite this was the first to enter the city the next day, 1 October, at 6:45.[6]

In the official history of Australia in the war it is told that at 05:00 on the morning of 1 October the 3rd Australian Light Horse Brigade under the command of Brigadier-General Wilson began to move from the northwest towards the centre of Damascus. Its mission was to take positions on the road to Homs. (This road was on the eastern side of Damascus, and in order to reach it the brigade had to cross the entire breadth of the city.) Leading the brigade was the 10th Regiment, and leading this regiment was the squadron of Major Timperley. The squadron advanced along the Barada River, with Major Timperley himself and Major Olden, the deputy commander of the 10th Regiment, riding at its head. A large crowd of people gathered in their way, and the Australian horsemen had to clear their way with drawn bayonets. When they arrived at the government house, the horsemen halted, and Timperley and Olden entered the building with drawn pistols and accompanied by a few soldiers. The time was between 06:30 and 07:00 in the morning. The two asked to see the governor, and Sa'id al-Jaza'iri came out to meet them. Olden, who was unaware of the situation inside the city, informed Sa'id that the city was surrounded by soldiers and that there was no point in further resistance. He demanded from him not to harass the entering soldiers. Sa'id answered: "In the name of the civil population of Damascus I welcome the British army," and he committed himself in writing to uphold Olden's demands. He even attached an Arab officer to the Australians in order to lead them to the road to Homs. This officer tried to persuade them to hold a victory parade in Damascus, and he did not understand "that the Australians were anxious to get clear of the city as soon as possible". Shortly after 07:00 Wilson's entire brigade had already vacated the city and had continued in pursuit of the Ottoman forces which had fled in the direction of Homs. This episode was summed up as follows in the first official summary of the campaigns of the Egyptian Expeditionary Force under the command of General Allenby, which was published in 1919: "Oct. 1 — [3rd Australian Light Horse Brigade] pushed on towards Damascus . . . and passed through the city at 06:00." As mentioned above, the exact time the brigade passed through the city was a little later, between 06:30 and 07:00. It should be added that the next forces that entered the city were patrols of the 14th Cavalry Brigade, which entered the city around 07:30 and reported that it was empty of Ottoman forces. (Chauvel wrote in his report that they entered at 06:00, but he apparently confused them with the Australians. Chauvel himself arrived at the government house only at 09:30.)[7]

The Arab version, based on the words of Saʻid al-Jazaʼiri, is almost completely identical to the Australian version, except for a few differences, which apparently cannot be avoided:

> Dawn had just broken on 1 October 1918, when the city was surrounded by an army of more than 10,000 British soldiers. The first to enter was an Australian major by the name of Arthur Olden. The amir [Saʻid] sent him a messenger who asked him what he wanted. He answered that he intended to take over the Hotel Victoria [where before this had been the headquarters of Jamal Pasha "the Lesser"] and to raise the British flag representing the first army that entered.

Afterwards Saʻid met with him personally, and according to his own account said to him that he had not conquered the city from the Ottomans because it had already become an independent city. Saʻid also instructed a pair of Arab officers to accompany the Australian soldiers (according to Saʻid, in order to supervise them so that they would not interfere in the affairs of the city). Later the vanguard of the Arab army entered the city, led by Sharif Nasir and accompanied by Colonel Lawrence.[8]

Concerning the time of entry of Lawrence and the Arabs into the city there are several versions. In the official British history of the war it is stated that Lawrence entered the city at 07:30 (apparently coupling his entry to the patrols of the 14th Cavalry

Brigade). Chauvel wrote the next day that at 08:00 he was informed that Lawrence and a number of Arab soldiers had already entered the city. Pichon delays the entry of Lawrence to 08:30. However, Lawrence himself wrote on the same day as follows: "Sharif Nasir with Major Stirling and myself moved into Damascus at 9 a.m."[9]

There were those who tried to explain why the soldiers of the Arab army were convinced that they were the first to enter the city. In the above-mentioned summary, concerning the campaigns of General Allenby, the following was stated: "The 14th Cavalry Brigade and Sherifian troops had entered Damascus on Oct. 1, but in so large a city it is not surprising that both detachments were ignorant of the arrival of the other, and that both thought that they were first in. On point of actual time a detachment of the 10th Australian Light Horse Regiment under Major Olden reached the Serail at 06:30 on Oct. 1, while Colonel Lawrence and Sherifian Camel Corps were a little later." (Concerning the entry of different forces into the city, from different places, it can be learned also from the testimony of the British officer Kirkbride. He entered the city through the Maydan quarter in the south in the morning hours of 1 October, and according to the reaction of the population it seems that at least in this region no other forces preceded him.) The official Australian history tries to explain also why the new forces that entered the city were not aware that the Australians had entered before them: "[Brigadier-General Wilson] sent back no messenger and left no troops in the city, but went on after the enemy with every man in his brigade. When, therefore, soon after he had cleared the streets, Lawrence rode into the town with a few Arab horsemen on the heels of the advance-guard of the 14th Cavalry Brigade, the Arabs believed that they shared with the Indians the honour of the first entry."[10]

When he entered Damascus, Lawrence went straight to the government house together with the tribal chiefs Nuri al-Sha'lan and 'Awda Abu Tayh. Joining them shortly thereafter were several al-Fatat members who had accompanied the army of the revolt. They were all stunned to find there the al-Jaza'iri brothers, who they had considered collaborators with and supporters of the Ottomans. Lawrence himself, as mentioned, had an unsettled account with 'Abd al-Qadir al-Jaza'iri. Therefore, after Shukri al-Ayyubi explained to Lawrence what had happened, Lawrence publicly announced that as Faysal's representative he had decided to depose them and to appoint al-Ayyubi as acting governor of the city. The al-Jaza'iri brothers took this hard.

Sa'id began to denounce Lawrence as being Christian and British, and 'Abd al-Qadir cursed Lawrence and drew a dagger. He would have fallen upon him had not Nuri al-Sha'lan and 'Awda Abu Tayh stood at Lawrence's sides. The al-Jaza'iri brothers, who were aware of the presence of Nuri al-Sha'lan's men and Nuri al-Sa'id's soldiers in the main square of the city, had no choice but to leave the building in great anger.

'Abd al-Qadir was not prepared to let this go by so easily. That night he gathered about 600 of his Algerian supporters and began to make fiery speeches against the Sharifs, that they were only servants of the Christians and their handiwork. He called for the expulsion from the city of the Sharifs and the British together. His men began to run riot, and joining them were the Druzes, who began looting. On the morning of 2 October the soldiers of the Arab army began to restore order in the city, using machine-guns against the rioters. The riots were suppressed within three hours, with about 20 bodies lying in the streets. By noon quiet reigned, with Nuri al-Sa'id's soldiers and Nuri al-Sha'lan's bedouins patrolling the streets and preventing any further attempt by the Algerians to run riot. 'Abd al-Qadir was caught and put in jail. Sa'id hid out at first, but was eventually caught and brought to the government house. The two would have been stood before a firing squad and executed had not Faysal arrived in Damascus on 3 October and announced a general amnesty. The al-Jaza'iri brothers were saved, but not for long.[11]

Within a short time Sa'id quarreled with Faysal, after he refused Faysal's request to place one of his houses at his disposal. 'Abd al-Qadir became involved in a confrontation with Faysal when he made plain to him that Faysal was no nobler than he by saying: "You are an Arab; so am I! You are from the race of the Prophet; so am I! You are from a family of amirs; so am I!" The al-Jaza'iris also quarreled with 'Ali Rida al-Rikabi, who replaced Shukri al-Ayyubi as governor of Damascus and wanted to put 'Abd al-Qadir back in jail for the above-mentioned riots. They began to undermine al-Rikabi and to try to persuade Faysal to replace him with another governor. Rumours were also spread — with the brothers' encouragement — that they were planning to carry out an uprising. All these factors, in addition to their very active past at the time of the Arab revolt and the liberation of Syria, brought Faysal to the conclusion that he could not maintain public order in Damascus and administer the city properly so long as the brothers were wandering around freely. He turned to Allenby with a request to arrest the two and deport them from the country. The request was answered in the positive.

On 7 November an arrest order was issued against the two. Sa'id was required to report to the authorities, and on his way to do this his automobile was stopped by two police officers and he was taken to the al-Maza prison. Ten days later he was transferred to Haifa, following an order from Allenby, and only in June 1919 was he permitted to return to Beirut. 'Abd al-Qadir spent the morning of 7 November at his grandfather's grave in the north of the city together with about 200 Algerian guests who had come from Safed and Tiberias. When he returned to his house, he found it surrounded by police and gendarmes. He went inside, and then the police prevented the other Algerians from joining him. One of the police officers went into the house after him and asked him to turn himself in. 'Abd al-Qadir refused. The officer went outside to get help, and then 'Abd al-Qadir went outside after him, jumped onto his horse and announced that he would ride by himself to the British commander and iron out the difficulties. The police surrounded the horse with rifles pointed, the horse made a frightening movement, the policemen sprung back, and 'Abd al-Qadir burst forth under a hail of bullets. He began to gallop up the street, ran into another police force, was hit in his abdomen and back and died three hours later.[12]

According to the original plan 'Ali Rida al-Rikabi was to be the governor of Damascus after the Ottomans left. Since he was not in the city on 1 October, Lawrence, as mentioned, appointed Shukri al-Ayyubi as temporary military governor. Al-Ayyubi did not show much suitability for the job (as noted, before the situation in the city was stabilized he released around 4,000 men from the Damascus jail, many of them criminals, which became a problem in itself during the following days). Therefore, as soon as al-Rikabi returned to the city he was appointed its military governor, according to Faysal's instruction. On 3 October Allenby approved the appointment of al-Rikabi as Chief Administrator of internal Syria (OETA, East), and on 5 October Faysal announced this in an official order. Shukri al-Ayyubi was given a new assignment, which will be described in the following paragraphs. In the meantime it became known to several of the al-'Ahd and al-Fatat leaders who had arrived in the city with the revolt army that Yasin al-Hashimi had managed to reach Damascus with the remnants of his corps, shortly before the city was taken, and was wounded and hiding in one of the houses in the Maydan quarter. They located him, he was made a member of the administrative committee of *al-Fatat*, and Faysal appointed him chief of the general staff of the new Syrian army which was to be established then.[13]

It has already been related above that on 30 September supporters of Sa'id al-Jaza'iri took over the Damascus telegraph office and had informed the various cities of Syria of the establishment of the Arab government in Damascus. One of the telegrams which went out that day was addressed to 'Umar al-Da'uq, the mayor of Beirut, who was asked to follow the example of Damascus and declare an Arab government in Beirut. Al-Da'uq was very perplexed to receive this telegram because until then he had not dealt with political subjects beyond the municipal plane. However, the Beiruti activists Ahmad Mukhtar Bayhum and Salim 'Ali Salam encouraged him to act in this spirit, and at a meeting attended by representatives of the important families of Beirut it was decided to set up a temporary Arab government in the name of the Damascus government. Thus, on 1 October 1918, an Arab government was established also in Beirut, headed by al-Da'uq, a government that was to last only one week.[14]

According to the Declaration to the Seven, the British were to recognize the independence of all the areas that would be liberated by the Arabs themselves. In this state of affairs there was room for the Arabs to assume that Beirut would belong to the independent Arab state. On the other hand, it was agreed by the British that Beirut and the coastal region would be turned over to the French, according to the Sykes-Picot agreement. And indeed, when the situation in Beirut became complicated in the next few days, Allenby sent a telegram to the War Office in which he complained about the issuance of the Declaration to the Seven without consulting him beforehand. He intimated that it was raising hopes among the Arab leaders which could not be realized owing to the terms of the Sykes-Picot agreement. Meanwhile, Lawrence advised Faysal to send a representative in his name to Beirut to declare an Arab government there in his name. Faysal agreed to the suggestion (apparently he had received a request in this spirit also from a number of Beirut notables), and he decided to send Shukri al-Ayyubi there. On 5 October at night al-Ayyubi left Damascus on his way to Beirut accompanied by 20 horsemen (according to another version, 100 horsemen). Before this, at a dinner attended by the French officer Coulondre, who was attached to the French high commission that was to be set up in Syria, Nuri al-Sa'id told about the sending of al-Ayyubi to Beirut. Coulondre left the dinner in the

middle, sent an urgent telegram to France to bring his government up to date on developments, and went himself to Beirut to
hasten the arrival of French forces there. The French protested
vehemently to the British Foreign Office and demanded the
removal of al-Ayyubi from Beirut. When Allenby found out
about all this, he reprimanded Lawrence for his initiating the
sending of al-Ayyubi, and made it clear to him that the coastal
region belonged to the French according to the Sykes-Picot
agreement.

In the late morning of 7 October Shukri al-Ayyubi and his
men arrived in Beirut. He settled himself in the government
house, declared himself military governor of the city in the name
of Faysal, and hoisted the Arab flag. He took over the governing
authority from 'Umar al-Da'uq and appointed Habib al-Sa'd the
civil governor of the city. On 8 October French forces landed in
Beirut led by Colonel de Piépape, who was to fill the post of
French military governor of Beirut. With him came also the
British 21st Corps under command of General Bulfin. The
French officer tried to persuade al-Ayyubi to leave, but in vain.
In the meantime Allenby ordered al-Ayyubi removed from Beirut and to take down the Arab flags that had been raised there.
British intelligence officers came to al-Ayyubi and informed him
of the termination of his mission. The flag that was raised over
the city hall was taken down (al-Da'uq was interested in cooperating with the French), but al-Ayyubi opposed taking down the
flag from above the government house and refused to leave his
office without a direct order from Faysal. Allenby instructed the
British liaison officer in Damascus to ask Faysal to send al-
Ayyubi an order in this spirit, and on 9 October he himself
instructed Bulfin to order al-Ayyubi to vacate the government
house by midnight. Bulfin did as required and informed al-
Ayyubi that if he did not leave the government house by midnight he would be evicted by force. All the Arab flags that had
been raised in the city were taken down. In this state of affairs
al-Ayyubi instructed the mayor and the police commanders to
obey the orders of the British, and when a British force arrived
at the government house at midnight it found that the Sharifs
had already left it. On 11 October de Piépape entered the government house and commenced functioning as military governor
of the city. Al-Ayyubi and his men returned to Damascus leaving behind Jamil al-Ulshi as liaison officer of the Arab army in
Beirut. All that Faysal could do was to protest and threaten to
submit his resignation.[15]

On 11 October a camelry force led by 'Ali Jawdat al-Ayyubi

left Damascus headed for Homs. It reached Homs on 14 October and after taking it continued north to Hama. On 19 October Hama was occupied in cooperation with an advance force of the 5th Cavalry Division. There the Arab force was joined by Arab officers who had deserted from the Ottoman army in Aleppo, among them the brothers 'Ali Rida and Tahsin al-'Askari (the brothers of Ja'far al-'Askari). 'Ali Jawdat al-Ayyubi fell ill and stayed behind in Hama, and the force continued on its way to Aleppo under the command of Tahsin 'Ali. Before his desertion 'Ali Rida al-'Askari was commandant of the gendarmerie of Aleppo and during the course of his duty he established relations with the tribes in the area. Then, before the attack on Aleppo, he sent letters to the tribal chiefs and urged them to join the Arab army. He was also the first to enter Aleppo, on 25 October, leading a force of tribesmen. The tribesmen were not evenly matched with the Ottoman forces that were still in the city, and they were scattered all over within a short time. At this juncture Nuri al-Sa'id reached the city with a number of British armoured cars, and in the evening the force led by Tahsin 'Ali also entered the city from the east. The battles lasted all night, and when the horsemen of the 5th Cavalry Division under the command of Major-General MacAndrew entered the city the next morning at 10:00, there was nothing left for them to do but remove the last remnants of the Ottomans. At 11:00 of 26 October it was all over. Nuri al-Sa'id began to organize the Arab government in the city, and as its military governor he appointed 'Ali Rida al-'Askari. However, the latter was replaced within a short time by Shukri al-Ayyubi, who had been unemployed since he was removed from Beirut.[16]

On 30 October 1918 an armistice was signed at the port of Mudros on the island of Lemnos aboard the British battleship "Agamemnon". Four centuries of Ottoman rule over the Arab countries had ended.

Summary, Conclusions, and Epilogue

The Arab revolt of Sharif Husayn of Mecca was not the only revolt against the Ottomans which was planned or carried out by the inhabitants of the Arab provinces of the Ottoman Empire during the First World War. It was, indeed, the first and only revolt that ended in success, yet this success overshadowed the very existence of many other revolt attempts during the period under discussion. Especially in the early period of the war rebellions were planned throughout Syria, Mount Lebanon, and also in Iraq, But their common denominator was their failure, either because they failed to reach the stage of execution at all or because they expired soon after they were begun.

These attempts were first made by the inhabitants of Mount Lebanon, several of whose activists tried to involve France, Britain, and Greece in a plan for an uprising against the Ottomans. The Allies were pre-occupied at the beginning of the war with other serious problems, and the lack of enthusiasm of their governments to help the Lebanese led to the demise of the plan. In the early period of the war the Syrian Decentralization Party and the Alliance Libanaise, both of them in Cairo, drew up similar plans for an outbreak of revolt in Mount Lebanon and Syria, but in the end nothing was done after the societies failed to reach an understanding with Britain and France. The Decentralization Party did cooperate with the British for a while and assisted them in spreading subversive propaganda in the Arab provinces of the Ottoman Empire. But eventually British lack of readiness to satisfy the party with official political declarations concerning the future of the Arab provinces (outside the Arabian Peninsula) led to the suspension of contacts between the party and the British.

A much more daring plan for revolt was concocted in early 1915 by the Syrian officer Amin Lutfi al-Hafiz. His plan to seize control of the Syrian coast from Latakia to the north of the Gulf of Iskenderun, exploiting the fact that most of the soldiers in Syria at the time were Arabs, was to co-occur with a British landing at Alexandretta. Because the British landing at the Gulf of Iskenderun never took place, his plan failed, despite the fact that the first steps in executing it had been taken. Another plan for severing the Ottoman lines of transportation from Anatolia to Syria and to assist an Allied invasion was devised at the same time by the former president of the "Literary Club", 'Abd al-Karim al-Khalil. A series of informings from various sources led to the exposure of the plan by the Ottoman authorities and to the capture of its organizers, several of whom paid for it with their lives.

Rebellious activities existed in the Levant also during the time of the Arab revolt. Some of the revolt ideas were thought up by the sons of Nuri al-Sha'lan, the paramount chief of the Ruwalla tribes, whose attitude towards the Arab revolt was vague until the final stage of the war. Other attempts and guerilla activities of various kinds were carried out in Syria and Mount Lebanon by the members of some of the most important Syrian and Lebanese families of this period (such as al-Mu'ayyad of Damascus and Haydar of Ba'albek) on the one hand, and by members of gangs such as Milhim Qasim on the other.

Besides the many revolt activities and attempts that were planned in the Levant during World War I, there were a small number of revolt plans and attempts also in Iraq. Their initiators were at first Iraqi officers serving in the Ottoman army, and later on embittered Shi'ites who could no longer bear the oppressive Ottoman yoke. However, a sign of what was going to happen in Iraq after the war was given by the uprising which broke out in Najaf in March 1918, against the British, and which was suppressed by them with force and determination.

The Ottoman authorities did not sit around idle in the face of the acts of the locals. Incriminating documents about the activities of the Syrian and Lebanese activists fell into their hands as a result of the treachery of the dragoman of the French consulate-general in Beirut. Another act of treachery, by one of the Decentralization Party activists, delivered into the hands of the authorities also the documents of this party. These documents, plus other information that came mainly from informings by locals, constituted an ample basis for the arrest of a considerable portion of the Arab activists and members of the secret societies that were operating in the Levant before and during the war. Many of them were executed in August 1915 and May 1916. The others were sentenced to prison terms or to exile in Anatolia.

However, at the same time that the revolt attempts that were planned in the various regions of the Arab provinces of the Empire were failing, the process began which was to end ultimately in the Arab revolt of Sharif Husayn of Mecca. In early 1915 the secret societies *al-Fatat* and *al-'Ahd* decided to unite their activity and to prepare a combined plan to start a general revolt against the Ottomans. The centre of the revolt was to be in Syria, basing itself on the Arab soldiers stationed there at the time. Since the planned revolt was to spread to the Arabian Peninsula, the members of the societies chose Sharif Husayn of Mecca as their partner in the revolt and also as its supreme leader. The emissary of the societies who transmitted this to Husayn did not hear any response at all from him, but in March 1915 Husayn sent his son Faysal to Damascus to verify the seriousness of the intentions of the societies. The leaders of the societies joined him in as a member, and after he reported to them on the contacts that his father had begun with the British for similar purposes, they formulated a list of conditions according to which they would agree to cooperate with the British in their war against the Empire. It was also agreed that after he brought his father up to date on the strength and willingness of the conspirators Faysal would return to Syria at the head of an army of Hijazi volunteers, and then the revolt would be proclaimed under his leadership. However, soon after he left Syria the authorities removed all the Arab divisions from the Levant and replaced them with loyal Turkish forces. The revolt plan in Syria became inapplicable.

The conditions that the leaders of *al-Fatat* and *al-'Ahd* submitted to Faysal constituted the basis for the letter Husayn sent in July 1915 to the British high commissioner in Egypt, Arthur Henry McMahon, in which he detailed his terms for cooperation with the British against the Empire. This letter, which started the McMahon-Husayn correspondence, was received with reservations by the British, who flinched from Husayn's demands, especially on the territorial plane. However, the desertion to British lines of the Iraqi officer and member of *al-'Ahd* Muhammad Sharif al-Faruqi, and the false information he gave to the British in Cairo concerning the strength and extent of the Arab movement, brought a complete turnabout in the British attitude towards Husayn. After some hesitation McMahon was authorized to send Husayn a letter of reply in which he informed him that the British government accepted his demands, including those concerning the borders of the future Arab state, with the exception of several territorial limitations.

While the McMahon-Husayn correspondence continued Faysal returned to Damascus as agreed upon at the time of his previous visit. However, when he arrived in the city and found out that all the Arab divisions on which the revolt was to be based had been removed from Syria, he realized that the revolt had to break out only in the Hijaz. Faysal slipped back to the Hijaz,

SUMMARY, CONCLUSIONS, AND EPILOGUE

and in June 1916 the Arab revolt broke out. Within less than
four months the rebels had taken Mecca, Jidda, Rabigh, Yanbu',
and Ta'if. Medina, on the other hand, was a different story. One
of the reasons why Medina held out in the early period of the
revolt was the lack of enthusiasm of the first commander of the
revolt, 'Aziz 'Ali al-Misri, to conquer it. Al-Misri, who was the
leader of al-'Ahd before the war, still advocated the program of
the society to establish a Turko-Arab empire on the pattern of
Austria-Hungary. Therefore, instead of acting in good faith to
conquer Medina, he planned to reach an understanding with its
Ottoman commander and with him to depose Husayn as a first
step in the realization of the bi-national empire plan.

'Aziz 'Ali al-Misri was not the only member of the societies
who joined the revolt. Forty members of al-Fatat and al-'Ahd
joined it in its various stages, and they comprised about a quarter of the members of al-Fatat and about a third of the members
of al-'Ahd. From a numerical point of view the members of the
societies were a drop in the sea of participants in the revolt,
whose four armies numbered at the peak of their strength over
10,000 regular soldiers and over 30,000 irregulars. The Hijazi
tribesmen constituted the main part of the revolt armies, but
besides them there began to arrive in the Hijaz Iraqi and Syrian
prisoners of war who had been captured by the British at the
various fronts and who preferred to join the revolt army rather
than remain in the prison camps. On the other hand, there were
many Arab prisoners who turned down the British offer to join
the revolt army. A British attempt to organize prisoners of war
into a separate military force, under the name "The Arab
Legion", failed utterly, and it was necessary to transfer them to
the revolt army. In addition to the prisoners of war, a small
number of deserters also joined the revolt, as well as Syrian civilians who had fled the oppressive Ottoman rule in Syria. On the
other hand, it should be pointed out that several of the most
prominent leaders of the Arab movement during this period,
such as Yasin al-Hashimi and 'Ali Rida al-Rikabi, did not join
the Arab revolt and continued to serve the Empire until the end
of the war.

In contrast to the meagre numerical participation of the society members in the revolt armies, their qualitative contribution
to them was decisive. The officer members of al-'Ahd who took
part in the revolt filled a most substantial part of the senior
posts in the revolt armies in the various stages. And if one looks
generally at the Iraqi and Syrian officers who took part in the
revolt, one finds that they literally took over all the senior and

middle command positions in the Arab revolt. The Iraqi officers
Ja'far al-'Askari, Nuri al-Sa'id, and Mawlud Mukhlis (the latter
two were members of *al-'Ahd*) led almost all the important
attacks made by the Northern Army after the occupation of
Aqaba in July 1917. The success of these attacks, on the other
hand, was only partial, and in fact most of the Ottoman strong-
holds in Transjordan held out until the final stage of the war.

The relations among the various elements that participated in
the revolt army were quite troubled. The most difficult relationships existed between the Iraqi and Syrian officers who took part
in the revolt. The latter felt themselves discriminated against, and
they claimed, with a large measure of justice, that the Iraqis were
taking over all the senior positions. In a few cases matters
reached the point of blows and pistol incidents. Attempts to
mediate between the Iraqis and Syrians did not go well. Husayn
himself detested both the Iraqis and the Syrians and did not
cease to suspect their intentions. The authority of his sons over
the officers was also only partial. The tense relations between
Husayn and the officers reached their peak in August 1918 when
Husayn publicly insulted Ja'far al-'Askari, the commander of the
Northern Army, by denying in the rebel newspaper *al-Qibla* that
al-'Askari was its commander. This incident almost caused the
disintegration of the Northern Army. On the eve of the great
offensive on Syria, and only by great efforts — including the use
of deceitful means — were the British able to smooth matters
over. Also the fact that Medina managed to hold out until the
end of the war is explained in great part by what was going on
within the Southern and Eastern Armies themselves. Not only
was the authority of 'Ali and 'Abdallah over the officers limited,
several of the Iraqi officers even displayed open sympathy for the
Ottomans and tried their best to sabotage the Arab military
effort to capture Medina.

While the soldiers of the Northern Army were fighting their
way north, the Syrian and Lebanese political activists living in
Egypt were preoccupied in heated debates on the political future
of Syria and Mount Lebanon after the war. If the idea of establishing the greater Arab state, of which Syria would be a part,
had begun to amass support after the outbreak of the Arab
revolt, towards the end of the war the support for this idea
began to wane. The troubled relations between the Syrians and
Iraqis in the Arab revolt army, between these two groups and
the Hashimite family, and between the Hashimite family and
some of the Syrian and Lebanese activists in Cairo, led to the
strengthening of separatist tendencies among the activists in

Cairo. Several of these activists approached the British in April 1918 with a request to clarify their attitude towards the future of the Arab countries, with the activists intimating that they preferred that an autonomous government be set up in Syria and that Syria and the Hijaz should not be considered one bloc. They took care to convince the British in Cairo of the strength and influence of the societies that they represented. After a short struggle with themselves, which was reminiscent of their hesitation following the information that Faruqi gave them and that led to the sending of McMahon's letter of 24 October, the British decided to accede to the appeal. In June 1918 the "Declaration to the Seven" was issued, in which the British in fact accepted the basic approach of the applicants.

The idea of separating Syria from the Hijaz was also the guiding idea of the Comité Central Syrien that was founded in Paris in 1917, but for entirely different motives. This society indeed wanted independence for Syria, but under the tight aegis of France. The society was involved in a French attempt to form a legion made up of Armenian and Syrian volunteers which would aid the French war effort at the Palestine front and in Syria. The French Légion d'Orient, which reminded one not a little of the Arab Legion that the British tried to form, did not achieve much greater success than that achieved by the Arab Legion, especially in regard to its Syrian volunteers. The attempts of the society to recruit volunteers for the Légion d'Orient in South America bore very limited fruits.

One of the reasons for the failure of the society's contacts with the Lebanese societies in South America was that the Lebanese activists in the various émigré communities were not prepared to be content with the separation of the Syrian question from the general Arab question, but insisted also on the separation of the Lebanese question from the Syrian one. The Lebanese societies in North and South America maintained good relations with France, but they wanted a separate Lebanese independence, under the aegis of France. Going farther than that was the Alliance Libanaise of Cairo, which was not prepared to be satisfied with less than absolute independence for Mount Lebanon, within its original borders, and under the guarantee of all the powers.

Thus, with the end of World War I, the Arab nation was divided into three main ideological trends: An Arab movement which strove to establish a single large Arab state in the territories of the Arab provinces of the Ottoman Empire; a Syrian movement which strove to establish a greater Syria which would include Mount Lebanon, Palestine, and Transjordan; and a Lebanese movement which strove for an independent Lebanon in extended borders. In Iraq, too, nationalist feelings began to seethe in this period; and they were to find expression in a revolt movement two years later.

*

'Aziz 'Ali al-Misri, the leader of *al-'Ahd* before the war, did not adapt himself to the changing circumstances, and he continued to advocate his society's idea of establishing a Turko-Arab empire on the pattern of Austria-Hungary. At the beginning of the war he proposed to the British to establish an independent Arab state which would include all the Arabic-speaking regions with the Alexandretta-Mosul-Persian border as its northern border. However, a follow-up of his statements and deeds during the war reveals that in the inner conflicts he had concerning the future of the Arab countries what ultimately won out was the idea of the Arabs remaining in the Empire in some sort of federal formula.

These views of his were no longer acceptable to his fellow society members, nor to the members of *al-Fatat*. Both resolved to start a revolt against the Ottomans and to achieve independence for the Arabs. Their view of the character of the future Arab state found expression both in the "Damascus Protocol", in which they demanded independence for all the regions from southern Anatolia in the north to the Indian Ocean in the south and from the Mediterranean Sea in the west to the Persian border in the east, and in the very fact of their appeal to Sharif Husayn, the man responsible for the holy places of Islam, to lead the planned revolt.

Sharif Husayn himself adopted the demands of the members of *al-'Ahd* and *al-Fatat*, and in his letter to McMahon in July 1915 he conditioned his cooperation with the British on their recognition of the independence of the Arab countries within the above borders. It should be emphasized that Egypt was not considered at the time to be part of the Arab world, not by Husayn and apparently not by most of the members of the societies either. On one occasion, when Husayn tried to convince the British that the royal title he had granted himself would not impair their status in Egypt, or the status of the French in North Africa, he explicitly pointed out that "Egypt is not an Arab country". (A different, and exceptional, opinion was expressed in 1918 by an anonymous pan-Arabist, who identified himself as

"Ahmad". In an article that he sent to the editor of the journal *The Near East* he expressed his desire for the realization of the "cherished dream of all Arabs . . . [to] establish an Arab kingdom extending over the whole of North Africa, including Egypt, as well as over the Peninsula of Arabia, Syria, Mesopotamia and Persian Arabistan, with Cairo as the seat of empire".)[1]

In the proclamation that Husayn broadcast after the outbreak of the Arab revolt he focussed on the Islamic element, and tried, using verses from the Qur'an and citations from the Hadith, to prove the betrayal by the CUP of the world of Islam, of the religion of Islam, and of the Muslims. However, beyond the attempt to incite the Muslims of the world against the CUP, he also spoke about the Arab nation and its suffering during the war. From his statements on this subject it becomes clear that he considered himself the leader and patron of the entire Arab nation, both in the Hijaz and in the other Arab provinces of the Ottoman Empire. In effect he considered himself responsible on three levels: (1) to the world of Islam; (2) to the Arabs in general; (3) to the Hijaz in particular. His solution for all this was absolute independence from the Ottoman Empire:

> The defence of the Hijaz from this evil and aggression, the observance of the rites of Islam that Allah has commanded, and the guarding of the Arabs and the Arab countries from the danger to which the Ottoman Empire is doomed because of the misbehaviour of this wicked society [that is, the CUP] — all of this will be achieved only by full independence and the cutting of all ties with these bloodthirsty conquerors and robbers.[2]

Husayn strove for the establishment of a single large Arab state in the territories from which the Ottomans would be expelled. But he did not go into detail about the form of the future Arab state after the war or about the relations between its various parts. His son Faysal, however, referred to this question in a proclamation that he issued in May 1917 and which was addressed "To All Our Brethren — The Syrian Arabs of All Creeds". In the proclamation he promised among other things that "The internal administration will be in each province of the Arab countries, according to the wishes of the inhabitants of that province . . . [and] will be also in accordance with the programme formerly laid down by the Arab Society of which I am a member . . . This is sanctioned by H.M. our King."[3]

Among the participants in the Arab revolt, with their various origins, the idea of a greater Arab state was considered the only legitimate idea on the field. Below the surface other currents were swirling; the Syrians felt they were fighting for Syria, and the Iraqis were thinking about Iraq. Among the Syrian and Lebanese communities throughout the world, on the other hand, the political activists were expressly divided into three trends, the Arab one, the Syrian, and the Lebanese, with the strength of each one of them changing with the place and time. The Lebanese and Syrians in the United States, for example, Christians and Muslims alike, were divided among the supporters of the Lebanese idea and of the Syrian idea, and one of their prominent journalists pointed out that "there was no such thing in America as a National Arab movement". In Cairo, on the other hand, all three trends gained support, with the supporters of Arab unity gaining over the others particularly in the period after the outbreak of the Arab revolt. They believed that Syria had to be under Husayn's sovereignty, as part of a federation or of a new Arab empire, which would include besides Syria the Arabian Peninsula and Iraq. This Syria would have autonomy and would administer its internal affairs separately from the Hijaz. Joining in this idea was Iskandar 'Ammun, the president of the Alliance Libanaise of Cairo, with the understanding that the Lebanon would continue to enjoy within the new framework the privileges that it had before the war and would also have its borders extended, as had been demanded for a long time. Others were willing to agree only to an Arab confederation, of which Syria would be a part, under the princedom of Faysal. There were those who opposed even that and forcefully maintained that Syria and the Lebanon should be taken out of the bosom of the Arab union. Some of them were prepared to accept Faysal as their ruler, on condition that he be a constitutional prince with no connection at all to the Hijaz. The others opposed even this.

The voices of those who were dubious about the wisdom of Syria being included in a greater Arab state, in which the Hijaz would be dominant, began to prevail in mid-1917. The Comité Central Syrien in Paris claimed that the Syrians would never agree to be ruled by bedouins. They shared, indeed, a common language and origin with the Arabs, but they were different from them in every other respect. The society vehemently rejected any possibility of Sharifite sovereignty over Syria, and its secretary-general Georges Samné published sharp articles in this spirit in its organ. The Syria-Mount Lebanon League of Liberation in New York also supported this view, and it called for the separation of the Arab question from the Syrian question.

As time went on the support of the advocates of Arab unity

for the Hashimite family weakened, and their enthusiasm for the Arab revolt waned. It was precisely their direct contact with Husayn and the Hijazis on the one hand and the Iraqis on the other which bit-by-bit led many pro-Hashimite activists to break away from the pan-Arab camp and to become Syrian activists, a process which intensified as the war drew to a close. The tense relations between the Syrian and Iraqi officers and the feeling of deprival of the Syrians in the Arab army, plus the difficult and stubborn personality of Husayn, brought many activists, who previously supported Husayn, to the conclusion that the Syrian question had to be detached from the Arab question. They were alarmed at the thought of masses of undisciplined bedouins entering Damascus and ruling over them together with the Iraqi officers, and this when they were the most advanced and cultured people of the Arab nation. It was activists of this type who submitted to the British in April 1918 the memorandum which led to the issuance of the "Declaration to the Seven". In September 1918 Clayton characterized them as "averse from any close connection with Arabia as represented by the king of Hejaz and his sons. They are, therefore, opposed in principle . . . to the Arab Movement as represented by the Sherifian leaders".[4] Sentiments like this of the Syrian activists found expression also in a petition against the involvement of the Hijazis in Damascus and for separating Syria from the other Arabic-speaking countries, which 200 Christian and Muslim activists in Cairo sent to the representatives of the Allies a few days after the liberation of Damascus.

Another reason for the apprehensions developed by the Syrians concerning Husayn's rule over them was the very fact of his status as guardian of the holy places of Islam. They felt that this would make him into a ruler by virtue of the religion, and his governmental capital would, of course, be Mecca. Opinions of this sort were expressed by the Christian activist Faris Nimr, who claimed that the upshot of Husayn's rule over Syria would be the negation of its independence, turning it into a Muslim theocracy, and impairing the equal status of the Christians in it. However, such opinions were also expressed by the Muslim activist Haqqi al-'Azm, who claimed that many of the Muslim Syrians shared the Christian apprehensions of a theocratic rule by Husayn and called for the detachment of Syria from the Hijaz.

And what was the alternative proposed by the Syrian activists? Absolute independence for Syria after the war, in its natural borders, and divided into four vilayets: the vilayet of Lebanon, the vilayet of Damascus, the vilayet of Aleppo, and the vilayet of

Palestine. Each vilayet would have an administrative council which would handle its internal affairs, and the seat of the general government of Syria would be in Damascus or Beirut (Decentralization Party leaders, mid-1915). Syria would become a confederation — "The United States of Syria", with each province administering its own internal affairs, just as in the United States or in Switzerland (Ibrahim Salim al-Najjar, April 1917). "The ultimate goal of the society is the liberation of Syria and the achievement of its independence . . . by way of a federal regime of provincial autonomies, in whose framework the various regions (the Lebanon — which already enjoys an autonomous regime — Palestine, etc.) will maintain their unique character and the unhampered development of their legitimate aspirations" (platform of the CCS, mid-1917). In spite of the differences in beliefs, the Syrians constituted a single nation, their country was one geographical unit, and their future was dependent on the political realization of this unity. A secular, democratic state must be established in Syria, and its inhabitants must cease to be guided by their religious sentiments (Georges Samné, September 1917). Greater Syria must be established, which would be divided into five (or six, if Palestine was included) cantons: The canton of Mount Lebanon, including Beirut, Sidon, Tripoli, and the Biqa'; the canton of Damascus, including Homs, Hama, the Syrian desert, Transjordan, and northern Palestine; the canton of Aleppo, including Latakia and the district of Alexandretta; the canton of Dayr al-Zur; the canton of Mardin; and the canton of Jerusalem (if this region was included in Syria). The cantons would constitute the independent Syrian kingdom, which would be united according to the Swiss or American model (Haqqi al-'Azm, early 1918). The Syrians were interested that there should be a decentralized regime, according to which Syria would be divided into vilayets each of which would administer its own internal affairs (Memorandum of the Seven, April 1918). An integral and independent Syria must be established. It would be a member of the Arab federation, though it would have its own king. Syria must be considered a unit in itself, with no connection to Iraq or the Hijaz. "Let the Federal Unity come later, and be formed piece by piece" (Faris Nimr, June 1918). "Syria must be the integral Syria" (Shukri Ghanim, July 1918). Absolute independence for a democratic and decentralized Syria (Syrian Union Party, late 1918). A Syrian federation must be established, which would be made up of autonomous provinces, in the framework of which the special autonomous status of Mount Lebanon would be preserved (the

Lebanese-Syrian Society of Egypt, early 1919).

As for the borders of the future Syria, there was more-or-less a unity of opinion among the various Syrian activists. Without doubt they had in mind the greater Syria, which was to include all of the Levant: The borders of Syria were the Mediterranean Sea in the west, the Taurus and Anti-Taurus mountains in the north, Mesopotamia and the Syrian desert in the east, the Arabian Peninsula in the south and Egypt in the southwest ("Count" Cressaty, 1915). "Syria . . . demands its unity within its natural borders, from the Taurus to Sinai, and from the Mediterranean Sea to the desert" (Georges Samné, August 1918). "The national borders of Syria are as follows: The Taurus mountains in the north, the Khabur and Euphrates Rivers in the east, the desert and Mada'in Salih in the south, the Red Sea, Gulf of Aqaba, Rafah, and the Mediterranean Sea in the west" (platform of the Syrian Union Party, early 1919).

These borders of Syria included Mount Lebanon, and were therefore not acceptable to the adherents of the Lebanese trend. The Syrian activists were aware of the unwillingness of most of the Lebanese activists to assent to the integration of Mount Lebanon in greater Syria. Haqqi al-'Azm attacked the Alliance Libanaise of Cairo for its activity in the cause of complete independence for the Lebanon with its severance from the rest of Syria. He claimed that this severance would cause great damage to all of Syria because just as the Lebanon could not exist alone so Syria could not live without it. The two countries were bound together politically, economically, commercially, and agriculturally. The Comité Central Syrien of Paris tried to persuade the Lebanese societies in South America to accept the principle of combining the Lebanon with Syria. These attempts were one of the factors for the failure of its recruiting mission there. The Syria-Mount Lebanon League of Liberation of New York decided that in order to prevent quarrels on this subject the discussion of the connection of the Lebanon to Syria had to be postponed until after the war. This postponement was necessary in its opinion not only to prevent tensions between Syrians and Lebanese, but also between Lebanese and Lebanese, since there were Lebanese who indeed advocated the integration of the Lebanon in Syria. The president of this society, the Lebanese Ayyub Thabit, for example, was one of the opponents of what he called the "separatist movement for Lebanese independence". Also the Greek Catholic native of Ba'albek, Nadra Mutran, claimed that the Lebanon constituted an integral part of Syria historically, ethnographically, and commercially. He opposed those who demanded independence for the Lebanon and claimed that not only were the Greek Catholics opposed to this initiative, but probably also the Greek Orthodox, the Muslims, and the Druzes. According to him, in the new Syria, where justice and equality would prevail, there would be no place for the fear of the Christians of the Lebanon for the Muslim majority that would be created as a result of uniting the two countries.

Most of the Lebanese activists did not share these views. To begin with, they were opposed to the idea of the greater Arab state, just as the Syrian activists were. They considered themselves first of all Lebanese and only afterwards Arabs. And there were those among them who believed that they were not Arabs at all but the direct descendants of the Phoenicians. The latter claimed that their right to independence arose from their being an entirely separate people from the Arabs or the Syrians. Their fears of the expansionist ambitions of the Hijaz increased after Husayn declared himself king of the Arab countries, and they reached their peak when Faysal arrived in Damascus. Iskandar 'Ammun, the president of the Alliance Libanaise of Cairo, who displayed a readiness for the integration of Mount Lebanon in the new Arab state, while still maintaining all its privileges, paid for this with the loss of his presidency after his fellow members accused him of having "sold his fatherland to the Arabs".

Still, an examination of the activities of the various Lebanese societies reveals that more than they worked against the idea of the greater Arab state they devoted their activity to the struggle against the greater Syrian state, probably because the fear of the establishment of such a state after the war seemed to them more real. The opposition of the Lebanese activists to the inclusion of Lebanon in greater Syria stemmed first of all from their fear of the large Muslim majority that would be created in the new state. Na'um Mukarzal, the president of the Lebanon League of Progress of New York, turned time and again to the French with a demand that two separate and independent administrations should be set up for Syria and the Lebanon. He based his demand on the differences of race and religion that existed, according to him, between the two countries and on the refusal of the Maronites to be included in a state where the majority of the population would be Arabs or Muslims. "We are not Arabs, and the calamities that we have suffered were caused only by religious laws that do not accord with our civilization." The Union Libanaise of Buenos Aires also opposed the combining of Lebanon to Syria and claimed that "we are first of all Lebanese". It refused outright to establish contact with any émigré society that did not demand the independence of the Lebanon (such as the CCS) and protested against anyone who tried to "drown" the Lebanese question in the Syrian one. "The Syrian question is one question and the Lebanese question is another, and we are unable not to separate the one from the other." Similar views (though with opposition to a solely French aegis) were held by the Alliance Libanaise of Cairo, which was against any political connection whatsoever between Mount Lebanon and Syria. In a response to the attacks of Haqqi al-'Azm on these ideas of the society, Antun al-Jumayyil, one of its leaders, replied that the Lebanon had always been independent and that there existed a "Lebanese nationalism". He emphasized the refusal of the Lebanese to reconcile themselves to the desire of some Syrians "that there should be no trace of the Lebanese question".

And what was the alternative proposed by the Lebanese activists? The ultimate national goal of the Lebanese was absolute independence (Yusuf al-Sawda, beginning of the war). Mount Lebanon must gain its independence, under French aegis (Na'um Mukarzal, 1916). Absolute independence for Mount Lebanon, with the return of its ancient borders (Union Libanaise, November 1917). Complete and absolute independence for Mount Lebanon, within its natural borders, under the guarantee of the great powers. The borders of Greater Lebanon should include the regions of Beirut, Tripoli, Tyre and Sidon, and the Biqa', and with this its area would in fact be more than doubled (Alliance Libanaise, 1917-18). The liberated Lebanon should become a democratic, constitutional principality or a republic (Auguste Adib, January 1918).

Among the officers of the Northern Army there were many Iraqis who believed that by their participation in the Arab revolt they were fighting for the independence of all the Arab countries, including their fatherland Iraq. Iraqi officers, who found themselves in Egypt under various circumstances, pressed the British officials there to tell them what Britain's attitude was towards the idea of an independent government in Iraq. At least on one occasion an Iraqi officer who was in a prison camp in Egypt explained his insistence on remaining in the camp by the fact that since he was an Iraqi there was nothing for him to look for in Syria. In Iraq itself the Arab revolt was not reverberating very much. The Iraqis, in the regions occupied by the British, were at most prepared to see in Husayn a religious leader, but not a political one. The orientalist Gertrude Bell, who was in Iraq at the time, wrote in 1918: "It is evident that there is not much here to encourage any pretensions on the part of the Sherif; there is still less ground for believing that there exists in the 'Iraq any genuine aspirations towards Arab unity." When the Iraqi sheikhs in the region of Baghdad spoke of the "Arab nation", this term had no political significance for them. "Their political horizon is bounded by Baghdad and Kufa, 'Amara and Basra are almost outside the circle of their interest, to say nothing of Syria and Morocco."[5] Bell also reported on the negative attitude shown by the Baghdadis, including the intellectuals among them, towards Syrian refugees who had fled from Syria to Iraq through the desert. They treated them as foreigners, and in one case the refugees were even called "execrable Syrians".

All this led Bell to conclude that the particularist forces that were dominating the Arab world would prevent Husayn from welding all the Arab countries into one stable state, and that if there existed any nationalism in the Arab countries it was only local.[6] The British officer Wyndham Deedes, who served in Egypt during the war, wrote in 1916: "It will never be possible to get all the Arabs of Syria, Iraq, Yemen and the others to acknowledge one temporal chief", and therefore the idea of establishing the great Arab kingdom was not realistic.[7] Cousse, the head of the French military mission in Jidda in 1918, tried to explain the origin of the constant quarrels between the Syrian and Iraqi officers in the armies of the Arab revolt: "The concept of Arab nationalism is too new, and perhaps also too artificial, for it to be accepted without debate. One can say therefore that before anything else they remain: Syrians or Iraqis."[8] In November 1918 Lawrence wrote in a report for the information of the British cabinet: "The greatest obstacle, from the war standpoint, to any Arab movement, was its greatest virtue in peace-time — the lack of solidarity between the various Arab movements."[9] Later on he said to one of his biographers that uniting the speakers of Arabic was not a realistic thing for this century and the next one, and he compared it to the prospect of achieving a union of speakers of English. He added: "I never dreamed of uniting even Hejaz and Syria. My conception was of a number of states."[10]

Not only outside observers reached the conclusion that it was unrealistic to establish one great Arab state, due to the many differences that existed among the various Arab peoples. Nadra Mutran said in 1916 that Arab unity was an unrealizable dream, owing to the different aspirations of each of the peoples of Syria, the Hijaz, Iraq, and Yemen.[11] In the same year a Syrian officer, a native of Aleppo by the name of Ahmad Mukhtar, who had been captured by the Russians, expressed the opinion that "Owing to different customs, nature, education and religion of the Arabs in the different provinces, they cannot all be ruled by the same laws. Decentralization must be the cardinal feature of the new Government. While in Hejaz and Yemen, where the population are Mohammedans, the Sheriat might be made the standard law; this could not apply to Syria and Irak for obvious reasons . . . The [Arab] kingdom should be divided into four provinces, Hejaz, Yemen, Syria, Irak. Each province to have a separate legislation and a governor elected by the people. Each province to enjoy a certain autonomy in the administration of its internal affairs, and freedom to develop its agriculture and industries . . ."[12] It is not known that this junior officer was a member of any of the Arab political societies before or during the war. It therefore seems that he was expressing the views of a broad stratum of the population, which though it perhaps dreamt of a utopian pan-Arab state, yet at the same time was aware of the difficulties and of the differences between the various Arab countries. The political activists knew how to express the dilemma better: In the *Correspondance d'Orient* it was written in July of that year: "There is no Arab question, but Arab questions."

The dualism of before the war, of the existence of particularist movements alongside the Arab movement, continued. In contrast to the pre-war period, the Arab movement became the dominant one for a while with the outbreak of the Arab revolt. However, towards the end of the war the enthusiasm of the Syrians for the revolt waned, and the Syrian and Lebanese tendencies grew stronger when the liberation of these countries became a real possibility. The local national movements that operated in the Fertile Crescent after the war were but a continuation of the national currents that emerged before the war and gained strength during it.

*

On the morning of 1 October 1918 the Australian cavalrymen of General Allenby entered Damascus, and with this they signalled the approaching end of the war. The war ended with the defeat of the Ottoman Empire and the occupation of the Arab countries by the British army. The members of the Arab societies, civilians and officers, then assumed the preeminent role in leading these countries to their independence. The members of *al-Fatat*, which expanded greatly after the war, were the actual administrators of the short-lived Syrian state headed by Faysal during the years 1918-20. The fall of Syria into the hands of the French in July 1920 signalled also the end of *al-Fatat*. The officers of *al-'Ahd*, Syrians and Iraqis, could no longer stay together after the confrontations between them during the Arab revolt. The society consequently split into *al-'Ahd al-Suri*, which became insignificant, and *al-'Ahd al-'Iraqi*, whose officers filled most of the senior posts in the new Syrian army of Faysal. However, these officers were not especially interested in the Syrian army, and their attention then turned to Iraq, where the British ruled. The officers began harassment operations against the British in Iraq from the Syrian-Iraqi border, operations which were a prelude to the Iraqi revolt of 1920.

The great Arab state was not established. The Arab states were founded separately one from another, and thus the ideology of the particularistic societies was realized. The society members, both those who belonged to the Arab trend and those who belonged to the local trends, assumed the highest positions in these states, with even the former adapting themselves to the new situation of separate states. The members of *al-'Ahd*, *al-Fatat*, and the Lebanese societies became the ministers, prime ministers, and presidents in Syria, Iraq, Transjordan, and Lebanon.

Notes

Chapter 1

1 FO 195/2460/3421: d56, Henry A. Cumberbatch (Beirut) to Louis Mallet (Istanbul) 5 Aug.1914. FO 371/2142: John Maxwell (Cairo) to Kitchener (London) 18 Oct.1914. MAE, Guerre 867: t147, Jules-Albert Defrance (Cairo) to MAE 5 Nov.1914. t62, Théophile Delcassé (Paris) to Defrance 13 Nov.1914. t213, Gabriel-Pierre Deville (Athens) to MAE 3 Dec.1914. t126, Delcassé to Deville 6 Dec.1914. FO 371/2147: t388, Francis Elliot (Athens) to FO 7 Dec.1914. t1173, FO to Francis Bertie (Paris) 9 Dec.1914. t550, Bertie to FO 10 Dec.1914. d273, Elliot to Grey (London) 14 Dec.1914. t1243, FO to Bertie 17 Dec.1914. MAE, Guerre 867: memo, British Embassy (Paris) 18 Dec.1914. FO 371/2147: t315, FO to Elliot 30 Dec.1914. MAE, Guerre 867: memo, British Embassy (Paris) 31 Dec.1914. t53-53bis, Delcassé to Paul-Pierre Cambon (London) 8 Jan.1915. Pierre de Margerie (Paris) to Defrance 8 Jan.1915. AN, 423AP 8: Ibrahim S. Naggiar, "Les Colonies Syriennes à l'étranger" (Paris) 23 Oct.1916. Antun Yamin, *Lubnan fil-Harb* (Beirut, 1919), p.11. See also Georges Adib Karam, *L'Opinion Publique Libanaise et la Question du Liban (1918-1920)* (Beirut, 1981), p.151. Meir Zamir, *The Formation of Modern Lebanon* (London, 1985), pp.34-35.

2 MAE, Guerre 867: t158, Defrance to MAE 12 Nov.1914. FO 371/2147: notes, 'Abdallah Sfer Pasha (Cairo) 19 and 20 Nov.1914, both enclosed with d180, Milne Cheetham (Cairo) to Grey 23 Nov.1914. AN, 423AP 8: Ibrahim S. Naggiar, "Les Colonies Syriennes à l'étranger" (Paris) 23 Oct.1916.

3 MAE, Guerre 867: Shukri Ghanim (Antibes) to Delcassé 14 Sept.1914.

4 The memo is enclosed with *ibid*: d614, Jean-Adrian Jusserand (Washington) to Delcassé 3 Nov.1914, and FO 371/2147: d358, Cecil Spring Rice (Washington) to Grey 2 Nov.1914. d575, FO to Spring Rice 18 Nov.1914. FO 371/2480: 1, K. al-Aswad (New York) to British Ambassador (Washington) 11 Feb.1915. d129, FO to Spring Rice 18 Mar.1915. FO 371/2492: 1, J. Maloof (Wilton, U.S.A.) to Grey 24 Oct.1915. 1165799/15, Maurice de Bunsen (London) to J. Maloof 10 Nov.1915.

5 FO 371/2482: t, Governor General of Canada to Secretary of State for the Colonies 30 Jan.1915.

6 Al-Qa'id al-'Amm lil-Jaysh al-Rabi' [Jamal Pasha], *Idahat 'an al-Masa'il al-Siyasiyya Allati Jarat Tadqiquha bi-Diwan al-Harb al-'Urfi al-Mutashakkil bi-'Aleyh* (Istanbul, 1916), pp.92-94. 'Aziz

Bek, *Suriya wa-Lubnan fil-Harb al-'Alamiyya: Al-Istikhbarat wal-Jasusiyya fil-Dawla al-'Uthmaniyya* (Beirut, 1933), pp.245-246. See also note by 'Abdallah Sfer Pasha 19 Nov.1914 in FO 371/2147.

7   FO 371/2140: t223, Cheetham to Grey 26 Oct.1914. t228, same to same 28 Oct.1914. L/P&S/11/95: t, SSI to Viceroy 31 Oct.1914. WP 134/1: "Notes obtained from a member of the Liberal Party in Turkey and Cairo named 'La Mirkazieh' who is now in Khartoum" [end of 1914?]. MAE, Guerre 868: d44, Defrance to Delcassé 4 Feb.1915. L/P&S/11/95: t, Arthur Henry McMahon (Cairo) to FSI (Delhi) 9 Feb.1915. FO 882/2: appendix to memo by Rashid Rida (Cairo) 12 Feb.1915. L/P&S/11/95: t, Percy Z. Cox (Basra) to FSI 13 Feb.1915. t, Vieroy to IO 16 Feb.1915. l, Cox to McMahon 18 Mar.1915. WP 134/5: l, Rashid Rida to Ibrahim Dimitri (Khartoum) 17 Apr.1915. L/P&S/11/95: t1377-B, Cox to FSI 11 July 1915. ISA 65/2855: "Shaikh Kamel al-Kassab — Notes made at interview held in Jerusalem on August 15, 1935". *Idahat*, p.94. 'Aziz Bek, *Suriya*, p.358. Amin Sa'id, *Al-Thawra al-'Arabiyya al-Kubra* (Cairo, [1934]), vol.1, pp.128-129. Idem, *Asrar al-Thawra al-'Arabiyya al-Kubra wa-Ma'sat al-Sharif Husayn* (Beirut, [1960]), pp.37-38.

8   FO 371/2140: t264, Cheetham to Grey 13 Nov.1914. t347, Grey to Cheetham 14 Nov.1914. Reuter's announcement. L/P&S/10/523: t269, Cheetham to Grey 15 Nov.1915. FO 371/2480: d23, MCMahon to Grey 15 Feb.1915. WP 134/2: l, Haqqi al-'Azm (Cairo) to Fu'ad al-Khatib (Khartoum) 18 Feb.1915. WP 134/5: l, Rashid Rida to Ibrahim Dimitri 17 Apr.1915. l, Reginald Wingate (Khartoum) to Hardinge (Delhi) 28 Apr.1915. Sa'id, *al-Thawra*, vol.1, p.129. See also Linda Carol Rose, *Britain in the Middle East 1914-1918: Design or Accident?* (Ph.D. Dissertation, Columbia University, 1969), pp.80-82.

9   MAE, Guerre 871: d355, Defrance to Aristide Briand (Paris) 16 Nov.1915.

10   FO 371/345: Annual Report for Turkey for 1906: "The Turkish Empire as a Military Factor" by H.C. Surtees, cited in G.P. Gooch and Harold Temperley (eds.), *British Documents on the Origins of the War 1898-1914* (London, 1926-36), vol.5, p.39.

11   FO 371/2480: note, Gilbert F. Clayton (Cairo) 3 Jan.1915 enclosed with d4, Cheetham to Grey 5 Jan.1915. t10, same to same 7 jan.1915. Cab 22/1/2: minutes of War Council 8 Jan.1915 cited in Jukka Nevakivi, "Lord Kitchener and the Partition of the Ottoman Empire, 1915-1916" in K. Bourne and D.C. Watt (eds.), *Studies in International History* (London, 1967), pp.321-322. WO 106/1570: "Expedition to Alexandretta" (MO2) 11 Jan.1915. WP 134/3: C.H.M. Doughty Wylie, "Note on a possible descent on Alexandretta" (SS Magellan) 10 Feb.1915. See also many French documents in MAE, Guerre 1060 cited in Jan Karl Tanenbaum, *France and the Arab Middle East 1914-1920* (Philadelphia, 1978), p.6. FO 800/48: McMahon to Grey 4 Feb.1915 and Grey to McMahon 8

Mar.1915, both cited in Tanenbaum, p.7. Jean Pichon, *Le Partage du Proche-Orient* (Paris, 1938), pp.24-26.

12 FO 882/15: r, Military Intelligence Office, WO (Cairo) 3 Sept.1915. FO 371/2490: 1B20/I/174(MO2), DMO (WO) to USS (FO) 27 Sept.1915. L/P&S/10/586: Summary no.2 of the Arab Bureau, by David G. Hogarth (Cairo) 12 June 1916. *AB* no.2 (Cairo) 12 June 1916, pp.14-15. *Idahat*, p.121. Ahmad Qadri, *Mudhakkirati 'an al-Thawra al-'Arabiyya al-Kubra* (Damascus, 1956), p.49. Anis al-Nusuli, *'Ishtu wa-Shahadtu* (Beirut, 1951), p.174. Many years later T.E. Lawrence wrote: "I am unrepentant about the Alexandretta scheme which was from the beginning to end, my invention, put forward necessarily through my chiefs ... Actually K[itchener] accepted it ... and then was met by a French ultimatum. A landing at Alexandretta in Feb.1915 would have handed over Syria and Mespot. to their native (Arab) troops." See David Garnett (ed.), *The Letters of T.E. Lawrence* (New York, 1939), pp.194-195.

13 Many documents about the Alexandretta invasion plan in Oct.-Nov.1915 and Oct.1917 may be found in FO 371/2480, WO 106/723 and WO 106/1570. See also George MacMunn and Cyril Falls, *Military Operations, Egypt and Palestine from the Outbreak of War with Germany to June 1917* (London, 1928), pp.77-83. Pichon, *Partage*, pp.27-28.

14 Qadri, p.49. 'Arabi [A.H.Y.], "Asrar al-Qadiyya al-'Arabiyya fi Sijn 'Aleyh", *Awraq Lubnaniyya* (Al-Hazimiyya, ed.1983), vol.2, p.36. *Idahat*, p.124. Kamal S. Salibi, "Beirut Under the Young Turks as Depicted in the Political Memoirs of Salim 'Ali Salam (1868-1938)" in Jacques Berque and Dominique Chevallier (eds.), *Les Arabes par leurs archives (XVIe-XXe siècles)* (Paris, 1976), p.212 citing Salam's memoirs p.43. See also MAE, Guerre 870: d293, Defrance to Delcassé 24 Sept.1915.

15 'Aziz Bek, *Suriya*, pp.194-196. Djemal Pasha, *Memories of a Turkish Statesman 1913-1919* (New York, [1922] rep.1973), pp.205-206.

16 'Aziz Bek, *Suriya*, pp.238-241. Idem, *Al-Istikhbarat wal-Jasusiyya fi Lubnan wa-Suriyya wa-Filastin khilala al-Harb al-'Alamiyya* (Beirut, 1937), p.131. 'Arabi, vol.1, pp.462-464.

17 'Aziz Bek, *Suriya*, pp.83-84, 242-248. Idem, *Al-Istikhbarat*, p.131. Djemal Pasha, pp.206-207. Salibi, pp.212-213 citing Salam's memoirs pp.43-44.

18 'Aziz Bek, *Suriya*, pp.249, 252. *Idahat*, p.124. Djemal Pasha, pp.212-213. Salibi, pp.213-214 citing Salam's memoirs pp.47, 49. Nasif Abi Zayd, *Ta'rikh al-'Asr al-Damawi* (Damascus, 1919), p.193.

19 ISA 65/2924: biography of 'Abd al-Karim al-Khalil by George Antonius. 'Arabi, vol.1, pp.462-463. Khayr al-Din al-Zirikli, *Al-A'lam* (Beirut, 3rd ed.1969), vol.4, p.178. Sulayman Musa, *Al-Husayn ibn 'Ali wal-Thawra al-'Arabiyya al-Kubra* (Amman, 1957), p.34.

20 Djemal Pasha, p.219. T.E. Lawrence, *Secret Despatches from Arabia* (London, n.d.), p.160. MG, 7N2145: note 9055-9/11, "Analyse du Rapport de l'Officier Interprète de 1ère classe Mercier, envoyé en Mission en Egypte" (Etat-Major de l'Armée, Section d'Afrique) 18 Dec.1917.

21 ISA 65/2784: "Notes collected in several interviews with Nasib Bey al-Bakri" [n.d.]. *AB* no.16 (Cairo) 18 Aug.1916, p.169. 'Aziz Bek, *al-Istikhbarat*, pp.323-331.

22 Sa'id, *al-Thawra*, vol.1, pp.93-95. Abi Zayd, pp.309-311. *Al-Manar* 23:3 29 Mar.1922, pp.207-208.

23 Abi Zayd, pp.204-208.

24 WO 157/735: Political and Economic Intelligence Summary No.12 (GSPI, GHQ, EEF) 12 Aug.1918. 'Aziz Bek, *al-Istikhbarat*, pp.156-157.

25 *AB* no.63 (Cairo) 18 Sept.1917, p.380. MG, 7N2141: note 76, L'Officier Interprète attaché à la Mission Militaire Française d'Egypte, "Faiz Bey Ben Ali El Mouayed" (Aqaba) 20 June 1918.

26 Ghassan R. Atiyyah, *Iraq 1908-1921: A Socio-Political Study* (Beirut, 1973), p.102, citing Iraqi officers Tawfiq Wahbi and Tahsin al-'Askari. Muhammad Tahir al-'Umari, *Ta'rikh Muqaddarat al-'Iraq al-Siyasiyya* (Baghdad, 1924-25), vol.2, pp.231-232.

27 Cab 17/177: Arabian Report N.S. No.XI 27 Sept.1916, citing army officers Shukri al-Shurbaji and Ahmad Shaykha. Arnold T. Wilson, *Loyalties: Mesopotamia 1914-1917* (London, [1930] 1936), p.72.

28 FO 371/2771: Arab Bureau Intelligence Summary no.5, by Hogarth 18 June 1916. *AB* no.5 (Cairo) 18 June 1916, pp.40-41. WO 106/922: *Personalities in the Area Occupied by the Mesopotamian Expeditionary Force, or Connected Therewith* (General Staff, MEF, 1920), p.196. L/P&S/20/C199: *Personalities — Baghdad and Kadhamain* (Baghdad, 1920), p.59. Arnold T. Wilson, *Mesopotamia 1917-1920: A Clash of Loyalties* (London, [1931] 1936), p.333.

29 Qahtan Ahmad 'Abush al-Tal'afari, *Thawrat Tal'afar 1920 wal-Harakat al-Wataniyya al-Ukhra fi Mintaqat al-Jazira* (Baghdad, 1969), pp.48-49, citing *Sada al-Ahrar* 158 9 May 1952 and 163 13 June 1952. FO 371/5231: t12708, HC (Baghdad) to IO 22 Oct.1920. FO 371/6349: *Personalities — Mosul, Arbil and Frontier* (Baghdad, 1921), p.9.

30 FO 371/3397: "Collection of Fortnightly Reports to Secretary of State for India by Civil Commissioner, MEF, from November 1st, 1917, to June 1st, 1918" (Baghdad, 1918), including Fortnightly Reports nos. 10-14, 15 Mar.-1 June 1918, pp.41-43, 48-49, 53-54, 57, 63-64, respectively. CO 696/1: "Reports of Administration for 1918 of Divisions and Districts of the Occupied Territories in Mesopotamia", including "Annual Report, Shamiyah Division, from 1 January to 31 December 1918", pp.69-70. 'Abd al-Razzaq al-Hasani, *Al-Thawra al-'Iraqiyya al-Kubra* (Sidon, [1952] 2nd

ed.1965), pp.56-57. 'Ali Al Bazirkan, *Al-Waqa'i' al-Haqiqiyya fil-Thawra al-'Iraqiyya* (Baghdad, 1954), pp.56-57.

Chapter 2

1 Djemal Pasha, pp.197-202. 'Aziz Bek, *Suriya*, p.108. Sa'id, *al-Thawra*, vol.1, pp.58-59. Mustafa al-Shihabi, *Al-Qawmiyya al-'Arabiyya: Ta'rikhuha wa-Qiwamuha wa-Maramiha — Muhadarat* (Cairo, [1959] 2nd ed.1961), pp.106-107. *Al-Manar* 19:2 15 July 1916, p.79.

2 'Aziz Bek, *al-Istikhbarat*, pp.206-207. On Falih Rifqi and his memoirs see Geoffrey Lewis, "An Ottoman Officer in Palestine, 1914-1918" in David Kushner (ed.), *Palestine in the Late Ottoman Period* (Jerusalem, 1986), pp.402-415.

3 *Al-Manar* 23:2 27 Feb.1922, p.131 (an article by Shakib Arslan). 'Aziz Bek, *Suriya*, pp.136, 149. Yamin, p.109. André Mandelstam, *Le Sort de l'empire ottoman* (Lausanne, 1917), pp.402-404. MAE, Guerre 874: t561, Defrance (Cairo) to MAE 23 Nov.1916.

4 Fa'iz al-Ghusayn, *Mudhakkirati 'an al-Thawra al-'Arabiyya* (Damascus, 1956), pp.44-45. Al-Shihabi, *al-Qawmiyya*, p.110. Pichon, *Partage*, p.22. Eugène Jung, *La Révolte arabe* (Paris, 1924-25), vol.2, pp.76-77. George Antonius, *The Arab Awakening: The Story of the Arab National Movement* (London, [1938] rep.1945), p.241. Nicholas Z. Ajay, *Mount Lebanon and the Wilayah of Beirut 1914-1918: The War Years* (Ph.D. Dissertation, Georgetown University, 1973), vol.1, pp.431-433, vol.2, p.60. On Salim 'Ali Salam see FO 371/4210: t30, Clayton (Cairo) to FO 7 Feb.1919.

5 'Aziz Bek, *al-Istikhbarat*, p.11. Al-Ghusayn, p.49.

6 MAE, Guerre 872: d177, Defrance to Briand 21 May 1916, enclosing reports of agent Konéri. Al-Ghusayn, p.50. Jirjis al-Khuri al-Maqdisi, *A'zam Harb fil-Ta'rikh wa-Kayfa Marrat Hawadithuha* (Beirut, 2nd ed.1927), pp.72-73. Sulayman Musa, *Al-Haraka al-'Arabiyya: Sirat al-Marhala al-Ula lil-Nahda al-'Arabiyya al-Haditha 1908-1924* (Beirut, 1970), pp.118, 121.

7 'Aziz Bek, *Suriya*, p.237.

8 MAE, Guerre 873: l, Louis-Maurice Bompard (Paris) to Briand 15 July 1916. t21, Henry Morgenthau (Istanbul) to Secretary of State (Washington) 11 Nov.1914 and t37, William J. Bryan (Washington) to Morgenthau 17 Nov.1914, both cited in United States Department of State, *Papers Relating to the Foreign Relations of the United States, 1914 Supplement: The World War* (Washington, 1928), pp.746-748.

9 MAE, Guerre 867: d428, Defrance to Delcassé 21 Nov.1914. MAE, Guerre 872: d177, Defrance to Briand 21 May 1916, enclosing reports of agent Konéri. MAE, Guerre 873: t401,

Philippe-Joseph Berthelot (Paris) to French Ambassador (Washington) 4 July 1916. L/P&S/11/118: Agence de la Presse Arabe
No.166 8 Nov.1917. MG, 17N489: note, Louis-Charles Mercier
(Cairo) 22 Apr.1918 enclosed with note 21, "Renseignements sur la
situation en Syrie" (Cairo) 24 Apr.1918. Abi Zayd, pp.233-234.
'Aziz Bek, *al-Istikhbarat*, pp.127-128. Sa'id, *al-Thawra*, vol.1,
pp.68-69. Mandelstam, p.342. Ajay, *Mount Lebanon*, vol.1,
pp.283-284, vol.2, p.64.

10 T1096, Morgenthau to Secretary of State 29 Sept.1915 cited in
United States Department of State, *Papers Relating to the Foreign
Relations of the United States, 1916 Supplement: The World War*
(Washington, 1929), p.815. FO 371/2491: note, American
Embassy (Paris) 5 Oct.1915 enclosed with d385, Bertie (Paris) to
Grey 13 Oct.1915. MAE, Guerre 871: d376, Defrance to Briand 8
Dec.1915. d826, Morgenthau to Secretary of State 4 Jan.1916 and
t1625, Hoffman Philip (Istanbul) to Secretary of State 3 Mar.1916,
both cited in *FRUS 1916*, pp.815-816, 818. MAE, Guerre 873:
t401, Berthelot to French Ambassador (Washington) 4 July 1916.
Note Verbale no. G1.84252/191, Ottoman Foreign Office (Istanbul)
2 July 1916 enclosed with d1517, Philip to Secretary of State 8 July
1916 cited in *FRUS 1916*, pp.822-823.

11 MAE, Guerre 872: d144, Defrance to Briand 21 April, 1916.
MAE, Guerre 873: t190-191, Defrance to MAE 31 May 1916.
Both the memo of the six dated 12 Mar.1913 and d131, Defrance
to Stéphen Pichon (Paris) 28 Mar.1913 were published in *Journal
de Beyrouth* 622 6 May 1916.

12 ISA 65/3253: "Two Years with the Enemy: Woman's Experience in
the Levant" (*Times* 15 Sept.1916). Sa'id, *al-Thawra*, vol.1, p.68.

13 MAE, Syrie-Liban 5: 1, Victor Augagneur (Le Tragas) to Pichon 12
Dec.1918. MAE, Syrie-Liban 6: t752, François Georges-Picot
(Cairo) to MAE 21 Dec.1918. MAE, Syrie-Liban 7: "Note pour le
Bureau de la Presse a.s. de Zalzal" 7 Jan.1919. FO 371/4214:
tEA2222, GHQ Egypt to WO 14 Feb.1919. 1, USS (FO) to DMI 1
Apr.1919. *Correspondance d'Orient* 2 15 Feb.1919, p.139.

14 Philip Hendrick Stoddard, *The Ottoman Government and the Arabs
1911-1918: A Preliminary Study of the Teşkilât-i Mahsusa* (Ph.D.
Dissertation, Princeton University, 1963), p.222. Djemal Pasha,
p.197. 'Aziz Bek, *Suriya*, p.66. List of French documents captured
by the Ottomans, including those captured in Damascus, is
enclosed with MAE, Guerre 876: d153, Defrance to Alexandre
Ribot (Paris) 23 Mar.1917.

15 T108, Morgenthau to Secretary of State 3 Dec.1914 cited in *FRUS
1914*, p.748. MAE, Guerre 873: t401, Berthelot to French Ambassador (Washington) 4 July 1916.

16 Muhammad 'Izzat Darwaza, *Nash'at al-Haraka al-'Arabiyya al-
Haditha* (Sidon, Beirut, [1971]), p.371. Sa'id, *al-Thawra*, vol.1,
pp.66-67. Abi Zayd, pp.196-197. 'Arabi, vol.1, p.464. Djemal
Pasha, p.208. Muhammad Kurd 'Ali, *Al-Mudhakkirat* (Damascus,

17 MAE, Guerre 867: t12, Defrance to MAE 8 Jan.1915. ISA
   65/2924: *al-Balagh* 29 Jan.1915. *Al-Ittihad al-'Uthmani* 25
   Feb.1915 cited in Ajay, *Mount Lebanon*, vol.1, p.274. Yamin,
   pp.63-64. Al-Maqdisi, p.44.

18 'Aziz Bek, *Suriya*, p.85.

19 *Al-Ittihad al-'Uthmani* 20 Nov.1914 cited in Ajay, *Mount Lebanon*,
   vol.1, p.276-277. Yusuf al-Hakim, *Bayrut wa-Lubnan fi 'Ahd
   Al 'Uthman* (Beirut, 1964), p.239. Sa'id, *al-Thawra*, vol.1, p.69.
   Al-Ghusayn, pp.47-48. Abi Zayd, pp.178-181. Djemal Pasha,
   p.198.

20 Yamin, pp.62-64. See also *al-Ahram*, 15 May 1916 enclosed with
   MAE, Guerre 873: d179, Defrance to Briand 23 May 1916.

21 Al-Ghusayn, pp.4-5, 11-13, 34. 'Arabi, vol.1, p.465. 'Aziz Bek,
   Suriya, pp.251-256. Djemal Pasha, pp.212-213. Stoddard, p.149.
   K.T. Khairallah, *Le Problème du Levant: Les Régions Arabes
   Libérées* (Paris, 1919), pp.79-80.

22 Al-Nusuli, pp.244-245. Yamin, pp.66-71. Sa'id, *al-Thawra*, vol.1,
   pp.60, 83-86. Al-Ghusayn, p.35. Al-Shihabi, *al-Qawmiyya*, p.107.
   'Arabi, vol.1, pp.565-566. Khairallah, *Problème*, p.80. For
   Jamal's announcement, as published in *al-Balagh* 21 Aug.1915, see
   "Bayan Jamal Pasha 'an Shuhada' 1915", *Awraq Lubnaniyya* (Al-
   Hazimiyya, ed.1983), vol.2, pp.204-208.

23 L/P&S/10/525: t1G1900, General, Force "D" (Basra) to Cairo, SSI
   and WO 2 Jan.1916. t1G1906, GOC, Force "D" to IO 4 Jan.1916.
   WP 136/3: "Mustapha Bey's Report" 27 Mar.1916. PRO
   30/57/48: 1 to HC 21 Apr.1916. Al-Ghusayn, pp.74-82. Stoddard,
   p.149.

24 *AB* no.2 (Cairo) 12 June 1916, p.13. ISA 65/2924: biographies of
   'Abd al-Ghani al-'Uraysi and Rafiq Rizq Sallum by George Anto-
   nius. *Idahat*, pp.49-50. Qadri, pp.50-52. Abi Zayd, p.191. Al-
   Nusuli, p.243. Kurd 'Ali, *al-Mudhakkirat*, vol.1, p.118. Djemal
   Pasha, p.214.

25 Al-Hakim, pp.236-238. Abi Zayd, pp.236-237. Yamin, p.64.

26 Sati' al-Husri, "Shuhada' al-'Uruba fil-Harb al-'Alamiyya al-Ula
   bi-Diyar al-Sha'm", *al-'Arabi*, 30 (1961), pp.22-25. 'Ali Fu'ad,
   Kayfa Ghazawna Misr: Mudhakkirat al-Jiniral al-Turki 'Ali Fu'ad
   ([Beirut], 1962), pp.5-6. Ahmad 'Izzat al-A'zami, *Al-Qadiyya
   al-'Arabiyya: Asbabuha, Muqaddimatuha, Tatawwuratuha wa-
   Nata'ijuha* (Baghdad, 1931-34), vol.6, p.108. Muhammad 'Izzat
   Darwaza, *Hawla al-Haraka al-'Arabiyya al-Haditha* (Sidon,
   1950-53), vol.1, p.44. *Al-Manar* 23:2 27 Feb.1922, pp.127,
   131-132; 23:3 29 Mar.1922, p.202. Sa'id, *al-Thawra*, vol.1, p.75.
   Al-Nusuli, p.243. Djemal Pasha, p.219. Stoddard, pp.150-151.

27 Qadri, pp.47-48. Al-Nusuli, pp.177-178. Djemal Pasha, pp.215,
   217. Anwar al-Rifa'i, *Jihad Nisf Qarn li-Sumuw al-Amir Sa'id
   Al 'Abd al-Qadir al-Jaza'iri* (Damascus, n.d.), pp.69-70.

28 Yamin, pp.75-83. Sa'id, *al-Thawra*, vol.1, pp.86-93. Al-Nusuli,

pp.246-248. Al-Rifa'i, p.75. Al-Shihabi, *al-Qawmiyya*, p.108. Musa, *al-Haraka*, pp.116-117. Khairallah, *Problème*, pp.86-87. Antonius, p.189. Stoddard, p.152. For Jamal's announcememt see *Journal de Beyrouth* 622 6 May 1916 and *al-Manar* 19:2 15 July 1916, pp.116-119. See also *AB* no.2 (Cairo) 12 June 1916, pp.13-17.

29 On the Husaynis see Hagana Archives (Tel-Aviv), L. Shneorson Papers 19: "Hadj Said Il Shawa of Gaza" [n.d.]. Al-A'zami, vol.3, pp.36-37. Sulayman Musa (ed.), *Al-Thawra al-'Arabiyya al-Kubra: Watha'iq wa-Asanid* (Amman, 1966), p.232. A.L. Tibawi, *Anglo-Arab Relations and the Question of Palestine 1914-1921* (London, 1978), p.166. On the Khazins see ISA 65/2856: *al-Sharq* 6 June 1916. MAE, Guerre 873: t216, Defrance to MAE 10 June 1916. t225, same to same 15 June 1916. Kairallah, *Problème*, p.82. Al-Hakim, p.239. Abi Zayd, p.232-233. Yamin, p.64.

30 *Al-Qibla* 52 11 Feb.1917. *Al-Manar* 23:3 29 Mar.1922, pp.208-209. Abi Zayd, pp.309-315, 318. Sa'id, *al-Thawra*, vol.1, pp.93-95. Qadri, pp.59-62. Al-A'zami, vol.6, pp.113-114. Antonius, pp.202-203. Qadri Qal'aji, *Jil al-Fida': Qissat al-Thawra al-Kubra wa-Nahdat al-'Arab* ([Amman, 1967]), pp.176-177.

31 *AB* no.13 (Cairo) 1 Aug.1916, p.128; no.14 (Cairo) 7 Aug.1916, pp.144-145; no.39 (Cairo) 19 Jan.1917, p.36, citing *al-Sharq* 11 Dec.1916. *Al-Mustaqbal* 37 10 Nov.1916. *Idahat*, pp.124-125. 'Aziz Bek, *Suriya*, pp.248-249. Abi Zayd, p.202.

32 *Idahat*, pp.49-50. See also Qadri, p.52 confirming this.

33 E.g. Darwaza, *Hawla*, vol.1, p.29 (Darwaza entered *al-Fatat* in 1916) and Musa, *al-Haraka*, p.34.

34 On the publication of *Idahat* see FO 141/654/356: 1, Clayton to Residency 4 Dec.1916 enclosing articles by Wilhelm Feldmann, *Berliner Tageblatt* end of Sept. and 14 Oct.1916. MAE, Guerre 876: d153, Defrance to Ribot 23 Mar.1917. Mandelstam, pp.344-349. Al-Husri, p.23.

35 *Al-Manar* 19:2 15 July 1916, pp.115-119. Al-A'zami, vol.6, pp.103ff. Mandelstam, pp.343ff. Yamin, pp.27-28.

36 E.g. Zeine N. Zeine, *The Emergence of Arab Nationalism* (New York, [1958] 3rd ed.1973), p.112. Also Musa, *al-Haraka*, p.119.

Chapter 3

1 Darwaza, *Nash'a*, p.503. Qadri, p.37. Al-A'zami, vol.4, pp.99-100. Al-Ghusayn, p.38. Sa'id, *al-Thawra*, vol.1, p.109. Sulayman Musa, "Jam'iyyat al-'Arabiyya al-Fatat", *al-'Arabi*, 151 (1971), pp.55-56.

2 Qadri, p.38. For a different version of this resolution see ISA 65/2855: *al-Jami'a al-Islamiyya* 4 Apr.1933 (English translation of that version see in Antonius, p.153).

3 Sa'id, *Asrar*, p.38. Al-Shihabi, *al-Qawmiyya*, p.106. Musa, *al-Haraka*, p.159. Idem, "Jam'iyya", p.55.

4 ISA 65/2855: "Shaikh Kamel al-Kassab — Notes made at interview held in Jerusalem on August 15, 1935". FO 371/2141: t251, Cheetham (Cairo) to Grey 9 Nov.1914 and minute of Kitchener. MAE, Guerre 871: d362, Defrance (Cairo) to Briand 25 Nov.1915. Sa'id, *Asrar*, pp.38-39, 235-236. Idem, *al-Thawra*, vol.1, p.108. Al-Ghusayn, pp.212-213. Qadri, p.37. Musa, *al-Haraka*, pp.129, 160.

5 FO 371/2486: "Note on Arab Movement" by Alfred C. Parker 21 Nov.1915. Fu'ad, p.55. Qadri, pp.39-40. ISA 65/2855: Ahmad Qadri, "Kayfa Ittasala al-Malik Faysal bil-Qadiyya al-'Arabiyya wa-Kayfa U'iddat al-Mu'iddat li-Idram al-Thawra al-'Arabiyya", *al-Jami'a al-Islamiyya* 4 Apr.1933. Sami 'Abd al-Hafiz al-Qaysi, *Yasin al-Hashimi wa-Dawruhu fil-Siyasa al-'Iraqiyya bayna 'Amay 1922-1936* (Basra, 1975), vol.1, pp.43-44.

6 FO 371/2490: 1, Ian Hamilton, General Commanding, Mediterranean Expeditionary Force (GHQ) to War Minister 25 Aug.1915. 1B20/I/174(MO2), DMO (WO) to USS (FO) 27 Sept.1915. 'Ali Jawdat, *Dhikrayat 'Ali Jawdat 1900-1958* (Beirut, 1967), p.31.

7 Muhammad al-Shurayqi, "Al-Shurayqi Yarthi al-Hashimi", *al-Istiqlal* 18:3116 4 Feb.1938, p.1. 'Abd al-Ghafur al-Badri, "Kayfa 'Araftu al-Hashimi?", *al-Istiqlal* 18:3105 21 Jan.1938, p.13. Al-Qaysi, vol.1, p.44. Al-Shihabi, *al-Qawmiyya*, pp.112-113. Ahad A'da' al-Jam'iyyat al-'Arabiyya [As'ad Daghir], *Thawrat al-'Arab: Muqaddimatuha, Asbabuha, Nata'ijuha* (Cairo, 1916), p.193. Jacques Benoist-Méchin, *Arabian Destiny* (London, 1957), pp.114-115.

8 WP 145/1: r, T.E. Lawrence (Yanbu') to Cyril E. Wilson (Jidda) 8 Jan.1917. *AB* no.42 (Cairo) 5 Feb.1917, p.80. MG, 7N2141: note 76, L'Officier Interprète attaché à la Mission Militaire Française d'Egypte, "La Famille des Bakris — Les Frères Fouzi et Nessib" (Aqaba) 20 June 1918. ISA 65/2784: "Notes collected in several interviews with Nasib Bey al-Bakri" [n.d.]. Sa'id, *al-Thawra*, vol.1, p.105. Al-Ghusayn, pp.202-203. Musa, *al-Husayn*, p.75. Idem, *al-Haraka*, pp.127-128. Antonius, p.149. T.E. Lawrence, *Seven Pillars of Wisdom* (New York, 1938), p.50. On the Baghdadi officer sent to Husayn see FO 882/15: Statement of Captain 'X' [Faruqi]" (Cairo) 12 Sept.1915. Al-'Umari, vol.1, p.219.

9 Musa, *al-Husayn*, p.38. Sa'id, *al-Thawra*, vol.1, pp.105-106. Al-Ghusayn, p.203. Antonius, p.150. Mrs. Steuart [Beatrice Caroline] Erskine, *King Faysal of 'Iraq* (London, 1933), p.40.

10 ISA 65/867: Lecture at Princeton by George Antonius, "The Expansion of Arab Nationalism" [1935]. ISA 65/2855: Qadri, "Kayfa", *al-Jami'a al-Islamiyya* 4 Apr.1933. "Safha Khatira min Ta'rikh al-Thawra al-'Arabiyya", *al-Jami'a al-Islamiyya* 12 Dec.1932. Al-A'zami, vol.4, pp.100-101. Sa'id, *al-Thawra*, vol.1, pp.108-109. Qadri, p.46. Al-Qaysi, vol.1, p.46. Erskine, p.42. Antonius, pp.152-153, 156.

11 *Ibid*, pp.157-158. See also Musa, *al-Husayn*, p.76.

12 Al-Sa‘id, *al-Thawra*, vol.1, p.106. Al-Ghusayn, p.204. Musa, *al-Husayn*, pp.38-39. Antonius, p.156. Erskine, pp.42-43. On the money see ISA 65/2784: "Notes collected in several interviews with Nasib Bey al-Bakri" [n.d.].

13 FO 141/736/2475: t, Cox (Basra) to Intrusive (Cairo) 2 Feb.1916. WP 145/1: r, Lawrence to Wilson 8 Jan.1917. *AB* no.1 (Cairo) 6 June 1916, p.7; no 42 (Cairo) 5 Feb.1917, p.80. NA 367/381: r17, William Yale (Cairo) to Leland Harrison (Washington) 4 Mar.1918. ISA 65/2855: Qadri, "Kayfa", *al-Jami‘a al-Islamiyya* 4 Apr.1933. Sa‘id, *al-Thawra*, vol.1, pp.107, 109. Idem, *Asrar*, pp.55-56. Qadri, p.46. Al-Ghusayn, pp.39-40, 204. Al-‘Umari, vol.1, p.219. Musa, *al-Husayn*, p.77. Erskine, pp.43-44. Antonius, pp.157, 159. William Yale, *The Near East* (Ann Arbor, [1958] ed.1968), pp.251-252.

14 ISA 65/867: Lecture by George Antonius, "The Expansion of Arab Nationalism" [1935]. Antonius, p.159. Lawrence, *Seven*, p.51. Erskine, p.44. Zeine, *Emergence*, p.117. Musa, *al-Husayn*, p.77.

15 Cab 17/177: Arabian Report N.S. No.XI 27 Sept.1916, citing army officer Shukri al-Shurbaji. FO 882/15: "Statement of Captain 'X' [Faruqi]" (Cairo) 12 Sept.1915. Al-‘Umari, vol.1, pp.220, 235. Jawdat, p.32. Sa‘id, *Asrar*, pp.58-59. Lawrence, *Seven*, p.48. Erskine, pp.44-45. Khairallah, *Problème*, p.96. Antonius, p.186. Stoddard, pp.147, 222.

16 *Al-Ahram* 15 May 1916 enclosed with MAE, Guerre 873: d179, Defrance to Briand 23 May 1916. *Al-Mustaqbal* 35 27 Oct.1916. Qadri, pp.43-44. Sa‘id, *al-Thawra*, vol.1, p.76.

17 FO 882/15: "Statement of Captain 'X' [Faruqi]" (Cairo) 12 Sept.1915. L/P&S/10/586: Arabian Report 23 Feb.1916. Cab 17/177: Arabian Report N.S. No.XI 27 Sept.1916. *Al-Kawkab* 19 5 Dec.1916. ISA 65/2924: biographies of ‘Arif al-Shihabi and Jalal al-Bukhari by George Antonius. Qadri, pp.40-42. Al-Ghusayn, p.41. Sulayman Musa, *Suwar min al-Butula* (Amman, 1968), pp.97-98. Muhammad Jamil Bayhum, *Suriyya wa-Lubnan 1918-1922* (Beirut, 1968), p.32.

18 ‘Abdallah ibn al-Husayn, *Mudhakkirati* (Jerusalem, 1945), pp.19-20. As‘ad Daghir, *Mudhakkirati ‘ala Hamish al-Qadiyya al-‘Arabiyya* (Cairo, n.d.[1959?]), p.86. Musa, *al-Husayn*, pp.18-19. *Al-Manar* 33:6 31 Oct.1933, p.557. ISA 65/2784: "Notes collected in several interviews with •Nasib Bey al-Bakri" [n.d.]. Antonius (p.103) is wrong in stating that the CUP leaders sent Husayn to Mecca.

19 ISA 65/2874a: l, Kitchener to Husayn 31 Oct.1914. For a somewhat different version of the letter see FO 371/2768.

20 For the official British version of the McMahon-Husayn correspondence see Cmd 5957: *Correspondence between Sir Henry McMahon His Majesty's High Commissioner at Cairo and the Sherif Hussein of Mecca July 1915 — March 1916* (London, 1939). On Husayn's letter of 14 July see also ‘Abdallah, pp.102-103.

21 FO 371/2490: 1, Ian Hamilton, General Commanding, Mediterranean Expeditionary Force (GHQ) to War Minister 25 Aug.1915 and minute signed by A.G.N. 10 Sept.1915. 1128226/15, FO to Secretary to the Army Council 15 Sept.1915.

22 FO 882/15: r, Military Intelligence Officer 3 Sept.1915. FO 141/732/70: t622, McMahon (Cairo) to FO 18 Oct.1915. Daghir, pp.82-83.

23 FO 882/15: "Statement by Captain 'X'" (Cairo) 12 Sept.1915.

24 Ibid: "Notes on Captain 'X' and his statement" by Na'um Shuqayr (Cairo) 12 Sept.1915.

25 FO 882/13: memo by Clayton (Cairo) 11 Oct.1915.

26 FO 882/15: Clayton to McMahon 11 Oct.1915. FO 371/2486: d121, McMahon to Grey 12 Oct.1915. t2012E, Maxwell (Cairo) to Kitchener 12 Oct.1915. WP 135/4: 1, Maxwell to Secretary (WO) 12 Oct.1915.

27 FO 371/2486: t8784, Kitchener (London) to Maxwell 13 Oct.1915. t2030E, Maxwell to Kitchener 16 Oct.1915.

28 Ibid: t "personal" , McMahon to Grey 18 Oct.1915.

29 Ibid: ts 626 and 627, McMahon to Grey 20 Oct.1915.

30 Many books and articles were written on this issue. See e.g. the comprehensive work of Elie Kedourie, In the Anglo-Arab Labyrinth: The McMahon-Husayn Correspondence and its Interpretations 1914-1939 (Cambridge, 1976). For the Arabic version of McMahon's letter of 24 Oct.1915 see FO 141/732/70.

31 For a discussion about Faruqi's allegations and proofs to their falsehood, see Eliezer Tauber, "The Role of Lieutenant Muhammad Sharif al-Faruqi", Asian and African Studies, 24 (1990), pp.17-50.

32 WO 158/624: "Summary of Historical Documents from the outbreak of War between Great Britain and Turkey 1914 to the outbreak of the Revolt of the Sherif of Mecca in June 1916" (Arab Bureau, Cairo) 29 Nov.1916, p.86. See also L/P&S/10/523: minute on d121, McMahon to Grey 12 Oct.1915: "The story fits in generally with what was already known from other sources".

33 WP 145/1: r, Lawrence to Wilson 8 Jan.1917. AB no.42 (Cairo) 5 Feb.1917, p.80. MAE, Guerre 875: note, "Le mouvement arabe — La situation au Hedjaz" enclosed with d71, Defrance to Briand 9 Feb.1917. ISA 65/2784: "Notes collected in several interviews with Nasib Bey al-Bakri" [n.d.]. "Safha Khatira min Ta'rikh al-Thawra al-'Arabiyya", al-Jami'a al-Islamiyya 12 Dec.1932. Sa'id, Asrar, pp.58-59. Lawrence, Seven, pp.51-52. Erskine, p.45.

34 R, Nasib al-Bakri (Medina) to Husayn 9 Mar.1916 cited in Sulayman Musa (ed.), Al-Murasalat al-Ta'rikhiyya 1914-1918 (Amman, 1973), vol.1, pp.61-63. Also in idem, al-Thawra, pp.48-51.

35 AB no.16 (Cairo) 18 Aug.1916, p.169. FO 882/4: "A Statement on my visit to Jeddah and Yenbo from 30th July to 17th August 1916" by Ibrahim Dimitri. MG, 7N2141: note 76, L'Officier Interprète attaché à la Mission Militaire Française d'Egypte, "La Famille des

Bakris — Les Frères Fouzi et Nessib" (Aqaba) 20 June 1918. ISA
65/2784: "Notes collected in several interviews with Nasib Bey al-
Bakri" [n.d.]. ISA 65/2855: "Safha Khatira", al-Jami'a al-
Islamiyya 12 Dec.1932. ISA 65/2856: al-Sharq 16 May 1916.
Muhammad 'Abidin Himada and Muhammad Taysir Zabyan,
Faysal ibn al-Husayn min al-Mahd ila al-Lahd (Damascus, 1933),
pp.27-28. Qadri, pp.47-49. Al-Ghusayn, pp.208-211. Sa'id, al-
Thawra, vol.1, pp.115-116. Bayhum, p.34. Erskine, p.46.

36 'Abdallah, pp.105-107. Sa'id, al-Thawra, vol.1, pp.110-111. Idem,
Asrar, pp.51-52. Musa, al-Thawra, p.34.

37 L, 'Ali (Medina) to Husayn 26 May 1916 cited in Musa, al-
Murasalat, vol.1, pp.74-75. WP 137/3: 1, Husayn to Ronald Storrs
n.d.[received on 5 June 1916]. AB no.52 (Cairo) 31 May 1917,
p.249. FO 882/7: "Summary of the Hejaz Revolt" by Hogarth
(General Staff, WO) 2nd ed. 30 Sept.1918.

38 WO 33/820 [No.5112]: tIG662, DMI Egypt to DMI 8 June 1916.
WP 140/3: "Notes on the Military Situation in the Hedjaz" by Wilson (HMS Dufferin) 11 Sept.1916. WO 157/735: "Military History
of the Arab Revolt" attached to Political Intelligence Summary
No.5 (GSPI, GHQ, EEF) 10 May 1918. FO 882/7: "Summary of
the Hejz Revolt" by Hogarth 30 Sept.1918. Military Operations I,
pp.225-226. Al-Qibla 1 14 Aug.1916. 'Abdallah, pp.107-108.
Musa, al-Husayn, pp.86, 90-92. Antonius, pp.194-195, 199.

39 Husayn's proclamation was published in various sources. See e.g.
Sa'id, al-Thawra, vol.1, pp.149-157, or al-'Umari, vol.1,
pp.257-268.

Chapter 4

1 FO 371/1968: t76, Cheetham (Cairo) to Grey 9 Aug.1914.
L/P&S/10/464: t87, FO to Cheetham 11 Aug.1914. FO 371/2140:
"Precis of Conversation with Abd El Aziz El Masri on 16 August,
1914" by R.E.M. Russell (Cairo) 17 Aug.1914 enclosed with d143,
Cheetham to Grey 24 Aug.1914. Antonius, p.155.

2 FO 371/2140: "Conversation with Aziz Bey El Masri" by Clayton
(Cairo) 30 Oct.1914 enclosed with d177, Cheetham to Grey 15
Nov.1914. Daghir, p.75.

3 FO 371/2140: t347, Grey (London) to Cheetham 14 Nov.1914.
t274, Cheetham to Grey 16 Nov.1914. L/P&S/11/88: t, SSI to
Viceroy 19 Nov.1914. FO 882/2: t550, Clayton to Wingate 21
Nov.1914. PRO 30/57/45: t331E, Maxwell (Cairo) to Kitchener 27
Nov.1914. FO 371/2140: t, SSI to Viceroy 27 Nov.1914.
L/P&S/11/88: tDS-102, FSI (Delhi) to Cox (Basra) 28 Nov.1914.
t82-B, Cox to FSI 3 Dec.1914. FO 371/2140: t, Viceroy to SSI 8
Dec.1914. t432, Grey to Cheetham 18 Dec.1914.

4 Ibid: r, Philip P. Graves 6 Dec.1914 enclosed with d203, Cheetham

to Grey,13 Dec.1914.

5 MAE, Guerre 869: note 52, "sur un entretien avec le Commandant Aziz Bey" by E. Maucorps (Cairo) 7 June 1915.

6 FO 882/2: l, Clayton[?] to Tyrrell 30 Oct.1915. FO 882/16: t, GOC Egypt to British Minister (Athens) 1 Nov.1915. Lord Birdwood, *Nuri as-Said: A Study in Arab Leadership* (London, 1959), pp.27, 33.

7 PRO 30/57/48: l, 'Aziz 'Ali al-Misri (Cairo) to Kitchener 5 Feb.1916.

8 FO 371/2767: t204, McMahon (Cairo) to FO 21 Mar.1916. t215, FO to McMahon 22 Mar.1916. L/P&S/10/525: t[draft], SSI to Viceroy 24 Mar.1916 and minute of Arthur Hirtzel. FO 882/15: l, Cairo to Lawrence (Basra) 26 Mar.1916. L/P&S/10/525: t[draft], Hirtzel (IO) to USS (FO) 28 Mar.1916. t1040, Percy Lake (Basra) to SSI 30 Mar.1916. t, Viceroy to SSI 31 Mar.1916. t[draft], Hirtzel (IO) to USS (FO) 31 Mar.1916. FO 882/13: tER491, Intrusive (Cairo) to Dirmilint (London) 31 Mar.1916. FO 371/2768: t232, McMahon to Grey 1 Apr.1916. memo, Austen Chamberlain (IO) to Grey 3 Apr.1916. FO 882/15: t, Lawrence (Basra) to Intrusive 8 Apr.1916. John Presland (pseud.) [Gladys Skelton], *Deedes Bey: A Study of Sir Wyndham Deedes* (London, 1942), pp.253-256.

9 FO 141/736/2475: tIG2508, Force "D" 16 Apr.1916 enclosed with t15548, Dirmilint to Intrusive 18 Apr.1916. tER512, Intrusive to Dirmilint 20 Apr.1916. note, "El Masri's party" n.d.[Apr.1916]. Presland, p.256.

10 FO 882/4: tIG851, Arbur (Cairo) to Dirmilint 7 July 1916. FO 371/2775: t807, McMahon to FO 24 Sept.1916. FO 371/2776: d270, McMahon to Grey 20 Oct.1916. FO 371/3381: "Interview with King Hussein at Jeddah on July 17th, 1918" by Wilson (Jidda) 17 July 1918. t39, Faruqi (Cairo) to Husayn 29 Aug.1916; t45, same to same 6 Sept.1916; t, 'Abdallah (Mecca) to Faruqi 7 Nov.1916, all cited in al-'Umari, vol.1, pp.293-294, 325. Also *ibid*, pp.319, 378. Daghir, p.89. Majid Khadduri, "'Aziz 'Ali Misri and the Arab Nationalist Movement" in Albert Hourani (ed.), *St Antony's Papers No.17 — Middle Eastern Affairs No.4* (London, 1965), p.152 (Khadduri interviewed al-Misri).

11 FO 141/462/1198: t, Wilson (Rabigh) 22 Sept.1916 enclosed with t807, McMahon to FO 24 Sept.1916. WP 141/6: d5, Wilson (Jidda) to McMahon 28 Sept.1916. MG, 7N2141: t417, René Doynel de Saint-Quentin (Cairo) to War Minister 24 Sept.1916. Daghir, p.90. Al-Ghusayn, pp.228-229. Jawdat, p.41. Sa'id, *al-Thawra*, vol.1, p.219. Lawrence, *Seven*, p.70.

12 WP 141/6: d5, Wilson to McMahon 28 Sept.1916. MAE, Guerre 1703: note, "Aziz El Masri" n.d.[Apr.? 1917]. FO 686/9: l, Fu'ad al-Khatib (Mecca) to Faruqi 10 Nov.1916. t, same to same 13 Nov.1916 cited in al-'Umari, vol.1, p.335. Also *ibid*, p.378.

13 WO 33/905 [No.6024]: tAB109, Arab Bureau to Sirdar (Khartoum) 30 Oct.1916. WP 143/1: tAB140, Arbur to Sirdar 2 Nov.1916.

MG, 7N2141: t417, Saint-Quentin to War Minister 5 Nov.1916.
FO 686/56: tAB160, Arbur to Wilson 5 Nov.1916. FO
141/736/2475: tW80, Hugh D. Pearson (Jidda) to Arbur 2
Jan.1917. FO 686/34: l, Wilson to Husayn 17 Jan.1917. H.V.F.
Winstone, *The Diaries of Parker Pasha* (London, 1983),
pp.154-158, 170. Maxwell Orme Johnson, "The Arab Bureau and
the Arab Revolt: Yanbu' to Aqaba", *Military Affairs*, 46:4 (1982),
pp.195-196. Suleiman Mousa, *T.E. Lawrence: An Arab View* (London, 1966), pp.21-22. Birdwood, p.47.

14 FO 141/462/1198: t27, Parker to Arab Bureau [26 Oct.1916]
enclosed with t943, McMahon to FO 30 Oct.1916. Cab 17/177:
Arabian Report N.S. No.XVI 2 Nov.1916. FO 686/56: tW525,
Wilson to RNO Port Sudan (for Parker) 8 Nov.1916. MG,
7N2141: t135, Cousse (Jidda) 14 Nov.1916 enclosed with t530, Defrance (Cairo) to MAE 16 Nov.1916. FO 686/55: tW595, Wilson to
Sirdar 16 Nov.1916. ts 845 and 846, Sirdar to Wilson 17
Nov.1916. tW602, Wilson to Sirdar 17 Nov.1916. WP 143A/6:
tAB250, Arbur to Sirdar 22 Nov.1916. FO 686/55: t, Parker to
Wilson 24 Nov.1916. t, Sirdar to Wilson 2 Dec.1916. t86, Parker
to Sirdar and Arbur 3 Dec.1916. FO 882/6: lJP25, Wilson to Wingate 8 Dec.1916. WP 144/1: tAB368, Arbur to Sirdar 8 Dec.1916.
MAE, Guerre 1690: t541, Saint-Quentin to MG 10 Dec.1916. FO
882/6: memo by Clayton 20 Dec.1916. *AB* no.36 (Cairo) 26
Dec.1916, p.554. MAE, Guerre 1703: note, "Aziz El Masri"
n.d.[Apr.? 1917]. Ronald Storrs, *Orientations* (London, 1937),
pp.209-210, 214-215. Winstone, *Diaries*, pp.171, 181. Al-'Umari,
vol.1, p.379.

15 FO 141/825/1198: l, Rosslyn E. Wemyss (Naval C-in-C, East Indies
and Egypt) 25 Jan.1917.

16 Jawdat, pp.41-46. Al-'Umari, vol.1, p.379, vol.2, pp.191-192. Al-Ghusayn, pp.238-239. Qal'aji, p.232 citing 'Ali Jawdat al-Ayyubi.
Khadduri, pp.153-154. Mousa, *Lawrence*, pp.22-24. Idem, "The
Role of Syrians and Iraqis in the Arab Revolt", *Middle East
Forum*, 43:1 (1967), p.9 citing Sati' al-Husri and 'Ali Jawdat al-Ayyubi.

17 FO 141/736/2475: tAB804, Arbur to Pearson 21 Feb.1917. tW458,
Pearson to Arbur 22 Feb.1917. MG, 7N2141: t99, Saint-Quentin
to MG 24 Feb.1917. FO 141/736/2475: t, RNO Port Sudan to
Arbur 25 Feb.1917. *AB* no.44 (Cairo) 12 Mar.1917, p.115. l, Wilson to Husayn 21 July 1917 cited in Musa, *al-Murasalat*, vol.1,
p.129. Daghir, pp.90-91. Jawdat, p.42. Sa'id, *al-Thawra*, vol.1,
p.219. Al-'Umari, vol.1, p.379.

18 *AB* no.44 (Cairo) 12 Mar.1917, p.115. FO 371/3396: d25, Arthur
H. Hardinge (Madrid) to Arthur James Balfour (London) 14
Jan.1918. d91, same to same 20 Feb.1918. Khadduri, pp.155-156.
"'Aziz al-Misri Yatahaddathu ila al-Ahram", *al-Ahram* 21 July
1959, p.3.

19 FO 371/3396: t177, Hardinge to FO 14 Feb.1918. t468, same to

same 4 May 1918. t482, FO to Hardinge 10 May 1918. d244, Hardinge to Balfour 18 May 1918. FO 371/3415: 1756/13(MI2), WO to USS (FO) 10 Nov.1918. d1053, FO to Derby (Paris) 19 Nov.1918. d884, George D. Grahame (Paris) to Balfour 23 Nov.1918. d1193, FO to Hardinge 27 Nov.1918. FO 371/4236: rM8110, H.E. Taylor (Madrid) 10 May 1919 enclosed with d338, Daniel Crackanthorpe (Madrid) to Curzon (London) 29 Aug.1919. t1492, FO to John de Robeck (Istanbul) 12 Sept.1919. Khadduri, p.156. "'Aziz al-Misri", p.3.

Chapter 5

1 FO 882/4: tIG882, Arbur to Dirmilint 3 July 1916. FO 141/461/1198: r, Kinahan Cornwallis (Cairo) 8 July 1916.

2 T, Faruqi (Cairo) to Husayn 24 July 1916 cited in al-'Umari, vol.1, pp.286-287. Daghir, p.94. Al-Ghusayn, p.229. FO 882/7: draft of "Situation of the Sherifian Revolt" (published in *AB* no.80 26 Feb.1918). Mousa, "Role", p.16.

3 L/P&S/10/599: tIG700, Officer in Charge of Intelligence (Cairo) to C-in-C (Simla) 15 June 1916. L/P&S/10/597: t, Viceroy to HC (Cairo) 17 June 1916. t, SSI to Viceroy 20 June 1916. FO 371/2773: t331S, Viceroy to Cairo and SSI 22 June 1916. t496, McMahon to India and FO 22 June 1916.

4 WO 158/624: 1, HC to Husayn 25 July 1916. L/P&S/10/598: t618, FO to McMahon 26 July 1916. t621, McMahon to FO 27 July 1916. t, Military Intelligence (Cairo) to DMI, FO and IO 30 July 1916. WP 139/1: ts IG1035, IG1036 and IG1402, Arbur to Governor General (Khartoum) 2 Aug.1916. FO 371/2774: t656, McMahon to FO 3 Aug.1916. WP 139/4: d2, Wilson (Jidda) to McMahon 17 Aug.1916. 1, Wingate (Khartoum) to Clayton (Cairo) 17 Aug.1916. FO 882/4: "A Statement on my visit to Jeddah and Yenbo from 30th July to 17th August 1916" by Ibrahim Dimitri. WP 141/6: d5, Wilson to McMahon 28 Sept.1916. ts, Faruqi to Husayn 3, 21, 22 and 24 July 1916; t, Husayn to Faruqi 28 July 1916; ts, Faruqi to Husayn 29 July, 1, 2, and 13 Aug.1916, all cited in al-'Umari, vol.1, pp.278-279, 285-292, vol.2, pp.61, 63, 70. Also *ibid*, p.179.

5 L/P&S/10/600: t, Viceroy to Cairo 16 Sept.1916. MAE, Guerre 1686: t419, Saint-Quentin (Cairo) to War Minister 25 Sept.1916. Al-Ghusayn, pp.157-158, 176-182. Jawdat, p.40. Al-'Umari, vol.2, p.179. Musa, *Suwar*, pp.125-126.

6 L/P&S/10/643: t, Sirdar (Khartoum) to FSI 1 Nov.1916. t895S, Viceroy to SSI and Sirdar 19 Nov.1916. t917S, Viceroy to Sirdar 23 Nov.1916. WP 143A/6: t972, Sirdar to Wilson 24 Nov.1916. t973, Sirdar to Foreign, Delhi 24 Nov.1916. L/P&S/10/586: Arabian Report N.S. No.XIX 29 Nov.1916. L/P&S/10/643: t, Sirdar

to Foreign, Delhi 5 Dec.1916. FO 371/3043: r, Parker to Arab Bureau 6 Dec.1916 enclosed with d368, McMahon to Balfour 22 Dec.1916. FO 882/6: IJP25, Wilson to Wingate 8 Dec.1916. L/P&S/10/643: t, Viceroy to SSI 14 Dec.1916. r18, Chelmsford and others (Delhi) to Chamberlain 23 Feb.1917. Winstone, *Diaries*, pp.181-182.

7 Ts, Musa'ad al-Yafi (Mecca) to Faruqi 11 and 14 Feb.1917. MAE, Guerre 1703: note, "Fouad El Khatib" n.d.[Apr.? 1917]. See also WO 33/905 [No.6665]: tAB694, Arab Bureau to DMI 4 Feb.1917.

8 FO 141/473/1805: t145, HC to FO 29 Feb.1916. Press communiqué (Headquarters, Cairo) 29 Feb.1917. WP 141/6: d5, Wilson to McMahon 28 Sept.1916. 1, Faruqi to Foreign Office (Mecca) 20 Dec.1916 cited in al-'Umari, vol.2, pp.77-78. FO 141/736/2475: tAB719, Arbur to Hubert W. Young (Jidda) 9 Feb.1917. MG, 7N2141: note 76, L'Officier Interprète attaché à la Mission Militaire Française d'Egypte, "Djafar El Askari" (Aqaba) 20 June 1918. Lawrence, *Seven*, pp.166-167. Erskine, pp.53-54. Birdwood, pp.47-49. *Military Operations I*, pp.106, 118, 128. Stoddard, pp.94-96. Al-'Umari, vol.2, pp.154-157. 'Abd al-Rahman Shahbandar, "Al-Kulunil Lurans", *al-Muqtataf*, 78 (1931), p.429.

9 L/P&S/10/643: t11348, Viceroy to SSI 1 Aug.1917. FO 371/3043: t, SSI to Viceroy 13 Aug.1917. L/P&S/10/643: t13578, Viceroy to HC Egypt and IO 9 Sept.1917. FO 371/3396: t4267, Viceroy to SSI 3 Apr.1918. 138008, DMI to USS (FO) 20 Apr.1918. L/P&S/11/110: "Arab Bureau Report for the month of July 1918" 1 Aug.1918.

10 On Mawlud Mukhlis see L/P&S/10/525: t2094, GOC Egypt (Cairo) to C-in-C (Delhi) 31 Oct.1915. Jawdat, p.38. Al-'Umari, vol.2, p.232. On Jamil al-Madfa'i see Birdwood, p.60.

11 On Ramadan al-Shallash see FO 686/47: 1, Faysal to Wilson n.d.[Sept.1917?]. WO 106/922: *Personalities*, p.167. FO 371/6349: *Personalities*, p.25. On Shurbaji and Shaykha see FO 371/2779: ts TL398 and TL404, Marsh (British Military Attaché to the Staff of the Russian Armies in the Caucasus) to DMI 18 and 19 Aug.1916. Cab 17/177: Arabian Report N.S. No.XI 27 Sept.1916. t, Faruqi to Husayn 12 Oct.1916 cited in al-'Umari, vol.2, p.75. WP 143/1: tAB149, Arbur to Sirdar 3 Nov.1916. MG, 7N2141: "Journal de marche du Lieutenant Lahlouh" (Jidda) 25 Apr.1917 enclosed with d209A, Edouard Brémond (Jidda) to War Minister 15 May 1917. On Arab deserters see also L/P&S/10/586: Arabian Report N.S. No.XXV 10 Jan.1917. FO 371/3048: t10, British Consul (Odessa) to FO 26 Jan.1917 and t202, FO to George W. Buchanan (Petrograd) 31 Jan.1917 (about a deserter in Dobrudja). Winstone, *Diaries*, p.178 (about deserters from Medina).

12 On the Ottoman Fourth Army see Ulrich Trumpener, *Germany and the Ottoman Empire 1914-1918* (Princeton, 1968), pp.103-104.

13 WP 146/5: 1, [Clayton] to DMI 17 Sept.1917. *AB* no.37 (Cairo) 4

Jan.1917, p.8; no.63 (Cairo) 18 Sept.1917, p.380; no.66 (Cairo) 21 Oct.1917, p.412. Qadri, pp.64-67. Al-Ghusayn, p.196. Saʿid, *Asrar*, pp.258-260. Idem, *al-Thawra*, vol.1, p.236. Lawrence, *Seven*, p.146.

14 David Hunter Miller, *My Diary at the Conference of Paris* (New York, 1924), vol.14, p.230.

15 Cab 17/177: Arabian Report N.S. No.XVIII 20 Nov.1916. L/P&S/11/131: t10W, Wingate (Cairo) to CIGS 17 Jan.1918.

16 FO 882/23: "Personalities: Arab Government of Syria" Mar.[?] 1920. Muhammad al-Mahdi al-Basir, *Taʾrikh al-Qadiyya al-ʿIraqiyya* (Baghdad, 1923), pp.111-112. Qadri, pp.64, 77. Jawdat, p.67. Al-Shurayqi, p.1. Saʿid, *Asrar*, pp.258-259 citing Salim ʿAbd al-Rahman. Al-Qaysi, pp.49, 54, 60-61. Musa, *Suwar*, p.186.

17 FO 882/16: 1, Lawrence (Cairo) to Clayton 10 July 1917. MAE, Syrie-Liban 1: d179, Defrance (Cairo) to Pichon 10 June 1918. Bordereau d'Envoi, MG to MAE 12 Aug.1918. ISA 65/2856: biographical details on al-Rikabi published in *al-Sharq*. Liman von Sanders, *Fünf Jahre Türkei* (Berlin, 1920), p.368. Garnett, p.226. Antonius, p.221. Saʿid, *Asrar*, p.259.

18 FO 882/24: *Who's Who in Damascus 1919* (Damascus) 14 May 1919, p.2. ISA 65/2856: "Note" on *al-Sharq* [n.d.]. ISA 65/3254: *al-Sharq* 23 Dec.1917. Kurd ʿAli, *al-Mudhakkirat*, vol.1, pp.107-108, 130. Abi Zayd, p.273.

19 WO 158/632: t1B, Egypforce (Cairo) to Troopers (London) 25 May 1917. WO 158/633: note, "The Arab Legion" n.d. FO 141/746/4833: t606, HC to FO 10 June 1917. FO 371/3043: t720, Balfour (London) to HC Egypt 26 July 1917. FO 141/746/4833: t538, HC to Governor General (Erkowit) 29 July 1917. WO 33/935 [No.7845]: t38730, CIGS to GOC Egypt 30 July 1917. WO 158/631: 1AL4, Pearson (Cairo) 20 Aug.1917. Edouard Brémond, *Le Hedjaz dans la guerre mondiale* (Paris, 1931), pp.184-185.

20 WO 158/632: tAB629, Arbur to General Baghdad 1 June 1917. WO 158/633: t635M, HC Egypt to Cox (Baghdad) 9 Sept.1917. "Al-Sariyya al-ʿArabiyya" (enrollment form in Arabic). "Oath taken in India, by Arab Officers, Prisoners of War, on their enlistment in the Arab Legion". "Oath taken in India by men Prisoners of War on their enlistment in the Arab Legion". 1, Pearson (Red Sea) to Clayton 17 Sept.1917.

21 WO 158/631: "Report on Work of Arab Legion for week ending Thursday 11th Oct.1917" by Pearson (Arab Legion) 10 Oct.1917. 1, A.J.P. Cramford (Ismailia) to Pearson 13 Oct.1917. MAE, Guerre 879: d11, Gaston Maugras [Cairo] to Ribot 15 Oct.1917, enclosing r, Robert Coulondre (Ismailia) to Maugras 13 Oct.1917. FO 141/746/4833: t1085, HC to FO 16 Oct.1917. WO 158/631: "Weekly Report of Progress of Arab Legion" by Hankey (Arab Legion) 18 and 24 Oct.1917. 1148/3032, Cadogan to GSI 25 Oct.1917. 1AL175, Pearson to GSI, GHQ, EEF 1 Nov.1917. "Weekly Report of Progress of the Arab Legion" by Pearson 8

Nov.1917. MG, 7N2145: "Compte-rendu de Mission" by Mercier (Cairo) 14 Nov.1917. WO 158/633: "Report on the Arab Legion at Ismailia" by Pearson 19 Nov.1917. MAE, Guerre 881: d16, Georges-Picot (Jerusalem) to Pichon 26 Dec.1917. Brémond, pp.187-192.

22 WO 158/633: "Report on the Arab Legion at Ismailia" by Pearson 19 Nov.1917. WP 147/3: 1. Clayton to Mark Sykes (London) 15 Dec.1917. MG, 7N2145: note 9055-9/11, "Analyse du Rapport de l'Officier Interprète de 1ère classe Mercier, envoyé en Mission en Egypte" 18 Dec.1917. Brémond, p.192.

23 WO 33/935 [No.8495]: t1160, Wingate [to CIGS] 2 Nov.1917 enclosed with t44707, CIGS to GOC Egypt 5 Nov.1917. FO 141/746/4833: t1161, HC to FO 2 Nov.1917. WO 33/935 [No.8504]: tIN4384, GOC Egypt to CIGS 6 Nov.1917. FO 141/746/4833: tCl4, Clayton to Arbur 20 Nov.1917. AB no.71 (Cairo) 27 Nov.1917, p.471. L/P&S/11/137: d4W, Wingate to Secretary of State for War 15 June 1918.

24 On al-Liwa al-Hashimi see al-'Umari, vol.2, p.234.

25 On al-Mafraza al-Shimaliyya see Jawdat, p.51. Al-'Umari, vol.2, p.266. Hubert Young, The Independent Arab (London, 1933), p.236.

26 FO 141/825/1198: 1, Wemyss (Naval C-in-C, East Indies and Egypt) 25 Jan.1917. Lawrence, Seven, p.164. Idem, Oriental Assembly (London, [1939] 4th imp.1944), p.108.

27 Al-'Umari, vol.2, pp.211-213. Sa'id, al-Thawra, vol.1, p.225. Musa, Suwar, p.130.

28 WO 33/935 [No.7726]: tAB942, Wingate to CIGS 10 July 1917. Al-Qibla 98 26 July 1917. L/P&S/11/137: d4W, Wingate to Secretary of State for War 15 June 1918. Military Operations I, p.240. Al-'Umari, vol.2, p.218.

29 Ibid, pp.214-216. Sa'id, al-Thawra, vol.1, p.225. Musa, Suwar, pp.132-133. Mousa, Lawrence, pp.60-61.

30 WP 146/9: 1, [Clayton] to DMI 9 Nov.1917. MG, 7N2145: Service d'information de la marine dans le Levant. Bulletin No.1 (Port Said) 13 Nov.1917. Lawrence, Seven, p.381. Al-'Umari, vol.2, p.234. Sa'id, al-Thawra, vol.1, p.227. Musa, Suwar, pp.124-136. Munib al-Madi and Sulayman Musa, Ta'rikh al-Urdunn fil-Qarn al-'Ishrin (Amman, 1959), pp.42, 45-46.

31 WO 33/946 [No.8875]: tAB986, Wingate to CIGS 14 Jan.1918. WO 33/946 [No.8970]: tAB14/Q, Arab Bureau to DMI 1 Feb.1918. t, Zayd (Tufayla) to Faysal 25 Jan.1918; 1, same to same 27 Jan.1918, both cited in Musa, al-Murasalat, vol.1, pp.170, 172-173. Mousa, Lawrence, p.134-135.

32 WO 158/634: t73114/80, Aqaba to Egypforce 14 Apr.1918. tGH336, Hedghog (Cairo) to GHQ, 1st Echelon 14 Apr.1918. tGH349, Hedghog to Jidda 14 Apr.1918. MAE, Guerre 886: t234, Defrance to MAE 17 Apr.1918, enclosing t72 (Jidda) 16 Apr.1918. t134, Saint-Quentin to War Minister 14 Apr.1918. WO 33/946

[No.9435]: tGH28/Q, Hijaz Operations Staff to DMI 21 Apr.1918. *AB* no.86 (Cairo) 21 Apr.1918, p.133. FO 882/7: r, Dawnay (Cairo) to CGS, GHQ, EEF 1 May 1918. MG, 7N2141: "Situation au Hedjaz — Compte-rendu mensuel (période du 7 avril au 7 mai 1918)" by Cousse 7 May 1918. Lawrence, *Seven*, pp.509, 518-519. Young, pp.164, 167-168. Brémond, pp.268-270. Birdwood, pp.62-65. Al-'Umari, vol.2, pp.241-249, 253. Sa'id, *Asrar*, pp.219-220. Idem, *al-Thawra*, vol.1, pp.229-230. Musa, *Suwar*, pp.138-141.

33 *AB* no.93 (Cairo) 18 June 1918, pp.203-204. Brémond, pp.279, 282. Liman von Sanders, p.321. Jawdat, p.48. Al-'Umari, vol.2, pp.262-264. Sa'id, *al-Thawra*, vol.1, pp.233-234.

34 WO 157/738: t699, Commandant (Aqaba) to Hedgehog 25 Sept.1918. Alec Kirkbride, *An Awakening: The Arab Campaign 1917-1918* (Tavistock, 1971), p.86. On the campaigns of the Arab army in general see also FO 371/3393: "Summary of the Hejaz Revolt" by Hogarth 30 Sept.1918.

35 L, Nasir (Aqaba) to Faysal 6 July 1917 cited in Musa, *al-Murasalat*, vol.1, p.125. FO 882/16: 1, Lawrence to Clayton 10 July 1917 (cited also in Garnett, pp.225-231). L/P&S/11/124: tAB959, Wingate to CIGS 13 July 1917. MAE, Guerre 884: t128, Georges-Picot (Cairo) to MAE 4 Mar.1918. MG, 7N2141: t337, Robert-Thomas Cosme (Cairo) to MAE 7 June 1918, enclosing t, Cousse 7 June 1918. note 76, L'Officier Interprète attaché à la Mission Militaire Française d'Egypte, "La Famille des Bakris — Les Frères Fouzi et Nessib" (Aqaba) 20 June 1918. Lawrence, *Seven*, p.228. Mousa, *Lawrence*, pp.52-53, 68-69, 72-73. Antonius, p.221. Sa'id, *al-Thawra*, vol.1, pp.235-238.

36 MG, 7N2141: "Journal de marche du Lieutenant Lahlouh" 25 Apr.1917 enclosed with d209A, Brémond (Jidda) to War Minister 15 May 1917. MAE, Guerre 878: t196, Defrance to MAE 11 Sept.1917. WO 158/634: 1, Pierce C. Joyce (Aqaba) to Clayton 12 Sept.1917. FO 882/7: draft of "Situation of the Sherifian Revolt" (published in *AB* no.80 26 Feb.1918). MAE, Guerre 884: d62, Defrance to Pichon 8 Mar.1918. MAE, PA 196/7: note 23, "Renseignements sur l'Emir Faysal sur son entourage et sa politique (Transmis par le R.P. Jaussen)" 22 Mar.1918. MAE, Syrie-Liban 1: 1, Haqqi al-'Azm (Cairo) to Jamil Mardam (Paris) 16 Apr.1918 and "Renseignements confidentiels" enclosed with d129, Defrance to Pichon 29 Apr.1918. MAE, Palestine 1: t265-266, Georges-Picot to MAE 19 May 1918. MG, 7N2141: r, Cousse to Defrance 16 June 1918. note 76, L'Officier Interprète attaché à la Mission Militaire Française d'Egypte, "Djafar El Askari" 20 June 1918. Brémond, p.215. Birdwood, p.59. Sa'id, *Asrar*, pp.239-241.

37 FO 686/52: 1, Nuri al-Kuwayri to J.R. Bassett (Jidda) 30 Aug.1917. MAE, PA 56/2: 1, Cousse to Defrance 30 May 1918. FO 686/52: r, W.A. Davenport 16 June 1918 and r, Mahmud al-Qaysuni (Mecca) to Wilson 30 June 1918, both enclosed with r12/16/Misc to

Director of Arab Bureau 18 July 1918. Brémond, pp.205-206, 228.
38 MAE, Guerre 1699: 1173, Mustafa Cherchali (Mecca) to Brémond 15 Oct.1917 enclosed with 1, Brémond to War Minister 17 Oct.1917. MAE, Guerre 879: d467, Defrance to Louis Barthou (Paris) 25 Oct.1917.
39 WO 158/619: t997, Commandant [Peake] (Aqaba) to GHQ 15 Dec.1918. t999, Commandant to Policy, GHQ 16 Dec.1918. tI7708/P, Policy, GHQ to Commandant 17 Dec.1918. t1004, Commandant to GHQ 17 Dec.1918. tI7709/P, Policy, GHQ to Briton (Damascus) 17 Dec.1918. tI7730/P, same to same 18 Dec.1918. t1009, Commandant to GHQ 19 Dec.1918. tI7770/P, Policy, GHQ to Briton 20 Dec.1918. t1014, Commandant to GHQ 22 Dec.1918. tI7780/P, Policy, GHQ to Briton 22 Dec.1918. tC755, Briton to Policy, GHQ 22 Dec.1918. tISL636, Policy, GHQ to Commandant 22 Dec.1918. tI7787/P, same to same 22 Dec.1918. t1021, Commandant to GHQ 23 Dec.1918. tI7811/P, GHQ to Commandant 25 Dec.1918. FO 371/4144: "The Akaba Incident", excerpt from AB no.108 11 Jan.1919.
40 NA 367/381: r10, Yale (Cairo) to Harrison (Washington) 31 Dec.1917. MAE, Guerre 884: d62, Defrance to Pichon 8 Mar.1918. MAE, Palestine 1: t265-266, Georges-Picot to MAE 19 May 1918. Kirkbride, p.46.
41 WP 143/7: r, Parker to Arbur 8 Nov.1916. AB no.54 (Cairo) 22 June 1917, p.276. FO 686/52: r, Davenport 16 June 1918 enclosed with r12/16/Misc to Director of Arab Bureau 18 July 1918. Al-Ghusayn, pp.232-233, 236. Jawdat, p.45. Winstone, Diaries, p.171.
42 MAE, Guerre 1691: t637-638, Defrance to MAE 21 Dec.1916. FO 371/3042: 1186/1171: Wemyss to Secretary of the Admiralty 9 Feb.1917. MAE, Guerre 1698: d400, Defrance to Ribot 5 Sept.1917. MAE, Guerre 1700: "Evénements politiques au Hedjaz — Mois d'octobre 1917" by Brémond (Cairo) 17 Nov.1917. FO 141/654/356: t156, HC to FO 23 Jan.1918. tW373 2.AB106, Bassett to Arbur 31 Jan.1918. FO 371/3381: "Interview with King Hussein at Jeddah on July 17th, 1918" by Wilson 17 July 1918. d20, Wilson (Red Sea) to Wingate 23 July 1918. 1, Rashid Rida (Cairo) to Husayn 18 Dec.1916 cited in Musa, al-Murasalat, vol.1, p.97. Jawdat, pp.45-46. Al-'Umari, vol.2, p.147. Sa'id, Asrar, pp.96, 236. Lawrence, Seven, p.167. Brémond, p.152. Stoddard, pp.140-141 citing Muhibb al-Din al-Khatib.
43 FO 371/3403: d14, Ronald W. Graham (London) to Clayton 19 July 1918. 1, Clayton to FO 15 Aug.1918. Al-Qibla 207 19 Aug.1918; 209 26 Aug.1918. MG, 7N2141: t86, Cousse to MG 24 Aug.1918. AB no.101 (Cairo) 27 Aug.1918, p.297. FO 882/13: tAB218, Arbur to 1st Echelon CPO 29 Aug.1918. FO 686/39: t526, Bassett to Husayn 30 Aug.1918. t527, same to same 31 Aug.1918. t, Husayn to British Agent [Bassett] (Jidda) 31 Aug.1918. MG, 7N2141: t379, Coulondre (Cairo) to MAE 31

Aug.1918. FO 882/13: t540, Commandant (Aqaba) to Arbur 2 Sept.1918. FO 686/52: tAB211, Arbur to Bassett 2 Sept.1918. FO 882/13: t543, Commandant to Arbur 2 Sept.1918. t074, Commandant to British Agent 3 Sept.1918. tAB263, Arbur to Bassett 3 Sept.1918. FO 686/39: t, Husayn to British Agent 3 Sept.1918. FO 686/52: tW738, Bassett to Arbur 4 Sept.1918. FO 686/39: t534, Bassett to Husayn 4 Sept.1918. t535, same to same 4 Sept.1918. MG, 7N2141: t386, Commissaire Jérusalem (Cairo) to MAE 4 Sept.1918. FO 686/39: t536, Bassett to Husayn 5 Sept.1918. FO 686/52: t, Husayn to A/British Agent 5 Sept.1918. tW739, Bassett to Arbur 5 Sept.1918. FO 882/13: tAB277, Arbur to Bassett 5 Sept.1918. FO 686/39: t540, [Bassett] to Husayn 5 Sept.1918. FO 882/13: t, Husayn to HC 5 Sept.1918. tAB292, [Arbur] to DAB (Jidda) and GHQ (Aqaba) 6 Sept.1918. FO 686/39: t545, Bassett to Husayn 6 Sept.1918. FO 371/3411: t1335, Wingate to FO 10 Sept.1918. FO 882/13: tP630, Chief Egypforce to Troopers 11 Sept.1918. FO 686/39: l, Wilson (Cairo) to Husayn 14 Sept.1918. MG, 7N2141: "Compte-rendu" 92, Cousse 19 Sept.1918. *AB* no.104 (Cairo) 24 Sept.1918, p.333. Lawrence, *Seven*, pp.576-579. Kirkbride, pp.46-47. Brémond, p.287. Shahbandar, "al-Kulunil", p.275.

44 Sulayman Musa (ed.), *Al-Thawra al-'Arabiyya al-Kubra: Al-Harb fil-Urdunn 1917-1918 — Mudhakkirat al-Amir Zayd* (Amman, 1976), pp.129-130 citing Zayd's memoirs 3 Oct.1918. FO 371/4144: "Discontent in Arab Army" excerpt from *AB* no.108 11 Jan.1919. Elie Kedourie, "The Surrender of Medina, January 1919", *MES*, 13:1 (1977), p.142.

45 WP 138/2: t, RNO (Port Sudan) to Hakimam (Erkowit) 3 July 1916. FO 141/461/1198: r, Cornwallis 8 July 1916. l, Lawrence (Wadi Safra) to Parker 24 Oct.1916 cited in Winstone, *Diaries*, p.163. Cab 17/177: Arabian Report N.S. No.XVI 2 Nov.1916. WP 143/7: r, Parker to Arbur 8 Nov.1916. "Opinion, expressed privately, by an Egyptian Officer, who returned recently from the Hejaz" (Khartoum) 25 Nov.1916.

46 MAE, Guerre 1690: t541, Saint-Quentin to MG 10 Dec.1916. MG, 7N2141: t77 (Jidda) 26 Feb.1917 enclosed with t170, Defrance to MAE 28 Feb.1917. t309, same to same 25 Apr.1917. FO 686/52: r, Davenport to Bassett 25 Apr.1918. MG, 7N2141: note 76, L'Officier Interprète attaché à la Mission Militaire Française d'Egypte, "Noury Ben Said" (Aqaba) 20 June 1918. FO 141/816/5986: t603, Commandant (Aqaba) to Arbur 12 Sept.1918. Jawdat, pp.44-45. Al-'Umari, vol.1, p.378, vol.2, p.210. Birdwood, p.52.

47 MAE, Arabie 20: 130CH, "Situation au Hedjaz — exposé sommaire des principaux événements militaires et politiques (7 février — 7 mars 1918)" by Cousse 7 Mar.1918. 135CH, Cousse to Cherchali 28 Mar.1918. 148CH, "Situation au Hedjaz — Compte-rendu mensuel 7 mars au 7 avril 1918)" by Cousse 7 Apr.1918. 163CH,

"Rapport mensuel du 7 mai au 15 juin 1918" by Lapadu Hargues (Jidda) 15 June 1918. FO 686/52: r, Davenport 16 June 1918. MG, 7N2141: note 25, "Rapport Mensuel — Situation au Hedjaz (1er mars au 31 mars)" by Depui (Jidda) 1 Apr.1919. Brémond, pp.228-229.

48 WP 137/6: 1, Fu'ad al-Khatib (Cairo) to Shahin Bey 26 June 1916. FO 141/783/5317: note, Symes, "Egypt and the Arab Movement" [Alexandria] 14 Aug.1917. NA 367/381: r2, Yale to Harrison 5 Nov.1917. Kirkbride, p.17. Rose, pp.178-179.

49 L/P&S/20/C131: *Personalities — Arabia* (Admiralty War Staff, Intelligence Division, April 1917), pp.100, 106, 108. FO 882/16: 1, Lawrence to Clayton 10 July 1917. *AB* no.64 (Cairo) 27 Sept.1917, p.393; no.65 (Cairo) 8 Oct.1917, p.398; no.72 (Cairo) 5 Dec.1917, p.490; no.97 (Cairo) 16 July 1918, p.254; no.100 (Cairo) 20 Aug.1918, p.279. MG, 7N2141: d77, Defrance to Pichon 14 Mar.1918. WO 157/738: t65018, Commandant (Aqaba) to Hedghog (Cairo) 18 Sept.1918. FO 371/3393: Appendix L to "Summary of the Hejaz Revolt" by Hogarth 30 Sept.1918. Lawrence, *Seven*, p.174. Brémond, p.286. George Stitt, *A Prince of Arabia: The Emir Shereef Ali Haider* (London, 1948), p.180. Mousa, *Lawrence*, pp.52-53. Qal'aji, pp.252-253.

50 FO 686/52: r, Davenport to Bassett 25 Apr.1918. r, Davenport 16 June 1918 and r, Mahmud al-Qaysuni to Wilson 30 June 1918, both enclosed with r12/16/Misc to Director of Arab Bureau 18 July 1918. MAE, Guerre 1693: d90, Defrance to Briand 26 Feb.1917. MG, 7N2141: t77 (Jidda) 26 Feb.1917 enclosed with t170, Defrance to MAE 28 Feb.1917. Brémond, p.229. Al-'Umari, vol.2, p.241. Musa, *Suwar*, p.138.

51 Lawrence, *Oriental Assembly*, p.141. In 1919 Faysal was more liberal when valuing Lawrence's role: "You know that out in the desert we often tie the camels head to tail in a long row, and then we put a little donkey at the head to lead the line. Lawrence has been that little donkey." See James T. Shotwell, *At the Paris Peace Conference* (New York, 1937), p.130.

52 Lawrence, *Oriental Assembly*, pp.110, 119.

53 MAE, Guerre 1699: "Bulletin de renseignements" by Brémond 26 Oct.1917. MAE, Guerre 1700: "Bulletin de renseignements" by Brémond 2 Dec.1917. MAE, Arabie 20: 130CH, "Situation au Hedjaz — exposé sommaire des principaux événements militaires et politiques (7 février — 7 mars 1918)" by Cousse 7 Mar.1918. *AB* n.83 (Cairo) 27 Mar.1918, p.93. FO 686/52: r, Davenport to Bassett 25 Apr.1918. 1, Davenport to H. Garland 30 May 1918. L/P&S/11/137: d4W, Wingate to Secretary of State for War 15 June 1918. FO 686/52: r, Davenport 16 June 1918 and r, Mahmud al-Qaysuni to Wilson 30 June 1918, both enclosed with r12/16/Misc to Director of Arab Bureau 18 July 1918. Jawdat, pp.42-43, 45-46. Brémond, pp.228-229. Kedourie, "Surrender", p.130.

54 FO 686/38: Jamal Pasha to Faysal 26 Nov.1917. Jamal Pasha to

Ja'far al-'Askari 26 Nov.1917. Jamal Pasha to 'Abdallah 5 Dec.1917. MG, 7N2141: t, Defrance to MAE 7 Jan.1918. t32, same to same 15 Jan.1918. NA 367/381: r11, Yale to Harrison 21 Jan.1918. MAE, Guerre 1700: t19, Cousse 25 Jan.1918 enclosed with t60, Defrance to MAE 25 Jan.1918. Antonius, pp.253, 256-257.

55 T, Faruqi (Cairo) to Foreign Office (Mecca) 25 Apr.1917 cited in al-'Umari, vol.2, p.105. FO 141/654/356: t, Sykes to HC enclosed with t22, Bassett to Arbur 6 May 1917. WP 145/7: "Note by Sheikh Fuad El Khatib taken by Lt Col Newcombe" enclosed with l, Clayton to Symes 27 May 1917. *Al-Manar* 22:6 6 June 1921, p.452; 33:10 15 Apr.1934, p.797. Sa'id, *al-Thawra*, vol.1, pp.301-303.

56 FO 371/3403: t655, Wingate to FO 8 Apr.1918. Faysal's conditions (Wahida) 10 June 1916 in Musa, *al-Murasalat*, vol.1, p.195.

57 FO 371/3060: t747, Horace G. Rumbold (Berne) to FO 30 Aug.1917. *Al-Manar* 23:2 27 Feb.1922, p.133 (an article by Shakib Arslan). On Ziya Gökalp's opinions see Uriel Heyd, *Foundations of Turkish Nationalism: The Life and Teachings of Ziya Gökalp* (London, 1950), p.131 and Ahmed Emin, *Turkey in the World War* (New Haven, 1930), p.207.

58 MAE, Arabie 1: t371, Coulondre to MAE 20 Aug.1918. MG, 6N193: t375, same to same 24 Aug.1918. FO 371/4182: *Times* 4 Sept.1919. Al-Rifa'i, pp.87-89, 92. Bayhum, pp.41-42, 67-68. Musa, *al-Husayn*, p.140. Mousa, *Lawrence*, pp.180-181.

59 l, Faruqi to Husayn 5 Dec.1915; ls, Husayn to Faruqi 1 Jan. and 18 Feb.1916; t, Faruqi [Jidda] to Husayn 3 July 1916, all cited in al-'Umari, vol.1, pp.219-225, 227, 280. See also *ibid*, p.274. FO 141/461/1198: Appendices II and III to Cornwallis' report 8 July 1916.

60 Ts, Faruqi to Husayn 19 July and 17 Sept.1916, cited in al-'Umari, vol.2, p.58, and vol.1, p.296, respectively. FO 686/56: tIG1539, Arbur to Wilson 29 Sept.1916.

61 FO 141/679/4088: t3, Faruqi to Husayn 10 July 1916. t,:'Abdallah (Mecca) to Wilson 29 Oct.1916 enclosed with t435, Wilson 29 Oct.1916 enclosed with t945, HC to FO 31 Oct.1916. MAE, Guerre 1687: t, 'Abdallah to French Foreign Minister 29 Oct.1916. t127, 'Abdallah to Russian Foreign Minister 29 Oct.1916 cited in E. Adamow, *Die Europäischen Mächte und die Türkei während des Weltkrieges — Die Aufteilung der asiatischen Türkei* (Dresden, 1932), p.161. FO 141/679/4088: t484, Wilson 4 Nov.1916 enclosed with t978, HC to FO 6 Nov.1916. *Al-Qibla* 22 30 Oct.1916; 23 2 Nov.1916; 24 6 Nov.1916. *Al-Manar* 22:6 6 June 1921, p.448. 'Abdallah, p.129. Sa'id, *Asrar*, pp.128-129. Jung, vol.2, pp.19-20.

62 FO 371/2782: d14, Wilson to McMahon 5 Nov.1916. FO 141/679/4088: t885, FO to McMahon 6 Nov.1916. WP 143/2: tW547, Wilson to Sirdar 9 Nov.1916. FO 371/2776: t12, Sirdar to FO 10 Nov.1916. FO 371/2782: t1004, McMahon to FO 13

Nov.1916. WP 143/2: tW571, Wilson to Sirdar 13 Nov.1916. t, McMahon to Sirdar 14 Nov.1916. FO 371/2782: d334, McMahon to Grey 21 Nov.1916, enclosing d15, Wilson to McMahon 11 Nov.1916. ts, Faruqi to Foreign Office (Mecca) 9, 17 and 18 Nov.1916, all cited in al-'Umari, vol.1, pp.326, 335-336.

63 T, Fu'ad al-Khatib (Mecca) to Faruqi 21 Nov.1916; t71, Faruqi to Fu'ad al-Khatib 25 Nov.1916, both cited in *ibid*, pp.337-338, 341-342. English translation of both in FO 686/9.

64 FO 141/679/4088: t973, FO to HC 11 Dec.1916. Reuter's telegram (Cairo) 26 Dec.1916. t80, Faruqi to Foreign Office (Mecca) 27 Dec.1916 cited in al-'Umari, vol.1, p.349. FO 882/19: 1, HC to Husayn 24 Jan.1917. L/P&S/10/637: note by IO, "King Husayn's Title" 14 Nov.1918.

65 L/P&S/10/601: 1, Husayn to McMahon 15 Sept.1916 enclosed with d276, McMahon to Grey 25 Oct.1916. WP 141/6: 1JP9, Wilson to McMahon 13 Oct.1916. FO 141/679/4088: t, McMahon to Sirdar 14 Nov.1916. FO 371/2782: d334, McMahon to Grey 21 Nov.1916. WP 144/1: t, McMahon to Sirdar 8 Dec.1916. *AB* no.36 (Cairo) 26 Dec.1916, p.555, cited also in Storrs, p.215.

66 WO 158/624: 1, McMahon to Husayn 25 July 1916. WP 139/1: t1G1035, Arbur to Wingate 2 Aug.1916. WP 139/4: d2, Wilson to McMahon 17 Aug.1916. WP 140/3: Arbur to Wingate 9 Sept.1916. FO 371/2776: d8, Wilson to McMahon n.d. enclosed with d280, McMahon to Grey 26 Oct.1916. FO 686/9: 1, Fu'ad al-Khatib to Faruqi 10 Nov.1916.

67 T, Faruqi to Foreign Office (Mecca) 8 June 1917; t, Fu'ad al-Khatib to Faruqi 8 June 1917; t, Faruqi to Mecca 9 June 1917; t, Fu'ad al-Khatib to Faruqi 9 June 1917, all cited in al-'Umari, vol.2, pp.120-123. FO 141/654/356: t617, Wingate to FO 12 June 1917. t647, FO to Wingate 27 June 1917. t691, Wingate to FO 1 July 1917.

68 Ts, Faruqi to Foreign Office (Mecca) 14 and 24 July 1917; t, Ahmad (Mecca) to Faruqi 26 July 1917; t, Faruqi to Foreign Office 27 July 1917; t, Ahmad to Faruqi 27 July 1917, all cited in al-'Umari, vol.2, pp.134-138.

69 MAE, Guerre 1704: t, Brémond to MG and MAE 15 Oct.1916. MAE, Guerre 1697: d346, Defrance to Ribot 28 July 1917. t, Foreign Office (Mecca) to Faruqi 24 Aug.1917; t, Faruqi to Foreign Office 24 Aug.1917; ts, Faruqi to Mecca 2 and 5 Sept.1917, all cited in al-'Umari, vol.2, pp.150-151. MG, 7N2141: t612, Defrance to MAE 17 Sept.1917. 1163, Cherchali to MAE 12 Oct.1917 enclosed with 1199, Brémond to MG 17 Oct.1917. *Al-Qibla* 78 14 May 1917. *Al-Manar* 24:8 13 Aug.1923, p.607; 28:1 3 Mar.1927, p.5.

70 MAE, Guerre 1699: 1173, Cherchali to Brémond 15 Oct.1917 enclosed with 1, Brémond to MG and MAE 17 Oct.1917. FO 686/30: tW1727, Wilson to Arbur 16 Oct.1917. MAE, Syrie-Liban 1: "Renseignements confidentiels" enclosed with d129, Defrance to

Pichon 29 Apr.1918. FO 686/30: tW708, Bassett to Arbur 8 Sept.1918. FO 141/816/5986: tAB305, Arbur to Commandant (Aqaba) 9 Sept.1918. FO 686/39: 1, Wilson to Husayn 14 Sept.1918. FO 141/816/5986: 1, HC to Husayn [15 Sept.1918]. t, Husayn to HC 28 Sept.1918. FO 686/30: tAB350, Arbur to British Agent (Jidda) 3 Oct.1918. 1, C.A.G. Mackintosh (Cairo) to Musa'ad al-Yafi (Mecca) 26 Nov.1918.

Chapter 6

1 MAE, Guerre 869: d202, Defrance (Cairo) to Delcassé 5 July 1915. d211, same to same 10 July 1915. *Al-Manar* 22:6 6 June 1921, pp.450-451.
2 FO 371/2490: r12, Sykes (Cairo) to C.E. Callwell (London) 14 July 1915. Presland, pp.243-244.
3 FO 371/2491: d520, Evelin Grant-Duff (Berne) to Grey 26 Oct.1915. FO 882/13: t9504, Kitchener (London) to Maxwell (Cairo) 4 Nov.1915. t2122E, Maxwell to Kitchener 4 Nov.1915. FO 371/2491: 1s, Habib Lutf Allah (London) to Grey 5 and 8 Nov.1915. t901, FO to McMahon (Cairo) 20 Nov.1915. FO 371/2768: t58, McMahon to FO 21 Jan.1916. d20, same to same 25 Jan.1916. t67, FO to McMahon 25 Jan.1916. d77, Hardinge (Madrid) to Grey 29 Feb.1916. t161, FO to Hardinge 8 Mar.1916. FO 371/2781: 1, Habib Lutf Allah (Madrid) to Grey 27 Aug.1916. FO 141/471/1731: d237, Hardinge to Balfour 12 May 1918. FO 371/5223: Defense Security Intelligence Report 8 Sept.1920. Presland, pp.247-249. Ahmad Shafiq Pasha, *Mudhakkirati fi Nisf Qarn* (Cairo, [1934]), vol.3, p.97.
4 MAE, Guerre 875: d71, Defrance to Briand 9 Feb.1917. d100, same to same 28 Feb.1917. MAE, Guerre 876: note (Cairo) 9 Jan.1917 enclosed with d184, Defrance to Ribot 10 Apr.1917.
5 FO 141/736/2475: 1, Rafiq al-'Azm (Cairo) to Husayn 27 Feb.1917. 1, Husayn to Rafiq al-'Azm 16 Mar.1917. t, Fu'ad al-Khatib (Mecca) to Faruqi (Cairo) 15 Apr.1917; t, Faruqi to Mecca 21 Apr.1917, both cited in al-'Umari, vol.2, pp.104-105.
6 L, Faruqi to Foreign Office (Mecca) 20 Dec.1916; 1, same to same 11 Apr.1917; t, same to same 9 June 1917; t, Fu'ad al-Khatib to Faruqi 9 June 1917; ts, Faruqi to Foreign Office 17 and 25 June 1917; t, Fu'ad al-Khatib to Faruqi 28 June 1917; 1, Faruqi to Foreign Office 29 June 1917, all cited in *ibid*, pp.78, 96, 122-123, 125, 127-129, 131-132.
7 MAE, Guerre 869: d210, Defrance to Delcassé 10 July 1915. d216, same to same 17 July 1915. t, Faruqi to Foreign Office (Mecca) 14 Dec.1916 cited in al-'Umari, vol.1, p.345. *AB* no.39 (Cairo) 19 Jan.1917, p.37. Cab 17/177: Arabian Report N.S. No.XXVII 24 Jan.1917. MAE, Guerre 875: note, "Le mouvement

arabe — La situation au Hedjaz" enclosed with d71, Defrance to Briand 9 Feb.1917. L/P&S/11/110: "Report on Moslem Propaganda" (Arab Bureau) 11 Feb.1917 enclosed with d35, Wingate (Cairo) to Balfour 22 Feb.1917. MAE, Guerre 876: d184: Defrance to Ribot 10 Apr.1917. Jung, vol.2, p.26. See also Bruce Cornelius Westrate, *Imperialists All: The Arab Bureau and the Evolution of British Policy in the Middle East, 1916-1920* (Ph.D. Dissertation, The University of Michigan, 1982), p.155.

8 Ts, Faruqi to Foreign Office (Mecca) 25 Apr. and 27 June 1917, both cited in al-'Umari, vol.2, pp.105-106, 130. MAE, Guerre 877: d5, Georges-Picot (Cairo) to Prime Minister 2 May 1917. WP 145/6: "Note of a meeting at the Residency, Cairo, on 12th May 1917". *Al-Manar* 21:4 28 June 1919, p.203; 22:6 6 June 1921, p.452. Shahbandar, "al-Kulunil", p.660. Sa'id, *Asrar*, pp.184-185, 191. Rose, pp.237-239.

9 FO 141/654/356: 1, Mackintosh (Cairo) to Clayton 22 Nov.1917, enclosing telegram from the Syrians (Cairo) to Balfour 20 Nov.1917. NA 367/381: r5, Yale (Cairo) to Harrison (Washington) 26 Nov.1917. r7, same to same 10 Dec.1917. r8, same to same 17 Dec.1917. r10, same to same 31 Dec.1917. Frank E. Manuel, *The Realities of American-Palestine Relations* (Washington, 1949), pp.187-188.

10 FO 882/17: r113/1/3744, Mackintosh to Clayton 27 Dec.1917, enclosing ls, Sulayman Nasif to Clayton 26 and 28 Dec.1917. FO 371/3398: 1, Sulayman Nasif and others (Cairo) to Sykes (London) 17 Jan.1918. 1, Sykes (in name of Syrians, Armenians and Zionists) 15 Feb.1918. Manuel, p.187.

11 NA 367/382: r22, Yale to Harrison 8 Apr.1918. CZA L4/768: 1, Cornwallis (Cairo) to Symes 20 Apr.1918. "The Arab Commission in Jaffa" by 'Isa al-Sifri (Jaffa) 22 May 1918. NA 367/383: r29, Yale to Harrison 27 May 1918. *AB* no.91 (Cairo) 4 June 1918, p.182. MAE, Arabie 1: d185A, Cousse (Jidda) to MAE 10 July 1918. CZA L4/768: *Mir'at al-Gharb* 15 Aug.1918 citing letter from Sulayman Nasif to *al-Kawkab* 14 June 1918. Manuel, p.188.

12 MG, 7N2145: d467, Defrance to MAE 25 Oct.1917. FO 371/3054: t1126, FO to Wingate 26 Nov.1917. t1281, Wingate to FO 28 Nov.1917. MAE, Syrie-Liban 56: 1, Haqqi al-'Azm (Cairo) to Georges Haddad (São Paulo) 1 Jan.1918 enclosed with d110, Defrance to Pichon 5 Apr.1918. NA 367/382: r23, Yale to Harrison 15 Apr.1918. Lawrence, *Secret Despatches*, p.158.

13 NA 367/381: r10, Yale to Harrison 31 Dec.1918. FO 882/17: r113/1/4577, Mackintosh to Clayton 25 Feb.1918. MAE, Syrie-Liban 1: 1, Haqqi al-'Azm to Jamil Mardam (Paris) 16 Apr.1918 enclosed with d129, Defrance to Pichon 29 Apr.1918. NA 367/382: r25, Yale to Harrison 29 Apr.1918.

14 MAE, PA 196/7: note 23, "Renseignements sur l'Emir Faysal sur son entourage et sa politique (Transmis par le R.P. Jaussen)" 22 Mar.1918. MAE, Syrie-Liban 56: 1, Haqqi al-'Azm to Georges

Haddad 4 Apr.1918 enclosed with d110, Defrance to Pichon 5 Apr.1918. MG, 7N2141: d45, Cherchali (Mecca) to MAE 12 Apr.1918. MAE, Syrie-Liban 1: d170, Defrance to Pichon 3 June 1918, enclosing an article by Haqqi al-'Azm. *Al-Qibla* 171 11 Apr.1918. Sa'id, *al-Thawra*, vol.1, p.310.

15 NA 367/382: r23, Yale to Harrison 15 Apr.1918. Sa'id, *Asrar*, pp.237, 243-245. Idem, *al-Thawra*, vol.2a, pp.37-38. Darwaza, *Hawla*, vol.1, pp.89-90.

16 FO 882/17: Memorandum by Seven Syrians [translated by 'Abd al-Rahman al-Shahbandar and Osmond Warlond] to HC 26 Apr.1918. Also in Sa'id, *al-Thawra*, vol.2a, pp.38-40.

17 The common version is of Antonius, p.433; Darwaza, *Hawla*, vol.1, p.90; Musa, *al-Haraka*, p.392; Wajih 'Alam al-Din, *Al-'Uhud al-Muta'alliqa bil-Watan al-'Arabi* (Beirut, 1965), p.82. Warlond's version is in FO 882/17: 1, Warlond to Clayton 17 July 1918. The same version may also be found in FO 882/24: note, "The AHD Committee or Committee of the Covenant" by Arab Bureau (Cairo) Apr.1919. The third version is of Sa'id, *Asrar*, p.246.

18 The summary of the Arab societies' activities is enclosed with the memo of the seven in FO 882/17.

19 *Ibid*: Warlond's original report on the Arab societies. 1, Warlond to Clayton 17 July 1918. *AB* no.90, "Arab Committees before the War" (Cairo) 24 May 1918, pp.165-167. NA 367/383: r28, Yale to Harrison 20 May 1918. *Al-Manar* 22:6 6 June 1921, p.461.

20 FO 371/3380: d90, Wingate to Balfour 7 May 1918.

21 *Ibid*: t736, FO to Wingate 7 June 1918. draft of the Declaration to the Seven, signed by M[ark] S[ykes], which was eventually sent as t753, FO to Wingate 11 June 1918. For the official version of the Declaration see Cmd 5964: *Statements made on behalf of His Majesty's Government during the year 1918 in regard to the Future Status of certain parts of the Ottoman Empire* (London, 1939), pp.5-6. FO 371/3381: d127, Wingate to Balfour 25 June 1918. FO 371/3383: tP695: GOC [Edmund Allenby] to WO 7 Oct.1918. Sa'id, *Asrar*, p.246. Idem, *al-Thawra*, vol.2a, p.40. 'Alam al-Din, pp.82-83.

22 FO 141/654/356: memo by Hogarth, "Conversation with Dr. Faris Nimr" (Arab Bureau) 13 June 1918. Also in *AB Supplementary Papers* no.5 (Cairo) 24 June 1918, pp.13-15.

23 MAE, Syrie-Liban 1: t359, Coulondre (Cairo) to MAE 11 Aug.1918. FO 141/654/356: "Appel aux grandes puissances libératrices de la Syrie" enclosed with 1, Haqqi al-'Azm and others to Wingate 25 Oct.1918.

24 MG, 7N2145: t384, Defrance to MAE 3 July 1918. MAE, Arabie 1: d213, Defrance to Pichon 13 July 1918. FO 371/3414: memo 4289, Italian Ambassador (London) 27 Oct.1918. t1807, Wingate to FO 4 Dec.1918. *Al-Manar* 22:6 6 June 1921, p.461. Sa'id, *Asrar*, pp.238-239.

25 L/P&S/11/146: 1, Michel Luṭf Allah (Cairo) 18 Jan.1919.

Al-Manar 21:4 28 June 1919, pp.202-203. Saʻid, *Asrar*, pp.241-243. Idem, *al-Thawra*, vol.2a, pp.37, 41. Al-Nusuli, p.25.

26 NA 367/381: r19, Yale to Harrison 18 Mar.1918, enclosing "Historical Review of the 'Alliance Libanaise'" (Cairo) 7 Feb.1918. MAE, Syrie-Liban 1: note ["sur l'Alliance Libanaise d'Egypte"] 10 Mar.1918 enclosed with d96, Defrance to Pichon 23 Mar.1918. FO 882/17: rEG76/18108, "B" Branch, Eastern Mediterranean, Special Intelligence Bureau (Cairo) to Director, Arab Bureau 18 June 1918.

27 FO 371/3048: d38, Wingate to Balfour 24 Feb.1917, enclosing 1, Alliance Libanaise (Cairo) to FO 22 Feb.1917. MAE, Guerre 875: d94, Defrance to Briand 26 Feb.1917, enclosing 1, Alliance Libanaise (Cairo) to MAE 22 Feb.1917. MAE, Guerre 876: d160, MAE to Defrance 19 Mar.1917. FO 371/3048: memo 1348, Italian Ambassador (London) to FO 20 Mar.1917. NA 367/381: "Historical Review of the 'Alliance Libanaise'" 7 Feb.1917 enclosed with r19, Yale to Harrison 18 Mar.1918. Adib Karam, p.151.

28 L, Faruqi to Foreign Office (Mecca) 11 Apr.1917 cited in al-ʻUmari, vol.2, p.97. NA 367/381: r19, Yale to Harrison 18 Mar.1918. WO 157/735: Political and Economic Intelligence Summary No.13 (GSPI, GHQ, EEF) 31 Aug.1918. Khairallah, *Problème*, p.71. Zamir, p.49. Lyne Lohéac, *Daoud Ammoun et la création de l'Etat Libanais* (Paris, 1978), p.71.

29 MAE, Guerre 881: d522, Defrance to Pichon 27 Dec.1917. MAE, Guerre 882: "Note pour le Bureau de la Presse a.s. de réunions de Libanais" 30 Jan.1918. Bishara Khalil al-Khuri, *Haqaʻiq Lubnaniyya* ([Beirut], 1960), vol.1, pp.83-84.

30 T, Faruqi to Foreign Office (Mecca) 9 May 1917; t, Fuʼad al-Khatib to Faruqi 14 May 1917; ts, Faruqi to Mecca 17 and 25 June 1917, all cited in al-ʻUmari, vol.2, pp.110-113, 127-128. FO 882/17: rEG76/18108, "B" Branch, Eastern Mediterranean, Special Intelligence Bureau to Director, Arab Bureau 18 June 1918. Saʻid, *al-Thawra*, vol.1, pp.301-302. Idem, *Asrar*, pp.184-185. Adib Karam, pp.151-152 citing Yusuf al-Sawda.

31 FO 686/30: tAB798, Arbur to Bassett (Jidda) 25 June 1917. ts, Faruqi to Foreign Office (Mecca) 20 June, 27 July, 1 and 3 Aug.1917, all cited in al-ʻUmari, vol.2, pp.126, 137-140. MAE, Guerre 878: d366, Defrance to Ribot 15 Aug.1917. MAE, Guerre 882: note, "L'Emir Fayssal" 3 Jan.1918 enclosed with d9, Defrance to Pichon 16 Jan.1918. MAE, Syrie-Liban 1: note 10 Mar.1918 enclosed with d96, Defrance to Pichon 23 Mar.1918. Lohéac, pp.71-72.

32 T, Faruqi to Mecca 17 May 1917 cited in al-ʻUmari, vol.2, p.113. MAE, Guerre 882: note, "L'Emir Fayssal" 3 Jan.1918 enclosed with d9, Defrance to Pichon 16 Jan.1918. MAE, Guerre 883: d46, same to same 8 Feb.1918. *al-Ittihad al-Lubnani* 28 Nov.1917 enclosed with 1, Michel Tuwayni to Pichon 12 Feb.1918. MAE, Guerre 884: note, "Renseignement sur l'Arabie" by Le Service

d'Information dans le Levant, enclosed with d59, Defrance to Pichon 26 Feb.1918. MAE, Syrie-Liban 1: d84, Coulondre (Jerusalem) to Pichon 5 Sept.1918. Sa'id, *Asrar*, pp.237-238.

33 NA 367/381 and FO 371/3398: Alliance Libanaise, *Mémorandum sur les aspirations des Libanais* (Cairo) 8 Jan.1918. FO 371/3398: d13, Wingate to Balfour 26 Jan.1918. NA 367/381: "Historical Review of the 'Alliance Libanaise'" 7 Feb.1917 enclosed with r19, Yale to Harrison 18 Mar.1918. Jung, vol.2, pp.76-78.

34 NA 367/381: r12, Yale to Harrison 28 Jan.1918, enclosing summary of Adib Pasha's opinions about the future government of Lebanon.

35 MAE, Syrie-Liban 1: 1, Shukri Ghanim (Paris) to Pichon 9 Mar.1918. *Al-Mustaqbal* 98 20 Mar.1918; 108 20 July 1918. Comité Central Syrien, *L'Opinion Syrienne à l'Etranger pendant la Guerre* (Paris, 1918), pp.15-16. Georges Samné, *La Syrie* (Paris, 1920), pp.516, 518. Jung, vol.2, pp.82-83.

36 FO 882/17: rEG76/18108, "B" Branch, Eastern Mediterranean, Special Intelligence Bureau to Director, Arab Bureau 18 June 1918. MAE, Syrie-Liban 1: d210, Defrance to Pichon 12 July 1918. FO 141/620/323: 1, Clayton to Coulondre 11 Aug.1918. FO 882/17: l113/1/7170, Director, Arab Bureau to CPO 15 Aug.1918. 1, Clayton to Director, Arab Bureau 17 Aug.1918. MAE, Syrie-Liban 1: d84, Coulondre to Pichon 5 Sept.1918.

37 MAE, Guerre 877: t, Le Comité de défense des intérêts syriens et libanais (Alexandria) to Ribot 21 June 1917. t436-437, Defrance to MAE 24 June 1917. MAE, Guerre 885: t, de Margerie (Paris) to Cairo 17 Mar.1918. MAE, Syrie-Liban 1: d187: Defrance to Pichon 15 June 1918. MAE, Syrie-Liban 4: "Information sur les milieux syriens d'Egypt" 5 Nov.1918 enclosed with Bordereau Récapitulatif, Marine Ministry to MAE 6 Nov.1918. MAE, Syrie-Liban 7: note by André-Miranda Malzac (Cairo) and program of "Association des Comités Libano-Syriens d'Egypte", both enclosed with d5, Pierre-Antonin Lefevre-Pontalis (Cairo) to Pichon 9 Jan.1919. Sa'id, *Asrar*, P.191. Idem, *al-Thawra*, vol.1, p.310.

38 MAE, Guerre 881: d510, Defrance to MAE 17 Dec.1917. MAE, Syrie-Liban 56: d188, Defrance to Pichon 15 July 1918. t251, Jean Gout (Paris) to Cairo 21 Sept.1918. t467, Lefvre-Pontalis to MAE 27 Sept.1918.

39 *Al-Qibla* 171 11 Apr.1918; 198 17 July 1918. MG, 7N2141: d45, Cherchali to MAE 12 Apr.1918. MAE, Arabie 1: d196A, Cousse 20 July 1918. Abi Zayd, p.104.

Chapter 7

1 MG, 6N197: note 6247-9/11, "sur un projet d'organisation d'Armée Syrienne" (Paris) 18 Aug.1917. MG, 7N2145: d336,

Defarnce (Cairo) to Ribot 26 July 1917 enclosed with d3179, MAE to MG 23 Aug.1917. note 9055-9/11, "Analyse du Rapport de l'Officier Interprète de 1ère classe Mercier, envoyé en Mission en Egypte" 18 Dec.1917, enclosing "Compte-rendu de Mission" by Mercier (Cairo) 14 and 20 Nov.1917. Benoist d'Azy, "L'Origine de la Légion d'Orient", *Revue d'Histoire Diplomatique*, 53:1 (1939), pp.12-22. R. de Gontaut-Biron, *Comment la France s'est installée en Syrie (1918-1919)* (Paris, 1922), pp.39-41, 53-54. Gustav Gautherot, *La France en Syrie et en Cilicie* (Courbevoie, 1920), pp.32-33. Samné, *Syrie*, pp.469-471, 514-515, 520-522. Jung, vol.2, p.48. 1, Faruqi (Cairo) to Foreign Office (Mecca) 19 Aug.1917 cited in al-'Umari, vol.2, p.146.

2 MAE, Guerre 867: note [on Nadra Mutran and his plans] 15 Jan.1915. MG, 7N2145: note 420-9/11, "sur M. Mautran, Président du Comité Franco-Syrien à Paris" (Paris) 31 Jan.1915. FO 371/2483: "Comité Littéraire Arabe" [Feb.1915]. Christopher M. Andrew and A.S. Kanya-Forstner, *The Climax of French Imperial Expansion 1914-1924* (Stanford, 1981), p.69.

3 Le Comte Cressaty (de Damas), *La Syrie française* (Paris, 1915). Nadra Moutran, *La Syrie de demain* (Paris, 1916), especially pp.135, 137-138, 141, 214-216, 221-222, 225, 228-229. On Cressaty's lectures see MAE, Guerre 872: leaflets announcing Cressaty's lectures 13 and 16 Apr.1916. Also *al-Mustaqbal* 7 14 Apr.1916.

4 MAE, Guerre 869: 1s, Shukri Ghanim (Paris) to Director (MAE) 29 June, 29 June enclosing his speech of 25 June, 5 and 11 July 1915. MAE, Guerre 883: *al-Ittihad al-Lubnani* 28 Nov.1917 enclosed with 1, Michel Tuwayni (Paris) to Pichon 12 Feb.1918. K.T. Khairallah, *La Question du Liban* (Paris, 1915), pp.42-44.

5 FO 371/2767: r, A.P. Albina (London) 6 Mar.1916. *Correspondance d'Orient* 145 10 July 1916, p.134.

6 *Al-Mustaqbal* 1 1 Mar.1916. MAE, Guerre 876: note (Cairo) 9 Jan.1917 enclosed with d184, Defrance to Ribot 10 Apr.1917. ISA 65/2710: 1, Albina (Cairo) to Sykes 10 Aug.1917. FO 371/3059: 1, Grahame (Paris) to Hardinge (London) 20 Aug.1917. MAE, Guerre 879: 1, Etienne Flandin (Paris) to MAE 10 Nov.1917. 1, MAE to Flandin 14 Nov.1917. NA 367/381: r6, Yale (Cairo) to Harrison 3 Dec.1917. MAE, Syrie-Liban 56: "Note à Monsieur Wiet au sujet de campagne de presse menée par K.T. Khairallah" [beginning of Sept.1918]. MAE, Syrie-Liban 57: 1, Shukri Ghanim to Gout n.d.[end of Nov.1919]. ts, Faruqi to Mecca 9 and 26 Aug.1917, both cited in al-'Umari, vol.2, pp.140, 150. Jung, vol.2, pp.20-21, 58, 67, 101. Al-A'zami, vol.4, pp.85-86. Khayriyya Qasimiyya (ed.), *'Awni 'Abd al-Hadi: Awraq Khassa* (Beirut, 1974), pp.15-16.

7 MAE, Guerre 876: 1, Shukri Ghanim to Ribot 4 Apr.1917. 12819-9/11, War Minister to Prime Minister 10 Apr.1917. note, MAE to Georges Leygues 13 Apr.1917.

8 MAE, Guerre 877: "Note pour le Président du Conseil" 2 May

1917. l, Shukri Ghanim to Ribot 8 May 1917. l, MAE to Shukri Ghanim 14 May 1917. AN, 423AP 8: "Comité Central Syrien" (Paris) 18 Jan.1918. Jung, vol.2, pp.55-56. Zamir, p.48.

9 MAE, Guerre 877: "Note pour Monsieur Jules Cambon, Secrétaire Général aux Affaires Etrangères" 15 May 1917. tl42, MAE to French Minister (Cairo) 14 June 1917. Al-Mustaqbal, 94 10 Feb.1918. Samné, Syrie, pp.490-491. Zamir, p.49.

10 Comité Central Syrien, p.31 (the society's complete program may be found in ibid, pp.30-33). Also in Al-Mustaqbal, 94 10 Feb.1918.

11 L, Faruqi to Foreign Office (Mecca) 19 Aug.1917 cited in al-'Umari, vol.2, pp.148-150. MAE, Guerre 1698: t573, Defrance to MAE 3 Sept.1917. d157, Brémond (Jidda) to MG and MAE 18 Sept.1917, enclosing excerpts of al-Qibla 112 13 Sept.1917. MAE, Guerre 1699: t314, Brémond to Defrance 27 Sept.1917 enclosed with t643, Defrance to MAE 27 Sept.1917. MG, 7N2141: note MA38751, Chef de la Mission Anglaise près du MG (Paris) to Goubet 30 Sept.1917. Samné, Syrie, p.495.

12 MAE, Guerre 878: l, Shukri Ghanim to Gout 26 July 1917. MAE, Guerre 879: letter from Egypt published in al-Zaman 16 Aug.1917, enclosed with l, Shukri Ghanim to Barthou 29 Oct.1917. MAE, Guerre 883: al-Ittihad al-Lubnani 28 Nov.1917 enclosed with l, Michel Tuwayni to Pichon 12 Feb.1918. MAE, Guerre 885: l, Directeur de la Sûreté générale (Paris) to MAE 14 Mar.1918. MAE, Guerre 886: 1401, MAE to Direction de la Sûreté générale 5 Apr.1918. MAE, Syrie-Liban 2: 1280A, Cousse (Jidda) to MAE 26 Sept.1918. Samné, Syrie, p.513. Jung, vol.2, p.83. Abdallah Sfer Pacha, Le Mandat Français et les traditions françaises en Syrie et au Liban (Paris, 1922), p.29.

13 MAE, Guerre 877: "Note pour Monsieur Jules Cambon, Secrétaire Général aux Affaires Etrangères a.s. Réception du Bureau du Comité Central Syrien" 15 May 1917. l, MAE to Military Government of Paris 18 May 1917. l, Shukri Ghanim to Ribot 22 May 1917. MAE, Guerre 883: al-Ittihad al-Lubnani 28 Nov.1917 enclosed with l, Michel Tuwayni to Pichon 12 Feb.1918. MAE, Syrie-Liban 1: l, Yusuf Darian (Cairo) to Wadi' Abi Samra (São Paulo) 26 Apr.1918 enclosed with d145, Defrance to Pichon 11 May 1918. Jung, vol.2, p.56. Qasimiyya, 'Awni, p.17.

14 Al-Mustaqbal 7 14 Apr.1916. MAE, Guerre 873: t, Torres (Secrétaire du Roi, Madrid) to Faris Najm (São Paulo) 17 July 1916. AN, 423AP 8: l, Faris Najm to Shukri Ghanim 27 July 1916. MAE, Guerre 873: t, Faris Najm to MAE 29 July 1916. MAE, Guerre 874: t, Faris Najm to Shukri Ghanim 17 Aug.1916. t, Faruqi to Foreign Office (Mecca) 1 June 1917 cited in al-'Umari, vol.2, p.118. MAE, Syrie-Liban 1: l, Darian to Wadi' Abi Samra 26 Apr.1918 enclosed with d145, Defrance to Pichon 11 May 1918. Jung, vol.2, p.26.

15 MAE, Guerre 878: t, Shukri Ghanim to César Lakah (São Paulo) [6 July 1917]. l, Shukri Ghanim to Ribot 7 July 1917. l, MAE to

Shukri Ghanim 11 July 1917. t, Comité Central Syrien (Paris) to Syrian community (São Paulo) 14 Sept.1917 enclosed with t350, de Margerie (Paris) to French Minister (Rio de Janeiro) 19 Sept.1917. NA 367/381: r6, Yale to Harrison 3 Dec.1917 citing l, Adib Koutiet (São Paulo) to Faris Nimr (Cairo) 2 Sept.1917. *Al-Mustaqbal* 85 10 Nov.1917; 86 20 Nov.1917; 87 30 Nov.1917; 88 10 Dec.1917. Comité Central Syrien, pp.22, 25. Jung, vol.2, p.82.

16 MAE, Guerre 879: "Note pour le Ministre" by de Margerie 26 Oct.1917. t440, de Margerie to French Minister (Rio de Janeiro) 9 Nov.1917. MAE, Guerre 885: t183, MAE to French Minister (Rio de Janeiro) 30 Mar.1918. MAE, Guerre 886: t291, Paul-Louis Claudel (Rio de Janeiro) to MAE 1 Apr.1918. MAE, Syrie-Liban 2: d81, Claudel to Pichon 17 Sept.1918. Comité Central Syrien, p.22. Samné, *Syrie*, pp.493-494. Abi Zayd, p.103.

17 MAE, Guerre 883: d7, Alexis-Jules Lefaivre (Montevideo) to Pichon 4 Feb.1918. *Al-Mustaqbal* 98 20 Mar.1918. Comité Central Syrien, pp.23, 26.

18 *Al-Mustaqbal* 21 27 July 1918. L/P&S/11/118: Agence de la Presse Arabe No.126 19 June 1917. MAE, Guerre 883: *al-Ittihad al-Lubnani* 1 Nov. and 1 Dec.1917 enclosed with l, Michel Tuwayni to Pichon 12 Feb.1918. d4, Henry Jullemier (Buenos Aires) to Pichon 6 Feb.1918. Comité Central Syrien, p.23. Jung, vol.2, pp.62, 83-84.

19 MAE, Guerre 883: "Déclaration du Comité de l'Union Libanaise", *al-Ittihad al-Lubnani* 1 Nov.1917; "A tous les Libanais du monde entier", *al-Ittihad al-Lubnani* 1 Dec.1917, both enclosed with l, Michel Tuwayni to Pichon 12 Feb.1918. MG, 7N2145: "Le Comité de l'Union Libanaise et la délégation de Paris", *al-Ittihad al-Lubnani* n.d.[beginning of 1918]. MAE, Guerre 883: d4, Jullemier to Pichon 6 Feb.1918. MAE, Guerre 885: l, César Lakah (Paris) to Shukri Ghanim 25 Mar.1918 enclosed with l, Shukri Ghanim to Gout 27 Mar.1918. t, MAE to French Minister (Buenos Aires) n.d.[end of Mar.1918]. MAE, Syrie-Liban 1: d656, Director (MAE) to Ministre du Blocus et des Régions libérées 16 May 1918. *Al-Mustaqbal* 106 30 June 1918. Samné, *Syrie*, p.494. Jung, vol.2, pp.79-82.

20 MAE, Guerre 883: d4, Jullemier to Pichon 6 Feb.1918. MAE, Guerre 1701: t22, Cherchali (Mecca) to MAE 22 Feb.1918 enclosed with t, Cousse to MAE 23 Feb.1918. l, Cherchali to Cousse 23 Feb.1918. MAE, Guerre 885: l, Directeur de la Sûreté générale (Paris) to MAE 14 Mar.1918. MG, 7N2145: "Le Comité de l'Union Libanaise appelle à l'engagement volontaire et à la souscription", *al-Ittihad al-Lubnani* 16 Apr.1918. MAE, Syrie-Liban 20: d, Fernand-Edouard Gaussen (Buenos Aires) to Pichon 26 Dec.1919. Samné, *Syrie*, p.494. Jung, vol.2, pp.80-84. Abi Zayd, p.104.

21 MG, 6N197: l, Shukri Ghanim to Paul Painléve 15 July 1917. note "au sujet de la constitution éventuelle d'une mission militaire

française chargée d'organiser 'l'Armée syrienne'" (Paris) 12 Aug.1917. note 6247-9/11, "sur un projet d'organisation d'Armée Syrienne" (Paris) 18 Aug.1917. l, War Minister (Paris) to Shukri Ghanim 9 Sept.1917. MG, 7N2145: "Compte-rendu de Mission" by Mercier 14 Nov.1917. note 9055-9/11, "Analyse du Rapport de l'Officier Interprète de 1ère classe Mercier, envoyé en Mission en Egypte" 18 Dec.1917.

22 MAE, Guerre 881: note by Shukri Ghanim (Comité Central Syrien) 18 Dec.1917.

23 MAE, Guerre 879: l, Shukri Ghanim to Barthou 8 Nov.1917. MAE, Guerre 881: note by J[ean] G[out] [24 Dec.1917], enclosing speeches of himself and of Sykes 23 Dec.1917. *Al-Mustaqbal* 91 10 Jan.1918. *Al-Manar* 21:1 2 Dec.1918, pp.34-36. Comité Central Syrien, pp.2-7. Samné, *Syrie*, pp.501-506.

24 *Al-Mustaqbal* 97 10 Mar.1918; 98 20 Mar.1918. Comité Central Syrien, pp.14-29. Samné, *Syrie*, pp.516-518.

25 MAE, Syrie-Liban 2: l, Georges Samné (Paris) to Gout 7 Oct.1918. l, Shukri Ghanim to Georges Clemenceau 9 Oct.1918. l, Shukri Ghanim to Pichon 11 Oct.1918. MAE, Syrie-Liban 5: l, Georges Samné to Gout 4 Dec.1918. Georges Samné, *La Question Syrienne: Exposé-solution-statut politique* (Paris, 1918), especially pp.3, 6, 18, 20-21, 27, 35-36, 44, 46. Idem, *Syrie*, p.599.

26 MAE, Syrie-Liban 2: "Note à son Excellence Monsieur Stéphen Pichon, Ministre des Affaires Etrangères" by Shukri Ghanim 10 Oct.1918. note by Gout 12 Oct.1918.

27 FO 371/2777: l, David Hederi and Elias Atallas (Brooklyn, New York) to Spring Rice (Washington) 20 May 1916 enclosed with d472, Spring Rice to Grey 22 May 1916. MAE, Guerre 872: l, United Syrian Party (Brooklyn, New York) to Robert Lansing (Washington) 20 May 1916 enclosed with d397, Jusserand (Washington) to Briand 20 May 1916. L/P&S/10/586: Albina, "The Arab Emigrants in the United States of America" annexed to Arabian Report No.XXIIA 15 July 1916. Also in *AB* no.19 (Cairo) 9 Sept.1916, pp.213, 215-216.

28 MAE, Guerre 869: l, Na'um Mukarzal and K. al-Aswad (New York) to Jusserand 29 May 1915 enclosed with d467, Jusserand to Delcassé 31 May 1915. memo by Lebanon League of Progress (New York) 4 June 1915 enclosed with d498, Jusserand to Delcassé 10 June 1916. L/P&S/10/586: Albina, "Arab Emigrants" annexed to Arabian Report No.XXIIA 15 July 1916. Also in *AB* no.19 (Cairo) 9 Sept.1916, p.214. MAE, Guerre 875: t1486, Gaston-Ernest Liébert (New York) to MAE 18 Dec.1916. WO 157/735: Political and Economic Intelligence Summary No.13 (GSPI, GHQ, EEF) 31 Aug.1918. Khairallah, *Problème*, p.72.

29 MAE, Guerre 869: d229, Defrance to Delcassé 23 July 1915, enclosing *al-Muqattam* 23 July 1915. MAE, Guerre 870: d309, same to same 8 Oct.1915, enclosing *al-Muqattam* 7 Oct.1915. d850, Jusserand to Delcassé 13 Oct.1915. Khairallah, *Problème*,

p.72. Moutran, p.134.

30 MAE, Guerre 872: 1, Na'um Mukarzal to Jusserand 23 Feb.1916 enclosed with d162, Jusserand to Briand 24 Feb.1916. t114, same to same n.d.[received on 25 Feb.1916]. MAE, Guerre 875: memo by Lebanon League of Progress [n.d.] enclosed with d40, Jusserand to Briand 15 Jan.1917.

31 MAE, Guerre 871: t44, Jusserand to MAE 22 Jan.1916. MAE, Guerre 878: t808, Liébert to MAE 26 July 1917. MAE, Guerre 879: t1145, same to same n.d.[received on 24 Oct.1917].

32 L/P&S/10/586: Albina, "Arab Emigrants" annexed to Arabian Report No.XXIIA 15 July 1916. Also in *AB* no.19 (Cairo) 9 Sept.1916, p.215. FO 371/3059: *L'Orient Arabe* 12 5 July 1917. MAE, Guerre 879: t1145, Liébert to MAE n.d.[received on 24 Oct.1917]. MAE, Guerre 883: *al-Ittihad al-Lubnani* 1 Dec.1917 enclosed with 1, Michel Tuwayni to Pichon 12 Feb.1918. *Al-Mustaqbal* 108 20 July 1918. MAE, Syrie-Liban 13: d29, Liébert to MAE 13 June 1919. Samné, *Syrie*, pp.491-492.

33 FO 371/3059: memo by Syria-Mount Lebanon League of Liberation (New York) [n.d.] enclosed with d55, Colville A. Barclay (Washington) to Balfour 30 June 1917. *Al-Mustaqbal* 108 20 July 1918. Samné, *Syrie*, p.492.

34 MAE, Guerre 884: t, Ayyub Thabit (New York) to Shukri Ghanim enclosed with 1, Shukri Ghanim to Pichon 26 Feb.1918. MAE, Syrie-Liban 1: memos by Syria-Mount Lebanon League of Liberation to Lansing (Washington) and to Woodrow Wilson (Washington) 10 May 1918, both enclosed with d222, Jusserand to Pichon 12 May 1918. *Al-Mustaqbal* 108 20 July 1918. Samné, *Syrie*, p.516.

35 MAE, Syrie-Liban 1: d2, Liébert to MAE 29 July 1918, enclosing ls, Ayyub Thabit to Liébert 22 July 1918.

36 MAE, Syrie-Liban 3: d37, Liébert to MAE 28 Oct.1918, enclosing Ayyub Thabit's speech 14 Oct.1918.

37 MAE, Guerre 879: note, "Projet de Congrès Syrien" enclosed with d899, MAE to Jusserand 25 Oct.1917. MAE, Guerre 884: d128, Jusserand to Pichon 4 Mar.1918. MAE, Syrie-Liban 2: "Note pour Monsieur Doyen" (Paris) 25 July 1918. WO 157/735: Political and Economic Intelligence Summary No.13 (GSPI, GHQ, EEF) 31 Aug.1918. Samné, *Syrie*, p.507.

Chapter 8

1 FO 882/23: "Personalities: Arab Government of Syria" Mar.[?] 1920. Cyril Falls, *Military Operations, Egypt and Palestine from June 1917 to the End of the War* (London, 1930), vol.2, p.586. H.S. Gullett, *The Official History of Australia in the War of 1914-1918*, vol.7: *The Australian Imperial Force in Sinai and*

Palestine 1914-1918 (Sydney, [1923] 3rd ed.1936), p.757. Young, pp.253-254. Brémond, p.306. Liman von Sanders, p.368. Muhammad Kurd 'Ali, *Kitab Khitat al-Sha'm* (Damascus, 1925), vol.3, pp.156-157.

2 MG, 7N2141: d152, Brémond (Jidda) to War Minister 15 Sept.1917, enclosing excerpts of *al-Qibla* 112 13 Sept.1917. MG, 17N489: note, Mercier (Cairo) 22 Apr.1918 enclosed with note 21, "Renseignements sur la situation en Syrie" (Cairo) 24 Apr.1918. MAE, Syrie-Liban 2: "Note sur le Prince Said" (Paris) 5 Oct.1918. MAE, PA 51/2: t296-300, Pichon (Paris) to Coulondre (Jerusalem) 6 Oct.1918. FO 371/4182: *Times* 4 Sept.1919. Lawrence, *Seven*, p.645. Al-Rifa'i, pp.79-82, 84. Al-Nusuli, p.16. Bayhum, pp.36-40, 71. Musa, *Suwar*, pp.67-69. Mousa, *Lawrence*, pp.107, 209. Jean Pichon, *Sur la Route des Indes un siècle après Bonaparte* (Paris, 1932), pp.142-143.

3 L, Fayasl (Dar'a) to Sa'id al-Jaza'iri [26 Sept.1918] [the letter was not received] cited in Bayhum, pp.74-75. WO 157/738: r, Lawrence (Damascus) to General Staff, GHQ 1 Oct.1918. FO 371/3383: tP690, GOC (in C, Egypt) to WO 6 Oct.1918. *AB* no.106 (Cairo) 22 Oct.1918, p.349. Lawrence, *Seven*, p.643. Gontaut-Biron, p.47. Pichon, *Sur la Route*, p.143. Philippe David, *Un Gouvernement arabe à Damas: Le Congrès Syrien* (Ph.D. Dissertation, Paris University, 1923), pp.8-9. Al-Rifa'i, pp.96-103. Abi Zayd, pp.429-431. Bayhum, pp.45-46, 48. Mousa, *Lawrence*, pp.209-210.

4 E.g. Musa, *al-Murasalat*, vol.1, p.213 citing t, Allenby to Husayn [1 Oct.1918] enclosed with t, Bassett (Jidda) to Husayn 2 Oct.1918. See also Zeine N. Zeine, *The Struggle for Arab Independence: Western Diplomacy and the Rise and Fall of Faysal's Kingdom in Syria* (Beirut, 1960), p.25. At the Paris Peace Conference Faysal stated that "the Arab army entered Damascus with General Allenby's forces". See Miller, *My Diary*, vol.14, p.233.

5 WO 95/4371: tCGL, Descorps to GSI, GSO, GHQ 1 Oct.1918. War Diary (GSO, GHQ, EEF) 1 Oct.1918. WO 33/960 [No.10180]: tEA1713, GOC-in-C, Egypt to WO 1 Oct.1918. WO 33/960 [No.10185]: tEA1715, same to same 2 Oct.1918. d, Allenby (GHQ, EEF) to War Minister 31 Oct.1918 cited in H. Pirie-Gordon (ed.), *A Brief Record of the Advance of the Egyptian Expeditionary Force under the command of General Sir Edmund H.H. Allenby, July 1917 to October 1918* (London, 2nd ed.1919), p.33. See also MG, 6N189: t4038/M, Commandant DFPS (Cairo) to MG 1 Oct.1918.

6 WO 95/4371: "Report by Lieutenant-General Sir H.G. Chauvel on the Capture of Damascus, and the arrangements made for the Civil Administration thereof" 2 Oct.1918. Beckles Willson, "Our Amazing Syrian Adventure", *The National Review*, 76 (1920), p.44. Pichon, *Partage*, p.152.

7 Gullett, pp.759-762. Pirie-Gordon, p.53. WO 95/4371: War Diary (GSO, GHQ, EEF) 1 Oct.1918. report by Chauvel 2 Oct.1918.

See also Elie Kedourie, "The Capture of Damascus, 1 October 1918" in idem, *The Chatham House Version and other Middle-Eastern Studies* (London, 1970), pp.33-47.

8 Al-Rifa'i, pp.103-106. Bayhum, p.51.

9 *Military Operations II*, vol.2, p.591. WO 95/4371: report by Chauvel 2 Oct.1918. Pichon, *Partage*, p.152. WO 157/738: r, Lawrence to General Staff, GHQ 1 Oct.1918.

10 Pirie-Gordon, page facing plate 51. Kirkbride, p.92. Gullett, p.762.

11 L/P&S/11/139: t97, Clayton (Cairo) to FO 7 Oct.1918. FO 371/3383: tC1, same to same 8 Oct.1918. MAE, Syrie-Liban 2: t12151, Sykes (London) to Gout and Picot 11 Oct.1918. *AB* no.106 (Cairo) 22 Oct.1918, pp.350, 356. FO 371/4182: *Times* 4 Sept.1919. Lawrence, *Seven*, pp.645-646, 648-649, 653. W.F. Stirling, *Safety Last* (London, 1953), p.95. Mousa, *Lawrence*, p.210. Pichon, *Sur la Route*, p.144. Qadri, p.74. Jawdat, p.67.

12 L/P&S/11/141: t176, Clayton to FO 8 Nov.1918. memo by W.F. Stirling (Damascus) to Sa'id al-Jaza'iri 9 Nov.1918 cited in Bayhum, pp.70-72. MG, 6N193: t589, Georges-Picot (through Cairo) to MAE 20 Nov.1918. MAE, Syrie-Liban 16: l, Sa'id al-Jaza'iri (Beirut) to MAE 10 Aug.1919 with enclosures. *Correspondance d'Orient* 206 30 Jan.1919, p.91. Gontaut-Biron, p.48. Bayhum, pp.55-57, 61-63. Al-Rifa'i, pp.123, 126, 132.

13 WO 157/738: r, Lawrence to General Staff, GHQ 1 Oct.1918. WO 95/4371: report by Chauvel 2 Oct.1918. L/P&S/11/139: t80, Clayton to FO 6 Oct.1918. t104, same to same 9 Oct.1918. t107, same to same 10 Oct.1918. *AB* no.106 (Cairo) 22 Oct.1918, p.350. *Military Operations II*, vol.2, p.593. Lawrence, *Seven*, pp.646, 659. Brémond, p.306. Qadri, pp.75, 77. Jawdat, p.67. Darwaza, *Hawla*, vol.1, pp.71-72. See also Kedourie, *Chatham*, pp.43-44.

14 FO 371/3383: tP689, GOC (in C, Egypt) to WO 6 Oct.1918. Al-Rifa'i, pp.101-102, 112, 114-115. Al-Nusuli, p.16.

15 MG, 6N193: t28, Coulondre (through Cairo) to MAE 5 Oct.1918. FO 371/3383: t80, Clayton to FO 6 Oct.1918. tP695, GOC (in C, Egypt) to WO 7 Oct.1918. L/P&S/11/139: t104, Clayton to FO 9 Oct.1918. t106, same to same 9 Oct.1918. MG, 6N196: t21, de Piépape (Beirut) enclosed with t81896, Ariane (Port Said) to Marine Ministry 10 Oct.1918. t82083, same to same 11 Oct.1918. FO 141/654/356: tEA1760, C-in-C, GHQ to HC 11 Oct.1918. WO 95/4371: tEA1768, Egypforce to Troopers 11 Oct.1918. FO 371/3412: t110, Clayton to FO 11 Oct.1918. t114, same to same 11 Oct.1918. L/P&S/11/140: t116, same to same 12 Oct.1918. FO 371/3384: t117, same to same 13 Oct.1918. MAE, PA 51/2: t469, Coulondre [Beirut] 16 Oct.1918. Pichon, *Sur la Route*, pp.157-158. Gautherot, pp.51-52. Willson, p.46. Qadri. p.78. Al-Rifa'i, p.120. Zeine, *Struggle*, pp.27-28, 31-32, 39. Jukka Nevakivi, *Britain, France and the Arab Middle East 1914-1920* (London, 1969), p.71.

16 FO 141/473/1805: tWO5, C-in-C, EEF to HC 20 Oct.1918.

t1818E, same to same 26 Oct.1918. WO 95/4371: tWO10, Egyp-
force to Troopers 26 Oct.1918. War Diary (GSO, GHQ, EEF) 26
Oct.1918. MG, 7N189: t5027/M, Commandant DFPS (Cairo) to
MG 28 Oct.1918. Pirie-Gordon, pp.34, 51. Young, p.263.
Al-'Umari, vol.2, pp.277-280. Sa'id, *al-Thawra*, vol.2a, pp.3-4.
Qadri, pp.80-81. Al-Nusuli, p.15.

Conclusion

1 FO 371/3407: 1, Gertrude L. Bell (Baghdad) to Hardinge 25 May
   1918. The article "The Aims of the Arabs" was sent from
   "Ahmad" (Baghdad) to the editor of *The Near East* (London) on 1
   May 1918 (FO 371/3412). On Husayn's opinion about Egypt see t,
   Fu'ad al-Khatib (Mecca) to Faruqi (Cairo) 21 Nov.1916 cited in
   al-'Umari, vol.1, p.338.
2 See e.g. Sa'id, *al-Thawra*, vol.1, p.156.
3 WP 145/7: Faysal ibn al-Husayn, "To All Our Brethren — The Syrian Arabs of All Creeds" [translated 28 May 1917].
4 FO 371/3384: d, Clayton (GHQ, EEF) to FO 21 Sept.1918.
5 FO 371/3407: 1, Bell to Hardinge 25 May 1918.
6 *Ibid.*
7 Presland, p.245.
8 MG, 7N2141: r, Cousse (Jidda) to Defrance (Cairo) 16 June 1918.
9 Lawrence's report 4 Nov.1918 cited in Garnett, p.265.
10 B.H. Liddell Hart, *T.E. Lawrence — In Arabia and After* (London,
   [1934] 1964), p.217.
11 Moutran, p.211.
12 Cab 17/177: Arabian Report N.S. No.XXIII 27 Dec.1916 Appendix C.

Bibliography

Documents

Britain

The Public Record Office, Kew, Richmond, Surrey.
  Cab 17: Committee of Imperial Defence
  CO 696: Iraq — Sessional Papers
  FO 141: Egypt — Correspondence
  FO 195: Turkey — Correspondence
  FO 371: Political
  FO 686: Jeddah Agency Papers
  FO 882: Arab Bureau Papers
  PRO 30/57: Kitchener Papers
  WO 33: Reports and Miscellaneous Papers
  WO 95: War Diaries
  WO 106: Director of Military Operations and Intelligence — Papers
  WO 157: War of 1914-1918 — Intelligence Summaries
  WO 158: War of 1914-1918 — Correspondence and Papers of Military Headquarters

India Office Library and Records, London.
  L/P&S/10: Departmental Papers — Political and Secret Separate Files
  L/P&S/11: Political and Secret Annual Files
  L/P&S/20: Political and Secret Library

School of Oriental Studies, University of Durham, Durham.
  Wingate Papers

France

Archives du Ministère des Affaires Etrangères, Paris.
  Guerre 1914-1918
      Affaires Musulmanes
      Turquie
  Levant 1918-1929
      Arabie-Hedjaz
      Palestine
      Syrie-Liban-Cilicie

Papiers d'Agents
    51: Coulondre (Robert)
    56: Defrance (Jules-Albert)
    196: Gout (Jean)

Archives du Ministère de la Guerre, Service Historique de l'Armée de Terre, Vincennes.
    Série N: Première Guerre Mondiale
        6N: Fonds Particuliers
        7N: L'Etat-Major de L'Armée
        17N: Missions Militaires Françaises

Archives Nationales, Paris.
    432AP: Papiers Etienne Flandin

Israel

Israel State Archives, Jerusalem.
    65: Deserted Documents Collection
        George Antonius Archives

Central Zionist Archives, Jerusalem.
    L4: Zionist Commission, Jaffa

United States

National Archives Microfilm Publications.
    Microcopy No.367: Records of the Department of State Relating to World War I and its Termination, 1914-1929

Official Publications and Collections of Documents

'Alam al-Din, Wajih (ed.), *Al-'Uhud al-Muta'alliqa bil-Watan al-'Arabi* (Beirut, 1965).

[Jamal Pasha] Al-Qa'id al-'Amm lil-Jaysh al-Rabi', *Idahat 'an al-Masa'il al-Siyasiyya Allati Jarat Tadqiquha bi-Diwan al-Harb al-'Urfi al-Mutashakkil bi-'Aleyh* (Istanbul, 1916).

Musa, Sulayman (ed.), *Al-Murasalat al-Ta'rikhiyya 1914-1918* (Amman, 1973).

Al-Thawra al-'Arabiyya al-Kubra: Watha'iq wa-Asanid (Amman, 1966).

Shibika, Makki (ed.), *Al-'Arab wal-Siyasa al-Baritaniyya fil-Harb al-'Alamiyya al-Ula* (Beirut, 1971).

Al-Watha'iq wal-Mu'ahadat fi Bilad al-'Arab (Damascus, [1937]).

Adamow, E. (ed.), *Die Europäischen Mächte und die Türkei während des Weltkrieges — Die Aufteilung der asiatischen Türkei* (Dresden, 1932).

Arab Bulletin 1916-1919

Cmd 5957: *Correspondence between Sir Henry McMahon His Majesty's High Commissioner at Cairo and the Sherif Hussein of Mecca July 1915 — March 1916* (London, 1939).

Cmd 5964: *Statements made on behalf of His Majesty's Government during the year 1918 in regard to the Future Status of certain parts of the Ottoman Empire* (London, 1939).

Cmd 5974: *Report of a Committee Set up to Consider Certain Correspondence between Sir Henry McMahon and the Sharif of Mecca in 1915 and 1916* (London, 1939).

Comité Central Syrien, *L'Opinion Syrienne à l'Etranger pendant la Guerre* (Paris, 1918).

[Djemal Pacha] Le Commandement de la IVe Armée Ottoman, *La Vérité sur la question syrienne* (Istanbul, 1916).

G., "Textes historiques sur le réveil arabe au Hedjaz", *Revue du Monde Musulman*, 46 (1921), pp.1-22; 47 (1921), pp.1-27; 50 (1922), pp.74-100; 57 (1924), pp.158-167.

Garnett, David (ed.), *The Letters of T.E. Lawrence* (New York, 1939).

Gooch, G.P. and Temperley, Harold (eds.), *British Documents on the Origins of the War 1898-1914* (London, 1926-1936).

United States Department of State, *Papers Relating to the Foreign Relations of the United States, 1914 Supplement: The World War* (Washington, 1928).

United States Department of State, *Papers Relating to the Foreign Relations of the United States, 1916 Supplement: The World War* (Washington, 1929).

Newspapers and Periodicals

Al-Manar (Cairo) 1915-1922, 1933-1934.
Al-Mustaqbal (Paris) 1916-1918.
Al-Qibla (Mecca) 1916-1918.
and many other single issues of newspapers and periodicals from Cairo, Beirut, Damascus, Paris, London, Buenos Aires and New York.

Books, Articles and Doctoral Dissertations

Arabic

'Abdallah ibn al-Husayn, *Mudhakkirati* (Jerusalem, 1945).

Abi Zayd, Nasif, *Ta'rikh al-'Asr al-Damawi* (Damascus, 1919).

'Arabi [A.H.Y.], "Asrar al-Qadiyya al-'Arabiyya fi Sijn 'Aleyh", *Awraq Lubnaniyya* (Al-Hazimiyya, ed.1983), vol.1, pts. 10-12; vol.2, pt.1.

Arslan, 'Adil, "Kalimat al-Amir 'Adil Arslan Ra'is al-Lajna al-Ta'biniyya", *al-Istiqlal* 18:3112 31 Jan.1938.

Al-A'zami, Ahmad 'Izzat, *Al-Qadiyya al-'Arabiyya: Asbabuha, Muqaddimatuha, Tatawwuratuha wa-Nata'ijuha* (Baghdad, 1931-1934).

'Aziz Bek, *Al-Istikhbarat wal-Jasusiyya fi Lubnan wa-Suriyya wa-Filastin khilala al-Harb al-'Alamiyya* (Beirut, 1937).

   Suriya wa-Lubnan fil-Harb al-'Alamiyya: Al-Istikhbarat wal-Jasusiyya fil-Dawla al-'Uthmaniyya (Beirut, 1933).

"'Aziz al-Misri Yatahaddathu ila al-Ahram", *al-Ahram* 21 July 1959.

Al-Badri, 'Abd al-Ghafur, "Kayfa 'Araftu al-Hashimi?", *al-Istiqlal* 18:3105 21 Jan.1938.

"Bayan Jamal Pasha 'an Shuhada' 1915", *Awraq Lubnaniyya* (Al-Hazimiyya, ed.1983), vol.2, pt.4.

Bayhum, Muhammad Jamil, *Suriyya wa-Lubnan 1918-1922* (Beirut, 1968).

Al Bazirkan, 'Ali, *Al-Waqa'i' al-Haqiqiyya fil-Thawra al-'Iraqiyya* (Baghdad, 1954).

Daghir, As'ad, *Mudhakkirati 'ala Hamish al-Qadiyya al-'Arabiyya* (Cairo, n.d.[1959?]).

[Daghir, As'ad] Ahad A'da' al-Jam'iyyat al-'Arabiyya, *Thawrat al-'Arab: Muqaddimatuha, Asbabuha, Nata'ijuha* (Cairo, 1916).

Darwaza, Muhammad 'Izzat, *Hawla al-Haraka al-'Arabiyya al-Haditha* (Sidon, 1950-1953).

   Nash'at al-Haraka al-'Arabiyya al-Haditha (Sidon, Beirut, [1971]).

Fu'ad, 'Ali, *Kayfa Ghazawna Misr: Mudhakkirat al-Jiniral al-Turki 'Ali Fu'ad* ([Beirut], 1962).

Al-Ghusayn, Fa'iz, *Mudhakkirati 'an al-Thawra al-'Arabiyya* (Damascus, 1956).

Al-Hakim, Yusuf, *Bayrut wa-Lubnan fi 'Ahd Al 'Uthman* (Beirut, 1964).

Al-Hasani, 'Abd al-Razzaq, *Al-Thawra al-'Iraqiyya al-Kubra* (Sidon, [1952] 2nd ed.1965).

Himada, Muhammad 'Abidin and Zabyan, Muhammad Taysir, *Faysal ibn al-Husayn min al-Mahd ila al-Lahd* (Damascus, 1933).

Al-Husri, Sati', "Shuhada' al-'Uruba fil-Harb al-'Alamiyya al-Ula bi-Diyar al-Sha'm", *al-'Arabi*, 30 (1961), pp.20-26.

Jawdat, 'Ali, *Dhikrayat 'Ali Jawdat 1900-1958* (Beirut, 1967).

Al-Khuri, Bishara Khalil, *Haqa'iq Lubnaniyya* ([Beirut], 1960).

Kurd 'Ali, Muhammad, *Kitab Khitat al-Sha'm* (Damascus, 1925).

Al-Mudhakkirat (Damascus, 1948).

Al-Madi, Munib and Musa, Sulayman, *Ta'rikh al-Urdunn fil-Qarn al-'Ishrin* (Amman, 1959).

Al-Maqdisi, Jirjis al-Khuri, *A'zam Harb fil-Ta'rikh wa-Kayfa Marrat Hawadithuha* (Beirut, 2nd ed.1927).

Musa, Sulayman, *Al-Haraka al-'Arabiyya: Sirat al-Marhala al-Ula lil-Nahda al-'Arabiyya al-Haditha 1908-1924* (Beirut, 1970).

Al-Husayn ibn 'Ali wal-Thawra al-'Arabiyya al-Kubra (Amman, 1957).

"Jam'iyyat al-'Arabiyya al-Fatat", *al-'Arabi*, 151 (1971), pp.52-59.

Suwar min al-Butula (Amman, 1968).

Al-Thawra al-'Arabiyya al-Kubra: Al-Harb fil-Urdunn 1917-1918 — Mudhakkirat al-Amir Zayd (Amman, 1976).

Al-Nusuli, Anis, *'Ishtu wa-Shahadtu* (Beirut, 1951).

Qadri, Ahmad, *Mudhakkirati 'an al-Thawra al-'Arabiyya al-Kubra* (Damascus, 1956).

Qal'aji, Qadri, *Jil al-Fida': Qissat al-Thawra al-Kubra wa-Nahdat al-'Arab* ([Amman, 1967]).

Qasimiyya, Khayriyya (ed.), *'Awni 'Abd al-Hadi: Awraq Khassa* (Beirut, 1974).

Al-Hukuma al-'Arabiyya fi Dimashq bayna 1918-1920 (Cairo, 1971).

Al-Qaysi, Sami 'Abd al-Hafiz, *Yasin al-Hashimi wa-Dawruhu fil-Siyasa al-'Iraqiyya bayna 'Amay 1922-1936* (Basra, 1975).

Al-Rifa'i, Anwar, *Jihad Nisf Qarn li-Sumuw al-Amir Sa'id Al 'Abd al-Qadir al-Jaza'iri* (Damascus, n.d.).

Sa'id, Amin, *Asrar al-Thawra al-'Arabiyya al-Kubra wa-Ma'sat al-Sharif Husayn* (Beirut, [1960]).

Al-Thawra al-'Arabiyya al-Kubra (Cairo, [1934]).

Al-Sakakini, Khalil, *Kadha Ana Ya Dunya* ([Jerusalem, 1955], [Beirut?], 2nd ed.1982).

Al-Sawda, Yusuf, *Fi Sabil Lubnan* (Alexandria, 1919).

Shahbandar, 'Abd al-Rahman, "Faysal ibn al-Husayn", *al-Muqtataf*, 83 (1933), pp.257-267

"Al-Kulunil Lurans", *al-Muqtataf*, 78 (1931), pp.269-276, 426-434, 655-663; 79 (1931), pp.37-44.

Shafiq Pasha, Ahmad, *Mudhakkirati fi Nisf Qarn* (Cairo, [1934]).

Al-Shihabi, Mustafa, *Muhadarat fil-Isti'mar* (Cairo, 1957).

Al-Qawmiyya al-'Arabiyya: Ta'rikhuha wa-Qiwamuha wa-Maramiha — Muhadarat (Cairo, [1959] 2nd ed.1961).

Al-Shurayqi, Muhammad,, "Al-Shurayqi Yarthi al-Hashimi", *al-Istiqlal* 18:3116 4 Feb.1938.

Subayh, Muhammad, *Batal La Nansahu: 'Aziz al-Misri wa-'Asruhu* (Beirut, Sidon, [1971]).

Al-Tal'afari, Qahtan Ahmad 'Abush, *Thawrat Tal'afar 1920 wal-Harakat al-Wataniyya al-Ukhra fi Mintaqat al-Jazira* (Baghdad, 1969).

Al-'Umari, Muhammad Tahir, *Ta'rikh Muqaddarat al-'Iraq al-Siyasiyya* (Baghdad, 1924-1925).

Wahba, Hafiz, *Jazirat al-'Arab fil-Qarn al-'Ishrin* (Cairo, 3rd ed.1956).
Yahya, Jalal, *Al-Thawra al-'Arabiyya* (Cairo, 1959).
Yamin, Antun, *Lubnan fil-Harb* (Beirut, 1919).
Al-Zirikli, Khayr al-Din, *Al-A'lam: Qamus Tarajim li-Ashhur al-Rijal wal-Nisa' min al-'Arab wal-Musta'ribin wal-Mustashriqin* (Beirut, 3rd ed.1969).

European Languages

Aboussouan, Benoit, *Le Problème politique Syrien* (Paris, 1925).
Adelson, Roger Dean, *The Formation of British Policy Towards the Middle East 1914-1918* (Ph.D. Dissertation, Washington University, 1972).
Adib Karam, Georges, *L'Opinion Publique Libanaise et la Question du Liban (1918-1920)* (Beirut, 1981).
Ajay, Nicholas Z., *Mount Lebanon and the Wilayah of Beirut 1914-1918: The War Years* (Ph.D. Dissertation, Georgetown University, 1973).
"Political Intrigue and Suppression in Lebanon during World War I", *IJMES*, 5:2 (1974), pp.140-160.
Andrew, Christopher M. and Kanya-Forstner, A.S., *The Climax of French Imperial Expansion 1914-1924* (Stanford, 1981).
"La France à la recherche de la Syrie intégrale 1914-1920", *Relations Internationales*, 19 (1979), pp.263-278.
Antonius, George, *The Arab Awakening: The Story of The Arab National Movement* (London, [1938] rep.1945).
Atiyyah, Ghassan R., *Iraq 1908-1921: A Socio-Political Study* (Beirut, 1973).
D'Azy, Benoist, "L'Origine de la Légion d'Orient", *Revue d'Histoire Diplomatique*, 53:1 (1939), pp.12-22.
Benoist-Méchin, Jacques, *Arabian Destiny* (London, 1957).
Birdwood, Lord, *Nuri as-Said: A Study in Arab Leadership* (London, 1959).
Brémond, Edouard, *Le Hedjaz dans la guerre mondiale* (Paris, 1931).
Busch, Briton Cooper, *Britain, India and the Arabs 1914-1921* (Berkeley, 1971).
Cressaty (de Damas), Le Comte, *La Syrie française* (Paris, 1915).
David, Philippe, *Un Gouvernement arabe à Damas: Le Congrès Syrien* (Ph.D. Dissertation, Paris University, 1923).
Dawn, C. Ernest, *From Ottomanism to Arabism: Essays on the Origins of Arab Nationalism* (Urbana, 1973).
Djemal Pasha, *Memories of a Turkish Statesman 1913-1919* (New York, [1922] rep.1973).
Emin, Ahmed, *Turkey in the World War* (New Haven, 1930).
Erskine, [Beatrice Caroline] Mrs. Steuart, *King Faysal of 'Iraq* (London, 1933).
Evans, Laurence, *United States Policy and the Partition of Turkey*

1914-1924 (Baltimore, 1965).

Falls, Cyril, *Military Operations, Egypt and Palestine from June 1917 to the End of the War* (London, 1930).

Friedman, Isaiah, "The McMahon-Hussein Correspondence and the Question of Palestine", *The Journal of Contemporary History*, 5:2,4 (1970), pp.83-122, 193-201.

The Question of Palestine 1914-1918: British-Jewish-Arab Relations (London, 1973).

Gautherot, Gustav, *La France en Syrie et en Cilicie* (Courbevoie, 1920).

Goldner, Werner Ernst, *The Role of Abdullah Ibn Husain, King of Jordan, in Arab Politics 1914-1951* (Ph.D. Dissertation, Stanford University, 1954).

Gontaut-Biron, R. de, *Comment la France s'est installée en Syrie (1918-1919)* (Paris, 1922).

Gottlieb, W.W., *Studies in Secret Diplomacy during the First World War* (London, 1957).

Groodt-Adant, Juliette de, *Geschichte des Französischen Einflusses in Syrien* (Köslin, 1941).

Gullett, H.S., *The Official History of Australia in the War of 1914-1918*, vol.7: *The Australian Imperial Force in Sinai and Palestine 1914-1918* (Sydney, [1923] 3rd ed.1936).

Haffar, Ahmad Rafic, *France in the Establishment of Greater Lebanon: A Study of French Expansionism on the Eve of the First World War* (Ph.D. Dissertation, Princeton University, 1961).

Heyd, Uriel, *Foundations of Turkish Nationalism: The Life and Teachings of Ziya Gökalp* (London, 1950).

Hogarth, D.G., "The Burden of Syria", *The Nineteenth Century and After*, 87 (1920), pp.387-395.

Howard, Harry N., *The Partition of Turkey: A Diplomatic History 1913-1923* (New York, [1931] 1966).

Ireland, Philip Willard, *'Iraq: A Study of Political Development* ([London, 1937] rep. New York, 1970).

Johnson, Maxwell Orme, "The Arab Bureau and the Arab Revolt: Yanbu' to Aqaba", *Military Affairs*, 46:4 (1982), pp.194-201.

Jung, Eugène, *La Révolte arabe* (Paris, 1924-1925).

Kedourie, Elie, *The Chatham House Version and other Middle-Eastern Studies* (London, 1970).

England and the Middle East: The Destruction of the Ottoman Empire 1914-1921 (London, [1956] 1978).

In the Anglo-Arab Labyrinth: The McMahon-Husayn Correspondence and its Interpretations 1914-1939 (Cambridge, 1976).

"The Surrender of Medina, January 1919", *MES*, 13:1 (1977), pp.124-143.

Khadduri, Majid, "'Aziz 'Ali Misri and the Arab Nationalist Movement" in Hourani, Albert (ed.), *St Antony's Papers No.17 — Middle Eastern Affairs No.4* (London, 1965), pp.140-163.

Khairallah, K.T., *Le Problème du Levant: Les Régions Arabes Libérées*

— *Syrie-Irak-Liban* (Paris, 1919).

La Question du Liban (Paris, 1915).

Khan, Rasheeduddin, "The Arab Revolt of 1916-1918", *Islamic Culture*, 35:4 (1961), pp.244-258.

"The Rise of Arab Nationalism and European Diplomacy 1908-1916", *Islamic Culture*, 36:3,4 (1962), pp.196-206, 245-255.

Kirkbride, Alec, *An Awakening: The Arab Campaign 1917-1918* (Tavistock, 1971).

Kostiner, Joseph, "The Hashemite 'Tribal Confederacy' of the Arab Revolt, 1916-1917" in Ingram, Edward (ed.), *National and International Politics in the Middle East: Essays in Honour of Elie Kedourie* (London, 1986), pp.126-143.

Lammens, H., *La Syrie: Précis historique* (Beirut, 1921).

Larcher, M., *La Guerre turque dans la guerre mondiale* (Paris, 1926).

Lawrence, T.E., *Oriental Assembly* (London, [1939] 4th imp.1944).

Secret Despatches from Arabia (London, n.d.).

Seven Pillars of Wisdom (New York, 1938).

Leslie, Shane, *Mark Sykes: His Life and Letters* (London, 1923).

Lewis, Geoffrey, "An Ottoman Officer in Palestine, 1914-1918" in Kushner, David (ed.), *Palestine in the Late Ottoman Period: Political, Social and Economic Transformation* (Jerusalem, 1986), pp.402-415.

Liddell Hart, B.H., *T.E. Lawrence — In Arabia and After* (London, [1934] 1964).

Lieshout, R.H., "'Keeping Better Educated Moslems Busy': Sir Reginald Wingate and the Origins of the Husayn-McMahon Correspondence", *The Historical Journal*, 27:2 (1984), pp.453-463.

Liman von Sanders, [Otto], *Fünf Jahre Türkei* (Berlin, 1920).

Lohéac, Lyne, *Daoud Ammoun et la création de l'Etat Libanais* (Paris, 1978).

MacMunn, George and Falls, Cyril, *Military Operations, Egypt and Palestine from the Outbreak of War with Germany to June 1917* (London, 1928).

Mandelstam, André, *Le Sort de l'empire ottoman* (Lausanne, 1917).

Manuel, Frank E., *The Realities of American-Palestine Relations* (Washington, 1949).

Meinertzhagen, Richard, *Middle East Diary 1917-1956* (London, 1959).

Moberly, F.J., *The Campaign in Mesopotamia 1914-1918* (London, 1923-1927).

Monroe, Elizabeth, *Britain's Moment in the Middle East 1914-1971* (London, revised ed.1981).

Mousa, Suleiman, "Arab Sources on Lawrence of Arabia: New Evidence", *The Army Quarterly and Defence Journal*, 116:2 (1986), pp.158-171.

"The Rise of Arab Nationalism and the Emergence of Transjordan" in Haddad, William W. and Ochsenwald, William (eds.), *Nationalism in a Non-National State* (Columbus, 1977), pp.239-263.

"The Role of Syrians and Iraqis in the Arab Revolt", *Middle East Forum*, 43:1 (1967), pp.5-17.

T.E. Lawrence: An Arab View (London, 1966).

Moutran, Nadra, *La Syrie de demain* (Paris, 1916).

Miller, David Hunter, *My Diary at the Conference of Paris* (New York, 1924).

Nadhmi, Wamidh J.O., *The Political, Intellectual and Social Roots of the Iraqi Independence Movement, 1920* (Ph.D. Dissertation, Durham University, 1974).

Nevakivi, Jukka, *Britain, France and the Arab Middle East 1914-1920* (London, 1969).

"Lord Kitchener and the Partition of the Ottoman Empire, 1915-1916" in Bourne, K. and Watt, D.C. (eds.), *Studies in International History: Essays Presented to W. Norton Medlicott* (London, 1967), pp.316-329.

Pichon, Jean, *Le Partage du Proche-Orient* (Paris, 1938).

Sur la Route des Indes un siècle après Bonaparte (Paris, 1932).

Pirie-Gordon, H. (ed.), *A Brief Record of the Advance of the Egyptian Expeditionary Force under the command of General Sir Edmund H.H. Allenby, July 1917 to October 1918* (London, 2nd ed.1919).

Presgrove, Barbara Ann, *Britain and the Middle East, 1914-1921: A Study in Personal Policy Making* (Ph.D. Dissertation, Florida State University, 1979).

Richard, Henry, *La Syrie et la Guerre* (Paris, 1916).

Rose, Linda Carol, *Britain in the Middle East 1914-1918: Design or Accident?* (Ph.D. Dissertation, Columbia University, 1969).

Sachar, Howard M., *The Emergence of the Middle East 1914-1924* (New York, 1969).

Salibi, Kamal S., "Beirut Under the Young Turks as Depicted in the Political Memoirs of Salim 'Ali Salam (1868-1938)" in Berque, Jacques, and Chevallier, Dominique (eds.), *Les Arabes par leurs archives (XVIe-XXe siècles)* (Paris, 1976).

Samné, Georges, *La Question Syrienne: Exposé-solution-statut politique* (Paris, 1918).

La Syrie (Paris, 1920).

Sfer Pacha, Abdallah, *Le Mandat Français et les traditions françaises en Syrie et au Liban* (Paris, 1922).

Shotwell, James T., *At the Paris Peace Conference* (New York, 1937).

[Skelton, Gladys] Presland, John (pseud.), *Deedes Bey: A Study of Sir Wyndham Deedes 1883-1923* (London, 1942).

Stirling, W.F., *Safety Last* (London, 1953).

Stitt, George, *A Prince of Arabia: The Emir Shereef Ali Haider* (London, 1948).

Stoddard, Philip Hendrick, *The Ottoman Government and the Arabs 1911 to 1918: A Preliminary Study of the Teşkilât-i Mahsusa* (Ph.D. Dissertation, Princeton University, 1963).

Storrs, Ronald, *Orientations* (London, 1937).

Tanenbaum, Jan Karl, *France and the Arab Middle East 1914-1920*

(Philadelphia, 1978).

Tauber, Eliezer, "The Role of Lieutenant Muhammad Sharif al-Faruqi: New Light on Anglo-Arab Relations during the First World War", *Asian and African Studies*, 24 (1990), pp.17-50.

"La Vérité sur la Question Syrienne: A Reconsideration", *Journal of Turkish Studies*, 15 (1991), pp.315-344.

Tibawi, A.L., *Anglo-Arab Relations and the Question of Palestine 1914-1921* (London, 1978).

A Modern History of Syria including Lebanon and Palestine (London, 1969).

Trumpener, Ulrich, *Germany and the Ottoman Empire 1914-1918* (Princeton, 1968).

Weintraub, Stanley and Rodelle (eds.), *Evolution of a Revolt: Early Postwar Writings of T.E. Lawrence* (Pennsylvania State University, 1968).

Westrate, Bruce Cornelius, *Imperialists All: The Arab Bureau and the Evolution of British Policy in the Middle East, 1916-1920* (Ph.D. Dissertation, The University of Michigan, 1982).

Willson, Beckles, "Our Amazing Syrian Adventure", *The National Review*, 76 (1920), pp.41-54.

Wilson, Arnold T., *Loyalties: Mesopotamia 1914-1917* (London, [1930] 1936).

Mesopotamia 1917-1920: A Clash of Loyalties (London, [1931] 1936).

Wingate, Ronald, *Wingate of the Sudan: The Life and Times of General Sir Reginald Wingate, Maker of the Anglo-Egyptian Sudan* (London, 1955).

Winstone, H.V.F., *The Diaries of Parker Pasha* (London, 1983).

The Illicit Adventure: The Story of Political and Military Intelligence in the Middle East from 1898 to 1926 (London, 1982).

Yale, William, *The Near East: A Modern History* (Ann Arbor, [1958] ed.1968).

Young, Hubert, *The Independent Arab* (London, 1933).

Zamir, Meir, *The Formation of Modern Lebanon* (London, 1985).

Zeine, Zeine N., *The Emergence of Arab Nationalism* (New York, [1958] 3rd ed.1973).

The Struggle for Arab Independence: Western Diplomacy and the Rise and Fall of Faysal's Kingdom in Syria (Beirut, 1960).

Index

Abaza, Subhi, 23
'Abbas Hilmi, Khedive, 168
'Abd al-Hadi, 'Awni, 2, 203, 206
'Abd al-Hadi, Salim al-Ahmad, 47, 54
'Abd al-Hamid II, Sultan, 1-2, 68, 95, 98
'Abd al-Nur, Thabit, 31, 126, 131
'Abd al-Rahman, 137
'Abd al-Rahman, Salim, 112, 115
'Abdallah, 61, 65, 69, 81, 93, 95, 114, 122, 136, 139, 145-146, 151, 153-154, 158-159, 248
'Abidin, Musallam, 47, 54
Abu al-Kulal, 'Atiyya, 32-34
Abu al-Lisal, 128
Abu Tayh, 'Awda, 128, 133, 238-239
Acre, 179
Adalia, 58
Adana, 19, 63, 70, 88
Aden, 63, 70, 118, 158
Adib, Auguste, 193, 195-196, 257
Agamemnon, 243
al-'Ahd, 7-8, 10, 20, 26, 29, 31, 53, 55, 57, 60-61, 63, 66, 70-73, 76-78, 83-84, 86, 96-98, 103-105, 110, 112-115, 123-127, 129, 131-132, 138-139, 151, 163, 183, 240, 245-248, 250, 260
al-'Ahd al-'Iraqi, 111, 127, 138, 260
al-'Ahd al-Suri, 138, 260
al-Ahram, 190, 193
al-'Ajam, Mahmud, 47, 54
al-'Alam, 8, 31
Aleppo, 4-5, 19-21, 45, 60, 64, 66-67, 73, 75, 144, 166, 179, 221, 243, 253-254, 258
Aleppo, vilayet of, 168
Alexandretta, 19-21, 65, 77-79,

84, 179, 244, 250, 254, 263
Alexandria, 11, 17, 58, 159, 165, 191, 196-197
'Aleyh, 24, 26-27, 31, 37-38, 44, 46-47, 50, 52-53, 56, 58, 68
Algeria, 172
'Ali, 62, 65, 80-81, 93, 95, 97, 114, 122-124, 136, 138-139, 146-147, 151-152, 248
'Ali, Caliph, 17
'Ali Haydar, 68, 148
'Ali, Sa'id, 145
'Ali, Tahsin, 125-127, 131-132, 243
Allenby, Gen. Edmund, 132, 142-144, 185, 202, 219, 232-242, 259, 295
Alliance Libanaise, 15-16, 24, 165, 169-170, 189-196, 198, 244, 249, 252, 255-257
Amadia, 63, 70
'Amara, 258
American consulate in Aleppo, 43
American consulate-general in Beirut, 40-41
American embassy in Istanbul, 39-41
American government, 41, 201
State Department, 40, 223, 228
American Lebanese Union, 229
American legation in Cairo, 162, 177, 191, 194-195
al-'Amili, Ahmad Sa'id, 23
Amman, 132-133, 137, 155
'Ammun, Iskandar, 5, 15, 52, 169, 189-190, 192-194, 198, 252, 256
'Ammun, Sa'id, 193
Anatolia, 21, 25, 27-28, 31, 38-39, 66, 78, 82, 86, 99, 116, 155, 179, 183, 220, 232, 244-245, 250
Andalusia, 17

Anglo-French declaration of Nov. 1918, 189, 197
Ansar, 24
Antioch, 20, 157, 179
Aqaba, 29, 110, 112, 115-116, 120-121, 125, 127-129, 135, 137-138, 162, 174, 178-179, 193, 211, 232, 248, 255
'Aql, Sa'id, 50, 55
Arab Agency in Cairo, 102, 157, 163, 174, 188, 194
Arab army, 29, 83, 86, 91-93, 97-98, 101-103, 105-108, 110-116, 120, 122, 127-129, 132-134, 136, 139-146, 148, 150-151, 155-156, 193, 233-240, 242-243, 247-248, 253, 258, 279, 295
    Eastern Army, 114, 122, 136, 139, 145-146, 150-153, 248
    Northern Army, 112, 114, 122, 127-128, 132, 134-137, 139-144, 146-147, 149, 162, 193, 248, 257
        Hashimite Brigade, 125-126, 128, 132, 278
        Northern Brigade, 126-127, 278
    Southern Army, 114, 122, 136, 138-139, 147, 150-153, 248
Arab Bulletin, 184
Arab Bureau, 77, 95, 110, 172, 174, 180, 184
Arab government, see Hijazi government
Arab Legion, 109-110, 117-121, 247, 249
Arab-Ottoman Brotherhood, 2, 53
Arab revolt, 10, 26-27, 29, 31, 51-52, 57, 59, 77, 80-81, 83, 92, 96, 101-105, 107, 109-120, 122, 127-128, 130-132, 134, 138, 144-145, 147-150, 153, 157-158, 161-162, 168, 170, 172-173, 182, 189, 193, 205-206, 239, 244-245, 247-248, 251-253, 257, 259-260, see also Arab army
Arab Revolutionary Society, 8, 53

Arab Youth society, 4
Arabian Peninsula, 3-4, 8, 18-19, 58, 60, 72-74, 87-88, 138, 163, 167, 169-170, 177-178, 181-182, 188, 203, 244, 246, 251-252, 255
Argentina, 215-218, 220
al-Armanazi, 'Ali, 46-47, 54
Armenia, 86
Armenians, 31, 174, 183, 200-202, 215, 223, 249
Arqash, Rizq Allah, 38, 41, 197-198
Arslan, Shakib, 36, 38, 155
al-As'ad, Kamil, 16, 24
al-'Asali, Shukri, 47, 50, 55, 183
Asia Minor, 14, 220
'Asim, 'Abd al-Rahman, 17
'Asir, 99
al-'Askari, 'Ali Rida, 111, 243
al-'Askari, Ja'far, 98, 108-109, 111, 124-126, 128-132, 134-135, 137, 140-144, 153, 169, 243, 248
al-'Askari, Tahsin, 111, 243
al-Aswad, K., 14
Athens, 12, 43, 77
al-'Atiqi, 'Abd al-'Aziz, 17
al-Atrash, Husayn, 133
al-Atrash, Nasib, 64-65
al-Atrash, Salim, 65
al-Atrash, Sultan, 114, 133, 149
Australia, 44, 236
Austria-Hungary, 7, 83, 88, 97-98, 155, 247, 250
Ayas Bay, 19
'Ayn Wahida, 129, 131
al-Ayyubi, 'Ali Jawdat, 7, 97, 103, 105, 107, 115, 123, 125-127, 140, 143, 151, 242-243
al-Ayyubi, Shukri, 27, 51-52, 65, 231, 233, 238-243
al-A'zami, 'Izzat, 56
al-'Azm, Haqqi, 18, 135, 138, 174, 178-179, 187, 197-198, 253-255, 257
al-'Azm Rafiq, 5, 16, 52, 58, 163, 169-170, 172-177, 180-182, 186,

189
'Azmi Bek, 36
'Azuri, Najib, 52

Ba'albek, 2, 27-28, 45, 54, 194,
    202, 245, 255
Baghdad, 4, 6-9, 30-31, 71, 84,
    86-87, 168, 173, 258
Baghdad, vilayet of, 91, 168
al-Bakri, 'Ata', 61
al-Bakri, Fawzi, 61-62, 108-109,
    173, 175, 177, 182-183
al-Bakri, Nasib, 26, 61-62, 78-79,
    111, 116, 133
al-Bakri, Sami, 158, 170
Balfour, Arthur James, 174-175
Balfour Declaration, 115, 149,
    173-174, 178
Balfour, Capt. Frank C.C., 32
Balkan War, 2, 4-5, 183
Bani Hasan, 30
al-Bani, Sa'id, 112
Banu Sa'b, 46
Banu Sakhr, 57
al-Baqqal, Najm, 32-34
Barada river, 236
Barakat, Da'ud, 15, 52, 190,
    192-193
al-Barakati, Sharaf 'Abd al-
    Muhsin, 164
Barrow, Maj.-Gen. G., 231, 234,
    236
al-Basat, Tawfiq, 47, 50, 55, 67
Basra, 6, 8, 17, 70, 84-85, 88, 258
Basra, vilayet of, 75, 168
Bassett, Lt.-Col. J.R., 149
Bavaria, 155-156, 169
Bayhum, Ahmad Mukhtar, 241
Beirut, 3, 5-7, 10, 17, 20, 22-24,
    27, 37, 41-42, 46-47, 49-51, 54,
    57-58, 66-67, 153, 166, 179,
    194, 197, 202, 204, 218, 221,
    226, 240-243, 254, 257
Beirut, vilayet of, 6-7, 22, 37, 168
Bell, Gertrude L., 257-258
Berlin, 99, 155
Biqa', 45, 54, 173, 179, 194, 196,

254, 257
Birejik, 63, 70
Black Hand society, 4
Black Sea, 184
Bolsheviks, 153-154, 184, 194, 219
Bombay, 105
Bordeaux, 200, 209, 228
Brackenbury, Gerald, 172
Bray, Capt. Norman N.E., 127
Brazil, 212-214
Brémond, Col. Edouard, 149
Breslau, 9
Britain, 5, 9, 14, 18-20, 63, 65,
    69-70, 72-76, 83-85, 87-89, 98,
    172-173, 177, 180, 182, 184,
    187, 189, 206, 219-220, 227,
    229, 244
British Agency in Jidda, 93, 95,
    104-105, 109, 140, 142-143,
    149, 158
British consulate in Aleppo, 5, 43
British consulate-general in Beirut,
    11, 42
British embassy in Istanbul, 4, 8
British government, 16, 18, 20,
    157, 160, 181, 185-186, 203,
    246, 258
    Foreign Office, 17-19, 83, 85,
        89-90, 100, 104, 168, 242
    India Office, 17-18, 85, 90, 107,
        109
    War Office, 90, 110, 235, 241
British Residency in Cairo, 58, 95
Brooklyn, 227
Buenos Aires, 215-218, 256
al-Bukhari, Jalal, 50, 55, 68
Bulfin, Gen., 242
Burj al-Barajna, 23
al-Burj Square (Beirut), 46, 48-51
Bursa, 28, 49
Bury, George Wyman, 26
Bushir, 17

Cairo, 3, 5-6, 8, 13, 16, 18-19, 43,
    45, 58, 71, 73, 76-77, 83-86,
    89-91, 93, 95, 103-104, 106,
    108, 110, 120, 135, 137-138,

143, 154, 157, 159-163, 165, 167, 169, 171-178, 180, 184, 186-191, 194-198, 211-212, 244, 246, 248-249, 251-253, 255-257
Canada, 15, 224
Carpathians, 66
Caucasus, 66, 110
Chatalja, 5
Chauvel, Lt.-Gen. H.G., 235, 237-238
Chile, 218
Churchill, Winston, 19-20
Cilicia, 99, 168, 202
Clayton, Gilbert F., 73-74, 77, 84-85, 89-90, 121, 174-176, 180, 183, 253
Cleveland, 229
Comité Central Syrien, 181, 195, 197-198, 202, 208-212, 214, 216-217, 219-222, 226-227, 230, 249, 252, 254-255, 257, 291
Comité de l'Orient, 209
Comité Franco-Syrien, 202
Comité Libanais de Paris, 13, 204-205
Comité Littéraire Arabe, 202-203
Committee of Union and Progress, 1-4, 6-7, 22, 31, 37, 68, 82, 87, 95, 99, 146, 183-185, 251, 270
Constantinople, see İstanbul
Correspondance d'Orient, 205, 210, 259
Coulondre, Robert, 241
counter-revolution of 1909, 1-2
Cousse, Lt.-Col., 149, 258
Cox, Percy Z., 85, 90, 160
Cressaty, "Count", 202-203, 255, 290
Crusades, 229
Cuba, 230
Cyprus, 12, 14, 200-201

al-Dabbuni, Da'ud, 4
Daghir, As'ad, 48, 172
Damascus, 2-3, 7-8, 21, 26-29, 35, 39, 42-43, 45, 48-52, 57-59,

61-65, 67-68, 72-73, 75, 78-80, 87, 111-112, 115-117, 133, 137, 144, 148-149, 166, 177, 179, 187-188, 202, 205, 212, 221, 231-243, 245-246, 253-254, 256, 259, 266, 295
Damascus Protocol, 59, 63-65, 70, 250
Damascus, vilayet of, 168, 225
al-Damluji, 'Abdallah, 85
Dar'a, 132-133
Dardanelles, 20
Darian, Yusuf, 190
Darwaza, Muhammad 'Izzat, 268
al-Da'uq, 'Umar, 241-242
Davenport, Maj. W.A., 150
Dawnay, Lt.-Col., 150
Dayr al-Zur, 110, 179, 254
Decentralization Party, 5-6, 8, 10, 15-19, 22-24, 27, 40, 42-46, 48, 53-56, 58, 67, 165, 169-172, 182-183, 189, 244-245, 254
Declaration to the Seven, 176, 180, 185-186, 189, 234, 241, 249, 253, 287
Deedes, Wyndham, 89-90, 167, 258
Delcassé, Théophile, 12-13
Desert Mounted Corps, 234-235
Diarbakr, 31, 45, 71-72, 181
Dobrudja, 276
Druzes, 26, 57, 64, 72, 78, 84, 114, 133, 149, 215, 223, 239, 256
al-Dulaymi, 'Abdallah, 103, 123, 125, 129-130
Dutch consulate in Beirut, 45

Egypt, 1, 5, 8, 11-15, 18-20, 22, 35, 39, 55, 58-60, 69-70, 73-74, 77, 83-89, 92, 95, 97-98, 102-110, 117-119, 121, 131, 135, 139-140, 146-148, 150, 158, 163, 165, 167-168, 171-172, 175, 182, 185, 191, 193, 196-197, 200-201, 203, 211-212, 214, 218, 246, 248,

250-251, 255, 257-258, 297
Egyptian army, 18, 161
Egyptian Expeditionary Force, 237
Egyptian government, 190
    finance ministry, 190, 193
Enver Pasha, 26-27, 35-36, 42, 49, 63, 66, 78, 80, 95-96, 108
Euphrates, 255

al-Fa'iz, Fawwaz, 57
Fahmi, Hasan, 124, 134
Fakhri Pasha, 20, 50
Farid Bek, 6
Faris, Bishop, 205, 211, 222
al-Faruqi, Muhammad Sharif, 66, 70-73, 75-77, 87, 89-91, 102-104, 109-110, 137, 154, 157-163, 169-171, 173, 191-192, 246, 249, 271
Fasu'a, 130
al-Fatat, 2-3, 7-8, 24, 26-27, 29, 47-48, 51, 53-57, 59-62, 64, 67-68, 71-73, 76-78, 111-116, 124, 132-133, 158, 163, 174, 182-185, 212, 231, 238, 240-241, 245-247, 250, 259-260, 268
al-Fatat (newspaper), 226
Faysal, 26, 29, 49, 52, 59, 62-65, 67, 78-81, 89, 93-95, 109, 112-117, 121-127, 129-130, 132-135, 137-138, 140-144, 146, 148-149, 153-156, 163, 174, 177-178, 186-187, 211, 232-233, 236, 238-242, 246, 251-252, 256, 259-260, 282, 295
Fertile Crescent, 1-2, 259
Foch, Gen. Ferdinand, 21
Foreign Legion, 200
Fournet, Admiral Dartige du, 19
Fourteen Points of President Wilson, 227
France, 9, 11-13, 20, 37, 39-40, 44, 48, 58, 72, 75, 86-87, 138, 154, 162, 167, 173, 177-178, 180, 184, 187, 189-191,

194-195, 197-198, 200-229, 242, 244, 249
French consulate in Aleppo, 4, 43
French consulate-general in Beirut, 11, 39-42, 45, 48, 51, 200, 245
French consulate-general in Damascus, 35, 42, 45
French embassy in Istanbul, 4, 39, 55
French government, 12, 20, 41, 160, 187, 197, 200, 203, 209, 211-212, 216, 221-222, 242
    foreign ministry, 42, 158, 190, 197-198, 200, 202, 205-212, 214, 217, 219-222, 227, 230
    war ministry, 200, 218
French legation in Haifa, 43
French legation in Jidda, 43
French military mission in Jidda, 93, 149-150, 258
French ministry in Cairo, 15, 41, 173, 197-198, 210
Fu'ad, 'Ali, 48
al-Funun, 226

Galicia, 66, 115
Gallipoli, 5, 19, 53, 66, 70-71, 110
Gaza, 43, 51, 219
German consulate-general in Beirut, 40
German embassy in Istanbul, 155
German government
    foreign ministry, 100
Germany, 9, 13, 88, 92, 98-100, 155-156, 167, 169, 171, 182, 184
Ghadir al-Hajj, 130-131
Ghalib Pasha, 63, 81
Ghanim, Shukri, 13-14, 52, 204-209, 211-214, 218-222, 254
al-Ghusayn, Fa'iz, 64, 67, 132, 139, 148, 156, 233
Goeben, 9
Gökalp, Ziya, 155, 283
Gout, Jean, 219-220, 227, 230
Graves, Philip P., 85-86, 172

Greece, 244
Greek Catholics, 256
Greek consulate-general in Beirut, 11
Greek government, 11-12
Greek Orthodox, 12, 197, 215, 256
Green Flag society, 4, 51, 56
Grey, Edward, 74-75, 159, 168

al-Ha'ik, Yusuf, 44, 46
Haddad, Jurji, 50, 55
al-Hafiz, Amin Lutfi, 7, 10, 19-21, 47, 50, 55, 71, 244
Haifa, 54, 179, 240
al-Hajj Radi, Sa'ad, 32-34
al-Hakim, Khalid, 163, 180, 183
al-Halabi, 'Abd al-Latif, 125
Halim, Sa'id, 49
Hama, 29, 54, 60, 67, 73, 75, 111, 179, 243, 254
Hamad, 'Umar, 47, 50, 55, 67
Hamada, Hasan, 183
Hamada, Khalil, 3
al-Hamawi, Tawfiq Abu Tawq, 105, 107, 123
Hamuda, Mahmud Hamdi, 135, 137
al-Hani, Yusuf, 41, 48
Haqiqat, 172
Haqqi, Ibrahim, 137
Harmoun Club, 214
al-Hasani, Badr al-Din, 49, 64-65, 117
al-Hasani, Taj al-Din, 117
Hasbaya, 27, 194, 214
al-Hashimi, Taha, 7
al-Hashimi, Yasin, 7, 60-62, 64-66, 76-77, 83, 115-116, 240, 247
Hashimites, 61, 92, 138-139, 153, 248, 253, see also Husayn; 'Ali; 'Abdallah; Faysal; Zayd
Hashimite government, see Hijazi government
Havana, 230
Hawran, 135, 221

Haydar, 'Ali, see 'Ali Haydar
Haydar, As'ad, 27
Haydar, Husayn, 27
Haydar, Ibrahim, 27
Haydar, Muhammad, 27
Haydar, Rustum, 2, 112
Haydar, Salih, 27, 47, 54, 67
Haydar, Yusuf, 27
Hijaz, 21, 26, 31, 47, 51-52, 59, 61-65, 67-69, 74, 78-82, 91-92, 94, 96-99, 102-105, 107-111, 117, 119, 128, 139-140, 145-147, 150-152, 155, 157-158, 160-161, 163, 167-170, 172, 177-180, 182, 187, 205, 210-211, 229, 246-247, 249, 251-254, 256, 258-259
Hijazi government, 96, 141, 162-163, 170-171, 176, 193, 210
foreign ministry, 154, 158, 162, 170-171, 191
war ministry, 141
Hijazi railway, 67, 81, 94, 127-128, 130-132
Hilla, 30
Hilmi, Muhammad, 136, 139, 145, 151-152
Hodgson, Maj.-Gen. H.W., 236
Hogarth, David G., 186-187
Homs, 3, 21, 29, 67, 73, 75, 179, 221, 236-237, 243, 254
House, Col. Edward, 229
al-Huda, 223
Husayn, 10, 26, 31, 49, 52, 55, 59, 61-66, 68-71, 73-82, 87, 89, 91-92, 94-98, 101-111, 115, 117-119, 136-137, 139-149, 151-152, 154-163, 168-182, 186-188, 191-193, 232, 244-248, 250-253, 256-258, 269-270, 272, 297
Husayn Kamil, Sultan, 52, 168
al-Husayni, Ahmad 'Arif, 51
al-Husayni, Mustafa, 51
al-Hushaymi, 'Abidin, 174
Huwaytat, 128

Ibn Rashid, 61, 178
Ibn Sa'ud, 4, 8, 17, 61, 71, 76, 95, 145, 163, 178
Ibrahim, Muhammad, 24
Idahat, 42, 53-54, 268
al-Idrisi, 71, 76, 168
India, 33, 73, 85-88, 90, 102-107, 109-110, 118, 121, 158
Indian government, 31, 107, 160
al-Inklizi, 'Abd al-Wahhab, 23-25, 50, 55
Iraq, 1, 3-4, 7-10, 17-19, 21, 29, 31-33, 61, 65, 67, 71-75, 77, 80, 83-91, 99, 102, 105, 109-110, 118, 145, 155, 158, 167, 170-172, 177-181, 183-184, 187-188, 203, 244-245, 250-252, 254-255, 257-260, 263
Iraqi revolt of 1920, 31, 260
Irwad, 201, 207
Iskenderun, Gulf of, 19-20, 244
Isma'iliya, 118, 120
Istanbul, 2-4, 7, 19, 21-22, 31, 35-36, 43, 49, 52-53, 62-64, 66, 68, 71, 74, 80, 83, 86, 88, 98-99, 109, 115, 156, 183
Italy, 1, 7, 183, 187, 194, 227
al-Ittihad al-Lubnani, 216
Izvestia, 153

Jabal al-Duruz, 29, 67, 112, 133, 149, 179, 233
Jabal 'Amil, 22, 24
Jafet, Ni'ma, 212-213
Jaffa, 43, 46, 176
Jamal Pasha, 16, 20-28, 35-36, 38, 42-43, 45-50, 52-54, 60-61, 66-67, 71, 78-81, 117, 148, 153-154, 183, 267-268
Jamal Pasha "the Lesser", 133, 154-156, 233, 237
Jamal Pasha III, 128
Jamal, Yusuf, 45
Jarablus, 45
Jardun, 130-132
Jawdat, 'Ali, *see* al-Ayyubi, 'Ali Jawdat

Jawf, 26, 67, 79
al-Jaza'iri, 'Abd al-Qadir, 232
al-Jaza'iri, 'Abd al-Qadir (grandson), 231-234, 238-240
al-Jaza'iri, 'Ali, 232
al-Jaza'iri, Sa'id, 49, 156, 231-234, 236-237, 239-241
al-Jaza'iri, Salim, 3, 5, 7, 20, 47, 50, 55, 109
al-Jaza'iri, Tahir, 68
al-Jaza'iri, 'Umar, 49-50, 55, 232
Jazirat Ibn 'Umar, 63, 70
Jellicoe, Admiral John, 21
Jenin, 54
Jerusalem, 24, 51, 176, 254
Jerusalem, sanjaq of, 168
Jews, 30, 72, 119, 174-176, 234
Jidda, 81, 92, 95-96, 103-104, 119, 139, 145, 149, 151, 154, 157, 159-160, 173, 188, 247
Jiyad fort (Mecca), 81
Joyce, Lt.-Col. Pierce C., 126, 129, 139, 144, 149-150
Jubran, Jubran Khalil, 226
al-Jumayyil, Antun, 190, 192, 198-199, 257
Juniyya, 14
Jurf al-Darwish, 131-132

Kamil, Mustafa, 165
Kamil Pasha, 68
Karachi, 106
Karak, 129
al-Karawi, Bahjat Salih, 126
Karbala, 30
al-Karmi, Sa'id, 46
Katana, 235
al-Kawkab, 172
al-Kaylani, 'Abd al-Rahman, 31
Kermanshah, 111
Kerr, Vice Admiral Mark, 19
Khabur river, 255
al-Khalil, 'Abd al-Karim, 2, 7, 10, 21-25, 27, 35-36, 44, 46-47, 54-55, 245
Khalil Bek, 49
Khalil Bek, Gen., 90-91

Khan al-Basha jail (Damascus), 51
al-Kharsa, 'Abd al-Qadir, 47, 54
Khartoum, 163
al-Khatib, 'Abd al-Qadir, 79
al-Khatib, Fu'ad, 104, 108, 119-120, 137, 154, 158-159, 161, 163, 192
al-Khatib, Muhibb al-Din, 17-18, 104, 139, 158, 183
al-Khatib, Sayf al-Din, 48, 50, 53, 55
Khayrallah, Khayrallah, 44, 204-205, 207, 222
al-Khazin, Farid, 51
al-Khazin, Farid, 193
al-Khazin, Philippe, 51
al-Khazin, Yusuf, 212
Khulqi, 'Ali, 119
al-Khuri, Emile, 193
al-Khuri, Faris, 27, 51-52, 233
Khurma, 145
King-Crane commission, 177
Kirkbride, Alec, 238
Kitchener, Lord, 19, 21, 63, 69-70, 74, 88-89, 98, 168, 263
Kufa, 30, 33, 258
Kurd 'Ali, Muhammad, 35, 117
Kurdistan, 99
Kurds, 86
Kut al-'Amara, 30, 32, 89-90
Kuwait, 99
al-Kuwayri, Nuri, 124, 136, 147

Lakah, César, 212-215, 217, 220
Lake, Gen. Percy, 90
Latakia, 21, 179, 244, 254
Lawrence, T.E., 26, 94, 101, 116, 127-128, 133, 142, 144, 146, 148-151, 232-233, 235-242, 258, 263, 282
Le Havre, 200
Le Temps, 204
Leachman, Lt.-Col. Gerard E., 33
Lebanese Cedar, 229
Lebanese Revival, see Society of the Lebanese Revival

Lebanese-Syrian Liberation Society, 230
Lebanese-Syrian Patriotic Society, 215
Lebanese-Syrian Society of Egypt, 197, 255
Lebanon, 1, 25, 51, 173, 179, 196, 226, 260
Lebanon League of Progress, 14, 223-229, 256
Lebanon, Mount, 5-8, 10-16, 26, 31, 36-37, 41-42, 44-45, 48, 51, 54, 99, 133, 154, 165-166, 168-170, 173, 189-192, 194-199, 203-207, 210-218, 223-227, 229, 244-245, 248-250, 252-257
Lebon, Commandant, 236
Légion d'Orient, 117, 193, 200-202, 208, 212-215, 217-219, 222, 226, 228, 249
Lemnos, 243
Levant, 10, 12, 25, 29, 35, 38, 46, 51, 59, 111, 148, 154, 201, 211-212, 216, 218-219, 222-223, 245-246, 255
Levin, Alter, 23
Liberal Moderate Party, 183
Libya, 1-2, 4, 7, 108, 153, 183
Liddell Hart, B.H., 101
Liman von Sanders, Gen. Otto, 233
Literary Club, 2-4, 7, 10, 20-22, 35, 53-56, 232, 245
London, 111, 140, 168, 172, 174-175, 185, 192
Lutf Allah, George, 170
Lutf Allah, Habib, 167-168
Lutf Allah, Michel, 167, 189

Ma'an, 112, 128-132, 137, 142-143, 149, 155
MacAndrew, Maj.-Gen. H.I.M., 236, 243
Mada'in Salih, 47, 68, 128, 255
al-Madfa'i, Jamil, 7, 110, 125-127, 130-131, 276
al-Madfa'i, Rashid, 93, 97, 103,

123-124, 126, 128, 146
al-Madfa'i, Sa'id, 134, 138
Madrid, 98-99, 168
al-Manar, 54, 163
Mandelstam, André, 54
Mansura, 165, 197
al-Maqdisi, An'am, 124
Mardam, Jamil, 203, 212-213, 220
Mardin, 63, 70, 179, 254
Marj 'Ayun, 194, 214
Marja Square (Damascus), 49-50
Maronites, 10-12, 133, 167, 177, 197, 200, 215-217, 225, 227, 229, 256
Marseille, 200, 209
Marshall, Capt., 32-34
Ma'ruf, Sheikh, 157
Maxwell, Gen. John, 11, 13, 74-75
Maydan (Damascus), 238, 240
al-Maza jail (Damascus), 240
McMahon, Arthur Henry, 18, 59, 69-70, 74-77, 87, 89-90, 104, 157-161, 168, 184, 246, 249-250, 271
McMahon-Husayn correspondence, 68-69, 75-77, 186, 246, 270
Mecca, 10, 17, 21, 26, 31, 49, 52, 59, 61-62, 65, 68-69, 80-82, 87, 91-92, 94-97, 101, 103, 108, 111, 134-136, 139-140, 144-148, 150, 153, 157-160, 162-163, 170, 176-177, 188, 192, 194, 211, 232, 244-247, 253, 270
Medina, 26, 59, 62, 69, 78-81, 92, 96-97, 110, 122, 128, 140, 145-146, 150-153, 155, 247-248, 276
Melchites, 215
Merida, 230
Mersina, 63, 70-72
Mesopotamia, see Iraq
Mexico, 230
al-Mihmisani, Mahmud, 46-47, 54
al-Mihmisani, Muhammad, 3, 46-47, 54, 58, 66-67

al-Mir'a, 198
Mir'at al-Gharb, 223
al-Misri, 'Aziz 'Ali, 3, 7-8, 52, 60, 70-71, 76-77, 83-100, 103, 108-109, 123, 140, 146, 151, 247, 250
Moderate Syrian Party, 177
Montevideo, 215
Morocco, 44, 99, 258
Mosul, 4, 7-8, 21, 31, 60, 71, 77, 84, 250
Mosul, vilayet of, 168, 181
al-Mu'ayyad al-'Azm, Shafiq, 28, 47, 50, 55
al-Mu'ayyad, Fa'iz, 28-29
al-Mu'ayyad, 'Umar, 28
Mu'allaqa, 27
Mudros, 77, 243
Muhammad Rashad, Sultan, 9
Muhammara, 85
Mukarzal, Na'um, 223, 225-227, 256-257
Mukhlis, Mawlud, 29-30, 110, 123-132, 134-135, 146, 149, 248, 276
Mukhtar, Ahmad, 258
Munif, 'Ali, 36
Muntafik, 6, 30
al-Muqattam, 162, 165, 167, 172, 178, 207, 211
al-Muraqib, 56
Muraywid, Ahmad, 68
Musa Dagh, 200
al-Mustaqbal, 206-207, 215
Mutawali Shi'ites, 22, 27-28, 133, 207
Mutran, Nadra, 202-203, 255, 258
Mutran, Nakhla, 45

al-Na'ib, Shukri, 124
Nablus, 2, 179, 202
Najaf, 30-33, 245
Najd, 4, 8, 61, 84, 95, 99
al-Najjar, Ibrahim Salim, 4, 13, 52, 206-207, 254
Najm, Faris, 212
Namiq, Isma'il, 125, 129

Napoleon, 1
al-Naqib, Sayyid Talib, 6, 52
al-Nashashibi, 'Ali, 50, 55
Nasif, Sulayman, 173, 175-176
Nasir, Sharif, 106, 133, 234, 237-238
Nasiriyya, 29-30
National Scientific Club, 7
al-Natur, Tawfiq, 2
Nazareth, 26
Near East, 251, 297
New Spirit Society, 229
New York, 5, 14, 195, 223, 225-229, 252, 255-256
Newcombe, Lt.-Col., 150
Nimr, Faris, 52, 167, 170, 172, 174-175, 177-178, 184, 187, 214, 253-254
Nu'ayma, Mikha'il, 226
Nuri, 'Abd al-Latif, 103, 139
Nuri, Badi', 6
Nusayris, 21, 72, 157, 207

Olden, Maj. Arthur C.N., 236-238
Orient Arabe, 207
Ottoman army, 2, 11-12, 17, 20, 27, 29, 31, 36-37, 59, 61, 63, 70-71, 75-76, 86, 89, 99, 110-111, 116, 119, 121, 132, 183-184, 200, 231, 233, 243, 245
    Fourth Army, 16, 23-24, 35, 37-38, 44, 48, 57, 59, 111, 133, 154, 276
    8th Corps, 59, 66, 115
    12th Corps, 59-60, 64, 66
    23rd Division, 59, 66
    24th Division, 115
    25th Division, 59, 64, 66
    27th Division, 59, 66
    35th Division, 59-60, 64-65, 71
    36th Division, 59-60, 64
    37th Division, 59, 66
Ottoman Empire, 1-7, 9-11, 13-17, 19, 22-25, 27, 35, 37-39, 41, 44-45, 50-52, 54, 57-59, 61,

63-64, 69, 73, 78, 80-89, 91-92, 97-99, 102, 117, 146, 153, 155-156, 166, 171-172, 181, 183-184, 190, 199-200, 208, 216, 219, 223, 225-227, 244-247, 249-251, 259
Ottoman General Security Service, 45
Ottoman government, 4, 7, 22, 106, 108, 155-156, 183
    foreign ministry, 41
    war ministry, 61
Ottoman parliament, 22, 24, 52, 183, 232
Ottoman police, 36, 45

al-Pachachi, Muzahim al-Amin, 85
Palestine, 29, 73-74, 87, 99, 110, 115, 121, 153, 166-168, 173-176, 178-179, 183, 188, 201-202, 210, 219, 222, 228-229, 249-250, 254
Paris, 2, 5, 7, 41, 45, 138, 181, 192, 195, 197-198, 202, 204-205, 208-209, 211-212, 214-218, 222, 230, 249, 252, 255
Paris Congress, 3, 7, 22, 44, 48, 202, 204, 223, 226
Paris Peace Conference, 100, 113, 229, 295
Parker, Lt.-Col. Alfred C., 106-107, 139, 145-146
Party of Liberty and Union, 21
Pauli, Petro, 50, 55-56
Payas, 21
Pearson, Lt.-Col. Hugh D., 118, 120-121
Persia, 70, 88
Persian Gulf, 8, 17, 63, 85-86, 172
Petra, 128
Petrograd, 192
Phoenicians, 194, 256
Pichon, Capt. Jean, 236, 238
Picot, François Georges-, 11-14, 39, 42, 138, 154, 172-173, 191,

219
Piépape, Col. de, 242
Pisani, Capt., 126, 149, 236
Port Said, 200, 207
Prussia, 155

al-Qadi, Nuri, 47, 54
Qadri, Ahmad, 2, 24, 27, 51, 56, 62, 112, 115-116
Qahtan, 3
al-Qahtaniyya, 3, 8, 20-21, 53-55, 183
Qal'at al-Mu'azzam, 127
Qal'at al-Zumurrud, 128
al-Qalqili, Muhammad, 17, 171
al-Qaltaqji, 'Abd al-Hamid, 51
Qasim, Milhim, 28, 245
al-Qassab, Kamil, 58-59, 135, 139, 158, 180, 182, 186, 188-189, 193
Qassab, Rashid, 123
al-Qaysuni, Mahmud, 98, 146-147, 152
al-Qibla, 104, 139, 141-142, 144, 188, 198, 248
al-Quwwatli, Shukri, 27, 51-52

Rabigh, 81, 92-97, 105-107, 119, 123, 127, 145, 150, 247
Rafah, 255
al-Rafi'i, 'Abd al-Ghani, 27
al-Rafi'i, Jamil, 157
Raji, Qasim, 125, 135
Rashaya, 27, 194, 214
al-Rawi, Ibrahim, 138, 153
al-Rawi, Jamil, 123, 152
Rayaq, 28, 233
Red Cross, 11
Red Sea, 18, 63, 70, 88, 96, 255
Reform Society of Basra, 6
Reform Society of Beirut, 6, 44, 48, 53, 55, 226
Renaissance Libanaise, 212-213
Reuters, 16, 18, 160
revolt army, see Arab army
Rida Pasha, 50

Rida, Rashid, 3-5, 16, 18, 48, 52, 54, 58, 140, 154, 158, 163, 166-168, 180, 189
Rifqi, Falih, 36, 265
al-Rihani, Amin, 226
al-Rikabi, 'Ali Rida, 56-57, 61-62, 64-65, 116-117, 231, 234, 239-240, 247
Rio de Janeiro, 212-214
Rome, 192
Romieu, Lt.-Col., 201
Rumelia, 183
Russell, Capt. R.E.M., 84
Russia, 9, 11, 184, 227
Russian consulate-general in Beirut, 11
Russian embassy in Istanbul, 54
Russian government foreign ministry, 153, 158
Ruwalla, 26-27, 47, 57, 60, 64, 114, 132, 148-149, 234, 245

al-Sa'ih, 226
Sabri, Da'ud, 153
Sabri, Sami, 153
al-Sa'd, Habib, 242
Safed, 240
Sa'id, Amin, 117
al-Sa'id, Hafiz, 46
Sa'id, Muhammad, 150
Sa'id, Mustafa, 152
al-Sa'id, Nuri, 7, 76, 85-87, 91-92, 94, 103-106, 109, 115, 119, 123-127, 129-132, 134-135, 138, 140, 143, 146-147, 156, 239, 241, 243, 248
Saladin, 153
Salam, Salim 'Ali, 22, 24-25, 37, 241, 265
Salih ibn Sharif, 17
Salim, Sultan, 80
Sallum, Rafiq Rizq, 48, 50, 53, 55, 119
Salt, 115, 144
Samna, 131
Samné, Georges, 198, 205-206, 208-211, 220-221, 252, 254-255

al-Sanusi, Sayyid Ahmad, 108
Sanusis, 7, 108
São Paulo, 5, 212-214
Sardist, Rasim, 103, 123, 129, 135, 141
Sarruf, Ya'qub, 162
al-Saruji, 'Izz al-Din, 67
al-Sawda, Yusuf, 191-192, 196, 257
al-Sayyid Salman, Mahdi, 32-33
Seven Pillars of Wisdom, 101, 150
al-Sha'b, 226
al-Shahbandar, 'Abd al-Rahman, 35, 52, 109, 172-173, 180-182, 186, 189
al-Sha'lan, Fawwaz, 26-27, 148
al-Sha'lan, Nawaf, 26, 57, 64, 67, 79, 149
al-Sha'lan, Nuri, 26-27, 47, 57, 60, 64, 68, 114, 132-133, 148-149, 238-239, 245
al-Shaliji, 'Abd al-Hamid, 127
al-Shallash, Ramadan, 110, 276
al-Sham'a, Rushdi, 47, 50, 55
Shamiyya, 32
al-Shanti, Muhammad, 43, 50, 55
al-Sharq, 109, 117
al-Shawa, Sa'id, 43, 51
Shawkat, Naji, 125
Shaykha, Ahmad, 111, 276
al-Shaykhali, Shakir 'Abd al-Wahhab, 125, 137
Shepheard's Hotel (Cairo), 173
al-Shihabi, 'Arif, 47, 50, 55, 67-68
Shi'ites, 30, 245
Shotwell, James T., 229
Shu'ayba, 29-30
Shuhada' Square, see al-Burj Square (Beirut)
Shukri Bek, 48
Shuqayr, Na'um, 71-73
Shuqayr, Sa'id, 167, 170, 175
al-Shuqayri, As'ad, 23
al-Shurbaji, Shukri, 111, 124, 276
Sidon, 22-24, 54, 173, 179, 194, 196, 254, 257
Sinai, 151, 221, 255
Society for the Defence of the

Rights of Syria and Lebanon, 173, 196-197
Society of the Arab Association, 3, 8
Society of the Islamic Revival, 31-32
Society of the Lebanese Revival, 6, 8, 51, 53, 55, 189, 197
Spain, 98-100, 168, 212
Stirling, Maj. W.F., 238
Storrs, Ronald, 95-96, 160
al-Subbi, Kazim, 32, 34
Sublime Porte, 97, 116, see also Ottoman government
Sudan, 18-19, 104, 165, 172
Suez, 17, 140, 161
Suez Canal, 13, 19-20, 35-36, 62, 64, 78-79, 210
Sufayr, 'Abdallah, 173, 196
al-Sulaymani, Khalid, 124-125
al-Sulh, Mukhtar, 77, 176, 183
al-Sulh, Rida, 22-25, 46, 116
al-Sulh, Riyad, 24
Sumerpur camp (India), 105, 107
al-Suwaydi, Thabit, 31
al-Suwaydi, Yusuf, 31
Switzerland, 98, 116, 167-168, 181, 254
Sykes, Mark, 117, 121, 138, 154, 167, 172-175, 185, 191, 205, 219-220, 227, 230
Sykes-Picot agreement, 149, 153-154, 172-173, 186, 191, 194, 219, 221, 241-242
Syria, 1, 3, 5, 7-8, 11, 13, 15, 17, 19-22, 25-27, 29-30, 35-38, 41, 43-44, 47-48, 51-55, 57-67, 69-74, 77-80, 83-84, 88-89, 92-93, 97, 99, 105, 109-111, 115-117, 119, 121-122, 126, 132, 134-135, 137-140, 144-145, 150, 154-155, 158, 162, 165-174, 177-185, 187-190, 194, 197-198, 202-207, 209-211, 213-223, 225-229, 233-234, 239, 241, 244-249, 251-260, 263
Syria-Mount Lebanon League of Liberation, 195, 226-229, 252,

255
Syria Welfare Committee, 174-177
Syrian army, 116, 241, 260
Syrian-Lebanese Patriotic Society, 212-213
Syrian-Lebanese Society, 230
Syrian Union Party, 167, 176, 180, 189, 254-255
Syrian Union Society, 223

Ta'if, 65, 68-69, 78, 81, 122, 247
Tabbara, Ahmad Hasan, 44-45, 50, 55
Tahsin, Hasan, 36
al-Takhayyumi, Marzuq, 126
Tal'at, 35-36, 43, 49, 53, 63, 155
Talib, Sayyid, see al-Naqib, Sayyid Talib
Tall al-Shihab, 232
Tallu, Na'if, 47, 54
al-Tamimi, Rafiq, 2, 112
Tangier, 172
Tanta, 165, 197
Taqla, Jubra'il, 193
Tariq ibn Ziyad, 17
Tarrad, Pietro, 38, 41
al-Tatari, 'Abd al-Karim, 123
Taurus Mts., 203, 210, 221, 255
Teskilât-i Mahsusa, 42, 66
Thabit, Ayyub, 38, 41, 226-229, 255
Thawrat al-'Arab, 172
Tiberias, 231, 240
Times, 86
Timperley, Maj. L.C., 236
Townshend, Gen. Charles, 90-91
Transjordan, 1, 26, 29, 112, 115, 122, 128-129, 132, 134, 144, 179, 248, 250, 254, 260
Tripoli (East), 27, 117, 173, 179, 194, 196, 207, 218, 254, 257
Tripoli (West), 4
Tufayla, 129
Tul Karm, 115
Tunisia, 167
Turanian nationalism, 2
Turkification policy, 2-3

Tuwayni, Michel, 41
Tyre, 24, 173, 194, 196, 257

al-Ulshi, Jamil, 242
'Uman, 88
'Umar, Caliph, 17
'Umar Tusun, Prince, 5
Union Libanaise, 215-217, 256-257
United States, 14-15, 37, 39, 161-162, 169, 179, 181-182, 184-185, 187, 191, 194, 198, 223, 226, 229, 252, 254
'Uraysi, 'Abd al-Ghani, 15, 35, 47-48, 50, 53, 55, 60-61, 67, 77
Urfa, 63, 70
Uruguay, 215

Van, 88
Vatican, 194
Venizelos, E., 12
Victoria Hotel (Damascus), 237
Von Stozingen mission, 80

al-Wadi, Hamid, 138
Wadi Khalid, 232
Wadi Musa, 128-129
Wafqi, Hasan, 125, 134-135
Wahib Pasha, 62-63, 68-69
Wajh, 124, 127-128, 132, 150, 154
Warlond, Osmond, 180-181, 183-186
Washington, 14, 223, 225, 227
Weizmann, Chaim, 174-176
Willson, Beckles, 235
Wilson, Lt.-Col. Cyril E., 149-151, 159-161
Wilson, Brig.-Gen. L.C., 236-238
Wilson, Woodrow, 188, 212, 227
Wingate, Reginald, 18, 104-105, 107, 113, 142-144, 160, 181, 185, 194, 196

Yahya, Imam, 71, 76, 168, 183

Yahya, Muhammad Ra'uf, 123
Yahya, Sa'id, 123
Yamin, Antun, 54
Yanbu', 81, 93-94, 123, 127, 247
Yarmuk valley, 232
Yazbak, Emile, 193
Yazdi, Muhammad Kazim, 33
Yemen, 80, 99, 167-168, 183, 258-259
Young Turk revolution, 1-3, 8, 68, 95
Young Turks, 1-3, 36, 95, 183

Yucatan, 230

Zahla, 15, 27-28
al-Zahrawi, 'Abd al-Hamid, 3, 5, 7, 47, 50, 55
Zaki Pasha, 35
Zalzal, Philippe, 39-40, 42
Zayd, 114, 129, 137, 141-144
Zayniyya, Khalil, 38, 41, 197
Zionists, 174-176